Richard

Best Wishes

Dele Ogun
25/4/18

A FATHERLESS PEOPLE

Dedication

To the memory of Jideofor Justice Ene, my brother-in-law, a joyful soul, who was mistaken for a member of the armed forces and killed by 'Boko Haram' forces in Maiduguri, Northern Nigeria, on 31 October 2012

DELE OGUN

A FATHERLESS PEOPLE

THE SECRET STORY OF HOW THE NIGERIANS MISSED THE ROAD TO THE PROMISED LAND

"You can't understand the culture of any country without knowing its history. You can't explain the politics without knowing the history"
William Hague, Former British Foreign Secretary

LAWLESS PUBLICATIONS
LONDON
2017

A FATHERLESS PEOPLE
The Secret Story of how the Nigerians
Missed the Road to the Promised Land

Published by
Lawless Publications Limited
3 Angel Gate
326 City Road
London EC1V 2PT
www.lawlesspublications.com

First published 2017

British Library Cataloguing in Publication Data
ISBN 978-0-9567682-3-0

Cover artwork and design: Mike Winter
Internal sketch drawings: Chiderah Bosah
Page Design: Luise Hemmer Pihl
Printed and bound by BELL & BAIN Limited

ACKNOWLEDGMENTS

My friend, Jonathan Mueller whose editorial discipline has given this multi-faceted story coherence. Roger Harding through whose generosity I have had the use of some rare photos from the era. Timothy Modu for allowing me access to rare documents from his late father, T.C. Modu's, Biafra archives. Nnedi Jane Ani who influenced the title; Maurice Asielu; Dele Osinuga, Jo Wealleans, Don Barton, Rev. John Papworth, the late John Coleman and Sir Peter Smithers and the many others who have contributed books, articles and commentaries wittingly and unwittingly. I give due credit to all the authors who have laboured ahead of me without whose efforts this work would not have been possible. And, finally, Esther and the children for the countless hours of family time given up to make this work a reality

CONTENTS

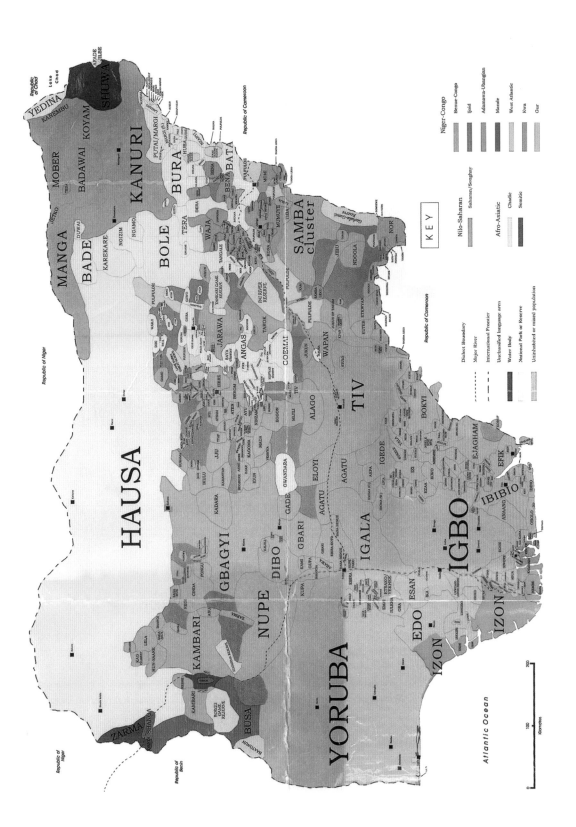

Nigeria's 371 Ethnic Groups

(Source: Okafor, 2016)

1 Abayon Cross River
2 Abua (Odual) Rivers
3 Achipa (Achipawa) Kebbi
4 Adim Cross River
5 Adun Cross River
6 Affade Yobe
7 Afizere Plateau
8 Afo Plateau
9 Agbo Cross River
10 Akaju-Ndem (Akajuk) Cross River
11 Akweya-Yachi Benue
12 Alago (Arago) Piateau
13 Amo Plateau
14 Anaguta Plateau
15 Anang Akwa lbom
16 Andoni Akwa lbom, Rivers
17 Angas Bauchi, Jigawa, Plateau
18 Ankwei Plateau
19 Anyima Cross River
20 Attakar (ataka) Kaduna
21 Auyoka (Auyokawa) Jigawa
22 Awori Lagos, Ogun
23 Ayu Kaduna
24 Babur Adamawa, Bomo, Taraba, Yobe
25 Bachama Adamawa
26 Bachere Cross River
27 Bada Plateau
28 Bade Yobe
29 Bahumono Cross River

30 Bakulung Taraba
31 Bali Taraba
32 Bambora (Bambarawa) Bauchi
33 Bambuko Taraba
34 Banda (Bandawa) Taraba
35 Banka (Bankalawa) Bauchi
36 Banso (Panso) Adamawa
37 Bara (Barawa) Bauchi
38 Barke Bauchi
39 Baruba (Barba) Niger

40 Bashiri (Bashirawa) Plateau
41 Bassa Kaduna, Kogi, Niger, Plateau
42 Batta Adamawa
43 Baushi Niger
44 Baya Adamawa
45 Bekwarra Cross River
46 Bele (Buli, Belewa) Bauchi
47 Betso (Bete) Taraba
48 Bette Cross River
49 Bilei Adamawa
50 Bille Adamawa
51 Bina (Binawa) Kaduna
52 Bini Edo
53 Birom Plateau
54 Bobua Taraba
55 Boki (Nki) Cross River

56 Bkkos Plateau
57 Boko (Bussawa, Bargawa) Niger
58 Bole (Bolewa) Bauchi, Yobe
59 Botlere Adamawa
60 Boma (Bomawa, Burmano) Bauchi
61 Bomboro Bauchi
62 Buduma Borno, Niger
63 Buji Plateau
64 Buli Bauchi
65 Bunu Kogi
66 Bura Adamawa
67 Burak Bauchi
68 Burma (Burmawa) Plateau
69 Buru Yobe
70 Buta (Butawa) Bauchi
71 Bwall Plateau
72 Bwatiye Adamawa
73 Bwazza Adamawa
74 Challa Plateau
75 Chama (Chamawa Fitilai) Bauchi
76 Chamba Taraba
77 Chamo Bauchi
78 Chibok (Chibbak) Yobe
79 Chinine Borno
80 Chip Plateau
81 Chokobo Plateau
82 Chukkol Taraba

83 Daba Adamawa
84 Dadiya Bauchi
85 Daka Adamawa
86 Dakarkari Niger, Kebbi

87 Danda (Dandawa) Kebbi
88 Dangsa Taraba
89 Daza (Dere, Derewa) Bauchi
90 Degema Rivers
91 Deno (Denawa) Bauchi
92 Dghwede Bomo
93 Diba Taraba
94 Doemak (Dumuk) Plateau
95 Ouguri Bauchi
96 Duka (Dukawa) Kebbi
97 Duma (Dumawa) Bauchi
98 Ebana (Ebani) Rivers
99 Ebirra (Igbirra) Edo, Kogi, Ondo
100 Ebu Edo, Kogi
101 Efik Cross River
102 Egbema Rivers
103 Egede (Igedde) Benue
104 Eggon Plateau
105 Egun (Gu) Lagos, Ogun
106 Ejagham Cross River
107 Ekajuk Cross River
108 Eket Akwa Ibom
109 Ekoi Cross River
110 Engenni (Ngene) Rivers
111 Epie Rivers
112 Esan (Ishan) Edo
113 Etche Rivers
114 Etolu (Etilo) Benue
115 Etsako Edo

116 Etung Cross River
117 Etuno Edo
118 Palli Adamawa
119 Pulani (Pulbe) Bauchi, Borno, Jigawa , Kaduna, Kano, Katsina, Kebbi , Niger, Sokoto, Taraba, Yobe, etc.
120 Fyam (Fyem) Plateau
121 Fyer(Fer) Plateau
122 Ga'anda Adamawa
123 Gade Niger
124 Galambi Bauchi
125 Gamergu-Mulgwa Bomo
126 Qanawuri Plateau
127 Gavako Borno
128 Gbedde Kogi
129 Gengle Taraba
130 Geji Bauchi
131 Gera (Gere, Gerawa) Bauchi
132 Geruma (Gerumawa) Plateau
133 Geruma (Gerumawa) Bauchi
134 Gingwak Bauchi
135 Gira Adamawa
136 Gizigz Adamawa
137 Goernai Plateau
138 Gokana (Kana) Rivers
139 Gombi Adamawa
140 Gornun (Gmun) Taraba
141 Gonia Taraba
142 Gubi (Gubawa) Bauchi
143 Gude Adamawa
144 Gudu Adamawa
145 Gure Kaduna
146 Gurmana Niger
147 Gururntum Bauchi
148 Gusu Plateau
149 Gwa (Gurawa) Adamawa
150 Gwamba Adamawa
151 Gwandara Kaduna, Niger, Plateau

152 Gwari (Gbari) Kaduna, Niger, Plateau
153 Gwom Taraba
154 Gwoza (Waha) Bomo
155 Gyem Bauchi
156 Hausa: Bauchi, Borno, Jigawa, Kaduna,Kano, Kastina, Kebbi, Niger,Taraba, Sokoto, etc
157 Higi (Hig) Borno, Adamawa
158 Holma Adamawa
159 Hona Adamawa
160 Ibeno Akwa lbom
161 Ibibio Akwa lbom
162 Ichen Adamawa
163 Idoma Benue, Taraba
164 Igalla Kogi
165 lgbo: Abia, Anambra, Benue, Delta, Ebonyi,Enugu, Imo, Rivers
166 ljumu Kogi
167 Ikorn Cross River
168 Irigwe Plateau
169 Isoko Delta
170 lsekiri (Itsekiri) Delta
171 lyala (lyalla) Cross River
172 lzondjo) Bayelsa, Delta, Ondo, Rivers
173 Jaba Kaduna
174 Jahuna (Jahunawa) Taraba
175 Jaku Bauchi
176 Jara (Jaar Jarawa Jarawa-Dutse) Bauchi
177 Jere (Jare, Jera, Jera, Jerawa) Bauchi, Plateau
178 Jero Taraba
179 Jibu Adamawa
180 Jidda-Abu Plateau
181 Jimbin (Jimbinawa) Bauchi
182 Jirai Adamawa
183 Jonjo (Jenjo) Taraba
184 Jukun

Bauchi, Benue,Taraba, Plateau

185 Kaba(Kabawa) Taraba
186 Kadara Taraba
187 Kafanchan Kaduna
188 Kagoro Kaduna
189 Kaje (Kache) Kaduna
190 Kajuru (Kajurawa) Kaduna
191 Kaka Adamawa
192 Kamaku (Karnukawa) Kaduna, Kebbi, Niger
193 Kambari Kebbi, Niger
194 Kambu Adamawa
195 Kamo Bauchi
196 Kanakuru (Dera) Adamawa, Borno
197 Kanembu Bomo
198 Kanikon Kaduna
199 Kantana Plateau
200 Kanufi Kaduna, Adamawa, Bomo, Kano,Niger, Jigawa, Plateau, Taraba, Yobe
201 Karekare (Karaikarai) Bauchi, Yobe
202 Karimjo Taraba
203 Kariya Bauchi
204 Katab (Kataf) Kaduna
205 Kenern (Koenoem) Plateau
206 Kenton Taraba
207 Kiballo (Kiwollo) Kaduna
208 Kilba Adamawa
209 Kirfi (Kirfawa) Bauchi
210 Koma Taraba
211 Kona Taraba
212 Koro (Kwaro) Kaduna, Niger
213 Kubi (Kubawa) Bauchi
214 Kudachano (Kudawa) Bauchi
215 Kugama Taraba
216 Kulere (Kaler) Plateau
217 Kunini Taraba
218 Kurama Jigawa,

Kaduna, Niger, Plateau
219 Kurdul Adamawa
220 Kushi Bauchi
221 Kuteb Taraba
222 Kutin Taraba
223 Kwalla Plateau
224 Kwami (Kwom) Bauchi
225 Kwanchi Taraba
226 Kwanka (Kwankwa) Bauchi, Plateau
227 Kwaro Plateau
228 Kwato Plateau
229 Kyenga (Kengawa) Sokoto
230 Laaru (Larawa) Niger
231 Lakka Adamawa
232 Lala Adamawa
233 Lama Taraba
234 Lamja Taraba
235 Lau Taraba
236 Ubbo Adamawa
237 Limono Bauchi, Plateau
238 Lopa (Lupa, Lopawa) Niger
239 Longuda (Lunguda) Adamawa, Bauchi
240 Mabo Plateau
241 Mada Kaduna, Plateau
242 Mama Plateau
243 Mambilla Adamawa
244 Manchok Kaduna
245 Mandara (Wandala) Bomo
246 Manga (Mangawa) Yobe
247 Margi (Marghi) Adamawa, Bomo
248 Matakarn Adamawa
249 Mbembe Cross River, Enugu
250 Mbol Adamawa
251 Mbube Cross River
252 Mbula Adamawa
253 Mbum Taraba
254 Memyang (Meryan)

Plateau
255 Miango Plateau
256 Miligili (Migili) Plateau
257 Miya (Miyawa) Bauchi
258 Mobber Bomo
259 Montol Plateau
260 Moruwa (Moro'a, Morwa) Kaduna
261 Muchaila Adamawa
262 Mumuye Taraba
263 Mundang Adamawa
264 Munga (Mupang) Plateau
265 Mushere Plateau
266 Mwahavul (Mwaghavul) Plateau
267 Ndoro Taraba
268 Ngamo Bauchi, Yobe
269 Ngizim Yobe
270 Ngweshe (Ndhang. Ngoshe-Ndhang) Adamawa, Borno
271 Ningi (Ningawa) Bauchi
272 Ninzam (Ninzo) Kaduna, Plateau
273 Njayi Adamawa
274 Nkim Cross River
275 Nkum Cross River
276 Nokere (Nakere) Plateau
277 Nunku Kaduna, Plateau
278 Nupe Niger
279 Nyandang Taraba
280 Ododop Cross River
281 Ogori Kwara
282 Okobo (Okkobor) Akwa lbom
283 Okpamheri Edo
284 Olulumo Cross River
285 Oron Akwa lbom
286 Owan Edo
287 Owe Kwara
288 Oworo Kwara

289 Pa'a (Pa'awa Afawa) Bauchi
290 Pai Plateau
291 Panyam Taraba
292 Pero Bauchi
293 Pire Adamawa
294 Pkanzom Taraba
295 Poll Taraba
296 Polchi Habe Bauchi
297 Pongo (Pongu) Niger
298 Potopo Taraba
299 Pyapun (Piapung) Plateau
300 Qua Cross River
301 Rebina (Rebinawa) Bauchi
302 Reshe Kebbi, Niger
303 Rindire (Rendre) Plateau
304 Rishuwa Kaduna
305 Ron Piateau
306 Rubu Niger
307 Rukuba Plateau
308 Rumada Kaduna
309 Rumaya Kaduna
310 Sakbe Taraba
311 Sanga Bauchi
312 Sate Taraba
313 Saya (Sayawa Za'ar) Bauchi
314 Segidi (Sigidawa) Bauchi
315 Shanga (Shangawa) Sokoto
316 Shangawa (Shangau) Plateau
317 Shan-Shan Plateau
318 Shira (Shirawa) Kano
319 Shomo Taraba
320 Shuwa Adamawa, Borno
321 Sikdi Plateau
322 Siri (Sirawa) Bauchi
323 Srubu (Surubu) Kaduna
324 Sukur Adamawa
325 Sura Plateau
326 Tangale Bauchi
327 Tarok Plateau, Taraba
328 Teme Adamawa
329 Tera (Terawa) Bauchi, Bomo
330 Teshena (Teshenawa) Kano
331 Tigon Adamawa
332 Tikar Taraba
333 Tiv Benue, Plateau, Taraba and Nasarawa
334 Tula Bauchi
335 Tur Adamawa
336 Ufia Benue
337 Ukelle Cross River
338 Ukwani (Kwale) Delta
339 Uncinda Kaduna, Kebbi, Niger, Sokoto
340 Uneme (Ineme) Edo
341 Ura (Ula) Niger
342 Urhobo Delta
343 Utonkong Benue
344 Uyanga Cross River
345 Vemgo Adamawa
346 Verre Adamawa
347 Vommi Taraba
348 Wagga Adamawa
349 Waja Bauchi
350 Waka Taraba
351 Warja (Warja) Jigawa
352 Warji Bauchi
353 Wula Adamawa
354 Wurbo Adamawa
355 Wurkun Taraba
356 Yache Cross River
357 Yagba Kwara
358 Yakurr (Yako) Cross River
359 Yalla Benue
360 Yandang Taraba
361 Yergan (Yergum) Plateau
362 Yoruba Kwara, Lagos, Ogun, Ondo, Oyo, Osun, Ekiti, Kogi
363 Yott Taraba
364 Yumu Niger
365 Yungur Adamawa
366 Yuom Plateau
367 Zabara Niger
368 Zaranda Bauchi
369 Zarma (Zarmawa) Kebbi
370 Zayam (Zeam) Bauchi
371 Zul (Zulawa) Bauchi

Introduction

During the negotiations for the independence of Nigeria the view of the Secretary of State at that time, with which I agreed, was that in Nigeria we should attempt to put together a large and powerful state with ample material resources, which would play a leading part in the affairs of the continent and the world.[1]

- Sir Peter Smithers

Every once in a while a book comes along that changes our understanding of the world in which we live. The 'turnaround book' for me was Professor Jared Diamond's '*Guns, Germs and Steel: A short History of Everybody*'. It explained, comprehensively and without any of the gaps in logic so often left by alternative religious and geneticist narratives, the pattern of human development that we see across the world today. Diamond's central argument is that the under-development of the southern hemisphere, and the relative over-development of the northern hemisphere, is neither the result of God's will as suggested by many believers nor a consequence of genetic differences.[i]. It is, Diamond says, the product of differences in geographical and climatic conditions.

It was the realisation, gained from this book, that the explanation for seemingly inexplicable human social conditions may not be beyond human understanding that led me to believe that there might equally be an explanation for the mystery that is Nigeria: a country of which so much is heard but about which so little is understood.

This work was further inspired and provoked by an admonition in the preface to another book; this one written by one of my own people, *The History of the Yoruba* by the Reverend Samuel Johnson:

> *Educated natives of Yoruba are well acquainted with the history of England, with that of Rome and Greece but of the history of their own country they know nothing whatever! This reproach it is one of the author's objects to remove*

The words struck home and struck deep. At the time Johnson wrote them, in 1897, his country was 'Yoruba'. By the time the book first saw the light of day in 1921, upon first

---

i As argued, for example, by Nicholas Wade in his book, *A Troublesome Inheritance: Genes, Race and Human History.*

publication, the Yoruba people (though not all of them) had been amalgamated with 370 other ethnic groups to become 'Nigeria'.

Being the land of my birth and of my formative years, the enquiry which Johnson's words set off was more than purely intellectual. Growing up, and then living, in England but forever looking back, I was keen to understand why it was that the evil of the slave trade had afflicted the land as it did. I then wanted to understand why colonisation followed so closely upon slavery and its abolition. Above all, I wanted to know the answer to the question, often asked of me by the new generation of young Nigerians, "what was there before Nigeria?"

Ajasa Street in Onikan, Lagos was the location of the family home at the time of my birth in 1962. Situated behind the old Federal Parliament building, in what is now Tafawa Balewa Square, the first air that I took in was heavy with the politics of the newly independent country. My father, a former clerk in the colonial service, was one of the many former 'colonial subjects' who came to the United Kingdom, in the early 1960s, to pursue further studies. He and others of his type were readying themselves for the new opportunities and responsibilities that independence promised. I wanted to understand the country's short journey from a colony status on 1 January 1900 to independence on 1 October 1960 and the effect of this period of tutelage upon the people and their politics. I only recently became aware that, before he became Premier of the Western Region of Nigeria, our next door neighbour, at number 20 Ajasa Street, was Samuel Ladoke Akintola, who plays a major part in Nigeria's post-independence story and specifically in the bloody turmoil that gripped that region from 1962 until the first military coup of January 1966.

When I was seven years old, my parents who were then living in the UK, sent for me to join the family and to be educated "like the white man's children". The Biafran War tragedy was just nearing its end at the time of my arrival. Each night we watched the unfolding tragedy with images of death and famine on the B.B.C. Nine O'Clock News without any inkling that I would one day become married to one of those young Biafran girls.

The initial resistance to the idea from both mothers sparked an interest into the origins of the antipathy between my wife's Igbo people and my own Yoruba people and into the Biafran story. As an extension of this, I wanted to get to the bottom of the rivalry between the Nigerians of the south (chiefly the Igbos and the Yoruba) on the one side and the Nigerians of the north (principally the Hausa and the Fulani) on the other side. Above all, I wanted to understand the reason for the state of underdevelopment which plagued the country even as it was so blessed with human and material resources.

It was a habit of mine, on the occasional return trips to my village, in the Yoruba heartland, to sit in on the traditional family meetings: an all-male assembly convened in the parlour of the oldest living male at which village affairs and family disputes were deliberated upon, as in a court of law. I recall how on one occasion, after a party to one dispute had made one too many appeals to Jesus Christ to be his witness as to the truth of what he was saying, my father's elder brother, uncle *Akingbehin*, suddenly exclaimed: *Ewo ni Jesu Christi yi ti iwo n pe? Se Okitipupa ni won bisi ni?* This translates to: *Who is this Jesus Christ that you keep calling? Was he born in Okitipupa?*[ii]

This incident stirred my curiosity as to the drivers of the foreign religious influences on my people. It emerged, in the course of the research, that a significant number of the colonial officers had been sons of clergymen[iii]. An interesting fact, in itself, which becomes all the more significant because one of the key challenges to the authority of the 'sons' came from the interest in western education which the 'fathers' had stimulated in the 'natives' in the course of their evangelism.

My research on the arrival of Christianity in Nigeria was to lead me to the realisation that the secondary school which I attended in London, Highbury Grove Boys Secondary School, in Highbury, Islington, stood on land which had belonged to the Church Missionary Society (CMS) which, in the 1830s, had spearheaded the push of Christianity into what was to become Nigeria[iv]. The first CMS training college had been opened in Highbury, in 1825 as the Highbury Missionary College. The Highbury Centre (formerly the Foreign Missions Club) which was established in 1893 'to provide accommodation to missionaries and Christian ministers in training' is still situated at Aberdeen Park which backs onto the old school complex. I recall how, as school boys, we used to see the nuns in their habits, the priests in their dog-collars, and various other pious-looking people, criss-crossing from Aberdeen Park to Highbury Fields without ever appreciating the significance of the location to Christianity in Africa. With some other members of my family being Muslims, and with the sound of the daily call to prayer in the vicinity of Omididun Street, Isale Eko (downtown Lagos), during the one year that I lived there with relatives, having imprinted itself on my memory, I wanted an understanding of how this faith, from Arabia, had first entered and then spread its reach across Nigeria. Above all, I was curious to discover how the fault line between the two faiths came to run through the centre of the country so perfectly-horizontally.

My reflections on all these issues began in earnest in the course of my attendance at the Nigerian Law School in Victoria Island Lagos, during the 1985-1986 academic year following my call to the English Bar. This was a period of transition for the country. The military regime of General Muhammadu Buhari and Major Tunde Idiagbon had just been overthrown, in August 1985, and General Ibrahim Babangida had taken over[v]. I wanted to understand why democracy had failed so badly in Nigeria and, also, the nature and origins of military rule in the country.

---

ii   *Okitipupa* was the administrative province within which our village fell during colonial rule
iii   'Of the ninety-five colonial governors for whose fathers' careers there is information, no fewer than thirty-four were the sons of Anglican clergymen' (Robert D Pearce, *Sir Bernard Bourdillon*, p.4)
iv   The grounds of the former stadium of Arsenal F.C., at Highbury, is believed to have originally formed part of the same land
v   At the time of writing general Buhari has re-emerged as a civilian president of Nigeria

In November 1995 the public hanging of the Ogoni activist, poet and playwright, Ken Saro-Wiwa was carried out. The hanging was at the insistence of General Sanni Abacha[vi] in contemptuous disregard of international pleas for clemency. The oil deposits in Saro-Wiwa's Niger-Delta region is what Nigeria's modern wealth is built upon and the UK's Shell Petroleum PLC is the main foreign oil operator in the region. I wanted to understand the oil politics of the country.

The colonisation of one people by another is engendered, and sustained, by complexes of superiority and inferiority. Like many myths, once such complexes have taken hold of human consciousness it requires super-human effort for them to be dislodged as intellectuals and historians begin to construct works of apparent reason upon these often dubious foundations. The following passage from the memoirs of Sir Bryan Sharwood-Smith, the last British Governor of Northern Nigeria is a case in point:

> *We were talking about the days when the ritual consumption of human flesh was a part of their daily life. Food was then desperately scarce and the maintenance of the aged and infirm who could no longer hunt or farm was more than the community could contrive, except for the few whose acquaintance with the supernatural made them valuable. The aged, it was conveniently believed, were prone to possession by evil spirits which would prey upon their fellows. Such as these, once identified, were put to the sacrifice and consumed. Over venturesome travellers from other parts and the victims of intertribal warfare met a like fate. In fact, here where we were sitting, they told me, was the site of the sacrificial altar.*
> *As I displayed interest, the old men, their tongues loosened by palm wine, began to describe in grisly detail, exactly how these things had been arranged. The persons of the condemned were secured, head downward, between two upright stakes, their limbs spread eagled. Beneath them burnt a slow, smoky fire. Around in anticipation, squatted the elders, each with his back against an upright slab of rock in the position to which his status entitled him. As life passed, boiling palm oil was introduced into the body, from above – I had heard enough*[2]

The Colonial Governor's account of events that were supposed to have taken place in the lifetime of my grandfather made me uncomfortable. It left me wondering how much of this was true rather than the product of myth and literary licence: in today's parlance "fake news". The instinctive scepticism that I felt over the account was reinforced by a documentary programme, that I watched in England, which featured an upside-down crucifixion during the time of the druids in Celtic-Britain which bore a striking resemblance to the method of ritual sacrifice that Mr Sharwood-Smith was attributing

vi   He had taken over from General Babaginda in a palace coup

16

to Nigeria. Yet, whatever a man of Sharwood-Smith's experience in Nigeria[vii] wrote in his memoirs, could not be lightly dismissed. These memoirs, published in 1969 as the Biafran war drew to a close, would have been amongst the leading reference materials for many commentaries, at the time, on the causes of that bloody conflict in which over two million are said to have died from a combination of machetes, bullets, bombs and starvation.

All the same, I had my own experiences to draw upon having been raised in the village by my grandmother during my early years with the extended influence of uncle Akingbehin and other relations. While I could accept that there would sometimes be the odd character, or two, whose habit was always to drink ogogoro[viii] to excess, I also knew that persons of such disposition were never known to be the custodians of reliable communal history. More than anything else, it was Sharwood-Smith's improbable tale, though solemnly told, of cannibalism and the eating of the aged, in 'the days when the ritual consumption of human flesh was a part of their daily life' that stirred me to look into these issues more closely.

It would be naive to deny that in times of war native fighters might not burn the corpse of their slain foe and, as a demonstration of fearlessness to their people and utter ruthlessness to their enemies, eat some part of the flesh of their slain opponent. However this tale of cannibalism as a habit, involving the roasting of human flesh with the addition of spices, born of scarcity of meat and a craving for flesh, as the Governor relayed, was quite another thing altogether. In any case, I had always thought it strange that it was in Africa, a part of the world which in the mind of the average Westerner is more known for its teeming wildlife than for its people, that it was said that humans consumed human flesh for want of meat. It was ironic because it was, after all, the abundance of the blessings from nature's bosom which God had chosen to lavish on the land that had induced Sharwood-Smith's government to first send its explorers, the David Livingstones and Mungo Parks etc., to scout and record the nature and extent of these blessings, before the traders and administrators then came out to harvest the bounty for repatriation back to their homeland. The straight-talking Lord Frederick Lugard, the chief British architect of 'Nigeria' (whose wife gave the country its name), admitted this much in his own memoirs:

> [T]he tropics are the heritage of mankind, and neither, on the one hand, has the suzerain Power a right to their exclusive exploitation, nor, on the other hand, have the races which inhabit them a right to deny their bounties to those who need them[3]

Sharwood-Smith's claim that, in the fiendish practice that he was reporting, the elderly were preyed upon was even more outlandish for me as one who had spent his early years

---

vii   He spent 37 years in Nigeria
viii   Local high-strength gin made from palm-wine

amongst villagers who, though rendered poor and miserable by the mismanagement of successive governments of nature's bounty, still held to the custom of tending the farms of neighbours who were too sick to toil, and of sending their young children to take meals across to the infirm, in the long-established tradition of care-in-the-community.

My interest in how Nigeria took the wrong turn led to an introduction to one of the elder statesmen whose political career straddled the before and the after of Nigerian Independence who was then living abroad in political exile from the Abacha regime.

Chief Anthony Enahoro's significance in the Nigeria story is testified to by the fact that his flight to Britain for refuge from charges of high treason in 1963, on a first round of exile in the wake of Nigeria's immediate post-Independence political crisis, filled the pages of the Hansard report on the UK Parliament's proceedings. Such was the political storm that blew up over the extradition of this small, yet extraordinary, man that it 'menaced the stability' of the Conservative Government of the day and contributed to its fall despite the fact that, in the end, it only granted the extradition request on the strict condition that he would not be executed. His thus deferred death, in December 2010, was noteable for being covered in the Obituary pages of all the leading British newspapers while his memorial service was conducted in Westminster Cathedral.

Enahoro was of the royal line in the Kingdom of Benin with which the royal court of Portugal first established diplomatic relations through the Portuguese explorers in the course of their quest for the new sea route to Asia, in the mid-fifteenth century. One of the many historical anecdotes that I picked up from him was one which had been passed down as to how the Portuguese had been extremely civil and respectful during these first visits. "What I have never been able to work out is, what caused them to change?" was the question he asked repeatedly in his closing years.

Being one of the first of a new generation of Nigerians in the diaspora who had been through the same primary, secondary and university education experience as the colonial administrators, and, more importantly, with the same opportunities for self-education that life in the West offers, I had more than a casual interest in the character of these young British men who had been made gods at such an early age:[4] even now their handiwork is deified by successive Nigerian leaders. The process of deification was captured in the words of Malcolm Muggeridge who it is said, went out to the empire in the 1920s:

> *From the moment of landing in Colombo, I was made conscious of my status as a Sahib. It was like suddenly inheriting a peerage and being addressed as My Lord. Just by virtue of being English and white, if you went to buy a ticket at a railway station, people made way for you. Similarly, in a shop. It was very insidious. At first I found it embarrassing and distasteful; then, though*

I continued to ridicule it, I came to count upon receiving special treatment. Finally, when for some reason it was not accorded, there was an impulse to become sulky and irritated. From that, it was but a small step to shouting and insisting, as, in the days of the Raj I saw happen often enough[5]

While some went in search of adventure, and the god-feeling to which Muggeridge was testifying, others were motivated by a sort of missionary idealism of the Victorian era.

Living in England, I had the good fortune of speaking with one or two of the key players on the Nigerian colonial scene in the course of which I was able to tease out some reflections. In one of the darkest moments of the country's recent political history, I had set out to bring together as many of them as I could trace for an on-camera discussion with Enahoro. The topic was to have been 'how the Nigerians missed the road to the promised land'. Britain being famous for the vibrancy of its 'old boy' networks, it was not long before I had drawn up an impressive list which included John Hilary Smith C.B.E., who had been Deputy Secretary to Nigeria's Prime Minister at Independence, Abubakar Tafawa Balewa. He was, in fact, still in post up until the time of Balewa's death in the first military coup on 15 January 1966. Unfortunately, that dialogue for posterity between the old colonialists and the old nationalist never happened.

There was, however, one former colonial officer with whom I enjoyed a longer correspondence, Mr Don Barton. That he had served in East Africa, and not Nigeria, was of little consequence in terms of understanding the character of the colonial cadets. It may, in fact, have accounted for he alone being prepared to engage on these issues after receiving my monograph on Nigeria which the Economic Research Council had published in 2002[6]. In the course of our correspondence, he provided the following insights from the perspective of a colonial administrator:

One characteristic of colonial rule was that whilst we were attached to our work, we were detached from any overriding local loyalties. After 50-60 years of colonialism, it was possible for Nigerians to accept decisions/advice of an alien District Officer (for example) knowing that he was detached, whereas it was later not possible to accept them from Nigerians of "other nationalities" and these potential local/internal frictions were concealed under the colonial umbrella. I've expressed that loudly, but nowhere was this scenario clearer than in the army. The Nigerian army could be loyal to a colonial government because in the context of local nationalities it was neutral. But after independence, these nationalities within the army developed national loyalties – or reverted to them. I think it probable that because these national loyalties were contained for several decades, the colonial governments of the day overlooked the potential for destruction so that the "independence constitution" was too optimistic.

I think we were all over-optimistic about "the state" and did not anticipate local frictions arising after independence – although there was certainly evidence of this in Nigeria. The state had functioned under colonial rule and there seemed no reason why this should not continue after independence. But in reality, nationalism was primarily a response to colonial rule, representing a wish for independence; there was no underlying sense of national unity in most cases – thus Tanzania and Zambia are perhaps exceptions. Primary loyalty was to family, clan and tribe – not to the country; in Tanzania even the district could be an alien concept, but what saved the day here was that there were no serious tribal rivalries, neither was any tribal group sufficiently large to aspire to dominate....

Which leads me on to the "Big Men" of politics. This is only a theory of mine, but I wonder if the origins go back to pre-colonial African societies. I know that there were many varieties of social structure, but the Chief in one form or another was a common feature. Whether elected or hereditary, in a pastoral/ agricultural society, his duties and responsibilities were not onerous or complex except, e.g., in times of war or other crisis. He governed in conformity with tradition, so decision-making was not difficult; he had a rule book as it were. The rewards were proportionately modest – status, limited power, respect and more of everything that everyone else had i.e. more food, milk, meat, wives perhaps more cattle, more clothes and better accommodation. Quantitavely better-off than his people, but qualitatively not much different – no enhanced medical care, private jet, shopping at Harrods i.e. he remained very much in touch with his people and close to them.

With the modern politician these links have become broken, and by misuse of power he has access to material rewards which "his" people can only dream about. In fact they are not "his people"; they are simply a means whereby he is enabled to feather his own nest.

One can perhaps argue from this that this process reflects my earlier remark about loyalty to family coming first rather than loyalty to country. It could explain what one might call the acceptable face of corruption; what it does not explain is the excess. By all means look after your family, but this does not require a fleet of Mercedes, a castle in Germany, shopping trips to New York and a bank account of billions in Switzerland.

Which brings us round to the question, "why do people vote for candidates who repeatedly let them down?" Is it gullibility, naiveté, a triumph of hope over experience – or because of local loyalties rather than appraisal of the "big picture"? Voting for personalities rather than policies clearly doesn't work. Going back in time, in traditional societies where chiefs were chosen, people clearly voted for the personality – but the personality was someone who they knew, who lived close by; policy was determined by the tribal rule book and not in dispute. In the circumstances of the time this arrangement probably worked very well; and if the chief did not come up to scratch he could be deposed, exiled or executed as custom required.

Incidentally, in referring to corruption in African affairs I am aware that it also exists in this country. A rich country can afford it, a poor country cannot; and it is the exception rather than the rule. Looking back it was only in the 1870s that recruitment to our senior civil service was by public examination rather than patronage, and that commissions and promotions in the army ceased to be by purchase and bribery of one's would-be commanding officer![7]

Against the backdrop of this introspective from this former colonial officer, we can begin the Nigeria story. We start where we should, at the very beginning, before 'Nigeria'.

10 July 2017

Chronology

Apr 19,	1775	US War of Independence begins
Nov 7,	1775	British procamation pledging freedom for slaves joining British forces
Nov 4,	1776	US Declaration of Independence
	1784	Rhode Island passes law liberating all newborn slaves
Dec	1783	William Pitt the Younger becomes British Prime Minister
May 22,	1787	Committee for the Abolition of the Slave Trade is formed under William Wilberforce
June 9,	1788	The Association for the Promoting the Discovery of the Interior Parts of Africa formed
Apr 12,	1799	Church Missionary Society established
May 29,	1804	Fulani Jihad against Hausa nation begins
May 25,	1807	Slave Trade abolished within the British Empire
May	1814	Napoleon Bonaparte defeated
Nov 1,	1814	Congress of Vienna
Oct 1,	1818	Congress of Aixle-Chapelle
	1830	Richard Lander identifies source of the river Niger
Nov 18,	1830	Palmerston becomes Foreign Minister
Aug 28,	1833	Abolition of Slavery
	1837	First publication of Thomas Fowell Buxton's *The African Slave Trade and its Remedy*
	1841	Niger Expedition
	1845	Kosoko dethrones King Akitoye of Lagos
Jul,	1846	Beginning of Abeokuta CMS Mission
Dec 25,	1851	British bombardment of Lagos
	1854	British depose King Pepple of Bonny
	1858	British Colonisation of India

	1859	Henry Townsend publishes first newspaper in Nigeria
	1860	Beginning of Yoruba civil war
Aug 6,	1861	British declare Lagos as a Colony
	1873	British war against the Ashante
	1884	Berlin Conference
	1884	Maxim gun invented
Jun 5,	1885	British declare Oil Rivers Protectorate
Jul,	1886	Grant of the Royal Charter to Niger Company
Sep 23,	1886	End of Yoruba civil war
Sep 19,	1887	British depose Jaja of Opobo
Jan 18,	1893	British treaty with Egba confirming independence of the Egba United Kingdom
	1894	British depose and deport Nana of the Tsekiri
Jan 22,	1895	Brassmen destroy Royal Niger Company depot at Akassa
Feb 22,	1895	Akassa massacre; British dethrone Koko of Nembe
Jan 27,	1897	British conquest of Bida
Feb 16,	1897	British conquest of Ilorin
Feb 18,	1897	British conquest of Benin
Jan 1,	1900	Charter of Royal Niger Company revoked and Protectorates of Northern and Southern Nigeria proclaimed
	1900	French conquest of Bornu
Feb3,	1903	British conquest of Kano
	1903	British conquest of Sokoto
	1903	British expedition against Tiv
Oct 16,	1905	British partitioning of Bengal, India
Feb 26,	1906	Amalgamation of Lagos Colony and Southern Nigeria under Governor Walter Egerton
Sep	1906	Frederick Lugard resigns as High Commissioner of Northern Nigeria
	1906	Oil exploration begins in Southern Nigeria
Nov	1908	Oil production begins in Southern Nigeria
	1911	Publication of E.D. Morel's *Nigeria: Its People and Its Probems*
May	1912	Frederick Lugard recalled to effect amalgamation of Southern Nigeria and Northern Nigeria
Jan 1,	1914	Amalgamation
Jul 18,	1914	World War I begins

24

Sep 1,	1914	Lugard revokes Egba Independence and amalgamates Egbaland with Nigeria
Jan 8,	1918	US President Woodrow Wilson proclaims his Fourteen Points and the creation of the League of Nations
Jun 13,	1918	Egba and Owu war against British rule begins
Jul 22,	1918	British defeat of Egba and Owu
Nov 11,	1918	World War I ends
Jun 28,	1918	Versailles Treaty imposing war reparations on Germany
Aug 8,	1919	Recall and retirement of Frederick Lugard as Governor General of Nigeria
Aug 8,	1919	Hugh Clifford becomes Governor of Nigeria
	1922	Clifford Constitution
	1923	Herbet Macaulay forms Nigerian National Democratic Party (NNDP), the first political party in Nigeria
	1923	Frederick Lugard publishes *The Dual Mandate*
	1923	Adolf Hitler publishes *Mein Kampf*
Nov 13,	1925	Graeme Thomson becomes Governor of Nigeria
	1929	The Great Depression begins
Dec	1929	British massacre of protesting women in eastern Nigeria
Jun 17,	1931	Donald Cameron becomes Governor of Nigeria
Mar 4,	1933	Franklin Delano Roosevelt becomes President of U.S.A.
Dec 31,	1933	Nnamdi Azikiwe's New Year Resolution
Aug 2,	1934	Adolf Hitiler becomes Chancellor of Nazi Germany
Nov	1934	Azikiwe completes his tour of Eastern Nigeria
Nov 1,	1935	Bernard Bourdillon becomes Governor of Nigeria
	1937	Bourdillon publishes his *Memorandum on the Future Political Development of Nigeria*
Jul	1937	Azikiwe returns to Nigeria from Ghana and launches *West African Pilot* Newspaper
Oct	1938	Nigerian Youth Movement wins Lagos elections
Apr 1,	1939	Bourdillon partitions Southern Nigeria
Sep	1939	World War II begins
May 10,	1940	Winston Churchill becomes British Prime Minister
Feb 20,	1941	Azikiwe resigns from Nigerian Youth Movement
Aug 14,	1941	U.S.President Roosevelt and British Prime Minister Churchill issue *The Atlantic Charter*
Dec 7.	1941	U.S.A. enters World War II against Nazi Germany

	1942	H.O. Davies resigns from Nigerian Youth Movement
Dec	1943	Arthur Richards becomes Governor of Nigeria
	1943	Formation of Igbo State Union
	1944	Azikiwe establishes National Council of Nigeria and the Cameroons (NCNC)
Apr 12,	1945	U.S. President Roosevelt dies
May 7,	1945	World War II ends
Jun	1945	General Strike
Jul 26,	1945	Clement Attlee becomes British Prime Minister
Jan 1,	1946	Richards Constitution formalising three regions published and reginal elections organised
May	1946	NCNC tour of Nigeria
Jan	1947	Richards Constitution comes into effect
Jun	1947	NCNC delegation to London
Aug 15,	1947	India granted independence
Feb 5,	1948	John MacPherson becomes Governor of Nigeria
May 14,	1948	Creation of the State of Israel
May	1948	Nigerianization Commission established
June	1948	Obafemi Awolowo forms Egbe Omo Oduduwa
Nov 18,	1949	Iva Valley massacre in Enugu
Jan	1950	National Conference held in Ibadan
Apr	1950	Zikist Movement outlawed
Jun 29	1951	Macpherson Constitution
Mar 21,	1951	Awolowo forms Action group as a political party
Oct 1,	1951	Northern Peoples Congress formed as a political party
Oct 26,	1951	Winstin Churchill returns as British Prime Minister
Nov	1951	Regional Assembly elections
Jan 29,	1952	First sitting of the new House of Representatives
	1952	First census
Jul 23,	1952	Colonel Abdul Nasser stages military coup in Egypt
Jan 20,	1953	Dwight Eisenhower becomes President of U.S.A.
Mar 31,	1953	Action Group motion demanding self-governance in 1956
May	1953	Araba riots and killings in Kano
May	1953	London Constitutional Conference
Oct 1,	1954	Lyttleton Constitution

Oct 1,	1954	Southern Cameroon becomes a separate region within Southern Nigeria
Nov	1954	Elections to Federal House of Representatives
Apr 6,	1955	Anthony Eden becomes British Prime Minister
Jun 15,	1955	James Robertson becomes Governor General of Nigeria
Dec	1955	Harold Smith comes to Nigeria
Jan	1956	Queen Elizabeth II visits Nigeria
May	1956	Western region elections
Jul 26,	1956	Nasser nationalizes Suez Canal
Oct 27,	1956	Israel invades Egypt, Six-Day Arab-Israeli War begins and Britain and France occupy the Canal Zone
Nov	1956	Northern region elections
Nov 6,	1956	Ceasefire in Arab-Israeli War
Dec 23,	1956	Last British troops retire from the Canal Zone
Jan	1957	Foster-Sutton Report into African Continental Bank published
Jan 10,	1957	Harold Macmillan becomes British Prime Minister
Mar	1957	Eastern Region and Southern Cameroons elections
Mar 7,	1957	Ghana granted indepencence
Sep 29,	1957	Lancaster House Constitutional Conference
Aug 8,	1957	Western and Eastern regions become self-governing
Aug 8,	1957	Tafawa Balewa appointed to office of Prime Minister
Jul	1958	Willink Commissiom Report published
Mar	1959	Northern Region becomes self-governing
Dec	1959	Independence elections
Dec	1959	Harold Macmillan delivers *Winds of Change* speech in South Africa
Aug	1960	Tiv uprising
Oct 1.	1960	Nigeria granted independence
Oct 1,	1960	NCP-NCNC alliance government take office with Balewa as Prime Minister
Nov 16,	1960	Nnamdi Azikiwe replaces James Robertson as Governor General of Nigeria
Dec 14,	1960	UN Resolution 1514 passed proclaiming the end of colonialism
Feb	1961	Plebiscites in Northern and Southern Cameroon
Feb	1962	Census
May 29,	1962	State of emergency declared in Western region

Oct 1,	1963	Nigeria becomes a Republic
Oct 1,	1963	Nnamdi Azikiwe becomes President of Nigeria
Jul	1964	Awolowo jailed on treason charges
Feb	1965	Maj.gen. Welby-Everard replaced as commander-in-chief of Nigerian army by Thomas Aguyi-Ironsi
Oct	1965	Regional Assembly elections
Jan 15,	1966	First military coup
Feb 23,	1966	Declaration of Niger-Delta Republic
May 24,	1966	Proclamation of Unification Decree No. 34 creating 'united Nigeria'
May 29,	1966	First round of programs against Igbos in northern Nigeria
Jul 29,	1966	Counter-coup and second round of programs against Igbos in northern Nigeria
Aug 3,	1966	Awolowo and Enahoro released from prison
Jul 29,	1966	Third round of programs against Igbos in northern Nigeria
Jan	1967	Aburi Accord
May 27,	1967	Decree dividing Nigeria into twelve states
May 30,	1967	Declaration of Biafra
Jul	1967	Biafra War begins
Aug 27,	1969	British House of Commons debate on Biafra War
May 30,	1969	American student Bruce Mayrock self-immolates in protest against Biafra War
Jan 11,	1970	Col. Ojukwu escapes from Biafra
Jan 15,	1970	Biafra surrender
Oct 6,	1973	Arab-Israeli War and onset of oil boom
Jul 29,	1975	Maj.Gen. Gowon overthrown in military coup by Murtala Muhammed
Feb 13,	1976	Murtala Muhammed assassinated and Olusegun Obasanjo becomes military ruler
	1976	Decision taken to move Nigerian capital from Lagos to Abuja
	1979	New Constitution dividing Nigeria into nineteen states and replacing pariamentary systen with presidential system
Oct 1,	1979	Return to civilian rule with Shehu Shagari as President
	1983	New presidential elections return Shagari to power
Dec 31,	1983	Shagari government overthrown by military coup and Gen. Buhari becomes military ruler
Aug 27,	1985	Buhari overthrown in military coup by Gen. Ibrahim Babangida

Apr, 22,	1990	Failed coup by Maj. Gideon Orkar
Jun 12,	1993	Presidential elections
Jun 23,	1993	Babangida annuls election results
Aug, 26,	1993	Babangida forced aside and Ernest Shonekan appointed interim President
Nov 18,	1993	Gen. Sanni Abacha removes Shonekan from power
May	1994	The National Democratic Coalition (NADECO) formed
June 23,	1994	Moshood Abiola declares himself winner of aborted June 12 elections and President and is jailed
Jun	1994	Abacha convenes National Constitutional Conference
Nov 10,	1995	Abacha regime hangs Ogoni activist Ken Saro-Wiwa
Jun 4,	1996	Abiola's wife Kudirat Abiola assassinated
Jun 8,	1998	Abache dies in office
Jul 7,	1998	Abiola dies in prison
	1999	National elections
May 29,	1999	Gen Obasanjo becomes President
Oct 26,	1999	Governor of Zamafara state in northern Nigeria announces plan to enforce sharia criminal law
Nov 20,	1999	Obasanjo government attacks and destroys Odi town in southern Nigeria
Nov 23	2002	Miss World pageant riots and killings in Kaduna
Mar	2003	U.S. and British Governments launch invasion of Iraq
May 29,	2003	Obasanjo returnerd to power for second term as President
May 29,	2007	Umaru Musa Yar' Adua becomes President
Nov 23,	2009	Goodluck Jonthan takes over from Musa Yar' Adua as President
Nov 23,	2011	Goodluck Jonathan becomes President after winning Presidential elections
May	2013	Operation restore Order launched against Boko Haram
Mar 17,	2014	Goodluck Jonathan convenes National Conference Dialogue
Apr 14,	2014	Announcement of Boko Haram kidnap of Chibok girls

BOOK 1
BEFORE NIGERIA

1. Slavery's End and Colonisation's Beginning

I entirely disclaim any disposition to erect a new empire in Africa. Remembering what has now been disclosed, of the affliction of that quarter of the globe, and of the horrors and abominations which every spot exhibits, and every hour produces[1]

Sir Thomas Fowell Buxton

ABOLITION IN AMERICA

It is often said that the Slave Trade came to an end because Industrialisation made it unprofitable. But, as at the middle of the eighteenth century when the Industrial Revolution is commonly said to have begun, abolition of the Trade was far from the minds of the main players. In fact, measures were still being introduced to enhance it:

In 1750 the slave trade was made even easier for British merchants: an [A]ct made the commerce entirely open, so that it was henceforth 'lawful for all His Majesty's subjects to trade and traffick to and from any port in Africa...[2]

British merchants were not, of course, alone in the Trade: it was the enterprise of the times for most of Western Europe and the Arab world. In Europe the focus was on the liberalisation of the Trade rather than the liberation of the traded:

In 1753 the Spanish Crown gave permission to Spanish companies to bring slaves directly from Africa to Cuba. The papal rule limiting trade with Africa to Portugal was at last, unceremoniously put aside[3]

33

France, for its part, having been compelled to surrender Canada and India to Britain, as the price of defeat in the Seven Year's War of 1756-63, was unabashed in recognising the importance of the Trade for its future:

> The French Prime Minister, Choiseul, sought immediately to develop new French interests in Africa so as to free its colonies in the West Indies from reliance on Britain, formally or informally, for the supply of slaves. That the provision of slaves was an essential part of French commercial policy he was left in no doubt. Thus in 1762 the Chamber of Commerce of Nantes declared: 'the African trade is precious not only because of gold and ivory, it is infinitely more so because of the blacks that it makes possible because only they are capable of carrying through the hard work which the agriculture and manufacturing [of sugar] demand[4]

Far from Industrialisation being the cause of Abolition, it was the super-profits made possible by the Trade which stimulated and sustained the Industrial Revolution; and it was Britain's position as the dominant player in the Trade that produced the situation where the Industrial Revolution began in Britain. A British historian, Niall Ferguson, acknowledges the traditional economic explanation as unconvincing:

> It is not easy to explain so profound a change in the ethics of a people. It used to be argued that slavery was abolished simply because it had ceased to be profitable, but all the evidence points the other way: in fact, it was abolished despite the fact that it was still profitable[5]

Even so, Ferguson was to advance an equally questionable theory of his own for this *"collective change of heart"*. His argument that it was a moral revolution that *"mobilize[d] not only legislators to ban the trade, but the Royal Navy to enforce the ban"*[6] still leaves the question as to what triggered this moral turn around? The Trade was, after all, a reflection of the prevailing morals of the times which explains why other European powers expressed so much scepticism over the British claim to have undergone a moral conversion:

> The efforts of Great Britain to put an end to it (the Slave Trade) are not attributed to good motives, but to commercial jealousy, and a desire to keep the monopoly of colonial produce in our hands. The grant of twenty millions may have done something to quench these narrow jealousies, but still, the nations of the continent will be slow to believe that we are entirely disinterested, [7]

The German state, which because it was still in formation had no hand in the Slave Trade, could claim some objectivity in its' questioning of British claims to having moved to a higher moral plain than other Europeans:

> *While the Germans are tormenting themselves with philosophical problems, the English, with their great practical understanding, laugh at us and win the world. Everybody knows their declamations against the slave trade; and while they have paled off on us all sorts of humane maxims as the foundations of their proceedings, it is at last discovered that their true motive is a practical object, which the English always notoriously require in order to act, and which should have been known before[8]*

What the evidence points to is that the 'practical object' which was the trigger for the abolition of the Slave Trade, and later slavery itself, was the loss by Britain of its American colonies in the American war of Independence of 1776.

NEGROES INSPIRED BY THE SPIRIT OF MARTYRDOM

When it started the American War of Independence was a purely domestic affair between the British and their American Colonies. However, in the French, the Dutch and the Spaniards, *'Perfidious Albion'*, as England was often referred to, had no shortage of neighbours with recent grievances to avenge. By the end of the war, in 1783, each one of these fellow European powers had joined the fight on the side of the American rebels. The shared objective was to prise Britain's 'First Empire' from her grip.

A point, which seems little appreciated, is that the African slaves in America had, through their combat role in this war, secured their own salvation. At the outset, the conflict was a matter of indifference to these slaves. The twist of fate came as both sides, the British and the rebels in turn, looked to the slaves for help in their war effort. It was the British side who first felt compelled to do so. All slaves who were prepared to run the risks of escaping from their masters to fight on the British side were promised liberation after the war. This devil's bargain was set out in a proclamation made, on 7 November 1775, by the British Governor General of the Colony of Virginia:

> *I do require every Person capable of bearing Arms to resort to His Majesty's STANDARD or be looked upon as Traitors to his Majesty's Crown and Government and therefore be liable to the Penalty the Law inflicts upon such offences, such as forfeiture of life, confiscation of lands &c &c. And I do hereby further declare all indented Servants, Negroes or others (appertaining to Rebels) free that are able and willing to bear Arms, they joining His Majesty's*

Troops as soon as may be for the more speedily reducing this Colony to a proper
sense of their Duty to His Majesty's Crown and Dignity[9]

With this pledge, the British side now had the most eager recruits that the history of warfare may, possibly, have ever known. Africans had been held in bondage, and transported, in their millions to lay the foundations of America because of their natural physical strength. Their long period of subjugation had been made possible and sustained only by careful efforts to deny them access to and training in the use of guns. By this proclamation Britain changed the rules of the game and the writing was on the wall for the end of slavery in America.

However neither Britain nor America was ready for a multicultural society at this time: one in which with blacks lived in freedom alongside whites. As it concerned the slaves, the words in the American Declaration of Independence were just fine words:

We hold these truths to be self-evident, that all men are created equal, that they
are endowed by their Creator with certain unalienable Rights that among these
are Life, Liberty and the pursuit of Happiness

An overnight transition from a way of life in which the one had been subjugated by the other was viewed with understandable concern; for who knew when the spirit of vengeance might rise amongst former slaves now trained in the use of guns and explosives especially now that their numbers were significant: 'In 1790 there had been less than sixty-thousand free Negroes in the United States. By 1820 there were a quarter of a million'.[10]

As part of the planning for the new independent America which they desired, the leaders of thought in America had already begun to address their minds to the question of the role and place of the imported Africans within American society. The question was a racial one: whether free blacks were to be allowed to live as equal citizens alongside whites and, if the answer was no, what was to become of them. Writing in 1781, Thomas Jefferson, who authored the words in the Declaration of Independence, did not shy away from recognising the unique problems that Abolition of the African Slave Trade posed: 'Among the Romans emancipation required but one effort.... the Slave, when made free, might mix with, without staining the blood of his master. But with us a second [step] is necessary, unknown to history. When freed, he is to be removed beyond the reach of mixture'.[11]

Samuel Hopkins, a clergyman from Connecticut, who had himself owned slaves in the past, was one of these early thinkers on the subject. His solution was what the European powers then adopted as the blueprint for colonisation of Africa:

In early April, 1773, Congressional clergyman Samuel Hopkins of Rhode Island,

Thomas Jefferson

William Wilberforce

the chief exponent of the still novel doctrine of benevolence, called upon the Reverend Dr Ezra Stiles, later President of Yale College, and unfolded his plan for training two missionaries for Africa. Hopkins was eager to test his theological concept of dynamic evangelical Calvinism that would carry Christianity to the unredeemed throughout the world. The dark-continent offered vast numbers of pagans and infidels, and Stiles suggested that they enlarge the project, organise a society, and send thirty or forty "well instructed Negroes...inspired with the Spirit of Martyrdom". In this way whites could compensate for "injury and injustice" of the slave trade, "that unhallowed Commerce of traffic in the Souls of Men[12]

This plan of removal marked the start of the colonisation programme for Africa.

Being the first of the original thirteeen colonies to declare its independence, Hopkins' Rhode Island State, in New England, already had the reputation as the pace-setting State. By 1774, the State had passed a law forbidding the importation of slaves. In 1784, the year after the War of Independence was won, the State followed up with a law which granted freedom to all slaves born within its boundaries after March 1785. In this way, New England (in the United States of America) could lay fair claim to having beaten *'Olde England'* to credit for leading the way in the abolition of slavery.

Hopkins had set up a school to teach emancipated slaves theology in preparation for missionary work in Africa. It was Hopkin's formula that the British were to copy and implement in Sierra Leone in the coming years.

ABOLITION IN EUROPE

The loss of America had immediate and major consequences in Britain not least in the appointment in December 1783 of a new Prime Minister in William Pitt the Younger.

Pitt was a pragmatist who saw things clearly. He knew that it was on the back of the slaves that so much development within a short period of time had been made possible for all the major powers. The slaves were the raw materials on which all enterprise depended: slave labour being cheap and plentiful, all that was needed was suitable land on which to deploy them. So long as the expanse of America belonged to Britain the country's status as the major player in the game was assured. With the loss of America, it now faced the prospect of relegation as against the other players, France, Netherlands and Spain together with the newly independent United States. This was a script that could not be allowed to play out: The game had to be stopped.

The strategy was dual-pronged. The medium-term element was to look for a way to forcibly take back the lost colonies by renewing the war: This came in the war of 1812. The immediate, and subtler, strategy was borne of the knowledge that the newly independent United States was banking upon the continued supply of cheap slave labour for its viability and development. Shutting off the supply of slaves, by abolition of the Slave Trade, would make the medium-term goal of re-taking the rebel colony easier. But what to do with the slaves who would then be emancipated?

The ink on the Treaty of Paris of 1783, which brought the long and bloody American War of Independence to a formal end, had barely dried before the former warring parties were acknowledging their common interests by exchanging ideas on what to do with the slaves who had been freed in the course of the war. By 1784 Britain's William Thornton was visiting Samuel Hopkins and by 1786 he had moved, permanently, to Philadelphia to study more closely the American scheme for missionary-led colonies in Africa.[13]

The first challenge for Pitt was to sell the case for abolition to the British people. On the one hand there were the British merchants, and West Indian plantation owners, who were now addicted to the super-profits which the trade generated; and then there were the ordinary citizens. Different persuasions were required for the different constituencies. For the slave traders and plantation owners only monetary compensation for loss of profits and amenities would do. For the citizenry a new moral narrative was what was needed.

However, there were a few amongst the informed public who had long felt appalled by slavery and the Slave Trade. The Quakers, for one, had long been of this view and there were individuals like Granville Sharpe who had been calling upon the judges, in various test cases, to outlaw the evil without success. Now, with the major change in policy signalled from the very top, what had been a fringe movement against the trade in slaves and slavery very quickly became the subject of election pledges. The Committee for the Abolition of the Slave Trade was formed in 1787 with William Wilberforce as its Founding Secretary. Its assigned mission was to gather the evidence of the scale and evil of the Trade, in all its sordid detail, in support of the campaign.

Selling the new moral code in a Parliament whose members had, all the while, been using their collective intellect to pass laws to facilitate and encourage the Trade - right down to the size and dimensions of the slave ships - was an especially difficult challenge. The Members of Parliament for Liverpool, a small port town which had grown into a great city on the back of the Trade, were especially keen to remind their fellow Honourable members, who were now in the abolition camp, of their past complicity in the Trade:

> [D]ifferent Acts of Parliament which I shall not detain the House with moving to have read, have encouraged the African Slave Trade. The Preamble of one which runs thus: "Whereas the Trade to Africa is highly beneficial...." to the acclaim of "Hear! Hear!"[14]

The pro-abolitionists, led by the Solicitor General, were not to be outdone:

I can well understand that nations as well as individuals may be guilty of the most immoral acts, from their not having the courage to inquire into all the circumstances of this Trade. But in that year [1796] this House had the courage to appoint a committee to investigate the complaints which were preferred against it.

The committee sat, and after a painful and anxious investigation, they reported to this House a great body of evidence, by which it is established beyond the possibility of dispute, that the African Slave Trade is carried on by rapine, robbery, and murder by encouraging and fomenting wars; by false accusations and imaginary crimes.

Thus are these unhappy beings, in order to supply this Traffik in human blood, torn from their families, relatives, and homes, not only in war, but profound peace, and after being sold in their native land, they are carried across the Atlantic, in the most deplorable state in which it is possible to convey them alive, and under circumstances of too much horror to bear reflection[15]

In a war between brothers few home secrets survive. On 25ᵗʰ March 1807, *'An Act for the Abolition of the Slave Trade'* was passed by the United Kingdom Parliament. It declared the Slave Trade illegal in any part of the British Empire. Slavery itself (as distinct from the trade in slaves) remained legal.

The British Government having taken the lead in Europe now took on the task of persuading its fellow European powers to follow its lead. The defeat of Napoleon, in May 1814, by a six-power European alliance, led by Britain, provided a perfect opportunity.

While the primary objective of the new Treaty of Paris which ended the war was to redraw the map of the European mainland to contain future French ambitions,[i] the British took the opportunity to insert a clause committing the restored Bourbon monarchy to the abolition of the French Slave Trade over a period of five years. The Congress of Vienna between the same great powers, which held from September 1814 to June 1815, to agree the new balance of power arrangement for Europe, also included a communique condemning the Slave Trade. Again, even though the Congress of Aix-la-Chappelle of 1818 was primarily concerned with the withdrawal of allied forces of occupation from France, the British managed to work into its agenda the question of the methods to be adopted for the suppression of the Slave Trade. Principal amongst these methodologies was a British proposal of a reciprocal right to stop and search ships on the high seas.

But there was suspicion over the motivation for Britain's new campaign. The Duke of Wellington, Britain's representative at the Congress, is reported to have sent a letter home to William Wilberforce warning:

i   By the creation of the German Federation on its Eastern border and the united kingdom of Netherlands and Belgium on its Northern boundary

[I]t is not believed that we are in earnest about it, or have abolished the trade on the score of its inhumanity. It is thought to have been a commercial speculation; and that having abolished the trade ourselves, with a view to preventing the undue increase of colonial produce in our stores, of which we could not dispose, we now want to prevent other nations from cultivating their colonies to the utmost of their power[16]

The suspicions were not without foundation especially when British evangelism on Abolition, relying initially on moral persuasion, was escalated to gunboat diplomacy as the British Navy was deployed to enforce the new moral code against the unpersuaded.

The truth of the matter was that Britain had seen opportunities for itself which could not easily be shared with those whose cooperation it was seeking to enlist: First was the opportunity to reduce the stain on its name as the lead nation in the Slave Trade by now being at the vanguard of what was being sold to the world as a moral re-awakening and then there was the opportunity to stop its commercial rivals from continuing the lucrative trade.

A NEW EMPIRE IN AFRICA

Even with the British Navy patrolling the West African coast to arrest slave ships, the volume of trade was unrelenting. There were just too many ships from too many nations. More significantly, with Britain's writ as ruler of the seas not being accepted by the ships of the newly independent United States, many slave ships escaped arrest by the simple expedient of hoisting an American flag. A new strategy was needed. That new strategy was to establish colonial settlements on the West African coast.
The viability of the scheme had been tested in Sierra Leone, Gambia and the Gold Coast (what is now Ghana). The original imperial plan was a grand one:

It appears to me well worthwhile to...establish, to the utmost extent possible, a confederacy with the chiefs from the Gambia on the West to Begharmi on the East; and from the Desert on the North, to the Gulf of Guinea on the South[17]

The vision for the land that was to become 'Nigeria' was taken from the work of an earlier author and explorer, McQueen, set out in a book titled *'View of North Central Africa'*:

The extent of a country and population whose improvements, labors, and wants would be dependent upon and stimulated to exertions by a settlement on the Niger, is prodigious, and altogether unequalled. The extent comprehends a country of nearly 40# of longitude from west to east, and through the greater part of this extent of 20# of latitude from north to south, a space almost equal to Europe. Where the confluence of the Tschadda [river Benue] with the Niger takes place, is the spot to erect the capital of our great African establishments. A city built there, under the protecting wings of Great Britain, would ere [before] long become the capital of Africa[18]

Within the new pro-Abolition climate, selling the new plan of colonisation of the same land that had been so blighted by the slave trade was going to be a hard job requiring the utmost craft and guile.

THOMAS FOWELL BUXTON

The man who had been identified for the job was Thomas Fowell Buxton the Member of Parliament for Weymouth.

The implementation of his plan had been long underway before Buxton, in 1837, released outlines of it for public consumption in a book titled *The African Slave Trade and Its Remedy*. It is a work to which much of British policy in relation to Nigeria over the 100 years following its first publication can be traced. In the book, Buxton provides graphic accounts of the horrors of the Slave Trade before proceeding to discuss the shortcomings of the measures that had been adopted towards Abolition, and then, finally, putting forward his audacious new solution. Borrowing from Congressman Hopkins' work, the case he made was powerful:

Our system hitherto has been to obtain the cooperation of European Powers, while we have paid very little attention to what might be done in Africa itself, for the suppression of the Slave Trade. Our efforts in that direction have been few, faint, and limited to isolated spots, and those by no means well chosen. To me it appears that the converse of this policy would have offered greater probabilities of success; that while no reasonable expectations can be entertained of overturning this gigantic evil through the agency and with the concurrence of the civilized world, there is a well-founded hope, amounting almost to certainty, that this object may be attained through the medium and with the concurrence of Africa herself. If, instead of our expensive and fruitless negotiations with Portugal, we had been, during the last twenty years, engaged in extending our intercourse with the nations of Africa, unfolding to them the capabilities of their soil, and the inexhaustible store of wealth which human labour might derive from its cultivation, and convincing them that the Slave Trade alone debars them from enjoying a vastly more affluent supply of our valuable commodities, and if we had leagued ourselves with them to suppress that baneful traffic, which is their enemy even more than it is ours, there is reason to believe that Africa would not have been what Africa is, in spite of all our exertions – one universal den of desolation, misery and crime[19]

Stripped off the emotive tones, the Remedy that Buxton was prescribing was colonisation, although he was careful not to call it by name as to do so ran the risk of exciting the jealous attentions of fellow European powers already suspicious of British motives. Only those who could read between the lines would have understood the true nature of the Remedy that was being proposed. Buxton wrote:

To these portions of Africa, in particular, Great Britain owes a heavy debt of justice, for the many years of misery which she inflicted upon them by making them the seats of the Slave Trade; a debt which she can only hope to repay, by carrying out the salutary measures which have proved so successful in the case of the Gold Coast. But as the injury was not limited to these localities only, so her redress should not terminate here: in order that her compensation may be ample, and her remedy efficient, they must be applied nearer the sources of the evil.

Our efforts, as far as they have gone, have been successful, and although our principal object has not been attained by them, we have proved what may be effected, by granting our protection, by encouraging commerce and agriculture, and by diffusing the blessings of Christianity. By adopting a similar policy in positions more favourable, and in connection with the other measures which I propose, I am led to believe we shall effectually check the Slave Trade, and produce a revolution in Africa, still more signal than that which has been already experienced in our present settlements[20]

Whose resistance would not be overcome by an admission that 'Great Britain owes a heavy debt of justice' with the promise of atonement by the 'granting of our protection'? But it was double-speak in its highest form. Buxton stressed the need for the utmost care to be taken:

Nothing, I apprehend, could be more unfortunate to the continent we wish to befriend, or more discreditable to ourselves than that Great Britain should give colour to the suspicion of being actuated by mercenary motives; an apology would thus be afforded to every other nation for any attempt it might make to thwart our purpose. We know, from the Duke of Wellington's dispatches, that the powers on the continent were absolutely incredulous as to the purity of the motives which prompted us, at the congress of Aix la Chapelle, to urge, beyond everything else, the extinction of the Slave Trade[21]

Knowing that the country's real motives for promoting Abolition had already come under strong suspicion, Buxton recommended that the commitment to abolish the Slave Trade should be coupled with a "pledge" that Britain would share, with those European partners who were ready to join the cause, all benefits that might accrue from the exercise. Central to this pledge was the policy of Free Trade. The priority was to avoid another war with the European neighbours as had occurred over America and India:

> *The proposal of a settlement in Africa, necessarily recalls to mind our vast empire in India: and, surely, no sober-minded statesman would desire to see renewed in another quarter of the globe, the career we have run in the East*[22]

In practical terms, this meant scaling down the original plan of creating one gigantic British colony on the West African coast, in the mould of India, running from Gambia right across the coast down to Congo.

The European powers apart, the other constituency from whom Buxton needed some buy-in for his Remedy were the people of Africa. To doubts about whether the grand plan of African colonisation in areas that had been so recently blighted by the Slave Trade would be practicable, the answers had been well researched by the explorers, "the travellers in Africa", who were now roaming the region:

> *[T]he natives, so far from shunning intercourse with us, and rejecting our overtures for peace and commerce, have been, in almost every case, eager and importunate that we should settle among them. If further progress had not been made, it is ourselves who have been to blame*[23]

The strategy paper correctly anticipated that resistance to the push into the interior was likely to come from the coastal chiefs, and the members of their court. These ones had grown rich through their role as agents and intermediaries in the illicit trade in the peoples of the interior and the trade in slaves was an enterprise to which they were as much addicted as their European principals and patrons:

> *We must then expect great opposition from the Chiefs on the coast. It appears indeed, from the journals of all the travellers in Africa, that every impediment has been thrown in their way, in order to prevent their proceeding into the interior of the country. It is, however, some consolation to learn from recent travellers, that the power of these chiefs has been greatly exaggerated*[24]

Part of the brief of the explorers, like Mungo Park and Hugh Clapperton, had been to investigate and report on the fighting capability of the peoples they visited. Based on these reports, the strategists at home had reason to be confident that the resistance of these chiefs could ultimately be overcome; if necessary by their forced removal. The intelligence gathering activities of the explorers also extended to gauging the attitude of the different native rulers towards Abolition:

> But whatever difficulties we may have to encounter with the chiefs on the coast (and I confess that, viewing their character, and the insalubrity of the climate near the sea, and at the mouths of the rivers, I apprehend that they will be far from light) there is good reason to believe that we shall find a much better disposition on the part of the Sultans and sovereigns of the interior, to receive, to treat, and to trade with us[25]

In this lay the early seeds of what would become a significant difference in the British relationship with the Sultans of the north and the leaders in the south of what would become Nigeria.

LORD PALMERSTON

If Buxton's '*Remedy*' was the intellectual framework for British foreign policy towards Africa, it was the British statesman, Lord Palmerston who, through his various offices of State, was responsible for its practical implementation.

At the headline level, Palmerston's 'Liberalism' translated into pushing on from the abolition of the Slave Trade to the abolition of slavery itself. In the sub-text this was to be achieved by getting the British slavers to make the switch from the business of the gathering and sale of Africa's people to the new enterprise of the gathering and sale of Africa's resources. It was out with the Slave Trade and in with Free Trade. Accordingly, the Abolition of Slavery Act was passed in 1833 under which slavery was made illegal throughout the British Empire.

The former slavers were not alone in re-making themselves. Realising that the new elixir of reform would be difficult to sell in the old keg of Toryism, on 18 November 1830, Palmerston, the grand old Tory, took up his position in the Foreign Office as part of a Whig government. From there he would move political boundaries across the globe as on a grand chess board. So delicious, in policy terms, was the new plan for Britain post-slavery that, in 1839, his new Whig party changed its name to the 'Liberal Party'.

THE ADVENT OF THE EDUCATED NATIVES

The *Association for Promoting the Discovery of the Interior Parts of Africa* (the African Association[ii]) was established in London, on June 9th 1788 on the back of William Thornton's study of the American colony initiative in Liberia for liberated American slaves. It was this Association that sent the famed explorers like Mungo Park and Hugh Clapperton, into the African interior as pathfinders.

The early work of these 'travellers' had led to Sierra Leone being identified as the most benign place on the coast of the continent to establish the first British Colony in West Africa. Initially it was for the settlement of those American slaves who had fought on the British side in the American War of Independence and who were now to be found, in significant numbers, on the streets of London[26]. Freetown, as the settlement was named, became the clearing house for the slaves re-captured by the Royal Navy in the course of Abolition. Here they were assessed for their potential with the less fortunate being shipped off to the Caribbean to work as slaves on the British plantations[27]. The apparent contradiction was explained by the fact that slavery was, at this time, still legal; it was only the trade in slaves that was not. Some of these *'returnees'* would later be transplanted into Yoruba land to play a key role in the conversion to Christianity of the natives and the subsequent British takeover.

Writing in 1837, Buxton states that, thirty years prior, 'a few liberated African boys were sent to England and educated at the expense of the African [Association], with a view to their aid in working out the general objects of the [Association] at Sierra Leone'. This experiment informed Buxton's call for 'the education of the sons of Africa in their own country, and by their own countrymen previously educated by Europeans'[28]. In the course of the Slave Trade, Africans had been deployed to capture other Africans to be taken to plantations in the Americas and the Caribbean. Now some of these former captives were to be deployed back to the West Coast of Africa to capture souls:

> *We have already seen the desirableness of educating and civilizing the inhabitants of Africa; and a number of facts have been brought to light, tending to show, that there is at least as great a readiness on their part to receive instruction, as on ours to communicate it; the question now remains- Who are to be the instructors? The climate is generally viewed as unfavourable to Europeans, and this being the case I have great satisfaction in finding, that from among the liberated Africans in our West Indian Colonies we are likely to be furnished with a number of persons, in whom are united the desirable qualifications of fitness for the climate, competency to act as teachers, and willingness to enter upon the work*[29]

The mission for these 're-captives' was to convert to the way of Christ the people of their

ii   Later, the Royal Geographic Society

Canterbury Cathedral

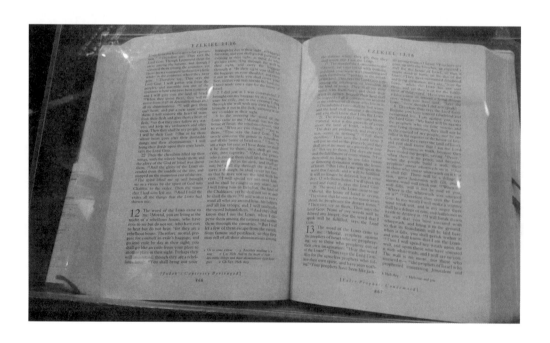

The Bible at Canterbury

homelands who, they would have been told, had sold them into slavery.

The relationship between Christianity, slave-owners and the education of slaves up until this point is best described as ambivalent. It was memorably captured in the autobiography of Frederick Douglas, the American Slave:

> *In August, 1832, my master attended a Methodist camp-meeting held in the Bayside, Talbot county, and there experienced religion. I indulged a faint hope that his conversion would lead him to emancipate his slaves, and that if he did not do this, it would at any rate, make him more kind and humane. I was disappointed in both these respects. It neither made him to be humane to his slaves nor to emancipate them. If it had any effect on his character, it made him more cruel and hateful in all his way; for I believe him to have been a much worse man after his conversion than before. Prior to his conversion, he relied upon his own depravity to shield and sustain him in his savage barbarity; but after his conversion, he found religious sanction and support for his slaveholding cruelty. He made the greatest pretensions to piety. His house was the house of prayer. He prayed morning, noon and night. He very soon distinguished himself among his brethren, and was soon made a class leader and exhorter. His activity in revivals was great, and he proved himself an instrument in the hands of the church in converting many souls. His house was the preacher's home. They used to take great pleasure in coming there to put up; for while he starved us, he stuffed them.....*
>
> *While I lived with my master in St. Michael's, there was a white young man, a Mr Wilson, who proposed to keep a Sabbath school for the instruction of such slaves as might be disposed to learn to read the New Testament. We met but three times, when Mr. West and Mr Fairbanks, both class-leaders, with many others, came upon us with sticks and other missiles, drove us off, and forbade us to meet again. Thus ended our little Sabbath school in the pious town of St Michael's*[30]

In the new climate of the drive towards colonisation, if the former slaves were to be effectively deployed to evangelize to their people they had to be educated. Their schooling centre was Fourah Bay College, Freetown, Sierra Leone; their curriculum was the Bible.

THE FLOW OF THE RIVER NIGER

Before roads and railways it was the rivers that served as the transportation highways into the various parts of the hinterland. The mighty river Niger was known, only its precise course was a mystery which the African Association, working with the Colonial

Office, resolved to get to the bottom of. The first explorer whom the African Association sent out in 1870 was Daniel Houghton an Irish soldier. He died in the Sahara desert. Mungo Park, a Scottish surgeon, came next. His first effort started on June 4th 1795. He returned to try to find the mouth of the River Niger in 1805-6. He was to die still trying.

Hugh Clapperton, a captain in the navy and the son of a surgeon, followed. His primary assignment was to explore the northern regions of West Africa working down from Tripoli down across Lake Chad and into Bornu. Having completed this assignment, he returned to the coast in December 1825 to try and unravel the mystery. He, too, died in the effort in 1827. It was his assistant on the venture, Richard Lander, a Cornishman, who, in 1830, finally succeeded in 'establishing that the River Niger entered the sea through oil rivers in present day Rivers State, Nigeria as the river flows eastwards'[31].

Having established that the river Niger ran from west to south-east and joined the Atlantic Ocean at the Bight of Benin, the drive into the hinterland could begin. The river Niger area was central to the vision of the new empire:

> By the Niger, the whole of Western Africa would be embraced; by the Sharry (which I have no doubt will be found navigable to the meridian of 25# east longitude) a communication would be opened with all nations inhabiting the unknown countries between the Niger and the Nile. British influence and enterprise would thereby penetrate into the remotest recesses of the country; new and boundless markets would be opened to our manufactures; a continent teeming with inexhaustible fertility would yield her riches to our traders; not merely a nation, but hundreds of nations, would be awakened from the lethargy of centuries, and become useful and active members of the great commonwealth of mankind[32]

A CHRISTIAN EMPIRE

The plan, at this stage, was to establish a Christian empire through the education of the natives in the way of Christ. It was a carefully considered strategy shaped, in part, by the lessons of recent history in the unsuccessful attempt to Christianise Native-American Indians:

> Within the last few years we have had occasion to review the whole course of our proceedings, and we have come to the conclusion, from a deliberate view of the past, that we erred in the plan which was originally adopted, in making civilisation the first object; for we cannot count on a single individual that we have brought to the full adoption of Christianity, in order to lead the way to other advantages[33]

The experience led to a Parliamentary Committee being set up, in 1833, to look into the key question of:

> *Whether the experience of the several missionary societies led to the belief that it would be advisable to begin with civilization in order to introduce Christianity, or with Christianity, in order to lead to civilization*[34].

The strategists will have been aided by the publication in 1776, the year that America won its Independence from Britain, of Edward Gibbon's *the Decline and Fall of the Roman Empire*. Gibbon showed how the the infusion of Christianity into the citizens of the greatest empire ever known had disengaged them from the pantheon of Roman gods, *Apollo*, *Janus*, *Mars* and *Jupiter*, to whom they had hitherto credited their greatness. With this precedent as a guide, there was every confidence that the arrival of Christianity would have a similarly transformative effect upon African traditional societies.

The other political calculation in the decision to take the Bible to the people of West Africa was the realisation that the rival faith of Islam was pushing down from across the Sahara. The despatch reports, from the explorers, of jihads whose true object was the expansion of the Islamic empire, helped to convince the Europeans of the merits of a religious cover for their own imperial advance. To arrest Islam's further southward penetration, Christian settlements were to be established at the southernmost points of the areas which Islam had already reached to serve as a buffer.

The work of taking the Bible to West Africa was the responsibility of the Church Missionary Society (CMS) which had been established on 12th April 1799, in anticipation of Abolition, with William Wilberforce as its Founding Vice-President. Its original name was the 'Society for Missions to Africa and the East'. The mission was to "preach the gospel to every creature". Its first task was the education and training of the 'recaptives' as native missionaries.

The moral case was to be based on a pressing need to turn the 'heathens' of these lands away from the ways of superstition and away from the practice of human sacrifice which it was said to spawn. Richard Lander's account of events which he claims to have observed in Badagry was sensational beyond the point of credibility with tales of ritual human sacrifice with 'smoking blood [gurgling]'[35]. With the home audience being fed reports like this, the case for the infusion of Christianity became compelling.

THE RE-CAPTIVES

Samuel Ajayi Crowther is of one of the most celebrated Africans of all times. He was born in 1809. Just two years previously the British Parliament had passed the law making the

Slave Trade, but not slavery itself, illegal. According to Crowther's own account, he was kidnapped as a young boy and sold into slavery. He had passed through 'the door of no return', through which the slaves passed before being loaded onto the slave ships on the Lagos coast, when the ship was arrested by a British anti-slavery patrol. If any native was qualified to preach the message of salvation, and of life after death, it would be a re-captive, like Ajayi Crowther.

Since it is by accounts of miracles that people are most readily converted to a faith, with the encouragement of the Church Missionary Society, Crowther had documented his own experience in a letter to one Reverend William Jowett, on 22 February 1837:

> *Rev. and Dear Sir*
>
> *As I think it will be interesting to you to know something of the conduct of Providence in my being brought to this Colony, where I have the happiness to enjoy the privilege of the Gospel, I give you a short account of it; hoping I may be excused if I should prove rather tedious in some particulars.*
>
> *I suppose sometimes about the commencement of the year 1821, I was in my native country, enjoying the comforts of father and mother, and the affectionate love of brothers and sisters. From this period I must date the unhappy, but which I am now taught, in other respects, to call blessed day, which I shall never forget in my life. I call it unhappy day, because it was the day in which I was violently turned out of my father's house, and separated from relations; and in which I was made to experience what is called to be in slavery – with regard to its being called blessed, it being the day which Providence had marked out for me to set out on my journey from the land of heathenism, superstition, and vice to a place where His Gospel is preached.*
>
> *For some years, war had been carried on in my [Oyo] Country, which was always attended with much devastation and bloodshed; the women, such men as had surrendered or were caught, with the children, were taken captives. The enemies who carried on these wars were principally the Oyo Mahomendans, with whom my country abounds – with the Foulahs [Fulbe], and such foreign slaves as had escaped from their owners, joined together, making a formidable force of about 20,000, who annoyed the whole country. They had no other employment but selling slaves to the Spaniards and Portuguese on the coast*[36]

The letter gives a sense of just how the experience of the evil of slavery made the minds of those who were rescued from it. Not only were they ready to embrace the religion of their saviours, they became passionate flag-bearers of the revolution amongst their people whom they would have held responsible for the misfortunes from which they had been freed. Crowther's letter ended with the following appeal:

That the time may come when the Heathen shall be fully given to Christ for His inheritance, and the uttermost part of the earth for His possession, is the earnest prayer of Your humble, thankful, and obedient servant,

Samuel Crowther[37]

Following the publication of Buxton's book in 1838, in the estimation of the British Government the time had most certainly come for Ajayi Crowther's prayer to be answered. Having demonstrated high intellectual ability, and a gift for languages, he was to play a key role in the 1841 Niger Mission to take Christianity Commerce and Civilization into what was to become Nigeria.

2. The Reverend Father, the Mujaddid, and the Sheikh

The demons soon discovered and abused the natural propensity of the human heart towards devotion, and, artfully withdrawing the adulation of mankind from their Creator, they usurped the place and honours of the Supreme Deity[1]
— Edward Gibbon

THE REVEREND FATHER

The Society for the Extinction of the African Slave Trade and the Civilisation of Africa was founded by Buxton in June 1839 to give practical expression to the Remedy he had prescribed in his book. His ownership of the project was made clear by the statement in its foundational documents: 'Sir Fowell Buxton emphatically declares that next to Christianity (the great and only effectual cure), the 'deliverance of Africa' is to be sought in 'calling out her own resources'. One of the stated main objects of the Association was to 'co-operate by every means in its power with the Government Expedition to Niger.

The 1841 Niger Mission, which was officially known as the African Colonization Expedition, was planned to shock and awe. Some insight into the scale of the expedition emerges from the following account:

> *The immediate plan was to send a massive expedition up the Niger at a cost of 100,000 pounds sterling, now worth more than 10,000,000. The expedition was not only to make a survey for the introduction of Christianity, commerce and civilisation, but also to impress Africans with the knowledge and power of British*

Industrial Revolution. On the three steamers, there were about 150 Europeans, and slightly more African auxiliaries, interpreters, stokers and other labourers. Even today, a trade delegation of that size would be deemed impressive. Among the Europeans, there were the naval officers and sailors and four government commissioners with authority to make treaties of friendship and commitment to abolition, acquire land at the confluence for a model farm, and explore the feasibility of stationing a consul on the Niger. There were scientists equipped with the latest instruments to make observations about the climate, the plants, animals, soils, weather, mineral resources and the people themselves, and their social and political institutions. There were commercial agents to report about the trade, the currency, and traffic on the river. There were agriculturalists to set up the model farm, and settle 24 Sierra Leonean farmers there under a superintendent and a chaplain. Besides the official chaplain who was in the captain's ship, the CMS nominated J.F. Crowther who had been studying Hausa with him, to act as chaplain in each of the other two ships. They were to carry out a feasibility study for the introduction of Christianity[2]

The Expedition was eventually grounded due to the high death toll amongst the white participants as a result of attacks from mosquitoes.

In preparation for his role in the venture, Ajayi Crowther had been sent from Sierra Leone to the Highbury Missionary College for his missionary education. However, the attempt to use Crowther, a Yoruba man, even though tutored in the Hausa language, to sell the Christian Gospel in Hausa-land was also a failure: ethnic identities were too hard-set for a member of one national group to evangelise effectively to the natives of another. As a result, Crowther was re-deployed to the Yoruba Mission in Abeokuta which was being spearheaded by the missionary Henry Townsend.

To prepare him for his new role, Crowther was sent back to Islington for further studies in the Yoruba language towards the mastery of which significant resources had been committed:

...the re-captives came back speaking the white man's language, and the white man came speaking the Yoruba language. The work of translation was thus of great advantage to the mission. There was a large concentration of Europeans involved in the study, each making his own contribution. Townsend with his printing press and monthly newspaper in Yoruba. Charles Gollmer helping to revise translations for linguistic consistency; David Hinderer, the mission expert in Hebrew, Bunyan's Pilgrim's Progress is still used today; Adolphus Mann, another German linguist, collecting Yoruba prayers and religious literature; Thomas Jefferson Bowen, the American Baptist, bringing American linguistics to supplement European linguistics in the study of Yoruba, but whose

Dictionary of the Yoruba Language was locked away in the huge volumes of the Smithsonian Contributions to Knowledge. The mission also had the largest concentration of native speakers of Yoruba among the agents as schoolmasters, catechists and ordained ministers, with Crowther at their head[47]

Crowther is credited with leading the work of translation of the Bible into the Yoruba language but the initiave was a British one. In this, they were drawing upon their own experiences following the first translation of the Bible into the English language, in 1611, at the instigation of King James I. The impact of the arrival of the alien faith on the established social order is, perhaps, best captured by Chinua Achebe, in his masterpiece *"Things Fall Apart"*. To his tragic-hero Okonkwo's question: "Does the white man understand our custom about land", the response is:

How can he when he does not even speak our tongue? But he says that our customs are bad; and our own brothers who have taken up his religion also say that our customs are bad. How do you think we can fight when even our own brothers have turned against us? The white man is very clever. He came quietly and peaceably with his religion. We were amused at his foolishness and allowed him to stay. Now he has won our brothers, and our clan can no longer act like one. He has put a knife on the things that held us together and we have fallen apart.[4]

THE MUJADDID

In today's Nigeria, owing to the work of the missionaries and early British Imperial policy, the people of the South can lay fair claim to being, generally, more educated than the people of the North. But it was not always so. In the days before modern transportation and communication it was the itinerant communities, rather than the settled, who were likely to be the best-informed and most-learned and the Fulani people could count themselves amongst them. For this reason, they were the principal agents for the spread of Islam in north-east Nigeria.

Shehu Uthman d'an Fodiyo, the Mujaddid, was a Fulani born, in 1754, in what was then Hausaland. In the competition for new followers between Islam and Christianity, the two faiths borrowed much from one another. Just as the community of Christians had grown quietly, and peacefully, within the belly of Rome until the movement was strong enough to withstand efforts of the established order to expel them, so too the Mujaddid had nurtured the growth of the community of the faithful, through his daily work as a religious teacher until, on 29 May 1804, he felt confident to declare a jihad against his Hausa hosts.

The declared purpose of the jihad was to establish *"true Islam"* in Hausaland. By the time the Sarki of Gobir (the then dominant kingdom in Hausaland) decided to take action the established order had been overwhelmed by the Fulani warriors of the faith[5]. The fall of Gobir (now renamed Sokoto) marked the beginning of the end of the Hausa nation.

The Mujaddid now had no shortage of volunteers to take up the green flag of jihad for the conquest of other Hausa States like Katsina and Kano. By 1807, d'an Fodiyo, had succeded in establishing a new Islamic State over the whole of Hausaland with its capital in Sokoto. He died in 1817 but the work of expanding his Islamic domain through holy war continued: 'four years before his death the Shehu had delegated great authority to his brother Abdullahi and his son Muhammad Bello. The former had responsibility for the lands to the west and south, the latter to the north and east'.[6] While Bello pushed the empire eastwards to the borders of the already Islamized state of Bornu and down to Bauchi and Adamawa and then through to Yola on the south side of the river Benue, Abdullahi pushed in a south-westerly direction into Nupe and, south of the river Niger, into Ilorin.

At every stage of the advance the trusted formula was re-used: instructors in the Koran built up the community of the faithful within the host community whilst waiting for the moment when the community could be turned into an army of conquerors. In some instances the forward march of the empire was assisted by the miscalculation of their hosts. The south-westerly drive, into the northern parts of Yoruba-land and the capture of Ilorin, discussed in the next chapter, is a leading example.

THE REALITY OF JIHAD

Islam had originated as a faith for the Arab peoples, to rival Christianity, in much the same way as the Christianity had taken hold amongst the people of Europe as a counter to Judaism. While the Jews, with their claim of being God's chosen people, were concerned to keep their status exclusive, the two newer faiths competed for recruits.

Proselytization and evangelism being, thus, at the heart of Christianity and Islam from their origins, and with both offering a truth which they claimed to be absolute, that their paths would clash was a certainty. The construction of rival Christian and Islamic empires, which saw the crown of the Holy Land of Jerusalem changing hands several times as jihads followed crusades and crusades followed upon jihads, was the ultimate manifestation of this competition. The defining contest, however, was to be the race for the souls of those whom both camps viewed as the heathen peoples of the world; the people of Africa who knew neither Christ nor Muhammad.

Until the sea route around Africa was opened up by the Portuguese, from around the middle of the fifteenth century, the only route through which new ideas, goods and weapons could enter the continent was from traders from the land of the Arabs, lying to the north of the Sahara desert. It was along these trade routes that Islam first came into the Nigeria space. One of the leading scholars on the history of Islam writes that Arab traders:

> ...created a commercial diaspora with a common religion, language, and legal system, the Shariah, a personal and extraterritorial divinely ordained law, which added to the mutual trust among merchants. Conversion to Islam thus became necessary for those who wished to join the commercial network[7]

In this entry phase, the promoters had been content for the new faith to gradually percolate down through the leaders while ordinary people were left to pursue their religious traditions. A new aggressive phase then saw a drive to establish a pure faith through jihad. In keeping with the tradition of all political revolutions, the revolution was rationalised by the expressed desire to cleanse the land of 'corruption, heathen practices and superstitions'.

That the Fulani-jihad within the 'Nigeria' space was, in fact, part of an internationally coordinated initiative is evidenced by the occurrence of similar jihadist drives, around the same time, all in the name of renewal of the faith[i]. These jihads were, in reality, the Islamic world's response to the aggressive forward march of the European-Christian empires. The Caliphate had watched the Christians use their mastery of the seas to take over much of the habitable planet: the Americas, Canada, Australia New Zealand as well as the southern parts of Africa. In 1804, the very year in which d'an Fodiyo launched his jihad in Hausaland, the British were in the final phase of their conquest of the whole of India which the Caliphate had been in contention for. These developments on the international stage manifested in West Africa as follows:

> In West Africa a major tradition of renewalist holy war (jihad) developed, with the result being the creation of a number of explicitly Islamic states. Jihads were proclaimed and jihad states were established in the Senegambia region during the eighteenth century. In the Futa Jallon region a teacher known as Karamoko Alfa (d.1751) declared a jihad in 1726 against non-Muslim elites and established a state ruled by a combination of warriors and scholars, which lasted until the French conquests of the region in the late nineteenth century. A similar jihad state was established in the Futa Toro region under the leadership of Sulayman Bal (d.1776). Muslim teachers who were part of the broader network of scholarship played an important role in the development of the ideology and the subsequent state structures. The tradition of militant reformism reached a climax with the

---

i   There was a jihad in north-west India in reaction to the British advance; in Chechnya, in reaction to Russian imperial claims; in Java, in response to the Dutch advances in Indonesia; in Algeria, after the French invasion of 1830; and in Somalia, in reaction to British, French and Italian encroachment

jihad of the scholar and reformist Uthman dan Fodio (1755-1817) in the area of modern Nigeria and beyond at the end of the eighteenth century [8]

By the time the British explorer Hugh Clapperton visited Sokoto, in 1824, Caliph Bello, the son of the Mujaddid, had become the undisputed head of the new Fulani Empire within the 'Nigeria' space. Clapperton's visit was part of the reconnaissance for the start of the British push into the hinterland which put the British and the Fulani on the pathway to eventual conflict. Both were alien powers who were making their formal entry into the 'Nigeria' space around about the same time, at the beginning of the 19th century. Both were using the cloak of religion as the cover for imperial expansion. In each case, they would first identify and target the local ruler or king to demonstrate the power of their prayers and medicines in competition with the traditional priests and healers; once the ruler had been converted, the work would begin to push the new faith down to the lower tiers within the society.

THE SHEIKH

The attempt by the Fulani to push eastwards into the Islamic kingdom of Bornu, in the area of north-east Nigeria, failed however. They were defeated when the Bornu ruling class, the Sayfawas, turned to another Islamic scholar-warrior, Sheikh Al-Kanemi, for help.

In every detail, excepting for the fact that he was not Fulani, Al Kanemi was a character in the mould of Shehu Uthman d'an Fodiyo:

> *He was a Kanembu (one of the ethnic groups of the Chad basin) who was born in Murzuk. His father, Muhammad Ninka, was a scholar of wide reputation. It was his quest for knowledge that made him leave Kanem for Murzuk in the central Saharan region*[9]

While with the Sheikh's help, the Bornu Kingdom survived the Fulani assault, it did not escape the Ilorin experience: Al Kanemi soon enough became the ruler of Bornu and, by 1846, the Sheikh's own family had become the new ruling dynasty in the land. Their reign lasted until 1893 when the dynasty was overthrown by another invader, from Sudan, by the name of Rabeh Zubair. In 1900, following the Berlin Conference of 1884, the Bornu Kingdom was carved up between Britain, Germany and France with different parts of it ending up in British Northern-Nigeria, German-Cameroon and French- Niger and Chad.

The Reverend Father, the Mujaddid and the Sheikh were not Nigerians in the strict sense of the word because the name *'Nigeria'* did not come into use until 1 January 1900, by which time they had, all, left the stage. Even so these three characters, from the three sides of the confluence of the Rivers Niger and Benue, were the local actors who did most to shape the country at the outset.

BOOK 2.
NIGERIA

3. Two Nigerias and the United Kingdom of Egbaland

'It is earnestly to be desired that all Christian powers should unite in one great Confederacy, for the purpose of calling into action the dormant energies of Africa'

Sir Thomas Fowell Buxton

THE ROYAL NIGER COMPANY

Back in England, abolition had required a massive propaganda campaign to attune the peoples' minds to the evil of slavery.

In this new moral climate which the Government had engineered, the implementation of Buxton's colonisation project required the greatest discretion. By the clever expedient of private companies, with private armies, being licensed by Government charter to establish the colonies as commercial ventures, complete with balance sheets and profit and loss accounts and dividends, the Government was able to distance itself from the early, invariably violent, groundwork for the construction of the colonies.

These companies were brought into existence by command, either by a Royal Charter or by an Act of Parliament, which would define the scope of the company's activities. With the cloak of such exclusive authority, the company's officers would then, effectively, act on the state's behalf while being answerable only to their private owners, and not to the general public. In this way, the Dutch used the *Dutch East India Company* for their colonial activities in Asia; Sweden had the *Swedish East India Company*; *the British East India Company* was used to midwife India while the *Royal Niger Company* was the corporate vehicle that was used to form Nigeria. After the politically sensitive groundwork of establishing the colonies had been done the companies were then taken into Government ownership by nationalisation.

GEORGE GOLDIE

George Goldie was educated at the Royal Military Academy in Woolwich. The youngest son of a Lieutenant Colonel in the British army, he was to Nigeria what Cecil Rhodes was to Rhodesia. It is said that but for his dislike of self-publicity, the country might well have, similarly, borne his name.

Before its Royal Charter was granted in July 1886, the *Royal Niger Company* was known as the *National African Company*. It had been formed, in 1879, as the *United Africa Company* (UAC) - the *"United"* epithet in the company's original name reflecting Goldie's work in bringing all British merchant interests, in the area of the River Niger, under one corporate roof to ensure that they would speak with one voice at the Berlin Conference of 1884.

Based in Asaba, in what was to become the Eastern Region of Nigeria, it was no ordinary company. Not only did it have its own army, in the form of the Niger Coast Constabulary, it dispensed its own justice through its own High Court. It was this company that carried out the wars of 'pacification'. Pacification and 'punitive expeditions' were euphemisms for the wars of conquest which the Company launched against the various ethnic groups in the course of the colonisation drive.

State-sanctioned wars of conquest of native peoples through a private company had the advantage of using private funds to prosecute the wars, saving the British taxpayer money in the process, whilst shielding the Imperial Government from direct responsibility for the bloodshed. It was a politically tidy arrangement for a bloody venture. Through these expeditions, it is said that Goldie managed to draw up over four hundred political treaties with the chiefs of the lower Niger and the Hausa states which is what Buxton's Society for the Extinction of the Slave Trade and for the Civilisation of Africa had called for.

These being documents drafted not just in English but in legal language for which no proper translation into plain English let alone the local language was available, it was easy enough for clauses to be inserted which had the effect of committing the signatories to ceding land to Britain. Those chiefs who refused to sign were simply deposed. Frederick Lugard would later admit to *'the naked deception of...'treaties' which were either not understood, or which the ruler had no power to make'*.

THE CONQUEST OF YORUBA LAND

The emergence of America in 1776 broadly marks the timing of the beginning of the fall of the Oyo or Yoruba Empire. At its height, it covered most of the 'Nigeria' space to the south and west of the confluence of the rivers Niger and Benue and extended further west through much of the present-day Republics of Benin and Togo, up to the lands of the Gha people of Ghana. Slave raids and slave wars, over the hundreds of years of the trade, had eaten into its bones but abolition of the trade, in 1807, brought no respite. The conflicts, in fact, intensified as the embargo on the sale of firearms to the natives, which had sustained the slave trade, now gave way to the policy of supplying arms to favoured tribes in proxy wars to break up the empire ahead of colonisation.

One by one, the tribes of the Yoruba nation which had historically recognised the sovereignty of the Alaafin of Oyo were encouraged, by British agents, to assert their independence. The end result was a series of revolutionary wars, over a period of close to one hundred years, amongst the major tribes: the Oyos, Ilorins, Ibadans, Ifes, Ekitis, Ijeshas, Ijebus and Egbas. It was the same strategy as had been used in the break up and destruction of the great Native American-Indian civilisations when the Indian tribes had been set against one another in destructive civil wars: the rise and fall of any particular tribe depending upon their willingness to work with the foriegn power since alliance meant protection and access to the best weapons.

THE MISSION TO ABEOKUTA AND THE EGBAS

The first foothold that the British gained, following the failure of the 1841 Niger Mission, was in Yoruba land amongst the Egba tribe when the Yoruba Christian Mission was started in July 1846.

As London, and the south-east of England, had been for the Romans, coming in with their new religion of Christianity, Egba land, with its newly established capital, Abeokuta, served as the gateway for British missionaries, traders and soldiers alike, into the rest of Yoruba country. Being a people with a fresh grievance - having been driven from their traditional homeland in what is now Ibadan by the then more powerful Oyo tribes - the Egba were ideal candidates for the role of the first partners in the imperial project. Christianity, with its message of hope and a new life for the oppressed and dispossessed, found enthusiastic welcome amongst them leading the missionary Henry Townsend to report to his CMS principals in England:

> *It is a great and merciful providence that while the door of access to the interior thro' the Niger is closed against us that God should give us favour in the sight*

of the Akus[i] by which we might reasonably hope to be as useful to the African race and eventually to penetrate to its remotest nation. I earnestly hope that as providence has opened a large field of usefulness that in like manner he will provide the means, and suitable agents, to enter upon the work he has prepared.

While Crowther had been sent from Sierra Leone to the Highbury Missionary College, the Englishman, Townsend had been admitted to the Highbury Missionary College in 1836 before being sent out to Sierra Leone, in that same year, to begin his missionary work. As Crowther was tutored in the English language, Townsend, while in Sierra Leone, took to learning the Yoruba language. The two of them, together with one Charles Gollmer, all of them ordained priests, were then assigned to begin the Yoruba mission in Abeokuta in January 1845 only for the death of the Egba chief Sodeke (who had given the missionaries a warm welcome on their earlier exploratory visit) to cause them to delay in Badagry until July 1846.

First access to the colonising power guaranteed a status of *primus inter pares* for Abeokuta and the Egbas. Thus the first church, St Peter's Church, was founded in Abeokuta in 1843. By the time Lagos became a colony in 1861 missionary work in that territory was still in its infancy.

With the first permanent mission being established by CMS in Abeokuta, in1846, came the first schools:

> *Because of their conviction that education was necessary for the Christian belief, the missionaries built schools for the Egba. It is impossible to estimate the number of western educated Africans resident at Abeokuta at this time. Adding the number of returnees from Sierra Leone to the young converts made in the period after 1850, there must have been a considerable number who could read and write*

These Educated Natives, who had become exposed to western education and ways, quickly put in place effective governance arrangements on western lines. George William Johnson, a re-captive who had relocated to Abeokuta from Sierra Leone, was a key figure:

> *By 1865, George William Johnson and his supporters had convinced [Basorun] Somoye and the other major chiefs to participate in an experimental form of central government. The name given to this new central system was the Egba United Board of Management (EUBM). Johnson's idea was to provide a more efficient bureaucratic mechanism which could be controlled by the [western educated Egba]. At first only western educated followers of Johnson belonged to*

---

i   The Yoruba language was referred to as Aku

the EUBM. The composition of the Board is not completely known, but Basorun Somoye was the head of the Board with the title of President-General. Other members of the Board, called Directors, were selected from the educated classes and after 1868 included some of the most important Ogboni chiefs[4]

Townsend was from a family of printers. His talent and training in the written word coupled with the competence he had acquired in the spoken Yoruba language made him a valuable aide for the Egba leaders in their communications with the British Crown and vice-versa. The relationship spawned benefits for both sides. Through the relationship, the Egba were transformed from a recently vanquished tribe, who had been driven from their homeland by the Oyo peoples, into the most powerful of the twenty-two tribes of the Yoruba nation. Abeokuta, their new capital, was twice saved from attempted invasions by the Dahomeans.

At the social-economic level, Abeokuta became the first seat of Western education through the work of the missionaries. Its competitive edge had been further boosted by the influx of educated former slaves from Sierra Leone and Brazil. At the socio-political level the Egba developed a level of unity that was unrivalled. Since it served British interests to have one paramount Egba chief to deal with rather than several Townsend had taken steps to strengthen the governance in the land, following Sodeke's death, by arranging for his successor, Sagbua, to be conferred with the title of before all the other Egba chiefs. In this way a clear hierarchy was established amongst the Egba chiefs who had hitherto regarded themselves as equals[5].

The main benefit for the British in the relationship was that in the Egba, they had a willing partner on the Yoruba mainland from whose territory, and with whose assistance, they were better able to project their power and influence into the rest of Yorubaland.

With their head start in education, and with the infusion of passion and radicalism from the freed slaves who had found a new home in their land, it was not long before the Egbas began to assert themselves even against their British benefactors. The attempt to collect customs duties on goods passing up the Ogun River to Abeokuta from Lagos was seen as a step too far by the British authorities.

When the British Government, by this time in Lagos, sought to assert its authority by imposing a blockade on the Egba, Johnson and his Egba United Board of Management colleagues struck back. An uprising against Europeans occurred on the weekend of 12-13 October 1867, known as the "Ifole" outbreak culminating in the expulsion of all Europeans from Egbaland and the closure of all mission schools and churches. In the recorded words of one Egba Chief: "it was written in the bible that Christian teachers should leave a town after 21 years and we had been 21 years in Abeokuta and it was time for us to go". On 30 October, all three missions, Methodist and Baptist as well as CMS left Abeokuta under escort.

In later years this impetuous action by the Egbas would have been answered with a punitive expedition and the deposition of the Egba chief who sanctioned it. But with the British foothold in the country not yet secure, it was an indignity they were prepared to bear for now. So instead of gunboats they had to rely on diplomacy to secure the lifting of the ban on Europeans, eight years later, in 1875.

This special relationship between the Egbas and the British, arising from the accident of first contact, explains the emergence of this tribe as as the most powerful tribe in Yorubaland and also their disproportionate influence within the wider Nigerian political setting. They amongst their illustrious sons some of the most famous Nigerians including the only Yorubas that have attained, in one way or another, the office of President of Nigeria namely Olusegun Obasanjo[ii], Ernest Sonekan and Moshood Abiola. To this impressive list is to be added some of the most significant social-political figures like Fela Anikulapo-Kuti (whose grandfather Reverend Ransome-Kuti had been one of the early converts to Christianity), and the Nobel Laureate, Wole Soyinka.

REGIME CHANGE IN LAGOS

As the British Isles had stood as an offshore-haven from the bloodletting which engulfed the European mainland during the Napoleonic wars of the early 1800s, so too the Island of Lagos, or to give its pre-Portuguese name *Eko*, stood in relation to the Yoruba mainland at this time. Again, as had happened with Britain itself, the Island saw its population, and wealth, swell on the back of the misery and conflict ravaging its mainland relations as it played the dual role of a home for refugees from the wars and a source of supplies for combatants. Until then Lagos was, literally the southern-most backwaters of the Oyo Empire.

The British, who by now had the coastal bases of Cape Town and Gibraltar and the offshore Island of Hong Kong as part of their collection of staging posts, recognised the island's potential as a more secure permanent base for the imperial designs on the Nigerian mainland than Abeokuta which was then plagued by repeated attacks from the Dahomeans and their Amazonian women warriors. A succession struggle for the crown of King of Lagos between King Akitoye and his nephew, Kosoko, provided the cover for the takeover of the island, and so on 22 July 1850 John Beecroft, the British Consul in Fernando Po, wrote to Palmerston:

> *Lagos is another point. If the legitimate [king] could be seen and communicated with, so as to make a treaty with him for the suppression of the foreign Slave Trade, and place him at Lagos, his former seat of Government, it would release*

---

ii   Strictly of the neighbouring Owu tribe but raised in Abeokuta *the people of Abeokuta from the jeopardy that they are continually in, from the King of Dahomey[6]*

When Kosoko seized the crown of Lagos from King Akitoye in 1845, Abeokuta was where the former King took refuge. From here Townsend, who never shied away from political entanglement, was able to enlist the support of the British Government for Akitoye's reinstatement leading Beecroft to report again, in 1851:

I have been informed by a person who was at Lagos that the massacre in 1845 was awful; he exterminated the whole of his uncle's family, about 2000, and the lagoon was a pest-house for weeks, owing to the dead carcasses in it[7]

Such deeply-felt grievances were always useful recruiting aides in the quest to extend British influence. With some encouragement, and more than a little letter-writing support, from Beecroft, the deposed King Akitoye is reported to have made a formal appeal for help from the British to regain his throne in Lagos:

I King Akitoye of Lagos, salute you and your great Queen and Government, and I wish you all happiness, peace and prosperity, May God bless your great Queen, and grant her a long and happy reign. I rejoice very much to see the day which has brought you, the Representative of England, to this town, particularly at this time when I am surrounded by dangers. Indeed, I very much need your protection, as my life is every moment at stake. I find myself obliged to solicit your assistance, and I am reduced to the necessity of begging your aid against an enemy who has seized my throne and kingdom. My humble prayer to you, Sir, the Representative of the English Government, who it is well known, is ever ready and desirous to protect the defenceless, to obtain redress for the grievance of the injured, and to check the triumphs of wickedness, is, that you would take Lagos under your protection, that you would plant the English flag there, and that you would re-establish me on my rightful throne at Lagos, and protect me under my flag: and with your help I promise to enter into a Treaty with England to abolish the Slave-Trade at Lagos, and to establish and carry on lawful trade, especially with English merchants [8]

That Akitoye was able to make this appeal illustrated not only the peripheral position of Lagos within the Oyo Empire but also evidenced the loose hold of the Empire on its territories. The appeal would also have been informed by the first hand insight which the deposed ruler would have had into how the Egbas had been greatly strengthed by cooperation with the British[9].

The Banks of the River Niger

The Mungo Park House, Asaba,
used as a warehouse of the Royal Niger Company

Palmerston wasted no time in accepting the invitation. On Christmas Day in 1851 the British gunboats began the bombardment of Lagos and on 1 January 1852 the grateful King Akitoye of Lagos, in appreciation, went aboard H.M.S. Penelope to sign a treaty pledging an open door, on most favoured terms, to British merchants and missionaries in Lagos and its associated territories[9].

Akitoye lasted just three weeks on the throne, from the date of signing this treaty, before his sudden death. His son, Dosumu, who succeeded him, lasted a little longer before he was deposed by the British authorities as they moved to take more direct control of Lagos. Beecroft wrote to the Foreign Secretary on 9 April 1860:[9]

> *There is a measure which, if adopted, would tend to put an end to the Slave Trade, and increase the legal commerce and industrial prosperity of this line of coast to an unlimited extent, the occupation of Lagos, either as a possession or by way of Protectorate*[10].

On August 6 1861, King Dosumu of Lagos duly climbed aboard H.M.S. *Prometheus* and, in return for a life pension, gave back to the British what they had given to him:

> *I, Dosunmu, do, with the consent and advice of my Council, give, transfer, and by these presents grant and confirm unto the Queen of Great Britain, her heirs and successors for ever, the port and Island of Lagos, with all the rights, profits and territories, and appurtenances whatsoever thereunto belonging, and as well the profits and revenue as the direct, full, and absolute dominion and sovereignty of the said port, island and premises, with all the royalties thereof, freely, fully, entirely and absolutely*[11]

With this Lagos became a British colony. This was an illustration of what Lugard described as *'the naked deception of treaty-making'* in which the so-called kings gave away land to which they had no legal right, on terms which they never understood.

THE YORUBA WARS

With the acquisition of Lagos, the British now had a very convenient offshore base from which to monitor and influence events on the Yoruba mainland, where wars were already raging, to await the moment to takeover. That these wars had been instigated can be deduced from the absence of any strategic objective for the warring parties. In his epic work, *The History of the Yoruba*, Samuel Johnson writes of Alaafin Abiodun, the ruler of the Oyo Empire, enjoying a long and peaceful reign and of how, in the wake of his death, the Oyo Empire became engulfed in these revolutionary fires as one newly-empowered chief after another began to assert his independence from Oyo:

> *Afonja the Kakanfo of Ilorin and Opele the Bale of Gbogun were the first to proclaim their independence, other chiefs soon followed their examples. This was the commencement of the breakup of the unity of the Yoruba kingdom, and the beginning of the tribal independence. Tribute was no longer paid to the King. The King's messengers and Ilaris no longer carried that dread as before, nor were they allowed to oppress people or enrich themselves with their goods as before*[12]

At one stage, the Oyo empire was simultaneously under assault on its northern borders from Fulani-jihadists from Sokoto; on its western flank from Dahomians (now Republic of Benin) with French support; and from the south by the Egbas and Ijebus with the help of guns and gunpowder acquired from their new British friends and trading partners in return for slaves. According to Johnson:

> 'the Owu war marked a definite period in Yoruba history. It was here for the first time [sic] gunpowder was used in war in this country, and it was followed by the devastation of the Egba townships and the foundation of modern Abeokuta and Ibadan'[13].

He dates this war, fought by an alliance of the *Ifes* in the east and *Ijebus* in the south against the *Owus* to around the time of the visit to the Alaafin of Oyo by a European traveller[iii].

AFONJA AND ILORIN

In the same way that Sodeke, the Egba war chief, had enlisted the support of Townsend and the British missionaries in Abeokuta as a measure to protect his Egba people, Afonja, the Ilorin war chief, sought the support of the Fulani Imam, Alimi, in his effort to position himself as the new centre of power in Yorubaland in rivalry to the Alaafin of Oyo. As Townsend had brought in the Yoruba returnees from Sierra Leone who later turned into a fighting force, so too Alimi brought with him followers who would before long turn into warriors of the faith.

It is, however, one of history's recurring lessons that whenever a ruling class have to turn to outsiders for help to maintain their rule, if they do not lose their right to rule to their assailants they lose it to their saviours. In 1824, while much of Yorubaland was pre-occupied with the Owu war, Alimi proclaimed a jihad in Ilorin just as Afonja was preparing to expel him and his followers. By its end, Afonja was killed and Yoruba Ilorin

---

iii   Clapperton is reported to have visited the Sultan of Sokoto in 1824

had joined Hausa Gobir to become an Emirate of the Fulani Empire.

The next most significant war in the disintegration of the Oyo Empire was the Ijaye War which started around the same time as the American Civil War. By this time missionaries and mercenaries were very much present in the land. Triggered by a succession crisis following the death, in 1858, of the ruling Alaafin, what began as a battle between Ibadan and Ijaye, on behalf of their rival candidates for the throne, saw, first, the Egbas, and then the Ijebus, joining in on the side of the Ijayes against the Ibadan forces. Other influences were to make their presence felt in this new conflagration as the Egbas gained access to new breech-loading rifles against the old Danish-made long-barreled muskets.

More significant was the direct involvement of foreigners in this domestic conflict. This emerges from Johnson's narrative about the ransom negotiations between Rev. D Hinderer of Ibadan and Ogunmola, the commander of the Ibadan army, over one Mr. Edward Roper, a British missionary who had been taken captive by the Ibadan forces on the conquest of Ijaye:

> We have learnt that white men live on eggs and milk and I will feed this one with parched corn...We know that this is not the actual white man of Ijaye, whom we often saw on the battlefield: this one only entered the town a few days ago, hence you have such easy terms, otherwise we should have killed him right out, for he fought us, and we had our eyes on him

Johnson in the same narrative spoke of *two "Afro-American" sharp-shooters who harassed the Ibadans a good deal with their rifles"*. These were likely to have been 'recaptives' who had been trained in the use of modern firearms.

The international dimension to the wars on the mainland was highlighted by the sudden death, on 28 February 1867, of Ogunmola, the Commander of the Ibadan army from smallpox contracted from a cloth he had been given in enemy territory[70]. Blankets infected with the lethal smallpox virus had been the principal instrument of death used to decimate the Native American Indians. Ogunmola's mysterious death was compounded by the equally sudden death within two months of both of his immediate subordinates in the line of command in the army[16].

The clearest evidence of the active participation of the Abeokuta missionaries in these conflicts comes from complaints made by Rev. David Hinderer, the then head of the CMS mission in Ibadan:

> [T]hese latter troubles we might have been.....spared, had the missionaries in Abeokuta treated us in a Christian spirit: but all we informed them of...& and advise[d] concerning Mr Mann &c. &c. was either treated with contempt or made mischief of by some party or other. Altogether, the part they acted during the Ijaye war, & now it seems also in this Jebu war - whatever their outward

profession may be – is a disgrace to the name of a missionary, & must prove a curse to the mission[17]

The defence to the accusations, put forward by Townsend, the head of the Abeokuta Mission, is equally revealing:

> *We don't think we have any right to interfere in their [i.e. Egba converts] going as they owe a duty to the law of their country as we do to ours. We have done the same, that is remained passive, in every war undertaken by the government, & when our converts go we exhort them to act as Xtians in it; we have not thought it right to command them not to go*[18]

The event which finally ended Yoruba independent military capacity was the great Yoruba civil war, the *Kiriji War*, which lasted 16 years until an armistice was brokered on 23 September 1886:

> *The Ijesas, Ekitis, Efons and other tribes hitherto subjected to the Ibadans formed an alliance which they termed Ekiti parapo i.e. the Ekiti confederation. They raised a formidable army and were determined not only to liberate themselves but to overrun the Oyo tribes right on to the Ibadan farms at the river Oba'*[19].

The confederate army were soon enough joined by Ibadan's old foes, the Egbas, the Ijebus and the Ilorins. Added to this was the introduction of new weapons of precision in the Snider–Enfield rifles acquired from Lagos that could fire ten rounds a minute. By 15 October 1881, the Alaafin of Oyo, now a King without a kingdom, was reduced to making this appeal to the British Governor of Lagos:

> *With all possible speed I beg that the Imperial Government-for which I have always a great respect- to come to my help. I crave your assistance both to come to settle this unfortunate war between the belligerent powers, and to stop the Dahomians who have made inroads into my kingdom'*[20].

Timing being critical in the power game, Downing Street was in no hurry to act. It was only after repeated entreaties from the Alaafin's messengers that, on 14 April 1882, the Governor of Lagos responded:

> *I appreciate the action of the King of Oyo in sending to the Governor of Lagos to ask him to send an officer to make peace between the Ibadans and the Ijesas. I thank the King of Oyo for the compliment he has paid to the English Government in doing this, showing that he believes in the honour of the English Government,*

and that he feels confident that an officer from the English Government will deal justly in this matter. The great Queen whom I serve, Her Most Gracious Majesty the Queen of England and Empress of India, has no other wishes than good wishes towards the entire African people. Her Majesty's instructions to her officers whom she sends to govern this colony are to promote by all proper means friendly intercourse between the people under their rule and the native tribes living near them. In doing this from time to time Her Majesty has approved the visits of her officers to many of the tribes neighbouring Lagos. But Her majesty has no desire to bring the inland tribes neighbouring Lagos under British rule, and though wicked people have said that if the white man comes into the interior he will take the country, I tell you publicly that my Queen has no wish to take your country[21]

It was another case of British double-speak as, by August of that same year, Rev. J B Wood, using the immunity accorded to missionaries, was sent in on a fact-finding tour to assess the potential for resistance amongst the warring chiefs to the planned Imperial takeover.[22] In further preparation for the new order, at the end of January 1886, Lagos was separated from the Gold Coast Colony, and, along with the Yoruba mainland, declared a Colony in its own right with Captain A C Moloney as its first Governor.

In July of the same year, with the Yoruba civil war effectively over, George Goldie's Royal Niger Company was granted its royal charter. With this it now had the seal and the authority of the imperial government for its actions to end the war and to secure new treaties. On 23 September 1886, with both sides having fought themselves to a standstill, after 16 years of civil war, the command came from Goldie's forces for both sides to lay down their arms. This is the point at which British rule in Yoruba land officially began. The only challenge which remained was from the French, at least so it appeared.

THE BERLIN CONFERENCE AND THE MAXIM GUN

In the same way that America's victory in its war of Independence from Britain, in 1783, propelled its emergence as a new force on the global stage, so too the spur for the rise of Germany to the stage can be traced to its defeat of France in the Franco-Prussian war of 1870. It had arrived too late to participate in the slave trade, and in the colonisation of India and the Americas, but the colonisation of Africa was still a work-in-progress at this time.

The new power in the club was determined not to be left out and so, on 19 May 1884, Otto von Bismarck, the Chancellor of Germany, sent a cablegram to Portugal. The recipient was Dr Gustav Nachtigal. The first inkling the British had of the new development was from the events that unfolded before their eyes on the coast of Cameroon in the summer of 1884:

> On 15 July Hewett was still engaged in palaver with the chiefs at Benin when a British naval officer brought him alarming news of a foreign gunboat in Cameroon. There was a report that those on board were negotiating a treaty with King Acqua and King Bell; however, the kings had agreed to give Hewett a week to make a counter offer. Hewett dropped everything. On the afternoon of 19 July, HMS Flirt steamed into the harbour at Bell Town. Hewett peered through the heat haze and then rubbed his eyes. Three foreign flags were flying from flagstaffs among the mangrove swamps. But they were not the red white and blue of the tricolour. They carried the black cross of the Kaiser's Germany. Five days earlier the famous German explorer, Dr Gustav Nachtigal, now Imperial Consul-General for the west coast of Africa, had been rowed ashore from the gunboat Mowe by a party of German Blue Jackets. He informed the astounded British traders that he was taking possession of Cameroon in the name of the German emperor. Bismarck had stolen a march on everyone. Nothing could now stop that 'unseemly and dangerous race'. The most feverish phase of the Scramble had begun[23]

The British plan had been for 'Nigeria' to include the whole of the territory that became German Cameroon. It was a plan that had now been disrupted by Bismarck's move. Lugard explained the development as follows:

> Germany on the other hand, found herself with a great and increasing industrial population in urgent need of raw materials and additional food supplies. Not content with the wholly unrestricted market offered by British colonies, where Germans were welcomed, and exercised every privilege equally with their British rivals, she not unnaturally desired to have colonies of her own[24]

Bismarck had all along disclaimed any interest in taking colonies in Africa to keep the European rivals off the scent. Having now proclaimed Germany's big-power status with the defeat of France, he saw, in the scramble for what remained of independent Africa, an opportunity to play the French off against their traditional rivals, Britain. It was no accident that it was Bismarck, himself, who hosted the Berlin Conference which began on 15 November 1884.

Popular commentary on the Berlin Conference of 1884 gives the impression that it was at the conference that the African continent was carved up and the boundaries of the African States were drawn whereas the conference was more concerned with agreeing the rules by which the game was to be played. The Berlin Act of 1885 which codified the result of the deliberations faithfully recorded the interested parties as follows:

> *In the Name of God Almighty.*
> *Her Majesty the Queen of the United Kingdom of Great Britain and Ireland, Empress of India; His Majesty the German Emperor, King of Prussia; His Majesty the King of Austria, King of Bohemia, etc. and Apostolic King of Hungary; His Majesty the King of the Belgians; His Majesty the King of Denmark; His Majesty the King of Spain; the President of the United States of America; the President of the French Republic; His Majesty the King of Italy; His Majesty the King of the Netherlands, Grand Duke of Luxembourg, etc.; His Majesty the King of Portugal and the Algarves, etc.; His Majesty the Emperor of all the Russias; His Majesty the King of Sweden and Norway, etc.; and His Majesty the Emperor of the Ottomans*

The Act of Navigation for the River Niger which came out of the conference deliberations spoke primarily to the two main contestants, Britain and France. Having first laid down the over-arching principle of toll-free navigation for ships of all nations, it went on to appoint these two powers as custodians of the river. The Act then went on, for the sake of good order, to set out how the interested parties were to announce their claim to each new territory to each other:

> *Any Power which henceforth takes possession of a tract of land on the coasts of the African continent outside of its present possessions, or which, being hitherto without such possessions, shall acquire them, as well as the Power which assumes a Protectorate there, shall accompany the respective act with a notification thereof, addressed to the other Signatory Powers of the present Act, in order to enable them, if need be, to make good any claims of their own*

Although the business of the Berlin Conference was conducted with the utmost civility between the delegates, the Act recognised that military force would be the ultimate determinant of any claim of ownership:

> *The Signatory Powers of the present Act recognize the obligation to insure the establishment of authority in the regions occupied by them on the coasts of the African continent sufficient to protect existing rights, and as the case may be, freedom of trade and of transit under the conditions agreed upon.*

This meant that any Power making a claim to a territory was obliged to show that it was, in actuality, the occupying power of the land; paper claims alone would not do. This required the subjugation of the native powers.

The other significant development in the year 1884 was the invention of the *Maxim* gun was invented. A machine gun with the emphasis on the word machine on account of its automated system for ejecting each spent cartridge and reloading. It was the principal weapon by which the British demonstrated effective presence in the construction of their empire. Winston Churchill, the future British Prime Minister, then a war journalist, is said to have described the Maxim gun as 'that mechanical scattering of death which the polite nations of the earth have brought to such monstrous perfection'[25].

From this point onwards the colonisation process was never going to meet any significant native resistance especially as a strict prohibition on the sale of arms to Africans was in place so that there was never any prospect of any equality of arms:

> *the one thing [the Berlin Act of 1885, and the Brussels Act of 1892] did succeed in effecting was the restriction of the import of arms of precision to the natives, theoretically as a check to the slave trade, but with the practical result of rendering the African more powerless than ever to resist conquest by Europeans*[26]

For his part Bismarck knew that the Conference would not be the final word on colonial possessions. He knew that a conflict lay ahead between Germany and Britain. In anticipation of this he ensured that Germany took territory next to the key British territories on the African continent: Cameroon to be next to Nigeria, Togo to be next to Ghana, Namibia to be within striking distance of what was then Rhodesia and Tanganyika[iv] to be next to Kenya.

THE COLONISATION OF YORUBALAND

Although, by this time, the Alaafin of Oyo was king of the Yorubas only in name, still in the battle of documents-of-title between the colonial powers, a treaty with him would still trump anything rival claimants might obtain. On 23 May 1888, Governor Moloney sent the Alaafin of Oyo an offer to help him reassemble the broken pieces of his Empire:

> *... 3. As you know, and every Yoruba knows, people to the west and to the north are not Yoruba; they differ in feelings and object from Yorubas. You will have doubtless learnt I always aim at making all Yoruba-speaking peoples one in heart as they are in tongue. Towards such unity I attach much importance to a definite and permanent understanding between these Yoruba-speaking peoples,*

---

iv   Now part of Tanzania

79

and this colony which is mainly inhabited by Yorubas. And where should I look first for sympathy and support but to Adeyemi, the Alaafin of Oyo the titular King of all Yoruba?

4. Between you and the Governor of the Queen's Colony of Lagos there should be ever friendship, goodwill which no foreign interference should be allowed to influence or disturb.

5. Yoruba land was comprised traditionally as regards its corners a few years ago of Yoruba proper, Egba, Ketu and Ijebu. Where is Ketu now? And from what direction was it destroyed?

6. Without the entertainment of the least desire to meddle with the government of such kingdoms as Yoruba, Egba or Ijebu, and with the assurance that not one yard of land is coveted by me, in feeling and sympathy for Yoruba union I desire that Lagos take the place of Ketu as the fourth corner.

7. If the accompanying document be agreeable to you, and embodies your wishes, sign it and return it to me

Alaafin Adeyemi signed the treaty under which he promised :

'that no cession of territory and no other Treaty or Agreement shall be made by me other than the one I have now made without the full understanding and consent of the Governor for the time being of the said Colony of Lagos'[28]

In return the Government of Lagos, on 23 July 1888, pledged to him '*a yearly dash of 200 bags of cowries*' conditional upon satisfactory observance of all terms, on 23 July 1888. Less than a year later, on 10 August 1889, the British and French signed the Treaty of Paris dividing the people of French Yoruba land (in the Republic of Benin and Togo) from their relations in British Yoruba land in what would become south-west Nigeria. The southernmost tip of the boundary between the Yoruba-speaking peoples is at the former slave port of Badagry.

The treaty with the Alaafin was ratified on 16 June 1890 but, in the broken kingdom, it meant little without the reassurance of separate treaties with the major tribes and so the Governor of Lagos proceeded to obtain these separate treaties from the Egba, the Ijebus, the Ibadans and the others:

Governor Carter left Lagos on the 3rd of January, 1893, for his tour, He was accompanied by a posse of Hausa soldiers, with Captain Bower, one of the officers who came out for the Ijebu war. The Maxim gun was en evidence throughout the whole way

THE COLONISATION OF THE NIGER DELTA

While British control of Yorubaland had been achieved through the agency of the missionaries and proxy wars, the colonisation of the Niger Delta was mainly led by trade and commercial relationships.

Until the arrival of European traders on the coast in the 15th century, the gateway to the outside world was overland across the Sahara. The ethnic groups situated at the mouths of the various inlets in the delta, where the river Niger meets the Atlantic, were far removed from this. With the arrival of the European traders on the Atlantic coast, these same groups now took centre stage: whatever it was that the Europeans wanted to buy, whether slaves or produce, was brought down from the hinterland to the coast for the chiefs of these communities to sell on. From this vantage point, the chiefs of the coastal communities secured access to the guns, the alcohol and other European merchandise before the inland communities. With first access to European manufactures, especially guns, these coastal communities became the first centres of power in what would become Nigeria.

However, with the slave trade giving way to the new ideology of free trade, and the former slave traders now turned into respectable merchants, the priority for the Europeans was now the removal of all impediments to the free movement of their wares and direct access to the produce suppliers in the interior. The interests of the former business partners were no longer aligned. With experience on their side, the European traders organised themselves to insist, with one voice, on direct access as the new terms of trade. Those terms shifted further in their favour when they insisted on exclusive power to adjudicate over the inevitable trade disputes:

> *...writing in 1854 Dr Baikie describes "a commercial or mercantile association" organized by some of the merchants at Bonny, "the members being the chief white and black traders in the place, and the chair occupied by the white supercargoes in monthly rotation. All disputes were brought before the court... and with the consent of the King, fines are levied on defaulters. If anyone refuses to submit to the decision of the court, or ignores its jurisdiction, he is tabooed and no one trades with him. The natives stand in much awe of it, and readily pay their debts when threatened with it*[30]

In quick time these trade courts were established in the major trading centres in the Niger Delta, in Calabar, Brass and Opobo and on the Benin River. The British consul, Mr Beecroft, doubled up as President of the courts to handle all appeals.

The discovery of crude oil was still some years away but there were abundant supplies of valuable palm oil and rubber to be found in the hinterland.

Control of the gateway into the hinterland having been the root of their power and their wealth, the rulers of these gateway ethnic groups were determined to resist the attempts of the European traders to gain direct access to the hinterland. The European traders and the chiefs of the hinterland peoples were even more united in their determination for direct dealings with each other. The British Navy which had long been stationed on the West African coast on the humanitarian exercise of arresting slave ships in the course of ending the Slave Trade, now saw its mission changed to bombing the coastal communities to clear the way for Free Trade. King Pepple of Bonny was one of the first to be dealt with:

> *In 1854, at the request of the merchants and chiefs alike, Mr Beecroft deposed King Pepple of Bonny, who was ruining the country by his crimes and the constant tribal warfare for which he was responsible. He was first sent to Fernando Po, and then to Ascension, and at length was permitted to visit England, where he was received with open arms by the heads of the missionary societies and leading members of the Government[31]*

Having been suitably educated to face the right way, he was then returned to his country and to his throne in 1861 at the request of the very same British merchants.

JAJA OF OPOBO

The changeover from slaves to palm oil not only shifted the balance of power from the gateway chiefs to the chiefs of the interior, it also shifted the balance of economic power in favour of the former slaves: 'the new men'[32], who now worked the oil palms.

Jaja of Opobo was one of these 'new men'. He had moved out to establish a new base in Opobo in 1869 in the wake of the succession crisis in Bonny and very quickly emerged as a leading player in the palm oil trade in Ijaw land. His practice of cutting out the British merchants, and trading directly with England, was the mirror image of the British merchants' policy of bypassing the gateway chiefs to deal directly with the oil palm producers. But it was never in the contemplation of the advocates of free trade that Africans would be given open access to markets in England. Something would have to give.

The first step was for the Oil Rivers to be sealed off from the meddling of competing European states and so, in preparation for the Berlin conference of 1884, standard form treaties of protection were signed with the chiefs in the area on the basis of which, on 5 June 1885, Britain was able to declare the *"Oil Rivers Protectorate"* over the land on both banks of the river Niger. Once the screen of the protectorate had been erected over the area, the work of bringing the peoples under effective control could begin.

One of the treaties was with Jaja himself but his version differed from the others in a material respect. Determined to preserve his claim to monopoly rights in respect of the palm oil trade in Opobo, the treaty which he signed omitted the clause guaranteeing freedom of trade. He had taken the precaution of asking the British authorities to spell out what they meant by the word 'protectorate'. The response he received, on 1 July 1884, was:

> *Dear Sir*
> *I write as you request with reference to the word "protection" as used in the proposed Treaty that the Queen does not want to take your country or your markets, but at the same time is anxious that no other nation should take them. She undertakes to extend her gracious favour and protection, which will leave your country still under your government.*
> *She has no wish to disturb your rule, though she is anxious to see your country get up as well as the countries of the other tribes with whom her people have so long been trading.*
> *Faithfully yours*
> *Edward Hyde Hewett*[33]

This being the same queen who had given him a sword of honour in appreciation for the men he had supplied for the British war effort against the Ashanti in 1873, Jaja had reason to believe the written assurance which had been given in her name. He was not to know that Britain's claim to the Niger area had been recognized by the Treaty of Berlin, of 1885, only on the strict condition that it would guarantee freedom of navigation of the river Niger, and therefore free access to the hinterland. Also, it was in 1886 that the same queen acceded to the request of George Goldie's Royal Niger Company for the grant of a royal charter conferring monopoly rights over trade in the Niger area and Goldie wasted no time in vigorously asserting the newly conferred rights.

When Goldie's move to fix the prices which the British merchants were to pay for produce ran into opposition from Jaja, he contrived to have him deported. Jaja was issued with an invitation to a meeting on board one of the British warships to hear the message of the British Government. Ever wary, he sought assurances that he would not be detained. By letter dated 18 September 1887 the assurance was earnestly given by the Acting Consul:

Sir

In reply to your note I beg to say that whatever Uranta may or may not have said to you is of no importance, and can affect in no way the issue of tomorrow's meeting. I have summoned you to attend in a friendly spirit. I hereby assure you that whether you accept or reject my proposals tomorrow no restraint whatever will be put upon you, you will be free to go as soon as you have heard the message of the Government.

If you do not attend the meeting no further consideration will be shown you, and you will simply be treated as an enemy of the British Government. I shall proclaim your deposition, and hand your markets over to the Bonny men.

If you attend tomorrow I pledge you my word that you will be free to come and go, but if you do not attend, I shall conclude you to be guilty of the charges brought against you and shall immediately proceed to carry out your punishment.

I am yours obediently

H.H. Johnston

Acting Consul[34]

Jaja obeyed the summons. No sooner was he on board than he was transported to Accra for trial before being deported to the Caribbean Island of St Vincent. He was never to see his homeland again.

NANA OF THE TSEKIRI

The experience of Nana Olomu, of the Tsekiri kingdom, was very similar. In 1885 he had been formally proclaimed by the British authorities as the *"executive power through which decrees of Her Majesty's Government and of the Consular Court are to be exercised and enforced"*[35]

However, by 1894 he was being issued with an *"invitation"* to talks on board one of the British Government's war-ships. His offence was that he was controlling the oil palm trade with the Urhobo people in the hinterland of his Tsekiri kingdom:

'For some 420 years, the selling and buying of commodities between the Europeans and Africans of the Benin coast had brought about a civilization, a culture contact, exchange of ideas and a mingling of peoples, about which the Urhobo people in the hinterland knew practically nothing'[36]

All that changed when, in October 1891, the British pushed up the Ethiope River to establish an administrative base for the new Niger Coast Protectorate and proceeded to

84

collect signatures to the standard treaties of protection from Urhobo chiefs who were only too happy to be free of their dependency on Nana and his Tsekiri people. The days of Nana's control of the oil palm trade were numbered.

Assured of support from Goldie, the Urhobos began to withhold payments. He retaliated by taking some Urhobo chiefs hostage as security for payment leading the British authorities to issue him with an "invitation". Knowing what had happened to Jaja, he refused to honour it. A bombardment of his kingdom followed, in 1894, before a blockade was imposed to smoke him out from his place of refuge. At the end of the punitive expedition he was deported.

FREDERICK WILLIAM KOKO OF NEMBE-BRASS

The evolution of the relationship between the British and the people of the Niger Delta, from missionary work to trading relationships and finally military conquest, can be seen from the experience of the Ijaw people and the Brassmen in particular.

Nembe-Brass was the location of one of the most successful CMS Missions in terms of converts to Christianity. Established in 1868, the Brassmen took to the new faith and used the education that came with it to enhance their trading activities: they learnt to keep written accounts and books and records. The highpoint of the success of the evangelism in the area was the conversion and baptism of the king, Ockiya, who renounced polygamy and changed his name to become Josiah Constantine.[37] On his death, in 1889, another recent convert, Frederick William Koko, a school teacher, was chosen as his successor[37].

The relationship between Goldie's Niger Company and the Brass chiefs had been a testing one since the beginning of the doctrine of free trade. They were gateway chiefs who showed more than the usual determination to keep the Europeans from gaining access to the interior. The relationship hardened following the grant of the Charter to the Royal Niger Company and the monopoly trading rights that came with it.

Had the Brassmen signed the standard form treaty that the Company was offering their land would have been counted as part of its territory. As it was, the chiefs refused to sign and so they were excluded. The Special Commissioner whom the Foreign Office later sent down to investigate the causes of the bloody conflict which ensued found as follows:

> ...in order to be able to trade legally on the Niger, any native of Brass, being technically regarded under the Company's laws as a foreigner in the Company's territory, would be required to comply with the same rules as affect the largest trading corporation. He would thus, I was told, be required to pay a yearly sum of £50 for licence to trade, with a further sum of £10, also yearly, for every

station he traded at, and he would then only be allowed to trade at such stations as had been declared open for that purpose, and nowhere else. He would next be required to pay £100 annually if he intended to trade in spirits, without which, I may remark, trade in the Delta is at present impossible. Having thus acquired the right to commence trade in the Niger Territory, he would on first entering have to report his arrival and obtain a clearance either at Akassa or higher up at the mouth of the Ekole Creek and pay the Company's duties[38]

The petition of grievances which King Koko had lodged on behalf of his people, in 1889, to protest at the anti-free trade practices of the Company had produced no satisfaction, and so he resolved to return to his beginnings and to take matters into is own hands. To begin with he renounced his Christian faith and other Brass chiefs followed his example:

Some years ago the Christian Party was much stronger and more powerful than their opponents; many Chiefs who were brought up as Christians have now gone back to fetishism, among these King Koko, the reason for this being that they had lost faith in the white man's god, who had allowed them to be oppressed, and their trade, their only means of livelihood, to be taken away from them without just cause or reason[39]

The point came when the Brassmen could endure the oppression no more. On 22 January 1895, King Koko organised a war party of more than 1500 men in war canoes to attack and destroy the Company's principal base at Akassa. The base was completely destroyed and ransacked. Many Company men were killed and several, including Europeans, were taken captive into the creeks. That there would be a bloody reprisal attack was assured despite Koko's protestations that his quarrel was not with the British but with the Company. That there was no difference between the British and the Company became clear when the Royal Navy, with some Marines, under the command of Rear Admiral Sir Frederick Bedford, launched an attack on Nembe that saw the town razed to the ground. The 'Akassa Massacre', as it came to be known, began at dawn on 20 February 1895 and finished at dusk:

At daybreak on February 22 we attacked and after an obstinate defence of a position naturally difficult, a landing was gallantly effected and Nembe was completely burned. In the evening the force was withdrawn, after King Koko's and other chiefs' houses were destroyed.[40]

The post-massacre Commission of Enquiry found the Brassmens' grievances to be well grounded. Peace terms were drawn up in April 1896 and some compensation was offered. When Koko rejected it he was promptly deposed, by the British, and declared an outlaw with a ransom of £200 placed on his head. He died in exile in 1898.

THE COLONISATION OF BENIN

The ancient Kingdom of Benin was next. The ground had been laid for the conquest by a treaty with the Oba of Benin, in March 1892, whose ostensible purpose was ending the slave trade and the practice of human sacrifice. The irony was that, as recently as 1880, the British missionaries were still owning slaves.[41]

With the experience of Jaja, Nana and King Koko before him, Oba Ovonramwen was concerned that he had been tricked into ceding land. He now took steps to renounce the treaty and to issue orders barring the British from the kingdom. But this was 1892 Benin and not 1867 Abeokuta. Since the imperial plan had no room for an independent kingdom within the Nigeria space, an excuse for an invasion was needed. Using the formula that had been used to good effect against Nana's Tsekiri kingdom, the Tsekiri's were now encouraged to withhold tribute due to the Oba. When he responded by stopping all supplies of palm oil to the Tsekiris, the British merchants demanded that action be taken to depose and deport him.

However, conquering Benin presented a greater challenge than the earlier conquest of Opobo and the Tsekiri's. The country had been trading with European nations since the first visits of the Portuguese in the middle of the fifteenth century in the course of which it had acquired guns and know-how. With knowledge of the tactics the British had used, in 1894, to invade and destroy *Brohomi*, the principal trading town in the Tsekiri kingdom, the Oba had had some time to fortify the defences of his kingdom. As a result, the first British attempt on Benin ended with the defeat and humiliation of the British forces. The invading force, led by a Lieutenant James Phillips, had tried to go in under the guise of a peace mission with weapons hidden. The Oba having received intelligence on the planned invasion, the Benin army launched a pre-emptive attack on 4 January 1897 in which the British invaders were routed with all but two killed.

To avenge the humiliation, a full invasion force was quickly assembled. On 12 January 1897, Rear Admiral Harry Rawson, who was commanding a squadron in South Africa, was appointed to lead the punitive expedition to sack Benin and capture the Oba.[42] He assembled an invasion force of around 1,200 including Royal Marines and the naval bombardment of Benin began on 9th February 1897. By 18th February the major towns in Benin had been razed and looted. The precious Benin Bronzes were carried off to England and the Oba was exiled to Calabar.

THE RIVALRY WITH THE FRENCH

The Berlin Act of 1885 which had laid the ground rules for European colonisation in West Africa required 'effective occupation' as proof of title to territory on the coast. It was, however, silent on the rules which were to apply to claims to territory in the interior and so the concerned powers simply made up their own. The result was a crude rule in terms that whoever could show effective occupation of any area of coastland was entitled to carry its claim into the hinterland for an indefinite distance and to treat that area as a sphere of influence.

This rough-and-ready solution produced two outcomes. The first is the odd situation where the state boundaries on the West African coast run in straight lines inwards from the coast. The second consequence, more specific to the 'Nigeria' story, was to bring the British and the French into conflict over an area on the western flank of what was to become Nigeria.

The territory was Borgu which bordered the eastern edge of Dahomey and the western borders of the Sokoto and Oyo Empires, not far from where Mungo Park had died. This is where Frederick John Dealtry Lugard, the man who finally formed *'Nigeria'*, made his entry onto the stage. He explained the background to the crisis:

> *The West African "colonies" at this time (1889) consisted of small settlements on the coast. Little or no attempt to develop their hinterlands was made until in 1895-96, France, in pursuance of her policy of linking up her various possessions in West Africa, alleging with truth the absence of any effective occupation, seized the interior lands, and threatened the territory immediately contiguous to these colonies.... Under Mr Chamberlain's energetic direction each of these colonies now bestirred itself to secure what was left of its hinterland. An epidemic of treaty-making and expeditions ensued, and eventually frontiers were fixed and delimited* [43]

News that leading Egba Chiefs had signed a treaty with the French who were based in Porto Novo[v], in circumstances where Egba territorial claims already extended as close to Lagos as Ebute Meta, injected new urgency into the matter[44]. As Lugard put it, this process was not without 'incidents', by which he meant campaigns of subjugation of native peoples. The agency through which these encounters were conducted was the West African Frontier Force[vi] which the unabashed imperialist Joseph Chamberlain, the British Secretary of State for the Colonies, had newly set up under Lugard's command.

Now that an army, funded by the British tax-payer, was enforcing the territorial claims of the Royal Niger Company, these lands which had previously been designated mere 'spheres of influence' were upgraded to 'protectorates':

---

v   Republic of Benin

vi   Which would evolve to become the Nigerian Army

The term "Protectorate" gradually changed its meaning from that of a pact with the ruler of a State, which maintained its internal but not its external sovereignty, to a declaration of the territorial status of a region included in the Empire, in which not only external, but in varying degrees the internal sovereignty also, had passed to the controlling Power, in many cases (since unexplored regions were included) without even the "treaty" consent of the people[45]

With the progression from '*spheres of influence*' to '*protectorates*', the embryo of the colony to be called Nigeria had begun to take form.

The French had first encountered Lugard in East Africa. There, whilst in the service of the Imperial British East Africa Company, he had been appointed to lead an expedition into to check French territorial advances. The tactics adopted by this gun-slinger led to a full scale religious civil war between British Protestants, French Catholics and Muslims as missionaries killed missionaries for the right to save the souls of the Ugandans. By the time these emissaries of Christ had slaughtered themselves in full view of the natives, not only were the Ugandans justly sceptical of the merits of this new God, but Lugard's name was like the anti-christ in French circles.

While his '*arraignment ... on charges of inhumanity and war mongering in Uganda*'[46] served to kill off his original aspiration of writing his name on the map of East Africa, his experience in taming French aspirations was precisely what Goldie's company was looking for. It was on the strength of this peculiar curriculum vitae that the Royal Niger Company chose Lugard to lead an expedition into Borgu in 1894. His assignment was to obtain treaties from the local chiefs for use in fending off French encroachments upon the river Niger. His tactics were, again, controversial:

At the town of Nikki, which was later to become the focus of British and French claims to Borgu, Lugard was unable even to secure a meeting with the African king. Instead he obtained the signatures of a local imam, or holy man, and two of the king's councillors (one of whom was the head butcher) to a pre-printed, formula treaty. He nevertheless wrote in the document that it had been made "between the king of Nikki (which is the capital of Borgu)" and the Royal Niger Company; the Arabic signature of the Imam was described on the treaty as "signature of native ruler". Lugard also inserted a name for the king in the treaty, which was later shown to be the name of a king who had been dead for six years[47]

This disregard of propriety would today be viewed by Nigerians as a '*419*[vii] of grand proportions. It set the early tone of official corruption that would become the bane of the country that Lugard was putting together.

---

vii   Section 419 of the Nigerian Criminal Code creates the offence of obtaining money or a pecuniary advantage by deception

THE DECLARATION OF THE COLONY
AND PROTECTORATE OF SOUTHERN NIGERIA

With Pepple, Jaja, Nana, Koko and the Benin Kingdom taken care of, the final obstacle to the realisation of Goldie's quest for a British monopoly of the Niger Delta trade was the French stake in his Royal Niger Company. This was dealt with by the simple expedient of buying out the French holding. The Igbos in the hinterland, and other nationalities in the South-East, were left to be dealt with later.

On 1 January 1900, the Foreign Office effectively nationalised the colonisation activities of the Royal Niger Company by revoking its charter. The Company's territories along the South-East coast, which had been known as the Niger Coast Protectorate, were amalgamated with the territories in the hinterland of the South-East (from which treaties of protection had yet to be obtained - principal amongst which was Igboland) and proclaimed the 'Protectorate of Southern Nigeria'. With this formal declaration, the colony of 'Southern Nigeria', which at this point was strictly South-Eastern Nigeria only, came into being. The first High Commissioner of the new colony was Sir Ralph Moor. He held the post from 1900 until his retirement, on health grounds, in 1903. His unexpected retirement provided the occasion for the second significant amalgamation bringing Yoruba land (excepting the still independent United Kingdom of Egbaland and the Emirate of Ilorin), then still officially known as the 'Lagos Colony', into Southern Nigeria.

This amalgamation of Southern Nigeria with Yorubaland under Sir Walter Egerton, the Governor of the Lagos Colony was initially informal. Moor's portfolio as High Commissioner of Southern Nigeria was simply added to Egerton's responsibilities as Governor of the Lagos Colony so that he held the two offices simultaneously. This de facto arrangement continued until 26 February 1906 when the Lagos Colony and the Protectorate of Southern Nigeria were formally amalgamated under the official title of 'The Colony and Protectorate of Southern Nigeria'[48].

The new country had its own flag and was divided into three provinces: Lagos and its hinterland with Lagos as the capital; a central province with Warri as its capital; and Calabar and its hinterland with Calabar as its capital.

THE SPECIAL CASE OF ABEOKUTA AND EGBALAND

The 16 year long Yoruba civil war officially ended in 1886 but it was 1893 before it came to a final end. Exhausted by the war effort, the warring tribes, having surrendered their arms as part of the British-imposed peace settlement, had little choice but to accept the standard terms Treaty of Protection. These template agreements had required a surrender of sovereignty symbolised by the appointment of a permanent British Resident as the ultimate power in the land. The terms of the Treaty of Protection which the Egba Chiefs signed with the British Government in 1893 was materially different. Under the terms of that treaty, Egbaland, with its capital in Abeokuta, was an independent state with only a defence pact with Britain. How this came about requires an explanation.

As we have seen, the Egba owed their unique treatment to the special relationship which they had cultivated with the British but even so independence had not simply been conceded to them on mere request; the Egba Chiefs had played their hand skilfully to secure it.

The long period of cohabitation with British traders and missionaries brought with it early access to education and firearms as well as the influx of ´recaptive` Sierra Leonians and Brazilians. For this reason the geo-political experience of the Egbas at this time bore some comparison with the Zulu people of South Africa in that what began as peaceful-coexistence soon became antagonistic, before ending up in war as the political ambitions on both sides came into conflict.

By the time the British were making their push inland with their standard form Treaties, the state of native governance and administration in Egbaland was already very advanced with a whole army of educated natives. Also it will be recalled that the Egba had, once before, their independence when in October 1867 they had expelled all Europeans from their land, only allowing them to return in 1875.

THE FRENCH CONNECTION

The other significant factor which set the Egbas apart and gave them leverage in negotiations with the British was interest from the French who were determined to use every possible means, short of direct conflict with Britain, to carve out for themselves a little more of the Nigeria space. With their strategic location on the western flank of what was to become Nigeria, on the border with French Dahomey (now Benin), the Egba found that they had more than one suitor and they were astute in playing the rivals off against each other:

> *Beginning in the early 1880s the Anglican missionary J.B. Wood with the dual support of the Protestant group in Egbaland and the important Chief Ogundipe gradually became the most important power at Abeokuta. Wood formed a tight-knit group of powerful Egba who were called the Christian Party and whose aims were the westernization of Abeokuta. The threat posed by this group to the traditional structure of Egba society was soon recognized and in a cumbersome fashion most of the chiefs tried to rid themselves of the Christian Party. The Christian Party was actually a pro-British Protestant group. Therefore it is not strange that some of its opponents should turn to the French for support. This*

dissatisfaction gave a young French trader, Edouard Viard, a brief moment of hope that he could gain control of Abeokuta for the French.

British authorities were not simply imagining a French threat to Abeokuta. French Roman Catholic missionaries had been at work there since 1880. Viard was potentially much more dangerous. In 1888 he signed a treaty with the chiefs of Ilaro, the major Egbado town. He then moved on to Abeokuta where he again concluded a treaty which would have made Abeokuta a French protectorate. In return he promised the chiefs that the French would build a railway from Porto Novo through Ilaro to Abeokuta[49]

It was by this exploitation of their experience from the long period of interaction with the British missionaries, and the competing interest from the French, that the Egba leaders were able to reject the standard-form treaties of protection that the British imposed on others, and to insist on properly negotiated terms. These terms were that the British either agreed to respect Egba sovereignty or the Egbas would join Francophone Africa:

On 18 January [1893], the Alake and the three major chiefs signed a treaty containing six sections....The Egba promised in the future not to close the roads and pledged themselves to improve trade with their neighbours. In section four the Alake and his associates promised to give every assistance to the spread of Christianity. Section five was for the Egba the most important since [Governor] Carter promised that so long as the other provisions in the treaty were adhered to, then Britain would not annex any part of Egbaland without consent of the lawful authorities. It further was stated that 'no aggressive action shall be taken against the said country and its independence shall be fully recognized'[50]

Thus it was that, at a time when laws in Lagos were passed in the name of the British Governor, in the United Kingdom of Egbaland laws were passed in the name of the Alake.

Not only was Egbaland sovereign and independent, continued French interest in the state compelled the British to promoting Egba unity. The British calculation was that a unified Egba kingdom would not only avoid the risk of some of the Egba chiefs doing their own deals with the French, it would also facilitate indirect rule[51]. To this end of strengthening central government in the independent kingdom, the Egba National Council was set up in 1898, with British help, complete with departments of state (Justice, Finance, Roads and Works, Public Order, Trade and agriculture and Sanitation) with a secretariat dominated by the western educated Egba:

The Egba National Council established in 1898 continued to grow since it was backed by both the British and the Alake's factions as well as most of the educated Egba. In 1902 the Council was considerably revised and the central government renamed the Egba United Government. By this time the position of secretary to the government carried great power and prestige for this officer was in charge of the everyday business of the government and could make or break the future of young educated Egba. Soon after the creation of the Egba United Government, the name Adeboyega Edun, the secretary, began to appear in British notes about Abeokuta. Edun had been a Methodist minister and had been known throughout most of his life as J. Henryson Samuel before changing his name and abandoning his first calling for politics. He was one of many Nigerians who gave up their European names in protest against the policies of the British government and the increasingly pro-white attitudes of the various Christian churches. All contemporary observers who left an account of Abeokuta in the days before the First World War agree that Secretary Edun was an amazingly competent administrator and politician who certainly earned his annual stipend of £250 per year. Within a short period he had become the de facto ruler of the Egba....

The central government came to be dominated more and more by Edun who was able to use the traditional authorities as cat's paws to gain his ends. It should be noted that Edun seems not to have been propelled by any sense of personal gain but rather was convinced that the future of the Egba lay in modernizing the state. In addition to creating a more efficient central government and civil service, the Egba United Government launched an ambitious scheme of road building and public works. The health service at Abeokuta provided medical care far above that available in any city with the exception of Lagos. Orders in Council also regulated the operations of markets and made individual chiefs responsible for maintaining roads, bridges, and eliminating health hazards. The most ambitious scheme of the Egba government was their lighting plant and advanced waterworks plant for Abeokuta. It had been obvious for years that the wells were not sufficient for the large population of Abeokuta. Impure water was the cause of much of the sickness and death among the residents. Edun's government in co-operation with the British decided to build a modern water system for the city[52]

THE CREATION OF NORTHERN NIGERIA

With no long-standing trading links with the territories north of the River Niger and Benue, and with Christian evangelisation having been limited to the territories in these areas which had not been claimed in the name of Islam, the colonisation of Northern Nigeria had to be achieved in short time by direct military conquest. In the open savannah lands in the North, as compared with the densely forested south, this was feasible especially with the Maxim gun.

THE CONQUEST OF THE EMIRATES OF NUPE AND ILORIN

The British preference was, nevertheless, to simply superimpose themselves on top of any existing order, whenever possible, rather than to see it dismantled as had happened with the Oyo Empire. It was a policy that had been applied to good effect in India where they had taken over an empire that had been in existence for more than three hundred years beforehand under a succession of alien imperial rulers, the last of which were the Moghuls.

The approach to the conquest of the Fulani Empire in north-west Nigeria was to first give a demonstration of the devastating capabilities of the Maxim gun before demanding the submission of the Emirs to British rule. Those who refused were deposed and replaced with more compliant alternatives.

Careful lessons had been taken from the history of the Roman Empire in the art of divide and rule, the first principle of which was to always ensure that those doing the policing have no affiliation with the policed. Thus it was veterans of the now disbanded Ibadan army that were deployed against the Fulani:

> *Ibadan never really settled down till after about eighteen months, when the Government of Lagos enlisted two battalions of men for military service in Northern Nigeria. This opening afforded relief to all those ardent spirits whose profession was arms, and with a wonderful celerity they imbibed and assimilated the new method of drill and discipline, by which they were led to a successful campaign*[53]

With the memory of the Fulani jihad in Ilorin still fresh, and the conquest of Ilorin being one of the strategic targets, the Yoruba recruits would have been suitably motivated. The first engagement was the conquest of Bida, the capital of the Nupe Emirate, on 27 January 1897:

> *On the 23rd January the Company's forces crossed the Niger and advanced towards Bida, and in spite of determined resistance by the Emir's followers, estimated at about 30,000 men, the town was taken four days later with the loss of one officer...seven men killed and nine men wounded. Another Emir*

was installed in the place of the former one, who had fled before the town was occupied, and the expedition at once re-crossed the Niger and moved on Ilorin.... The fire of the guns and Maxims, as at Bida proved decisive and Ilorin was occupied on the 16th February 1897[54].

THE CONQUEST OF THE SOKOTO CALIPHATE

The recent southern outgrowths of the Fulani Empire having been taken, the next target was the conquest of the Empire, itself. But first there was the important matter of the formal declaration of the "Protectorate of Northern Nigeria", on 1st January 1900. The man chosen for the job of High Commissioner was Lugard:

> *Arriving at the end of December 1899, I took over the administration from the Royal Niger Company, and the Union Flag was hoisted in place of the Company's at 7.20 a.m. at Lokoja, on January 1st 1900, in presence of a parade of all arms, at which all civilians were present in uniform*[55]

Lugard's conquest of the Sokoto Caliphate was done on the sly and in secrecy even from the Colonial Office. 'There were no vital national interests at stake; there were no white settlers and no vast deposits of gold and diamonds[56]. It was carried out by Lugard with an eye on the territory's strategic importance in the imperial control of the resource-rich Southern Nigeria. But the move had been given tacit clearance, from beyond the Colonial Office, most likely from Joseph Chamerlain, the Colonial Secretary, on the understanding that it was done quickly and successfully and delivered as a *fait accompli*. It was the very reason that Lugard had been chosen as the first High Commissioner and he was in a hurry to get the job done:

> *The report for 1901 did not appear until 1903, and that for 1902 and the first eventful months of 1903 was published in 1904. These were not so much plain factual reports as deliberate attempts to sway public opinion, attempts to prove as authoritative truth that conquest was forced upon him.*
> *The next objective in the propaganda campaign was the 'vindication' of the 'pacification' of the Northern Emirates planned in 1902 and carried out in early 1903. The Colonial Office's first intimation of such a campaign being planned was a Reuters report on 5 December 1902, and there were embarrassing questions in the House of Commons before the Christmas recess, to which, of all personages, it was the Postmaster-General, Austen Chamberlain, in his father's absence in South Africa, who replied as best he could without information, denying any*

*plan to attack Kano, and surmising that Lugard's moves must be measures to
protect the Anglo-French Boundary Commission. It was not until Parliament
reassembled in the following February, when the success of the Kano expedition
was mentioned in the King's speech, that Parliament paid any further attention.
By then the Kano campaign was over, and a practically deserted Sokoto was
about to be reoccupied. The field campaign was over, Lugard was rebuked for
secrecy before the act, but given the credit for a speedy victory...* [57]

That Lugard had approval for the attack that he launched against the Fulani Empire
is clear from the fact that he could not have done it without Treasury approval for the
enlargement of the West African Frontier Force. The increase that Lugard had sought
was for an additional 750 men, '*the Treasury ...not only allowed £50,000 for 1,400
men, but also sanctioned the largest grant-in-aid ever £405,000*'[58].

The first to fall was the Emirate of Kontagora which put Lugard's forces on the
southern edge of the Fulani Empire. To keep the Caliphate off the scent of what was
afoot, he wrote a letter to the Sultan of Sokoto, on 18 March 1901, to explain his
action:

> *In the name of the Most Merciful God,*
> *Peace be to the Generous Prophet*
> *Salutations, peace and numberless honours....*
> *In the case of the Emir of Bida, I have made the Makum Emir instead of Abu-
> Bakri, which proves to you that I have no hostility to the Fulanis or to your
> religion, provided only that the Emir of a country rules justly and without
> oppression. In the case of Kontagora...I desire that the people shall return and
> live in peace under a just ruler, and I write to you to appoint a man who will
> rule justly, and if he does so, I will support him and uphold his power; send him
> to me with a letter and I will install him as Emir of Kontagora with pomp and
> honour. But warn him that if he acts treacherously and with deceit, he will share
> the fate of Kontagora the Gwamachi* [59]

However, this Sultan was not ready to concede to Lugard the right to install and remove
emirs in the empire as he wished. His response left the British in no doubt about his
attitude toward their ambitions under his reign:

> *From us to you. I do not consent that any one from you should ever dwell with
> us. I will never agree with you. Between us and you there are no dealings except
> as between Mussulmans and Unbelievers, War, as God Almighty has enjoined
> on us. There is no power or strength save in God on high.*
> *This with salutations* [60]

It was just the response Lugard wanted. The Emirate of Yola, on the southern borders of the still separate Islamic Empire of Bornu, in the north-east, was the next target conquered in September 1901. After this came the conquest of Kano, the heartland of the Hausa before the conquest of their lands by the Fulani. Through clever exploitation of recent history, including continuing slavery, the necessary groundwork had already been done to encourage insurrection amongst the Hausa against their Fulani overlords:

> *The time had now come when the relative strength of the [Colonial] Government and the Fulani Empire had to be settled. It was believed (and subsequently proved) that the sympathies of the peasantry would be with the British in a struggle with the slave raiders. The Fulanis were aliens ruling over a subject people whom they had antagonized by decades of slave-raiding and injustice[61]*

The excuse for the attack on Kano was provided by an earlier confrontation in Keffi. In that clash Capt. Moloney, the British Resident, had been killed and the ruler who was seen to be responsible for his death had taken refuge in Kano. By this time, the British forces had moved up to within striking distance of Kano following an appeal to Lugard by the Emir of Zaria for help in dealing with some local trouble:

> *…It was clear that the Colonial Office was prepared to sanction an invasion of Kano only if it could be proved that it was necessary as a pre-emptive i.e. defensive measure…However, Lugard had no compunction about reassuring them on this score, and in January 1903, when preparations had been completed and queries were still being received, he offered to cancel the proposed expedition. With the troops poised to advance, he knew that the Office would not take this step, and that the expedition would be allowed to proceed. Lugard's real attitude was summed up at the time in a conversation he had with [Reginald] Popham-Lobb, when 'he was pleased at the way he had bustled up the Colonial Office, otherwise they would have left the north half of the protectorate for years'*

When an ultimatum given to the Emir of Kano to handover the fugitive ruler of Keffi was rebuffed, a strong force, including four Maxim guns, began the assault on the walled city and captured it on 3 February 1903:

> *As it turned out, there was little opposition. A heavy fire was opened from the walls, but the guns soon effected a breach, and the defenders fled as soon as the storming party appeared, losing heavily in their flight from the town at the hands of the troops sent to cut them off. The British casualties consisted of fourteen wounded….It was found that the Emir of Kano had left the city some weeks earlier to pay a visit to the Sultan of Sokoto, but he now returned towards*

Kano with a large army determined to fight. His chiefs, however, were not anxious for battle, and a considerable proportion deserted him. Leaving the still loyal portion under the command of the Waziris, he fled to Gobir, where he was subsequently captured, and the Waziri's troops were opposed by the British force, which moved out of Kano in search of them[62]

All that remained now was Sokoto itself.

THE SUBJUGATION OF THE FULANI

The Fulani and the British were both strangers to the land. Both had come into the Nigeria space around about the same time, from opposites ends of the territory, but with similar imperial ambitions. This was the final showdown for hegemony:

Friendly messages to the Sultan received only evasive replies, and the troops were opposed before Sokoto by a force of about 1,500 horse and 3000 foot. Fanatics charged the British square in twos and threes, but there was little real resistance, our casualties amounting to one carrier killed and two wounded. The enemy losses were about 70 killed and 200 wounded. The Sultan fled before the battle and did not return, but a few days later most of the Sokoto chiefs tendered their submission to the High Commissioner, who had followed the troops, with a small escort, first to Kano and then to Sokoto[63]

With Sokoto having fallen, the Fulani Empire now belonged to Britain. It only remained for the conquest of the "native" invaders to be justified to the home audience back in Britain:

The annual reports for the first years show the first workings out of this justification. For this the Fulani rulers had to be both good and bad. Strange ideas of race and of intelligence had to make them 'decadent', 'degenerate', and 'cruel' enough to be attacked and conquered, whether they resisted or not, and yet in the next breath they could be 'born rulers' and 'incomparably above the negroid tribes in ability' – and so fitted, if they submitted promptly, to be used in the new command structure[64]

It only remained for Lugard, the High Commissioner, to lay out for the Fulani leaders the new terms of engagement within the new order:

The chiefs were now asked to nominate a successor to the fugitive Sultan, and their choice being approved by the High Commissioner, the new Sultan, Atahiru, was installed with full ceremonial, after the terms on which he was appointed had been carefully explained to him. These included the abolition of slave-raiding and the recognition of British suzerainty, and were coupled with an assurance that the existing system of law and the Muhammadan religion would not be interfered with. The statement by the High Commissioner that their religion would be respected was received with audible expressions of pleasure and satisfaction by the large crowd which witnessed the installation. Sir Frederick Lugard then proceeded to Katsina, where the Emir peaceably accepted the Government's terms, and to Kano, where a new Emir was installed on the usual conditions[65]

This handshake and accord between the Fulani chiefs and their British conquerors would set the shape of things to come.

THE CONQUEST OF THE BORNU EMIRATE

The greater part of Shehu, al-Kanemi's old Bornu Empire lies in what is now south-east Niger, south-west Chad and north-west Cameroon. These being territories falling within the French zone of influence, it was to the French that the task of conquest fell.

An invading army from Sudan that had usurped the Bornu throne was driven out by the French in 1900. They then restored the deposed Shehu to power on the condition that he pay them a substantial reward for their services. When he refused he was deposed and replaced by one of his more compliant relations who was only too happy to acknowledge the debt.

The terms agreed at the Berlin Conference meant that the French were unable to keep that part of the Bornu Empire lying within the British zone of influence. Now that the British were ready to claim their property they did so in return for taking over the debt which the Shehu owed to the French. Thus, British Bornu became part of Nigeria by subrogation rather than by British military conquest as with the rest of the north.

THE CONQUEST OF THE TIV

In the middle ground between Islamic Northern Nigeria and Southern Nigeria lay a multitude of ethnic groups who were neither Christian nor Muslim. Principal amongst these were the Tiv, a warrior people who guarded their independence fiercely with their bows and poisoned arrows. The Fulani had tried and failed to conquer them. While Lugard had taken just three years to conquer the Fulani Empire, the effort to subdue the Tiv which had begun in 1900 ran on for years and they were only finally brought under British rule in 1914 when a treaty was signed.

The first assault came in 1900 after Tiv fighters with their poisoned arrows had annihilated the white men who were attempting to put up the telegraph lines across their farmlands. The reprisal attack with Maxim guns was well under way before Lugard had to explain his actions to the Colonial Office:

> *The Tivs are a most intractable people and nothing except extremely severe chastisement of this sort can prevent them from lawless murders or induce them to allow the telegraph to be constructed through their country.*

Even so by 1906 Lugard had to send troops, known as the Munshi Expeditionary force under the command of Lt. Colonel Hasler, back in to Tiv country in an effort to subdue them but still the Tiv resisted. In the end they were one of the last parts of Northern Nigeria to be brought under British rule.

LUGARD'S RULE IN NORTHERN NIGERIA

Born in 1858, in Madras India, Frederick John Dealtry Lugard was a short lovable rogue with a high pitched voice. He lost both his belief in Christ and his belief in love after he was jilted by a *'remarried divorcee in Lucknow, whose identity remains shrouded in mystery by his biographer'*[66]. With a heart now badly crushed by this set back, he set his mind on leaving England to find release from his emotional torment. He was to find it in the harassment of the French in their claims to lands in West Africa.

Three of his uncles were army officers and his own father, an army chaplain, had held the rank of Lieutenant Colonel while his mother was a CMS missionary. Fate ordained that he would find love again in a woman of equally hard head and heart, Flora Louisa Shaw. Several years his senior, and the daughter of a major general, she was a journalist who had risen to become Colonial Editor of the highly-influential *Times* newspaper in Britain.

Lugard and Shaw were ardent imperialists who fed off each other's enthusiasm, offices and abilities. This was an age when a select group of Englishmen were carving their names onto the face of the planet and Shaw had worked closely with the greatest British imperialist of them all, Cecil Rhodes, who had earned the accolade of having the colony that he had carved out for Britain in the south of the continent, being named 'Rhodesia' in 1895. The year of Rhodes' death, 1902, was the year of Lugard and Shaw's marriage. The only offspring from their union was the country which Lugard put together and which she said should be called 'Nigeria':

> *In an essay, which first appeared in The Times on 8 January 1897, she suggested the name "Nigeria" for the British Protectorate on the Niger River. In*

her essay she was making a case for a shorter term that would be used for the "agglomeration of pagan and Mohamedan States" that was functioning under the official title, "Royal Niger Company Territories....She then put forward this argument...: "The name Nigeria applying to no other part of Africa may without offence to any neighbours be accepted as co-extensive with the territories over which the Royal Niger Company has extended British influence, and may serve to differentiate them equally from the colonies of Lagos and the Niger Protectorate on the coast and from the French territories of the upper Niger"[67]

The Lugards had given careful thought to the form of administration that was to be adopted in Northern Nigeria and it was the India model that they fixed upon as Mrs Lugard explained:

In India, before the coming of the Europeans, native races of a lower order than the present ruling castes allowed themselves to be driven by successive invasions down to the sea shores of the extreme south, or up into the wild fastness of the hills. It is equally true of Nigeria....In India the great 'native' invasions were from the North....So it has been with Nigeria....As in India, so in Nigeria. We meant to trade but conquest was forced upon us. Having conquered we are now obliged to administer, and the hope that lies before us is to develop from the small beginnings which have been made in Nigeria such another great prosperous dominion as our ancestors have created for us in India.[68]

'INDIRECT RULE'

There would be a conscious effort to maintain distance between the ruling power, Britain, and the natives by the reinstatement and elevation of the conquered Fulani rulers in a system that Lugard called *'indirect rule'*. The essence of indirect rule was the British ruling without being seen to be doing so by relying upon the strict control of policy and personnel. The High Commissioner would appoint the Sultan and all the Emirs and other key officials of the Native Administration who, to all appearances, would be the effective rulers of the territory but their rule was conditional upon them following the High Commissioner's orders as communicated to them by the Resident. Provided the Emir and the Native Administration ruled in accordance with the High Commissioner's policy, as relayed through the Resident, they enjoyed a state of semi-independence:

[The Resident's] main object, one which he must ever bear in mind, is to create a situation resembling as far as possible that which existed, or might be imagined to have existed, were a thoroughly able, well-meaning, liberal Emir ruling over a unit untouched by foreign influence. He must as far as possible keep

his authority in the background and concealed, if not from the emir and his immediate entourage, at all events from the people generally[69]

To maintain the appearance of natives, rather than white men, being in charge Colonial office control over the finances of the Emir and the Native Administration had to be as light as possible. To begin with, the Emir was allowed total discretion over the revenue and expenditure of the Native Administration's funds without having to render any account. Only later, as Northern Nigeria struggled to balance its books, was some restraint placed on the Emirs' financial management by putting him and the members of his administration on salaries and introducing some budgetary disciplines. Even so, under what was called the Native Treasury system, the Emir had complete control of the funds under his management and of any surplus.

Through this arrangement of the Emir with his Native Administration and Native Treasury, controlled from behind the scenes by the British Resident, Lugard exercised maximum control of Northern Nigeria without undermining the prestige of the Emir.

The conquest of Northern Nigeria had been a very personal project for the Lugards and so the form of rule that they adopted was also very personal, with the minimum of officialdom and the maximum of close family involvement:

> *Not to have a normal Secretariat made sense only if the policy being followed could not be subjected to the ordinary process of discussion and formulation. Since Lugard's plan was fully formed, and too secret, too personal for a Secretariat, he was driven to nepotism to secure the appointment of his own brother, an army officer like himself, as 'Chief Clerk' in his office, and the appointment of a personal friend to command his army*[70]

With his wife as the Colonial Editor for the *Times* newspaper, Lugard sought to dispense with the input and control of the permanent officials in the Colonial Office by not taking holidays to avoid handing over to an Acting Governor.[128] To this end, unusually for a colonial administrator in West Africa, he planned for his wife to live in Nigeria with him:

> *Lady Lugard when they were going to be married, represented the great benefit which the Protectorate would derive from their both residing in it, and induced Mr. Chamberlain to sanction the expenditure required to build and furnish for them at Zungeru on what she considered a suitable scale*

The family enterprise ran into difficulty only when it emerged that due to Mrs Lugard's poor health she could not live in Nigeria. Undaunted, Lugard came up with a scheme, which he termed 'continuous administration', whereby he would rule Northern

Nigeria from his home in London for six months in each year: he would have a seat within the Colonial Office in London from which he would do his work as Governor so while technically on leave he would still be working.

Lugard's proposal would have fundamentally undermined the role of the Colonial Office and so the permanent officials killed it leading Lugard to resign in protest, in 1906. He left Nigeria to become Governor of Hong Kong but he would return, later, in an attempt to make 'One Nigeria'.

THE BACKGROUND TO THE AMALGAMATION

The point was made earlier in this work that the original British plan was to have one single large colony across tropical West Africa until that plan was compromised by the need to accommodate French, and then German, territorial ambitions in the area. Following the conquest of Benin in 1897, the British now had effective control of the whole of the Niger coast and attention could be given to the strategy for the hinterland.

The Niger Committee was commissioned to consider and advise on 'the future administration of the three territories Lagos, Niger Coast Protectorate and Niger Company's Territories' and in August 1898 it advised the eventual establishment of a Governor General for the whole of the territories, resident in the territories. But we feel that the appointment of a Govenor General is inadvisable for now'.[72]"One Nigeria" was a nice-sounding slogan that had been adapted from the British Prime Minister, Benjamin Disraeli's "One Nation" British election campaign in 1872. But how were the two very different Nigerias, North and South, which had now been brought into existence, complete with frontier controls,[73] to be made into one? The initial approach recognised the reality of the differences between the two Nigerias to the point that it produced two types of British colonial administrators, those recruited for Northern Nigeria, schooled in Arabic, and those for Southern Nigeria. The other key question was what was to be done about the – still – independent United Kingdom of Egbaland?

4. Lugard's 'One Nigeria' Mission

North and South managed to develop in strikingly different patterns – so different that they seemed more like the products of the influence of different ruling powers than the offspring of the same Secretary of State, brought up by the same Ministry, the Colonial Office[1]

I.F. Nicolson

MILITARY RULE IN THE NORTH AND CIVIL RULE IN THE SOUTH

The difference in the form of administration between North and South manifested in the different provision made in the foundational constitutional documents for the two new countries for deputisation in the event of the absence or incapacity of the High Commissioner. While the 'Orders in Council' for the South stipulated that the stand-in must be a civilian, the one for the North was explicit in providing for a senior military officer. The contrasting provision reflected the different methods by which the two countries had been brought under British rule.

CIVIL RULE IN THE SOUTH

The colonisation of the South was largely led by missionaries and traders in a form of soft-colonisation which evolved over a period of more than one hundred years. It was only in the closing stages of the 19th century that blood was spilt. This softer approach was not the result of any magnanimity on the part of the British. It was, rather, dictated by the conditions.

The experience of the failed Niger Expedition of 1841 had been an early warning of the lethal hostility of the dense forest terrain and the mosquito-harbouring climate. Direct military assault would have required protracted and costly warfare without any assurance of success contrary to the policy of constructing the empire 'on the cheap'. Instead, at least since the time the Portuguese first visited Benin in the mid-16th century, civil relationship through the coastal trade had been established with the people of Lagos and the southern coastal communities. The foundation upon which the empire in the South was built was, therefore, the re-tuning of minds through spiritual and educational tutelage. Thus, when the time came for political relationships to be superimposed upon the established trade and civil relationships, the administrators had to be civilian.

Lagos, for example, had been a crown colony since 1861 and not just a protectorate[i]. As this offshore island had always been intended as a staging post for the colonisation of the Nigerian mainland, it was being administered with a focus on bringing the best out of the environment and the people. The approach to administration and development in the colony bore comparison with other British colonies in Australia, New Zealand and the Caribbean at the time. It had harbour works, a railway, a racecourse and a canal. Marshland was reclaimed and a sewerage system was planned. The first High Commissioner for Lagos and the Yoruba Protectorate, William MacGregor, set the mold:

He began life as the second of eight children of a farm worker in Towie, Aberdeenshire, in a tiny cottage. Poverty seemed likely to deprive him of the opportunity for higher education, but his brilliance and application at the village school greatly impressed the local schoolmaster, minister and doctor. They were able to arrange that the boy remained a kind of pupil teacher at the village school, while studying, during intervals when not working at the plough or as a herdsman, for a bursary at the Aberdeen Grammar School. MacGregor, who is said to have learned his arithmetic table as a boy from the cover of a copy of the Shorter Catechism which he read while herding his cattle, won the bursary and reached the grammar school at the age of nineteen. In two years he was at University, graduating M.B. in 1872 and M.D. in 1874. Later, he made himself, in the words of the Dictionary of National Biography, an 'excellent linguist, botanist and ethnologist'[2]

This was a governor to whose personal story the educated Yoruba could relate. Lagos being the seat of the colonial government, its people had the advantage of direct exposure to the merits and possibilities of education as demonstrated by the white colonial administrators who lived amongst them and there was a genuine commitment to educating and training the Lagosians to become proper Englishmen[ii]. Even more

---

i   For the difference see the preceding page

ii   Following Lugard's return to Nigeria in 1912 there was an attempt to introduce racial segregation

inspiring to the Lagosians than the liberal colonial administrators was the sight of Sierra Leonians and Caribbeans employed in the colonial service. Henry Carr was one such member of the African Diaspora who, at this early stage, headed the Education Department and the Inspectorate of Schools:

> *Lagos was already an examination centre for Matriculation, and for the degrees of B.A. and LL.B. of the University of London...The civil service which linked the departments, through the Colonial Secretariat, with the Governor and the central organs of government was a surprisingly sophisticated one, with standards of competitive entrance and advancement higher than it would be practicable to enforce sixty years later in some parts of Nigeria. Entrance to the lowest clerical grade was by competitive examination in a very practical group of subjects. They were arithmetic, handwriting, English composition (writing 'a clear and grammatical account' of some recent local occurrence, and writing a simple letter), dictation, conversation, and knowledge of Yoruba....All promotions were centrally regulated 'by merit and ability and not necessarily by seniority nor length of service'. The probation period was six months, and annual confidential reports to the Secretariat by heads of departments had to include details of each clerk's ability, intelligence, and – showing how deep the Victorian zeal for self-help had bitten – 'endeavours after self-improvement since joining the service'....[3]*

Thus, for several decades before the Amalgamation, Lagos had been on a fast-track of development on British lines. A way of life had become established:

> *There was electric light in the street, there were telephones, printing presses, newspapers. Amidst the white officials, and not segregated from them by separate residential areas and hospital facilities, there was an educated elite of 'Black Englishmen' – doctors (four out of the Government establishment of sixteen), clergy, pastors, teachers, lawyers, police officers, journalists, senior clerks (when 'clerk' corresponded nearly in the civil service with what is now administrative status, and the Governor's confidential clerk, for instance, an African, was also clerk to the Legislative Council). And of course, there were substantial business men, traders, middle-men, some of them frequent visitors to Liverpool, some with sons and daughters being educated overseas[4]*

On the political front, there was the Lagos Legislative Council with its *"unofficial"* members. These were Lagosians selected by the Governor and approved by the Secretary of State. The Governor passed laws for the Colony *"with the advice and consent of the Legislative Council"*.

Lagos. June. 1911. Messrs. Pickering & Berthoud Ltd. Staff
W. J. Guby. J. V. Wilson. A. C. Christhel. J. Martin. H. J. Menkens.

Lagos. 12th March 1912. Refreshments at Government House after the swearing in of F. S. James C.M.G. as Acting Governor of Southern Nigeria.

The approach to administration in Calabar, the then capital of the Eastern province, was along the same progressive and liberal lines:

> *Like MacGregor in Lagos, McDonald was a steadfast believer in consulting native opinion and in basing policy firmly on the wishes and aspirations revealed in the process of consultation. It may not have been Scottish egalitarianism which inspired this respect for African self-determination; but these men may have been influenced by the unhappy ancestral memories of the MacGregors and the MacDonalds – memories of the terrible mistakes made by alien governments in the treatment of the Scottish Highland clans[5]*

The Governor who, above all others, drove the development agenda for the South was Walter Egerton; Governor of Lagos (and the Yoruba mainland) from 1904 to 1906 before becoming Governor of Southern Nigeria, from 28 February 1906 when Lagos and Yorubaland was formally united with the Southern Nigeria Protectorate up until 1912 when he was replaced by Lugard. To his post as the new Governor of Lagos he was bringing years of experience as a colonial administrator in the Far East.

He had a clear appreciation of the resource potential of Southern Nigeria and his management philosophy was to spend whatever was necessary to generate what was possible even if that meant deficit financing in the short term. His development programme was energetic. The experience from Malaysia enabled him to introduce the cultivation of rubber and the development of rubber plantations. He pushed for the expansion of the railway network and telegraph lines. With respect to the territorial boundaries of his territory, he argued forcefully for the re-unification of Ilorin with the rest of Yorubaland. The least known credit to his scorecard was the support he gave to the search for and the discovery of oil in Nigeria by John Simon Bergheim.

The big oil-find that Bergheim, an American engineer, had made in Galicia in Austrian Poland enabled him to say to Egerton with conviction that there was oil in Southern Nigeria and that with some financial contribution from the government he would find it. It was just the kind of development proposition that Egerton loved. In 1907 the Southern Nigeria Mining Regulation (Oil) Ordinance was passed and drilling, by Bergheim's Nigerian Bitumen Company, began. By November 1908 Bergheim was able to repay Egerton's faith with the announcement that he had found oil. By September 1909 his company was producing two thousand barrels of oil a day.[6]

Despite this new and major boost to Southern Nigeria's resource base, Egerton still faced an uphill struggle with the Colonial Office to carry through his development agenda. He was labelled 'extravagant'[7] even though by 1912, when he was replaced as Governor of Southern Nigeria, he had built up accumulated reserves of nearly £1,000,000.[8]

Lagos. 3rd June 1912. Kings Birthday Gymkana

Lagos 3rd June. 1912. Kings Birthday. Review of Troops.

The administrators of the South's *'deliberate effort to teach, to elevate and to influence by direct contact'* with their wards, to set them on the road to development stood in marked contrast to the approach in the North.

The military character of the administration was sealed by the choice of Lugard, the conquering soldier, as the colony's first High Commissioner:

> *He had the soldier's love of discipline and of ranks, each rank obedient through the official hierarchy to its head; for him law and authority proceeded downwards; they were not working arrangements evolved through discussion and democratic process[9]*

In his *Political Memoranda* Lugard placed the emphasis on pomp, pageantry and strict protocol. A proper distance was to be observed between those who were born to rule and those whom they ruled.[10] While the Governors of Southern Nigeria - MacGregor, Moor and Egerton - were pursuing a radical agenda of transformation of the country and its peoples through health, infrastructure and education programmes including the planting in Lagos (and Calabar) of the first seeds of democratic government, those administering Northern Nigeria were pursuing the conservative agenda laid down by Lugard:

> *....the Fulani Emirs, or captains were to be incorporated into Lugard's hierarchy of military command. In this system they were to be the 'Viceroy's Commissioned Officers', sworn in publicly with full military ceremonial to serve and obey the King. They were gazetted, in five grades according to their importance, paid substantial salaries, and presented with their staves of office 'by the High Commissioner personally, when possible, at a Review Parade of Troops, in the presence of the Resident and of their assembled people. Protocol was detailed: no chief should sit on a chair in the presence of the High Commissioner; those of the first grade would be provided with raised dais, such as 'a native bed covered with rugs and carpets'. 'All other grades will sit on mats and carpets on the ground'. Only chiefs of the first and second grades would be allowed 'royal trumpets'; no one except a chief could wear a sword, or assume special dress and titles. The symbolic presents given by the High Commissioner to the new Emir of Kano when he was installed were a sword, a dagger, and an umbrella[11]*

There was a class of Fulani Emirs who were not prepared to accept the indignity of being crowned by those who, according to their faith, were infidels. These Lugard ruthlessly deposed, and eliminated. The others, who accepted his terms, knew that their personal security and their office was assured so long as they remained obedient. The outlines of Nigeria as it would become, a top-down unitary system in which the governors, military and civilian, keep faith with the central power, rather than with the people they govern, out of the instinct for self-preservation, can be discerned in these foundations which Lugard laid in Northern Nigeria.

Another piece of the Nigerian political matrix originated by Lugard as the first High Commissioner of Northern Nigeria was the legal immunity for those at the apex of the power structure:

> But: 'The important Chiefs, and the persons holding high rank in a Native State, will never be arrested, or kept under detention in the common prison or otherwise, unless such extreme measures are necessitated by a very serious political crisis[12]

Tradesmen and missionaries from the South were discouraged and soldiers were used as administrators. Even the judicial system was modelled on military courts allowing him to justify the exclusion of professionally-trained lawyers from the trial process:

> Objection has been taken in some quarters to the appointment of military officers as civil residents. Failing the supply of men with African administrative experience I have found that selected Army officers are an admirable class of men for this work. They are gentlemen; their training teaches them prompt decision; their education in military law gives them a knowledge of the rules of evidence and judicial procedure sufficient when supplemented by a little special study to meet the requirements of a not too technical system of court work, and their training in topography enables them to carry out the surveys of all their journeys[13]

THE ECONOMICS OF AMALGAMATION

The adoption of different systems of administration in the North and South was not of itself problematic since the peoples of each territory were secure in their own space. The problem which has plagued Nigerians, even up to the present, was the appointment of Lugard in 1912 to unite the two territories in pursuit of the ideal of 'One Nigeria', a British policy objective borne of two calculations, one short term the other long term. The short-term calculation was administrative costs. The longer-term reckoning was the protection of the imperial hold on the territories, particularly on the resource-rich Southern Nigeria. It was a case of 'unite and rule'.

The Niger Committee had counselled delay for the amalgamation for the practical reason of the difficulty of finding the man with the right experience and physical constitution to cope with the climate. Even after Lugard had proved his mettle by his pacification and rule of Northern Nigeria, further delay came from the Colonial Office's battle to keep Southern Nigeria from Treasury control.

Imperial policy was that colonies should be self-funding. As long as the Colonial Office did not need Treasury funds the permanent officials at the Colonial Office could enjoy maximum control of policy within the territory in their interface between the Colonial Governor and the Colonial Secretary. With Southern Nigeria yielding annual surpluses and Northern Nigeria producing annual deficits, these officials were protective of the freedom of action they enjoyed over Southern Nigeria:

> *In London and in Northern Nigeria it was assumed that until the entire country was pacified and a strong government established throughout, a substantial military force, maintained at substantial expense, would be necessary. The colony itself was unable to generate funds for either its civil government or for a military force. During the years 1899-1913 an annual contribution was received from Southern Nigeria. This never exceeded £75,000. Therefore an annual grant-in-aid of revenue from the British Treasury, the major source of income for Northern Nigeria, was necessary.[14]*

The funding challenge in Northern Nigeria hit crisis point in the 1911/1912 budget which showed the need for a substantial Treasury grant in the sum of £365,000. With such a level of dependency, it was looking as if the Colonial Office would have to submit to Treasury control. To avoid this, it proposed a scheme of Amalgamation of Northern Nigeria with Southern Nigeria requiring an annual grant from the Treasury of £100,000 for a fixed period of five years on terms that, thereafter, the Colonial Office would 'do all that could be done to secure the financial stability of the amalgamated Nigeria'.[15]

On 12, October 1912 the scheme was approved. The decision that remained was the long-deferred one of who was to effect the amalgamation. The man making the decision was the Colonial Secretary, Lewis Vernon Harcourt.

Having overseen the amalgamation of Lagos and the Yoruba mainland with the East with the creation of Southern Nigeria in 1906, and implemented a successful economic development programme which had yielded annual budget surpluses, Egerton was the obvious choice for the job if the agenda for the amalgamated territory was development on the Southern Nigeria model. But this was not the plan. Instead it was Lugard's model of administration that was decided upon and the choice of Lugard for the job logically followed: 'they could not have Lugard's ideas without Lugard':

> *Lugard was formally appointed governor of Northern and Southern Nigeria in May 1912. He left for Nigeria in September for a survey, returned to England in the spring, and presented his amalgamation plan to the Colonial Office on 9th*

May 1913. The essence of the plan was as follows: Almagamated Nigeria was to be divided into Northern and Southern provinces. The original colony of Lagos (a strip 110 miles long and from four to twenty miles wide) was detached from the Southern Province and separately administered, and the Southern Nigeria Legislative Council restricted to Lagos. The Governor General would legislate for the rest of Nigeria with the advice of an executive council, composed of officials from his staff. There would be two Lieutenant Governors, one for Northern and one for Southern Nigeria, and an Administrator for Lagos. Some departments would be fully amalgamated; others would be supervised by deputy heads with separate establishments in the North and South and come directly under the respective Lieutenant Governors. The only significant unifying institution would be the Governor General, who would be in a 'strongly authoritarian position', as all financial estimates would emanate from him.[16]

Lugard, might have been amused by his deification by the Nigerian President, Goodluck Ebele Jonathan, when, at the official celebrations for the centenary of the amalgamation he said that, "The amalgamation of Nigeria was not a mistake but an Act of God". The flippancy of Jonathan's remark is rivalled only by the words of the British Colonial Secretary, Lord Harcourt, in the run up to the amalgamation, on 1 January 1914:

We have released Northern Nigeria from the leading strings of the Treasury. The promising and well-conducted youth is now on an allowance of his own and is about to effect an alliance with a Southern lady of means. I have issued the special licence and Sir Frederick Lugard will perform the ceremony. May the Union be fruitful and the couple constant

Upon Lugard's appointment, Egerton left Nigeria to become Govenor of British Guiana.

Lugard now sought to secure a return to Nigeria on his own terms by reviving his proposal of 'continuous administration'. Harcourt, who considered Lugard indispensable to the amalgamation project, approved a modified version of the scheme allowing Lugard to run Nigeria from London for four months in each year. As a reward for Harcourt's support, Lugard named the new port on the Bonny River, which Egerton had initiated, 'Port Harcourt'.

The impact of Lugard's assumption of responsibility for Southern Nigeria was immediate and dramatic. By the time of the handover, Bergheim's Nigerian Bitumen Company was just fifty miles away from today's oil fields in its search for oil in Southern Nigeria. A decision on the company's appeal for more financial support from the government was pending when, in September 1912, Bergheim was killed in a car crash. The death of his company, already financially challenged, followed very quickly afterwards:

Sir Walter Egerton, an enthusiastic supporter of economic development who had actively encouraged and worked with the Nigerian Bitumen Corporation, had left Nigeria. The new man, Sir Frederick Lugard, was more interested in administration than oil. He recommended, in May 1913, that no further money be lent and that the Company be asked to repay the original loan[17]

Lugard had his own economic development plan for Nigeria and Britain and he coined the phrase the '*Dual Mandate*' to explain it:

The aims of West African administration are comparatively simple. Unconcerned with that large range of subjects which provide material for the domestic legislation of most civilized countries, its problems are confined to two main branches:
The treatment of native races, who are centuries behind ourselves in mental evolution, and the steps by which they may be gradually brought to a higher plane of civilization and progress; and economic development by which these tropical countries may develop a trade which shall benefit our own industrial classes by the production, on the one hand, of the raw materials – rubber, oils, cotton, hides, etc. – which form the staples of our own manufactures, and by the absorption in return of our manufactured cottons, hardware and other goods[18]

He was equally forthright in his explanation of the division of functions in relation to the exploitation of Nigeria's resources. The natural resources taken from the land would be returned as finished articles for the use and comfort of Nigerians:

[The] tropics are the heritage of mankind…and neither, on the one hand, has the suzerain Power a right to their exclusive exploitation, nor, on the other hand, have the races which inhabit them a right to deny their bounties to those who need them. The responsibility for adequate development rests on the custodian on behalf of civilisation – and not on behalf of civilisation alone, for much of these products is returned to the tropics converted into articles for the use and comfort of its peoples[19]

LUGARD'S EDUCATION POLICY

By the time Britain declared the Protectorate of Northern Nigeria on 1 January 1900, a steely determination had set in amongst the imperial strategists to atone for the mistakes of the past which had led to the first Empire in America being lost to the rebel settlers and also to a slipping grip on the second.

Lagos 1st June 1912. Test match Europeans v. Natives

Lagos 1921. Government House.

There was real concern that the model of administration which had been pursued in Southern Nigeria over the preceding fifty years, based on Western education and the Christian teachings on the equality of all men, was producing a situation where the empire's hold on Southern Nigeria was at risk of being lost to nationalists. Early signs that the virus of nationalism had taken hold amongst the educated natives had made it necessary to create the offence of sedition in Southern Nigeria:

> The government responded to the outburst of political agitation and press criticism in 1908 by passing the Seditious Offenses Ordinance in 1909. Articulate Lagosians regarded the act as an intolerable and un-British stifling of criticism. In moving the rejection of the bill in the Legislative Council, the Honorable Sapara Williams pointed out that the "freedom of the Press is the great Palladium of British Liberty....Sedition is a thing incompatible with the character of the Yoruba people, and has no place in their constitution...Hyper-sensitive officials may come tomorrow who will see sedition in every criticism, and crime in every mass meeting"[20]

In the same way as Thomas Buxton had made the case for the colonisation of what became Southern Nigeria in the wake of Abolition, another intellectual, Edmund Dene Morel, was chosen to make the, seemingly impossible, case for preferring the feudal system of administration in Northern Nigeria to the liberal system prevailing in the South. The choice of Morel was a shrewd one as he was widely regarded as a friend of Africa, following his exposé on King Leopold of Belgium's atrocities in the Belgian Congo in his highly-acclaimed book *Red Rubber*.

Secure in his reputation for liberal thinking on African issues, Morel was able to make the case for the defence and extension of Lugard's system of governance in Northern Nigeria with gusto in another book which he published in 1911, *Nigeria: Its People and its Problems*[21] in which he dressed an argument for the defence of the imperial hold in the most liberal garments. The central plank of his case was the proper form of education for the native peoples drawing on the experience of the British Empire in India:

> The predominant characteristic of our educational methods – official and unofficial – in Western Africa hitherto may be summed up in one world – denationalisation. The result is so notoriously unsatisfactory as to need no specific illustration. If readers of Mr Valentine Chirol's book on India will turn to his chapters on the failure of our educational methods there, and substitute West Africa for India, they will be furnished with a replica of the situation on the West Coast of Africa. It is not an exact replica – for the reason that while the ties of caste are a deterrent to denationalization, such deterrent is non-existent in West Africa. But there is not one charge that Mr Chirol brings against the Indian

system that could not be equally brought against the West African system, and identical consequences are ensuing[22]

By *'denationalisation'* Morel really meant the lack of respect for established order, both Indian traditional and British colonial, which the extension of education on European lines was encouraging in the beneficiaries. In his assessment, the blame for the emergence of this trend within Nigeria lay squarely with the missionaries and the British colonial administrators in Southern Nigeria:

> *We are barely beginning to realize that the policy, or rather impolicy, of the last half-century has been a hideous example of misdirected effort, and there is hardly an administrator who does not contemplate the development of the "educated native problem" with the gravest foreboding.*
> *The object of the Northern Nigeria Administration is to set on foot an educational system throughout the country which shall save the Protectorate from these follies, while at the same time affording the rising generation the intellectual pabulum we are bound to provide, and ultimately laying the basis for a native civil service*[23]

The alarm that Morel was sounding, over the threat to the imperial hold posed by educated natives, was not altogether new. As far back as 1862, Henry Townsend, the head of the British Mission in Abeokuta, had sounded the same alarm when he engineered the re-posting of a missionary colleague who was perceived to be encouraging too much learning:

> *As the war matter between Abeokuta and Ibadan became complicated and battle shifted from Ijaye to Ijebu country, Townsend engaged in a conflict at home with his colleague, Gottlieb Frederick Buhler, who was in charge of the training institution. As a man who saw no value in what he considered too much book learning for Africans he loathed the academic emphasis in Buhler's curriculum. Townsend, like many CMS missionaries in West Africa in the mid-nineteenth century, believed that too much book learning only fans the vanities of African young people. They were of the view that basic training as evangelists and scripture readers was all they needed. In reality, part of their unstated fear was that they would not be able to keep well educated converts forever under their thumb as mission agents*[24]

That the concerns which were being voiced about the 'educated natives' were not entirely misplaced became clear within church politics after Henry Townsend had tried to block the ordination of Ajayi-Crowther as the first African bishop. Members of the African clergy reacted by declaring their independence of the Anglican Church and establishing the Native Church. The irony was that it was Townsend himself who had made the most telling contributions to the spread of education amongst the Yoruba generally and to the political strength of the Egba in particular. In 1859, drawing upon his experience as a member of a printing family, he had established the first newspaper in the land, 'Iwe Irohin'. He had intended it as a propaganda instrument to aid the Egba in their war against Ibadan but this head start has ensured the predominance of the southern media till today, especially in the south-west. The concern that western education was corroding the grip on Southern Nigeria drove Lugard and Morel to resolve to insulate the North from the virus by declaring western education for the native in Northern Nigeria to be a sin; in modern parlance Boko Haram:

> *Let us, rendered wise by experience elsewhere, set our faces like flint against the "Europeanizing" of Northern Nigeria*[25]

There would be education but it would be restricted to intellectual development for the sons of the Emirs; education for the masses would be limited to technical education:

> *It is at Nassarawa, a beautifully situated and healthy spot a few miles outside Kano, close by the Emir's country residence, that the first Government schools have been started. They consist at present of the Mallami School, or technical school with carpenters, blacksmiths, leather-workers and agricultural classes. The creation of a primary and secondary school will follow as soon as the work is sufficiently advanced*[26]

Divorced from the agenda of the perpetuation of the imperial hold, the case which Morel made for his education plan for Northern Nigeria was powerful, calling for a focus on the local and practical, rather than the international and enlightening:

> *The Mallamai school was full of special interest, being composed of grown men from eighteen to thirty; for these are the teachers of tomorrow....I attended the geography lesson which was then going forward, and found these future leaders studying, not the configuration of the Alps or the names of the English counties, but the map of Africa, the rivers, mountain ranges and political divisions of their own continent; not the distances between Berlin and St. Petersburg, Rome and Paris, but between Kano and Lokoja, Zaria and Yola and the routes to follow to reach those places from a given spot. The various classes, I observed, were not puzzling over, to them, incomprehensible stories about St. Bernard dogs rescuing snow-bound travellers or busy bees improving shining hours, but becoming acquainted with the proverbs and folk-lore of their own land; not*

being edified with the properties of the mangel-wurzel or the potentialities of the strawberry, but instructed in the culture requirements of yams, sweet potatoes, and sugar-cane. I did not see rows of lads in European costume, unsuited to the climate, hideous (out here) and vehicles for the propagation of tuberculosis, but decently clothed in their own graceful, healthy African garb[27]

In short what was being proposed was a programme of education that would preserve and sustain the existing order of rule by the Emirs by helping the people to be content with their condition of life:

> *The diffusion of education throughout the country, and especially the education of the sons of the native rulers, is particularly desirable in order to avoid the present danger of a separate educated class (in West Africa chiefly confined to the coast cities) in rivalry with the accepted rulers of the people.*
>
> *The impact of European civilisation on tropical races had indeed a tendency to undermine that respect for authority which is the basis of the social order. The authority of the head, whether of the tribe, the village or the family is weakened – tendencies which, as Lord Macdonell observed, are probably inseparable from that emancipation of thought which results from our education system and needs the control of scholastic discipline....[28]*

As Lugard took up office in 1912 to effect the amalgamation, his agenda was to shore up and underpin the British colonial grip on Nigeria using the following three key three pillars of educational policy recommended by E.D.Morel for the North: the adoption of a programme of education which placed the development of character before intellect; the promotion of Islam and Koranic education and the exclusion of missionaries and western education.

CHARACTER BEFORE INTELLECT

With Lugard's military background and emphasis on unquestioning obedience by government officials, Morel's argument for an education policy that emphasised the development of habits of obedience had a natural appeal to him. Lugard wrote:

> *these results may best be achieved by placing the formation of character before the training of the intellect...I speak of the controlling force and guiding principle which ministers through creeds and systems of philosophy to spiritual needs – the force which inspires a man to a sense of duty, to unswerving integrity and loyalty, whether in the public or private relations of life[29]*

Building on this, Morel explained the different approach to education in the two Nigerias:

> *The treatment of the problem of education must necessarily differ widely in Moslem and non-Moslem countries. In the former there already exists a literate class, held in respect by the illiterate peasantry. The goal of their ambition is to read the Koran, and to study the laws and traditions of Islam. No Mohamedan considers that he can claim to be properly educated unless he is able to do this. His outlook is towards the literature of the East - not of the West. In countries where Arabic is not the spoken vernacular (as it is in the Sudan), secular education, and the reading of their own language in the Roman character, does not offer to this class the same attractions as it does to non-Moslem natives. Arabic, says Blyden, is learnt for religion and for entrance to heaven, English for the things of this world[30]*

If Northern Nigeria was to be effectively protected from the virus of intellectual development, as Lugard and Morel proposed, then such education as there was to be had to be conducted in the vernacular language. At the very least, this would serve to keep western books out of popular reach:

> *For one thing, the preservation of the national tongue is aimed at, the general teaching being given in the vernacular, +for the present in Hausa – the lingua franca of the country – although in course of time, as the system extends, classes in Fulfulde (Fulani), Kanuri (the language of Bornu), and perhaps Nupe, will doubtless suggest themselves; not however, to the exclusion of Hausa, but in combination with it[31]*

Lugard's promotion of the preservation and use of the Hausa language in Northern Nigeria[iii] stood in contrast with his policy for Southern Nigeria Lugard where he warned against the preservation of the native tongues:

> *Elsewhere English must form the medium of instruction, and of intercommunication between tribes, as it has already to some extent done in West Africa...I concur with Lord Kimberley's dictum, that though instruction in English must of necessity at first be given through the medium of the vernacular, Government encouragement should not be exerted to stimulate or preserve these native tongues[32]*

PROMOTE ISLAM, THE CALIPHATE AND KORANIC EDUCATION

It was Morel who also provided the intellectual and moral support for Lugard's decision to base imperial rule in the amalgamated territory upon the Fulani, imperial foundations

---

iii   The BBC Hausa service, funded by the Foreign Office, became a key instrument of this policy

120

Lagos. 14th Aug. 1921.

Campbell Street. Lagos 1922. Catholic Cathedral.

already existing in Northern Nigeria:

> *All the good work accomplished in Northern Nigeria during the last seven years can be flung away by a refusal to benefit from experience in other parts of the world. In pleading...that where in Nigeria national life has already expanded through the exercise of its own internal forces into organized communities, possessing their own laws and customs, their own machinery of government and their own well-defined characteristics, that national life shall be protected, preserved and strengthened to enable it to bear the strains of the new conditions, one is pleading, it seems to me, for the true welfare of the people and for the highest concept of Imperialism[33]*

Thus, just as the British ruled India through the princely rulers, they were set to rule Northern Nigeria through the maintenance and strengthening of the Sokoto Caliphate. For this reason, not only was the feudal structure of the Sokoto Empire not dismantled, the British extended it, first over the separate Bornu Empire in the north-east and then, through the agency of further British conquests, over the many non-Islamic tribes in the middle regions of the country.

As part of the policy of strengthening and preserving the established order in Northern Nigeria, Koranic education was to be promoted. Morel wrote:

> *One other fact needs chronicling in connection with these national schools. It is the intention of the Administration to insist that all pupils receive careful religious instruction from teachers of their own creed. When I visited the schools, lessons in reading and writing the Koran were being given by a Kano Mallam specially selected by the Emir of Kano, somewhat on the model of the Egyptian schools. It is earnestly to be hoped that the Colonial Office will resist any attempt at interference with this policy. Interference would be disastrous....To allow a weakening of the spiritual forces at work among the people of the Northern Hausa States would be to perpetuate a cruel wrong upon those who have come under our protection and from thenceforth are our wards[34]*

If the Fulani were to be the new partners, and their rule of Northern Nigeria was to be preserved and extended, the earlier narrative that had been used to justify their conquest had to be re-written. In the new narrative, the Fulani conquest of the Hausa was explained as a civilising mission led by 'a great Fulani reformer':

> *There is evidence that in the middle and towards the close of the eighteenth century the Hausa Kings were relapsing into paganism...It was at this period that the spark of a spiritual renascence arose in the most northerly of the Hausa States,*

Gober. Othman Fodio, a Fulani, ultimately the leader of the uprising, was above all, a moral and spiritual reformer, as was his teacher the Mallam Jibrila....The root causes of the Fulani outburst were spiritual in their nature. Othman led a moral and spiritual revival, among a people who, like all negroes and negroids, are naturally more accessible to spiritual influences than are the white peoples of the earth... [iv] *One of the obvious duties of the Administration is to continue the work of the great Fulani reformer in everywhere extending and broadening the intellectual horizon, and doing nothing to weaken the national spiritual influences of the people of the land. The creation of a system of education which shall be truly national is imperative at this moment when the whole fabric of native society is being shaken by disturbing elements. The field is clear; the slate is clean. We are here unfettered by those bitter experiences of the West Coast of Africa and of India which are perpetual reminders of past blunders and daily handicaps to true progress.* [35]

KEEP THE MISSIONARIES OUT

The competition for converts within the 'Nigeria' space had seen Anglicans jostling with Catholics and the two contesting with Muslims to mark out exclusive spheres of spiritual influence. Action had to be taken to force the rival groups of saviours to sit around a conference table, in 1911, to map out their territorial claims 'within which each particular sect should be free to teach according to its own dogmas, without aggression from others'. [36]

The initiative was informed by Lugard's experience in Uganda where, in similar circumstances, bloody warfare had broken out between the rival religious denominations. It was this conference that accounts for the distribution of different Christian denominations in Nigeria today: the confluence of the River Niger is the dividing line between the different denominations with most to the east Catholic; most to the west Anglican; while those in the middle are Methodists. An even more significant outcome of the conference was the near-perfectly horizontal line across the country north of which no Christian mission, of any denomination, was permitted to enter. If the existing feudal order of the Fulani was to be preserved and Koranic education promoted, then there was no place in Northern Nigeria for Christian missionaries since it is the very essence of Christian teaching to uproot all aspects of the traditional order.

The Colonial Office had seen how missionary education had first uprooted the traditional faiths in Southern Nigeria before the new native revolutionaries began to use their new learning against the imperial order itself:

---

iv   Morel was equally enthusing in his advocacy of alcoholic spirits for Southern Nigeria

The missionary is a revolutionary and he has to be so, for to preach and plant Christianity means to make a full-frontal attack on the beliefs, the customs and apprehensions of life and the world, and by implication (because tribal religions are primarily social realities) on the social structure and bases of primitive society[37]

For the pragmatic British, in the face of a clash of interests between state and faith, the interests of the state would always take precedence. Although the missionaries had been the state's first partners in the construction of the empire in Nigeria, the new partnership with the Fulani leaders meant that the advancement of Christianity had to be arrested. Morel met the issue head on:

the advent of the missionary into the organized Mohammedan provinces of the north before the country is ripe to receive them, would be a positive danger, besides being an act perilously akin to a breach of faith....There is a field in pagan Northern and pagan Southern Nigeria sufficiently extensive to occupy all the energies of all the missions put together, without invading the heart of Moslem Nigeria. The advent of Christian missions into Kano or Katsina or Sokoto, for example, would be regarded as an act of aggression. Their presence in Zaria is a great mistake, and I make bold to assert that it is only comparable to a man smoking a pipe on a barrel of gunpowder. We hold this newly occupied country by the force of our prestige, far more than by the very small number of native troops in our service. That it is the duty of Government to prevent the introduction of elements, whatever their character and however lofty their motives, whose presence is calculated to cause unrest, is sufficiently self-evident as not to need emphasizing...The establishment of Christian missions in the Mohammedan Emirates would not succeed in damning up the self-propelling currents of Islamic propaganda which are permeating Nigerian paganism. That is the true problem which the Churches have to face[38]

THE AMALGAMATION AND THE REVOCATION OF EGBA INDEPENDENCE

The practicalities of fusing Northern and Southern Nigeria were far from straightforward. The problem was not only the differences of religion, culture and language between the people but also how, by 1914, the different approaches to colonial administration that had been applied in the two protectorates had led to differences in the culture and character of the colonial administrators themselves:

The administrative and military officials appointed direct to [Northern] Nigeria through the Patronage Private Secretary were for the most part public-school, 'officer class'...in contrast to the traders, the missionaries, the sea captains, and the specialist officials...from the industrial north, from Scotland, Wales and Ireland, some of them dissenters in religion, with radical sympathies in politics[39]

The success of the earlier amalgamation of the Colony of Lagos with the Protectorate of Southern Nigeria was due not so much to the fact that the two sides of the union were ethnically similar but to the fact that the same administrative and development policies were being pursued in both parts. The South benefitted from policies traceable back to the early-victorian humanitarian imperialists aimed at popular advancement through trade and education led by civilian administrators in a system of direct rule. The problem with the marriage with the North that Lugard brokered was that Northern Nigeria was being run with completely different policies in which soldiers managed a system of indirect rule through the Emirs:

> *...The plain facts ought to have been clear. Southern Nigeria, with its cash crops, expanding mission schools, growing numbers of wage earners and clerical workers, African entrepreneurs and petty capitalists, was a success in the terms of European imperialism, whose purpose was the integration of such regions into the British and world trading system. How was the feudal North, with its conservatism, Muslim law, and emirate government to be brought into this system and its administrative poverty brought to an end? The choice of Lugard in effect turned this question upside down. With his return to Nigeria there could be no question of devising measures whereby the Northern administration would be adapted to the new conditions. Instead the South would have to bend to Northern dogmas[40]*

It was going to require much more than the ring-fencing measures which Morel had recommended. The plan Lugard adopted was to first arrest and then remove those influences from Southern Nigeria itself.

THE REVOCATION OF EGBA INDEPENDENCE

Abeokuta, in the then still independent kingdom of Egbaland, represented all the Colonial Office's worst fears for the future direction of Southern Nigeria as things then were. Morel gave the following account:

Abeokuta, the capital of the Egba united Government" (whose authority extends over 1869 square miles), its mass corrugated iron roofs glaring beneath the huge outcrop of granitic rock where its founders first settled a hundred years ago, offers the curious picture of a Europeanized African town in the fullest sense of the term, but with this unique feature, that its administration and the administration of the district, of which it is the capital, is conducted by natives – i.e. by the Alake (the head chief) in council.

It is, of course, that the British Commissioner wields very great influence, but he is invested with no legal powers of intervention whatever, because the British treaty with the Egba section of the Yoruba people recognizes their independence in all internal affairs; and all Government notices and pronouncements posted up in the town are signed by the Alake and the Alake's secretary. The Commissioner, Mr Young, finds himself indeed, in a position where the utmost tact is required...The whole machinery of administration is on the European pattern, with its Secretariat, Treasury, Public Works Department, Police, Prison, Printing Offices, Post Office, etc. – all managed by Europeanized Africans. I visited most of the Government departments, the prison, the printing offices, and was impressed with the industry and business-like air which reigned within them. The revenues, thanks to the Commissioner, are in a healthy state. Excellent roads have been and are being constructed. A water supply is being arranged for out of a loan of £30,000 advanced by the Southern Nigeria Government. Labour-saving machinery is being introduced at the Commissioner's suggestion. An imposing college is in course of erection. It is all very remarkable and interesting. Whether it is durable is a matter which I shall have occasion to discuss later.[41]

The real concern was not whether this state of native governance and administration was "durable" but whether it was desirable. A viable and successful independent native-led mini-state existing alongside British-administered Nigeria was inimical to the plan to hold the colony for the long term.The independence granted to Egbaland back in 1893, a necessary and convenient expedient at the time to stave off competing French interests, was now intolerable.

Lugard's first priority was to bring Egbaland into Nigeria and the groundwork had begun ahead of his arrival. The first stage had been to use financial inducements to persuade the independent state to accept the appointment of a British Resident:

As British control was extended over most of Nigeria, the Lagos government attempted to undermine Egba independence whenever possible. Proximity aided this process. So, too, did the radical departure of the Egba United Government from established Egba norms. The Alake attempting to increase his powers and

Edun and associates trying to modernize the state needed as much support as they could obtain from the Lagos government. However, the Egba remained suspicious of the British and did not automatically concur with every scheme put forward by Lagos. Thus in 1907 the Egba rejected the offer of an annual payment of £300 to the Alake and the expenditure of £2,000 on construction and repair of roads in Egbaland. All the Lagos authorities wished in return was for a European to be appointed president of the Egba Court, the British commissioner to sit on the Council, and a British auditor to review the accounts. Edun and the Council could see through this thinly disguised take-over move and agreed only to accept the British auditor. However, it was stipulated that the auditor would be paid from Egba not British funds[42]

The one thing that the independent Egba state lacked, and which any truly independent state must have, was the means to ensure its own internal security. All it had, under the terms of the 1893 treaty, was a security-guarantee with the British which, while sufficient to keep the Egba safe from all other aggressors, left them vulnerable to pressure from the guardians themselves. It only needed an internal security crisis to arise for the nominally independent state to be forced into the arms of the Lagos government. The first opportunity to clip the wings of the independent mini-state came, in 1907, following the death, in custody, of an old man:

There was considerable disorder in the Egba state in the wake of the Ariwo incident of 1907. Secretary Edun charged an old man, Odugbemi Ariwo of Ikija, with sedition and sent the police to arrest him. The old man died while being arrested[43]

The Lagos government's price for helping to restore order after this incident was the acceptance by the Egba government of P.C.V. Young as a permanent British commissioner. The next stage, following the arrival of Lugard, was the complete abrogation of the 1893 treaty:

One of the most troublesome problems Lugard confronted in developing his plans for a united Nigeria was the presence upon the very borders of the Colony of the independent Egba state. It is not surprising that he set the abrogation of the treaties whereby Britain recognized Egba independence as one of the first goals of his administration. However, he had to be very careful to educate the Colonial Office to the necessity of any overt actions against the Egba. With all the stresses inherent in the composite government at Abeokuta, it was functioning more harmoniously than many Yoruba areas then under direct British control. Edun, his western educated associates, and the Alake were friendly toward the

Lagos government. The new institutions of the Egba state were modelled on those of Britain and there were many educated Egba in Lagos whose loyalty was not questioned. Lugard's task was not to put down an unruly government which threatened the lives and property of British nationals. Instead he had to find some way to subvert a friendly government[44]

There was little point in re-inventing the wheel; all that was needed was another old man to be sacrificed. The opportunity came, not long after the amalgamation of North and South on 1 January 1914, with the arrest of a 75 year old village chief, Shobiyi Ponlade:

In early June 1914, a boundary dispute developed between the Egba and the Ijebu at Iperu. Mr Edun, accompanied by J.O. George, President of the Native Court, Commissioner Young, and others, visited the site of the conflict. On their way back to Abeokuta they stopped at Ponlade's town. They had noted that the road to Fidiwa was neglected, and Polande was informed that he should see to the road work at once. He replied that he was a subject of the Alake and took no order from Edun or from a British representative. Edun decided to teach Ponlade a lesson and ordered his arrest for insubordination. For reasons that are unclear, the British Commissioner, Young, took an active part in the arrest of the old man on 17 June 1914[45]

The old man's subsequent death in custody on 1 July 1914 led to a level of unrest which forced the Egba government to call on the Lagos Government for military assistance. On 1 September 1914, Lugard got his prize with a formal treaty that he signed with the Alake surrendering the independence of Egbaland. It was equivalent to a military coup as those responsible for the security of the state forced the government to hand over power.

Having brought Egbaland into Nigeria, Lugard embarked on a course of developmental vandalism by systematically uprooting and dismantling the governance model that had become established in Southern Nigeria. His first target was the elaborate judicial system, with its trappings of barristers in wigs and gowns, circuit judges and appeals to the Supreme Court for both natives and non-natives. In its place he imposed a system of justice for cases involving natives along the lines operating in Northern Nigeria. In these new courts lawyers were banned and the Resident doubled-up as the judge.

The seeds of democracy, which had only recently been sown, were also to be dug up. The Legislative Council which had since the amalgamation of the South in 1906 been legislating for both the Lagos Colony and the Protectorate of Southern Nigeria had its legislative powers pegged back to Lagos alone. For the rest of Southern Nigeria, he set up a Nigeria Council which was little more than the equivalent of a company annual general meeting with no legislative powers.[46]

AN UNCONSUMMATED UNION AND THE EXPULSION OF LUGARD

The beginning of the end of Lugard's reign, and of British rule in Nigeria, came with his attempt to impose direct taxation in the South. Although, in November 1903, Lugard had delivered a paper to the Royal Geographical Society in which he had warned against attempting 'to enforce direct taxation in the very early stages of British rule'[47], the five year fixed funding deal that had been agreed with the Treasury to support the amalgamation now forced him to abandon his own counsel.

Northern Nigeria having been created through conquest, and with its system of indirect rule through the existing feudal order, it had been possible to impose direct taxation without resistance. His attempt to extend the policy to Southern Nigeria even as he was closing down the avenues of representation that previous governors of Southern Nigeria had introduced was a provocative policy mix. As had happened with the American Revolution that led to declaration of independence from Britain, the attempt to impose direct taxation in Yorubaland lit a fuse:

> *Sir Frederick had decided very early in his administration to apply the northern system of rule to the southern areas as far as possible. This meant salaried officials with well-defined powers operating under the direction of a single African executive. There was a fundamental flaw in Lugard's conceptualization. However similar a Yoruba Oba and his court might have appeared to be in comparison to a northern Emir and council, there were basic differences. No Yoruba Oba possessed the autocratic power of his northern counterpart. There were many overt and covert checks on his authority. This was even more true at Abeokuta than elsewhere in Yorubaland. No Yoruba chief had ever collected direct taxes from his people on a regular basis while the Hausa and Fulani had accepted this practice as a standard procedure for centuries. Any system of tribute in Yorubaland was not correlated with direct taxes. Even in sophisticated Abeokuta under the United Egba Government, the needed revenues had been raised by customs duties or use taxes. Lugard however regarded the levy of a direct tax as the very foundation of his system[48]*

A sensitization campaign, led by the Alake, to sell the new tax regime to his Egba people, made little impact. The Alake's influence had been diminished by his perceived surrender of Egba independence to the British. Egba and Owu groups now armed themselves to fight the tax and to free themselves from British rule.

The uprising was timed to coincide with the season of heavy rains. This, together with the dense forestry, they calculated, would give them a fighting chance against the superior weaponry of a British army back from engagements on the war front with German forces. It was a valiant effort which lasted from 13 June 1918 to 22 July 1918:

The presence of an unusually large number of regular troops enabled Lugard and Cunliffe to snuff out the possibility for the dissidents to score a major success during the first week of the disturbances. In all, the British used seventy European officers and 2,800 Nigerian rank and file against the Egba and Owu rebels. The British led troops were infantry. The quick success of the campaign can be attributed to the full complement of machine guns used by the British. Casualties for the British forces engaged were very low considering the intensity of some of the fighting. Lieutenant-Colonel Feneran reported eight rank and file and two civilian carriers killed. There were eighty-two wounded. Of these, four were Europeans and sixty-seven were Nigerian soldiers. Casualty figures for the Egba and Owu could only be approximate since many of the engagements were in forested areas and the rebellious forces removed their casualties. The number reported by the British, 564 killed, was in all probability a conservative estimate. The rough figure of 600 dead which appears in most accounts, therefore seems as accurate a figure of Egba and Owu losses as one is likely to have. Colonel Beattie in early 1919 characterised the nature of the Abeokuta campaign as well as any British military observer at that time could. He wrote, 'These operations were on an unusually large scale for West Africa against a serious uprising offering determined resistance[49]

A significant factor in the failure of the Egba uprising against British rule and for the restoration of Egba independence was that it lacked the external support which all revolutionary uprisings against imperial regimes need to succeed. Also, the schism that had developed between the Egba and the rest of the Yorubaland through their past collaborations with the British meant that they were unable to generate support for their struggle even internally amongst other Yoruba tribes.

But there was a victory of sorts for the rebels. It came with the sudden end of Lugard's tenure as Governor General. The report which followed the news of Lugard's retirement in the *Lagos Weekly Record*, of February1919, best captures the state of the relationship as it was between Lugard and the "educated natives":

The God of the Negro

The news of the retirement of Sir Frederick Lugard from the Governor Generalship of Nigeria, which was flashed down by Reuters during the latter part of January, has been received with great joy and gladness by the loyal natives of Nigeria. So overwhelming is the peoples' emotion that almost in every nook and corner but chiefly in the inmost recesses of their hearts they have offered and continue to offer day by day some silent prayer to the God of the Negro for his tender mercies in delivering his dusky children from the baneful effects of an inglorious administration which constitutes not only a standing disgrace to the cherished traditions of British colonial policy in West Africa but is also a positive libel upon the accepted principles of British culture.

Sir Frederick has earned the notorious distinction of being the originator of a system of government – the product of his exuberant imagination – entitled the Nigerian System….

To the natives of Nigeria in particular and of West Africa in general the 'Nigerian System' is the most infernal system that has ever been devised since the days of the Spanish Inquisition for the express purpose of humiliating and depressing the units of any loyal and progressive community. Its nefarious laws and ordinances read like the weird contents of some musty-fusty documents unearthed in far off Cathay.

Its 25 lashes, its public floggings of general offenders stripped naked in the public markets, its maintenance of so called 'white prestige' at all costs, its subjection of the Judiciary to the Executive, and its obnoxious Criminal Code bespeak an administrative system which is the exact prototype of German kultur in Africa and is in diametrical opposition to the traditionary [sic] principles of British justice and fair play.

Its abhorrence of legal practitioners and denial to natives of the principles and procedure of British Courts of Justice; its judicial folly in investing District Commissioners – whose innocence of English law and practice has been officially and naively admitted in an apologetic memorandum by the retired Chief Justice of Nigeria; its detestation of educated natives as the bête noire that haunts its political and ideological dreams per diem et per noctem and their shabby treatment as the convenient scapegoats of official blunders and misrule, and its manifestly provocative and harsh rules and regulations breathe undeniably the spirit and atmosphere of the barrack rooms.

There can be no question that as the conquering hero of punitive expeditions, the widener of imperial outposts by means of the sword, and as the High Commissioner of newly conquered territories subject to military control, Sir Frederick has had a distinguished career and has been amply decorated by the Imperial Government. But on the other hand, as the administrator of progressive African communities, we regret we cannot help but write Sir Frederick down as a Huge Failure. Judged by the light of modern conscience in its treatment of subject races, Sir Frederick is a hopeless anachronism; so hopeless indeed that as the byproduct of a bygone age, cast upon a time that would not understand him, yet he persisted in his fitful attempts to force the new wine of the law of social expansion of subject races – the inspiring ideals of twentieth century civilization – into the old bottles of military subjugation, domination and terrorism, with the result that the old bottles have invariably been burst and riots and massacres have become rampant….

The gaiety and external splendor of the regal courts of the Emirs, though superimposed upon a social stratum of abject woe and misery among the masses, fired Sir Frederick's oriental imagination, exalted as he was to the position of demi-god by the zarkings of the Emirs to him in public. But Sir Frederick forgot that by postulating the success of his system upon the demonstration of Force, the instillation of Fear and the fascination of a mercenary bait, he was practically leaning upon a broken reed; for already the schoolmaster is abroad and the rapidity and subtlety with which liberal influences are absorbed by any given community through contact not only baffle research but also escapes detection. For the communication of thought, New York is nearer to Lagos today than Lagos was to Ibadan some 20 years ago; whilst the daily occurrences in such remote places as Japan and Australia are discussed with accuracy and ease the following morning in West Africa, simply because the world is linked together by thought, and distances have been annihilated. When in the fullness of time the natives of the Northern Provinces, in spite of Sir Frederick's preventative policy, shall taste of the fruit of the tree of knowledge and, as the wisdom of the serpent hath represented, they shall be 'as gods knowing good and evil' (Sicut dii scientes bona et mala); when the bogey or fetish of white prestige shall with increased knowledge among the masses die a natural death, then shall it be a sorry day for Sir Fredericks repressive policy, and the very evil which he has long dreaded shall be reduced to political certainty by those very methods which he had devised for its prevention. Let us hope that in the interim wiser and more liberal policies shall intervene to prevent the occurrence of such a large catastrophe as the volcanic eruption of a Jihad or holy war in the Northern Provinces.

In the light of the foregoing, it was quite natural that Sir Frederick's policy should meet with such lamentable and disastrous failure in the Colony and Southern Provinces; for through liberal and sympathetic policy of previous administrations the darkness of ignorance had been dispelled by the erection of secondary schools as centres for the dissemination of knowledge; and their wonderful product – the Educated native – had been evolved in the normal course of events as the repository of the liberal and national aspirations of the people and the doughty champion of Right, Liberty and Justice. Through his mighty exertions, the Native Press – that struggling institution in West Africa – was called into existence as the vehicle of thought for giving articulate expression to the sentiments of the people and for ventilating their grievances under the Crown Colony system of government.

True to his disposition, Sir Frederick loathed the Educated Native and lived in constant dread of the Native Press, which at every turn foreshadowed his sinister movements, and he seemed to be blinded and confused by the intense glare of its searchlight criticisms invariably supported by a logic which is equally pitiless and irrefragable. The contests between Sir Fredrick, the Educated Native and the Native Press over his manifold administrative schemes were intellectual contests pure and simple; and in every such encounter the honours remained with the Educated Native and the Native Press; for Sir Frederick was hopelessly out of date, and it was quite easy to knock the bottom out of any political or administrative scheme deriving its solitary sanction from the dictum of my will is my law and the autocratic power conferred by the indiscretion of a Secretary of State for the Colonies. Again the bogey of white prestige had been given a decent burial ever since the early days of the old Colony and Protectorate of Lagos and any latent or induced fear of the white man was confined only to babes and sucklings. To crown it all, the people had for over sixty years been reared under the traditional principles of British Justice and fair play, and had been living as respectable members of a decent and well-ordered community with all the external indications and paraphernalia of modern progress. The wealth, intelligence and social independence of the educated natives galled Sir Frederick to the very bone. The very atmosphere proved uncongenial to his autocratic bearings and the flights of his oriental imagination. To descend from the intoxicating air of a demi-god in the Northern Provinces to the level of the first member in the community in the Colony and Southern Provinces was more than enough for Sir Frederick's kidney and he therefore determined upon a drastic change of affairs.

In order to wreak his vengeance upon the educated native, Sir Frederick began to set back the hand of the clock of progress by lowering the standard of education in the colony. King's College, which was founded by Sir Walter Egerton with the ambitious intention of preparing its students for complete graduation in London University, degenerated into a secondary school of the old regime. So deplorable was the state of affairs that many capable teachers of the old regime threw up their appointments in the Assisted Schools and started private schools of their own merely for the purpose of maintaining the efficiency of the old regime.....

Next, Sir Frederick introduced his revolutionary changes in the Judicial System which has been bitterly criticized on all sides, and with the Provincial Courts Ordinance, the Criminal Code and the Newspaper Ordinance, he attempted to break the backs of the educated natives and muzzle up the Native Press. But the educated natives, fighting for their very existence in defence of their sacred rights and privileges and in defence of their country and people, cheerfully entered the list against Sir Frederick. Being adepts in organized publicity, they brought home to the conscience of the British Nation the dangers that would arise out of successful prosecution of Sir Frederick's policy, since it would entail not only the social and economic enslavement of the natives but also the legal swindling and confiscation of their inherent and inalienable rights to their ancestral lands. Such gross injustice and un-British principles could have but one natural result and that is the gradual weaning away of the hearts and affections of the natives from the folds of the British Empire. The conscience of the British Nation, always alive to its vital interests, caught up the plaintive cry of the educated natives and looked with great disfavor upon Sir Frederick's reactionary schemes…Sir Frederick has indeed performed a miraculous achievement; for within the short space of 4 years he has transformed the proverbial loyalty of a liberty-loving people into a hot bed of disaffection and has been responsible for more massacres and riots than those of previous administrations.....

Today on the chessboard of imperial politics the question of questions with all loyal natives is whether Great Britain is definitely pledged to the maintenance of her former humanitarian and sympathetic policy in West Africa, or whether her future policy is to derive its sanction from the Nigerian System. If the former, she can, to her heart's content, count upon the well-tried loyalty of her African subjects but if the latter, then the natives will be compelled to claim the right of self-determination before the League of Nations....

Lugard's recall, in 1919, was an admission that the attempt to fuse the two Nigerias into one by imposing the system of governance operating in Northern Nigeria on Southern Nigeria had failed. The combined forces of the Egba and Owu rebels and the Lagos press had forced him out. His replacement as Governor General of Nigeria, Sir Hugh Clifford, set about introducing reforms to repair Lugard's vandalism in the South.

Clifford was a colonial administrator in the progressive mold that Southern Nigeria had been accustomed to. Though the son of a General in the British Army, he had found his ways more civilian and so elected for a career in the civil service. A gifted writer, he had served as Colonial Secretary in Trinidad, and as Governor in Malaya and Ghana before being moved to Nigeria to replace Lugard.

As much as he scorned Lugard's attempt to extend feudalism to Southern Nigeria, he was equally forthright in his criticism of some of the more grandiose ideas of a Nigeria united under the rule of the South held by some of the educated natives:

> *It can only be described as farcical to suppose that ...Nigeria can be represented by a handful of gentlemen drawn from a half-dozen coast tribes – men born and bred in British-administered towns situated on the seashore, who in the safety of British protection, have peacefully pursued their studies under British teachers, in British schools, in order to enable them to become ministers of the Christian religion, or learned in the laws of England; whose eyes are fixed, not upon African native history or tradition or policy, nor upon their own tribal obligations and the duties to their natural rulers which immemorial custom should impose upon them, but upon political theories evolved by Europeans to fit a wholly different set of circumstances, arising out of a wholly different environment, for the government of peoples who have arrived at a wholly different stage of civilization..[50]*

The compromise position was a return to separate policies of administration for North and South.

The constitution which he introduced in 1922, whilst retaining rule by proclamation of the Governor-General for Northern Nigeria, restored, in Southern Nigeria, the green shoots of democracy, which Lugard had dug up, by reinstating the Legislative Council and by going further to provide for electoral seats for the first time in Lagos and Calabar. Of the forty-six members of the new Legislative Council, nineteen were to be unofficial members of whom ten would be Nigerians with four of these being elected members: Lagos having three elected seats and Calabar having one electoral seat.

It was on the back of the Clifford Constitution of 1922 that party politics began in Southern Nigeria. In 1923, Herbert Macaulay, the grandson of Bishop Ajayi Crowther, founded the first political party in Nigeria, the Nigerian National Democratic Party (NNDP) at the age of sixty. His father being the founder, and the first principal, of the prestigious CMS Grammar School in Lagos, he had obtained a degree in land surveying and civil engineering in Plymouth in 1893. Macaulay's NNDP, with its youth wing, the Nigeria Young Democrats and its newspaper the *Lagos Daily News*, dominated Lagos politics up until shortly before the Second World War:

The Lagos Daily News, of which Herbert Macauley was proprietor and editor at the time, was an inflammatory sheet: ultra-radical, intensely nationalistic, virulently and implacably anti-white. Africans who were friendly with white men, or who went to the length of dining and wining with them, were denounced as imperialist agents, and branded as having sold Nigeria for their personal gains and advancement[51]

THE WOMEN'S UPRISING

Although titled the *Lagos Daily News*, Macauley's publication was concerned with national issues. One such issue to which it gave extensive coverage was the brutal murder of protesting women in eastern Nigeria, in 1929, by colonial forces. As with the Abeokuta uprising, it was the attempt to introduce the Northern system of direct taxation that triggered the revolt.

Eastern Nigeria was the last frontier for the British administration in their attempt to introduce direct taxation into Southern Nigeria. The need to force the pace was driven by two factors. The first was the desire to ensure that the eastern province shared the tax burden with the rest of the country; the second was the onset of the Great Depression in 1929. In the North, and to a leser extent in the Yoruba country, the imposition of direct taxation had been facilitated by the power and authority of the traditional rulers who served as tax collectors. In the east where there was no tradition of rule by chiefs and emirs, the Colonial Office found itself having to introduce a system of indirect rule by creating chiefs by Colonial Office Warrant. Getting these 'Warrant Chiefs' to collect taxes at a time when there authority had yet to be accepted, in the middle of an economic depression, brought the colonial authorities into direct conflict with the women of eastern Nigeria.

The initiative was driven by the new Governor, Graeme Thomson, who succeeded Hugh Clifford on 13 November 1925. A graduate of New College, Oxford, Thomson had started his career as a civil servant in the Admiralty where he rose to become the Director of Shipping for the Ministry of Shipping and Admiralty in 1917. He joined the colonial service after the First World War and served as Chief Secretary for Ceylon in 1919 and had been Governor of British Guiana since 1922 prior to his arrival in Nigeria.

The crisis began with a confrontation in November 1929 between a local man, Mark Emeruwa, and a local woman, Nwanyewura both natives of the Oloko area in Bende Division. Emeruwa while conducting a count of women, children and livestock in the area on the authority of the Warrant Chief ran into insolent defiance from Nwanyewura. When the encounter turned physical the women of Oloko rallied:

Palm fronds and leafy branches in each hand, wrappers tightly warped [sic] chest high, and some with naked breasts in full glare, the women sang chants of woe and distressed alarm. The emotions were strong wherever the threat on

Nwanyewura's life was recounted from women to woman. The women's dance, Nwaobiala, was a dance of defiance, performed with contempt, an act of rebellion when it was called for. Many women, young and old, knew that there was cause for concern. As Nwanyewura's story circulated a message gradually emerged: all women of the province were summoned to a palaver, a meeting on the imminent women's tax. If it was not resisted it would lead to their collective penury[52]

The women next proceeded to 'sit on' the Warrant Chief himself by effectively camping en masse outside his residence demanding his removal and trial.

The colonial government first sought to contain the protest by acceding to the women's demands. In this it misjudged the power of the market womens' network. In short order, the action had spread to other eastern provinces and the cause had broadened to rejection of the white man's presence in their land:

They would go to Owerrinta to demolish the Native Court; that they did not want the Native Court to hear cases any longer; and that all white men should return to their country so that the land in this area might remain as it was many years ago before the advent of the white man

"Our grievances are that the land is changed – we are all dying. It is a long time since the Chiefs and the people who know book....have been oppressing us. We are telling you that we have been oppressed. The new Chiefs are also receiving bribes. Since the white men came, our oil does not fetch money. Our Kernels do not fetch money. If we take goats or yams to market to sell, Court messengers who wear a uniform take all these things from us"[53]

By the time the protest movement reached Aba it numbered over 10,000 women demanding the removal of all Warrant Chiefs. Matters came to a deadly climax on 14 December 1929 in Abak, Calabar when soldiers with rapid fire machine-guns were deployed against the women. The following is the platoon commander's account:

They came running a few paces and then walking a few paces in much the same way as they had attacked Abak the day before. I considered it futile to try to use words in order to disperse the mob judging by the situation I considered very dangerous. The force of troops was small and in a hand to hand struggle with these mad women it was possible that some sort of reverse would have been sustained and the whole country would have been up. I therefore asked Lt. Browning to disperse the mob with FIRE![54]

When the shooting stopped, eighteen women were dead in Abak and another thirty-one women were killed in similar circumstances two days later in Opobo. Although a government enquiry predictably whitewashed the incidents of slaughter of unarmed women by machine-gun fire, the massacre rendered Thomson's continuance as Governor untenable and, on 17 June 1931, he was replaced by Donald Cameron.

Cameron had been serving as Governor of Tanganyika while Thomson had been in charge of Nigeria but he was no stranger to Nigeria having worked in the Nigerian civil service as Central Secretary under Lugard. The son of a sugar planter in British Guiana who married a kindred spirit, Gertrude Giltens, the daughter of a sugar planter in, he was a firm believer in Lugard's ideas about indirect rule and his appointment as Governor of Nigeria marked the return of Lugard's influence. Even so, in contrast to his predecessor, Thomson, and his successor, Bourdillon, his tenure as Governor was relatively eneventful. The only political figure of note that he had to deal with was Herbert Macaulay.

Although Macaulay's dominance of Lagos politics in the 1920s and'30s is shown by how his party won all the seats in the Lagos elections in 1923, 1928 and 1933, his politics was very much local under the rule of the British Crown rather than challenging it:

> *If ever there was a black English gentleman of his era, it was Herbert Macaulay. Always impeccably dressed in starched, spotlessly white suit, a black bow tie knotted painstakingly, white buck shoes, and sporting a white Panama hat, he was the object of much adulation by the populace. One imagined that he typified the term 'Victorian gentleman'. He certainly bore himself like one[55]*

This dandy politician, whose gripe was with the British colonial administrators rather than with colonialism, marked the first phase of political activism in Southern Nigeria. A second, and more radical, phase came with the arrival of a new generation of graduates. The formal changing of the guard came in 1938, by which time Macaulay was age seventy-five, with the emergence of the Niger Youth Movement:

> *Until 1938, nomination and election to the three Lagos seats in the Legislative Council had usually been settled within the confines of Herbert Macaulay's home. In the October,1938, elections, however, the Youth Movement, which had in the meantime established its own journal, the Daily Service, launched a vigorous campaign and defeated Macaulay's party[56]*

The Second World War (1939 to 1945) was to change the intensity of the battle between the colonialists and the educated natives in a way that neither side could have imagined before the war's outbreak.

5.
The Hot and Cold Wars and the End of Colonialism

...There never has been, there isn't now, and there never will be, any race of people fit to serve as masters over their fellow men...'

Franklin Delano Roosevelt

THE AFTERMATH OF THE FIRST WORLD WAR

The beginning of the end of the slave trade started with a turn of events in the British-American relationship climaxing in the American War of Independence. The end of colonialism, which replaced the slave trade, can also be explained by a turn of events in the same relationship. An understanding of these events is important for an understanding of the events which occured in Nigeria which culminated in the grant of Independence on 1 October 1960.

The United States having digested its own continental expanse, had been content to stand back from the scramble for colonies in Africa and Asia. With its own experience as the first overseas colony of the British Empire, and the first to have gained independence, America understood that the underlying cause of the First World War was the business of empires.

It had been a war between the Haves (Britain, France and Russia) and the Have-nots (Germany, Italy and Japan). The USA's decisive intervention on the side of the colonial powers earned for it the opportunity to change the world order. President Woodrow Wilson's Fourteen Points, which he proclaimed on 8 January 1918, was the first indication that the end days of colonialism were nearing but it was only a tentative signal. Point Five was a latter-day equivalent of the first steps towards abolition of the slave trade:

A free, open-minded, and absolutely impartial adjustment of all colonial claims, based upon a strict observance of the principle that in determining all questions of sovereignty the interests of the populations concerned must have equal weight with the equitable claims of the government whose title is to be determined.

A pronouncement of more significance for the future of colonialism was Point Fourteen which introduced the idea of the League of Nations. Hitherto the single most powerful colonial power served as the de facto ruler of the world and arbitrator of state claims. Now global sovereignty was to be pooled amongst a college of great powers.

The last attempt to regulate the uncivilised game of colonisation had been the Berlin Conference of 1884. That effort failed because it focused simply on the regulation of the game between the main players and paid no mind to the interests of the Have Nots let alone the interests of the colonised. In, again, simply focusing on the ground rules of the game to be observed by the colonial powers (and on punishing and reforming the conduct of the defeated powers), the terms of the peace agreement struck at Versailles in 1919 left the door open for a repeat of history. Those peace terms had stripped Germany of the few colonies in Africa that Bismarck had acquired by turning these territories into League of Nations-mandated territories to be administered by Britain and France. In this modern application of the Parable of the Talents, the Haves received a distribution of more colonial territory from the Have-nots. It was a focus on the outward manifestations of an ambition at the expense of an understanding of what was driving that ambition. One man on whom the lesson was not lost was Adolf Hitler.

Writing from his prison cell, in 1924, Hitler saw the land and colonial question which had led to the First World War as unfinished business. In his view, Germany had too small a proportion of the earth's land to be considered a great power:

> *In an era when the earth is gradually being divided up among the states, some of which embrace almost entire continents, we cannot speak of a world power in connection with a formation whose political mother country is limited to the absurd area of five hundred thousand square kilometres.*
>
> *From the territorial point of view, the area of the German Reich vanishes completely as compared with the so-called world powers. Let no one cite England as a proof to the contrary, for England in reality is merely the great capital of the British world empire which calls nearly a quarter of the earth's surface its own. In addition, we must regard as giant states, first of all the American Union, then Russia and China. All are spatial formations having in part an area more than ten times greater than the present German Reich...Thus, in the world today we see a number of power states , some of which not only far surpass the strength of our German nation in population, but whose area above all is the chief support of their political power[1]*

It was a matter of time before the German war machine broke free of the shackles placed on it by the Versailles Treaty. When the time came, all that could be done was to fall back upon hurried attempts at appeasement. The envelope which Britain's Prime Minister, Neville Chamberlain waved on his return from Munich, when he proclaimed "peace in our time", is believed to have contained an agreement that Germany's former colonies would be returned together with the transfer of Nigeria to the Germans. The deal failed. It was not to West Africa that Hitler was looking to satisfy the German nation's hunger for land:

> It must be said that such a territorial policy cannot be fulfilled in the Cameroons, but today almost exclusively in Europe. We must therefore coolly and objectively adopt the standpoint that it can certainly not have been the intention of Heaven to give one people fifty times as much land and soil in this world as another. In this case we must not let political boundaries obscure for us the boundaries of eternal justice. If this earth really has room for all to live in, let us be given the soil we need for our livelihood.
> True they will not willingly do this. But then the law of self-preservation goes into effect; and what is refused to amicable methods, it is up to the fist to take[2]

On 1 September 1939 history duly repeated itself when the Second World War started with Germany's invasion of Poland in furtherance of Hitler's policy of looking to Eastern Europe to seize the land that Germany wanted. The new war, which touched every continent and consumed more than 100 million lives, saw a new line up of 'Haves', Britain, France, Russia, China and their allies pitted against the 'Have Nots', led by Germany, Japan and Italy.

There was a tragic irony in the fact that this war, between the self-acclaimed civilised nations of the world, was to draw in, in large quantities, the human and material resources of those who they were competing to civilize. The story of the Yoruba man Isaac Fadoyebo[i], one of the 100,000 or so African troops who the British deployed to fight the Japanese in the rainforests of Burma during the war, was but one of many.

A NEW AMERICAN DECLARATION OF INDEPENDENCE

To begin with, the United States was, once again, able to stand back from the conflict but the cycle of history was completed when the British Prime Minister, Winston Churchill, travelled to America to make a plea for America to repeat the rescue mission of the First World War by entering the war against Nazi Germany.

Franklin Delano Roosevelt had brought America out of the Great Depression with

---

i   As told in the Al Jazeera film "The Burma Boy"

his New Deal economic programme but it was in the field of foreign affairs that his greatness was to become manifest. He was astute in realising that the First World War had ended without any clear vision of the principles upon which the world was to live in peace after the war. Guided by the shortcomings in President Woodrow Wilson's Fourteen Points he was determined not to repeat the mistake of failing to secure a clear agreement on the shape of the new post-war order before committing American lives to the war:

> *Leaving to one side for the moment the fact that Nazism is hateful, and that our natural interests, our hearts, are with the British. But there's another angle. We've got to make it clear to the British from the very outset that we don't intend to be simply a good-time Charlie who can be used to help the British Empire out of a tight spot, and then be forgotten forever[3]*

The discussion between the American President and the British Prime Minister over the future of the British Empire is interesting:

> *Roosevelt: "I can't believe that we can fight a war against fascist slavery, and at the same time not work to free people all over the world from a backward colonial policy."*
> *Churchill: "What about the Philippines?"*
> *Roosevelt: "I'm glad you mentioned them. They get their independence, you know, in 1946. And they've gotten modern sanitation, modern education, their rate of illiteracy has gone steadily down..."*
> *Churchill: "There can be no tampering with the Empire's economic agreements."*
> *Roosevelt: "They are artificial..."*
> *Churchill: "They are the foundation of our greatness."*
> *Roosevelt: "The peace...cannot include any continued despotism. The structure of the peace demands and will get equality of peoples. Equality of peoples involves the utmost freedom of competitive trade..."*
> *Churchill: "Mr President...I believe you are trying to do away with the British Empire. Every idea you entertain about the structure of the post war world demonstrates it. But in spite of that...we know that you constitute our only hope. And...you know that we know it. You know that we know that without America, the Empire won't stand."[4]*

In the new deal for the post-war world that was recorded in the terms of the Atlantic Charter which Roosevelt and Churchill signed on 14 August 1941, there was to be no place for colonialism. The Charter committed the signatory powers to:

....respect the right of all peoples to choose the form of government under which they will live; and that they wish to see sovereign rights and self-government restored to those who have been forcibly deprived of them[5]

Even so it was simply a declaration of intent. The procedure and timescale by which the colonial states were to be granted their independence had still to be worked out.

What Roosevelt envisaged was that at the end of the war the United Nations would replace the colonial powers, Britain, France and the Netherlands, as the arbiters of the national interests of their colonial subjects. They would effectively hold their colonies on trust under a mandate from the UN by which they would be charged with the responsibility of 'bringing education, raising standards of living, improving the health conditions – of all the backward, depressed colonial areas of the world'. The decision on whether any colony was ready for independence was to have been taken out of the interested hands of the colonial powers and placed with the United Nations as a whole. That none of this happened was the result of a twist of fate that saw President Roosevelt die on 12 April 1945, just weeks before the German surrender on 7 May 1945.

With Roosevelt gone, the defenders of the old world order took rapid steps to ensure that the vision was buried quickly with the man. The winds of change that Roosevelt had whipped up with the Atlantic Charter suddenly died.

The Cold War and the Vietnam War

Warrior nations need enemies and if there is none they must create one for it is the source of their internal strength and unity. Britain is before anything else a warrior nation. Thus, even before the final surrender of Germany, for which the three great powers, Britain, America and the USSR had pooled blood, sweat and tears, to achieve, new battle lines were being drawn between Britain and America, on the one side, and the new enemy, the USSR. Roosevelt's war against imperialism, the war to end all wars, was relegated to the background by those in charge of U.S. foreign policy. In fact the fear of communism became the strongest argument in favour of the need to slow the wind of decolonisation.

This remarkable U-turn in American foreign policy towards colonialism that Churchill managed to pull off left the field open for Russia to assume the mantle of the champion of the free world and anti-colonial crusader. Anthony Eden summed up the situation as he flew to Washington in 1956 to make a fresh appeal for America to line up on the British side in the new war; the Cold War against Russia and the defence of colonialism:

The visit of Marshall Bulganin and Mr Kruschev to India and Burma had not helped us. Western leadership had been put on the defensive by the anti-colonial manifesto they had flourished there. It was necessary that we and the United States should draw closer together on this prickly topic and find words to express a common philosophy[6]

With Roosevelt gone and with America now lined up against the new enemy, the British Empire had a new lease of life.

However, it was to prove only a short reprieve before differences between Britain and America over war strategy to help France keep hold of its colony French Indo-China (Vietnam) led the Americans to serve a final and formal notice on the British and the French to dismantle their colonial empires.

The American administration, under Dwight D. Eisenhower, had been proceeding on the basis that the new common enemy was communism in all its manifestations. When that enemy, with the active sponsorship of Communist China, surfaced in Vietnam to drive the French out, Eisenhower expected British support for intervention, knowing that that support was vital for the administration's hopes to get US Congressional approval for the deployment of US troops. The larger strategic objective for the Americans appears to have been to gain a foothold in South East Asia for any future war against China.

For its part, while the Churchill government was keen on American help to contain Communist influence in Europe, it was less enthusiastic over the prospect of the Americans gaining influence in South East Asia. When Churchill withheld British support for the American intervention, the Eisenhower administration saw this as a grave betrayal. The Americans, having gone too far with their planning and too public with their agenda, now found themselves having to go into Vietnam alone.

The change in the attitude of the Eisenhower administration towards Britain and France was swift. To the Chinese slogan *'Asia for the Asians'*, the United States was now resolved to add *'Arabia for the Arabs'* and *'Africa for the Africans'* and, indeed, *'Europe for the Europeans'*. It was intended as a reminder to Churchill of just how much Britain still depended on America in its renewed claim to be a major player on the world stage.

Harold Macmillan was in no doubt about the altered state of the power relationship between Britain and America:

Perhaps the most noticeable, and painful, difference between our position now and when we were last in office (1945) is our relationship to US. Then we were on an equal footing – a respected ally. Then it was the Churchill – Roosevelt combination (or its aftermath). Now we are treated by the Americans with a mixture of patronising pity and contempt. They treat us worse than they do any country in Europe. They undermine our political and commercial influence all over the world[7]

Britain's role in the creation of the State of Israel, on 14 May 1948, immediately upon the British mandate for Palestine coming to an end had already ignited the fuse of anti-colonialism in the Middle East. Egypt and the Suez Crisis was where the United States was to show that there was to be no turning back, this time around, from its renewed resolve to dismantle the British Empire.

Under the terms of the Anglo-Egyptian Treaty of 1936 that had been entered into in the run-up to the Second World War, Britain had been permitted to use the Suez Canal Zone as its main military base in the region. The war having since ended, the priority for the Arab states was to get the remaining British forces in the Zone out of the area.

The Egyptians sought to do this in 1951 by unilaterally revoking the Treaty. The British retaliated by taking early steps to de-couple Sudan from Egypt by announcing their plans to introduce self-government for Sudan with effect from 1 January 1956[ii].

This was the opportunity for the Americans to wade in on Egypt's side in its bid to be formally unified with Sudan under the rule of their King Farouk only for Farouk's reign to come to a sudden and dramatic end when he was ousted from power by a military coup, led by Colonel Abdul Nasser, on 23 July 1952.

If the new American policy towards the British Empire had been unstated previously, it became clearer to Churchill and his Foreign Secretary, Anthony Eden as they were preparing to fly to Washington on 24 June 1954:

> *Before leaving England, the Prime Minister and I had read a report from Washington of a meeting between Mr Dulles [American Secretary of State] and some leading American journalist. According to an account which our Embassy thought reliable, the Secretary of State had declared his conviction that American policy in the Middle East, as well as in Asia, had been badly handicapped by a tendency to support British and French 'colonial' views. He was reported to have spoken of his determination to talk bluntly about the Middle East, and of his aim to 'shift policies'*[8]

It was against the backdrop of this altered geo-political landscape that negotiations with the newly confident, Nasser-led Egypt led to an agreement, in July 1954, providing for the removal of all British troops from the Suez Canal in 1956. A British attempt to get the Egyptians to participate in the new Middle-East Defence Organisation which Britain was trying to put in place in anticipation of the planned final withdrawal of its troops from the Canal Zone failed when Nasser insisted that the troop withdrawal must be completed before he would even discuss the plan. On 26 July 1956, Nasser now moved to nationalize the Suez Canal.

---

ii   Which had, since 1899, been jointly-administered by Britain and Egypt under the terms of a Condominium Agreement

This being the main artery of Middle-East oil supplies to Western Europe, it was an attack on the very jugular of the Colonial Powers. Coming on the back of the Iranian nationalization of British oil interests, and with Nasser's general anti-colonial rhetoric, this was the defining challenge to the future of European empires. The British quickly rallied their fellow Colonial Powers, France and the Netherlands, to meet the challenge: The plan was for concerted action through the United Nations if possible and for direct military action if necessary. Meanwhile, the USSR, in keeping with its new mantle as the champion of anti-colonialism, stood behind Egypt. The outcome of the standoff would, once again, depend on which side the United States chose to come down on.

Without American backing for military action by the Colonial Powers, Nasser could make his moves with confidence. He had already rejected the compromise proposals which had been put forward by the eighteen-nation committee that the UN appointed to look into the matter. Everything now turned upon how he would respond to the alternative proposals of the Canal Users Club which had been brokered by the Americans themselves. When the Americans made a public announcement ruling out the use of force to resolve the issue, Eden said "the words were an advertisement to Nasser that he could reject the project with impunity"[9]. This was precisely what Nasser did.

As the American administration had done over Vietnam, the British government had gone too far with its own preparations over Egypt, and too public with its threats of action, to pull back without complete loss of face. The British and French preparations for military action to take back the Canal had been underway since July 1956[10] and had only been held back by the process of referral to the United Nations which the Americans had engineered. It was therefore more than just coincidence when, on 27 October 1956, Israel invaded Egypt and the British and French forces quickly used the opportunity to take control of the Canal Zone.

The United States government was not deceived. The US Vice President, Richard Nixon, responded by using the platform of the United Nations to make a formal announcement of America's break from British and French colonial policies:

> *For the first time in history we have shown independence of Anglo-French policies towards Asia and Africa which seemed to us to reflect the colonial tradition. This declaration of independence has had an electrifying effect throughout the world*[11]

This American declaration of independence in relation to foreign affairs was to have a dramatic impact on the course of history in Africa and Asia.

To begin with the British set out to defy the United States. However their Achilles heel was too well known to the Americans who, at this time, were still bank-rolling the European post-war economic revival and the reconstruction efforts with their Marshall Plan of financial aid. Knowing the financial vulnerability of the British, it was a simple enough measure to launch economic warfare against Britain to bring it to heel:

> *A run on the pound, at a speed which threatened disaster to our whole economic position, had developed in the world's financial markets*[12]

Harold Macmillan, Chancellor of the Exchequer at the time, wrote in his diary on 25th September 1956:

> *The state of our reserves, and the pressure on Sterling, made me very anxious. If this situation goes on too long it may well overcome us, and we be driven to devaluation or bankruptcy. It is all very sad; because, apart from Suez, we were really beginning to make real progress*[13]

A ceasefire was quickly declared on 6 November 1956 followed by UN resolutions demanding the withdrawal of British, French and Israeli forces from Egypt. The withdrawal of British troops was completed on 23 December 1956.

The Americans had now retrieved the crown of champions of anti-colonialism from the Soviet Union. They were in no mood to allow the British (and the French) to sleep on the job of liquidating the colonial empires[iii]. This was the unseen background to the spate of Independence ceremonies which followed across the globe.

However, this would not be the first time that the end of the British Empire had been proclaimed only for those who had come to witness its burial to discover that it had found new life:

> *Churchill in his old age had no heart for decolonization. His Foreign Secretary, Eden, proved to be a complacent gradualist. Only Harold Macmillan, Minister of Defence, seemed to have some sort of vision of moving towards 'a third British Empire'*[14]

---

iii   UN resolution 1514 of 14 December 1960 formally proclaimed the end of colonisation

6.
The
Bourdillon
Mask

"It really begins to look more than likely that our likeable, lazy northerner will be handed over to the tender mercies of the southern 'trousered apes' within a few years. It is a deplorable prospect but Abubakar Tafawa Balewa is almost playing a lone hand in our defence..."

Robert Hepburn Wright

The educated natives challenge to the 'demi-gods' of Empire was a modern re-run of the Biblical story of the Tower of Babel. It was to be dealt with in the same way, by the promotion of confusion and disunity amongst the people.

The divide between Northern Nigeria and Southern Nigeria ran so deep that it reflected in the character and attitudes of the colonial administrators themselves to the point that it was said that 'if all Nigerians had withdrawn from the country there would have been a civil war between the two groups of Europeans'. The colonial administrators who were posted to the North loved the people and their ways and resented the South and their peoples as much as their native wards:

I had asked in London if I might be posted to the Northern Provinces of Nigeria rather than to the South. The North seemed to me to resemble far more closely the northern India that I had known. It was predominantly Muslim, and it had a lingua franca, Hausa, that like the Indian Urdu could be spoken fluently by Europeans. Finally, it was horse country and would be, I thought, a far freer and more unfettered place in which to live than the forest-clothed South[1]

Similarly those who were posted to the South fell in love with the Southerners and shared a contempt for the "lazy" Northerners and their ways with their Southern wards:

> *The British in the North despised the educated Igbo and Yoruba from the South, but nevertheless they had to employ them as clerks, storekeepers and railwaymen in the North as there were no educated Northerners. They were seen as troublemakers like the missionaries: the sort of people who see injustice everywhere and protest to the newspapers*[2]

A clandestine war against the educated natives would endure, in one form or another, up to and beyond independence in 1960.

That the Lugardists' views about the intrinsic inadequacies of these natives was nothing more than self-serving rhetoric is clear from their actions which brought about the country's failure. The scheme was rolled out in stages over a period of forty years from Lugard's recall from Nigeria, in 1919, to Nigeria's Independence elections in 1959. In this battle the colonial administrators in the North held all the aces given the British Government's determination to hold on to Nigeria especially in the face of new and significant threats to the Empire which had arisen before, during and after the Second World War.

Just as slavery became unsustainable after both sides in the American War of Independence enlisted the help of those they had previously subjugated, so too the appeal by the colonial powers to their colonial subjects for help during the War had begun to undermine the imperial hold. The following was a public appeal issued by the Colonial Government on 3 September 1939:

> *The British Government at home will want all the produce it can get from this country – such as palm produce, groundnuts, cotton, etc. – and the prices of these are likely to rise. Every farmer will find that it will pay him to grow more and more of them, and however much he grows he may be certain of a market and feel that he is doing what he can to help win the war*[3]

With the Japanese having captured British Singapore and pressing hard on British Burma and with British India in their sights, the Empire had come full circle from the American War of Independence. Once again it found itself offering the promise of freedom to its captives (collectively now, rather than individually) in return for their support in its moment of extremis. Such a retreat by the Empire on one flank could not be kept secret for long from the other flanks of the empire.

Having been bombarded throughout the war with appeals to make sacrifices for the fight against fascism and for the course of liberty and democracy, the educated natives had high expectations of change after the war was won. With knowledge of the challenges that had been thrown down to the Empire, in India, in Iran, and then in Egypt, and with encouraging noises coming from the Russian and American governments, they began to organise themselves for a dash "towards colonial freedom".

The Yoruba were singled out as the main trouble makers who were already following the example of the Hindus in India:

> *It is among the Yorubas that Christian missionary propaganda has obtained most of its converts in West Africa...with Christian missionary teaching, Western education, or, more accurately, and, generally, semi-education (and indifferent at that) has, of course, gone hand in hand, and it is amongst the Yorubas almost exclusively, so far as Southern Nigeria is concerned, that the problem of the "educated native" and what his part is to be in the future of the country arises and threatens to become acute[4]*

Their potential for trouble had been demonstrated towards the end of the First World War with the joint uprising of the Egba and Owu tribes which had engaged the colonial army in an internal war for six weeks. Before the Second World War, a key part of the containment strategy had been to keep the Yorubas out of the Nigerian Army, but then the exigencies of the war effort dictated otherwise:

> *Army life was not confined to white troops; more than 100,000 Nigerians served in the military forces during the war. Two divisions, with more than 30,000 men, had experience in the Middle East, East Africa, Burma, and India...It is therefore not surprising to find ex-servicemen among the more militant leaders of the nationalist movement during the post war period[5]*

With freedom of assembly and speech severely curtailed at home, the best place to exercise it was in the very bosom of the Empire itself, in Britain:

> *It is not coincidence that most of the efforts to awaken respect for an appreciation of African culture started among African students abroad. Also, while abroad students could observe the white man as he actually is – stupid and intelligent, cruel and kind, evil and virtuous, filthy and immaculate, irrational and rational – and thus become aware of the universalities of human nature and behaviour.... The doctrine of white superiority, and with it the justification for imperial rule, was crushed by their devastating critique of the white man as he is versus the pretentiousness of his ideals[6]*

THE NATIONALISTS

Armed with the direct experiences of the war sacrifices that had been made by their people, and with learning acquired from British educational institutions, like the Inns of Court School of Law and through interaction with Indian students in Britain, a few of the educated natives now emerged as frontline activists in a formal campaign for Nigerian independence. These were many in number but four in particular, were the lead actors. These four were H.O. Davies, Obafemi Awolowo, Anthony Enahoro and Nnamdi Azikiwe. Each of the four was brilliant in his own way and could have made competent leaders of the country but none of them ever did.

At varying times they were on the same side and at other times they were at war with one another. All had a background in journalism. Two were Yoruba (one a Lagosian the other Ijebu), one was Edo and the fourth was Igbo. Two had come through serious financial challenges from a young age including long bouts of unemployment. Two would be tried and jailed for treason. Each would encounter Miss Margery Perham (Lugard's biographer), at an early stage in their political journey. Their story in the struggle for independence for Nigeria is as much the story of their personal and ideological struggles with one another as with the British.

HEZEKIAH OLADIPO DAVIES

Born in Lagos, his name at birth was Hezekiah Oladipo Ogunmade. His grandfather, Prince Ogunmade 'of the Ogunmade royal house of Lagos', had been a witness to the ceremony at which King Docemo had ceded Lagos to the British in 1861[7]. For this reason he had a special attachment to issues concerning the political future of Lagos.

Davies's education epitomised the problem that those concerned with the longevity of the Empire had with the system of education in Southern Nigeria. There was little that was beyond his intellect. Having shown an early gift in mathematics he was appointed as an assistant master at the prestigious Kings College to teach maths. In 1925, he was 'the only student who passed in Nigeria (possibly in West Africa)'[8] the Matriculation Examination for admission to the University of London. He almost invariably finished first in the order of merit in examinations, from the Higher Civil Service Entrance Examination to his first degree as a Bachelor of Commerce from the London School of Economics, to his second degree in law from the same university before gaining admission to the English Bar in 1946. A gifted writer, after a period of work in the Secretariat of Northern Nigeria in Kaduna from 1926 to 1930, he had first planned to pursue a career in journalism before later deciding to pursue a career in law.

He was a pioneer in several of the institutions that were to play a key role in the independence struggle including the Trade Union Movement, the Lagos Youth Movement (later renamed the Nigerian Youth Movement). He was editor of the Movement's newspaper, the *Daily Service* and had a leading role with the *Nigerian Morning Post* and the *Sunday Post*. A Wesleyan, he served in the First Republic Government from 1960 to 1964 as Federal Minister of State in the Ministry of Industries.

His commitment to the 'One Nigeria' ideal was total and without reservation. All sectional ideology was anathema to him whether it came from the Hausa-Fulani, the Igbos or his own Yoruba people or indeed the British. He would entertain any form of rule, democratic, military, feudal, provided it stood any chance of preserving Nigeria as configured by Lugard:

> Let all who wish to destroy the unity of Nigeria realize that it is the common heritage of 32,000,000 people. Our fathers throughout the country toiled and suffered together in those harsh pioneering days to build up Nigeria from a geographical expression. Citizens of Nigeria in the remote parts of the country are today, nourished by the sacrifice of our fathers who died toiling for Nigeria as one country – as co-messengers, labourers, etc. We therefore owe a duty to preserve such hard-won unity for generations yet unborn[9]

While studying in London, he found inspiration for the 'one nation one people regardless of religious and linguistic differences' ideology in the philosophy of the Congress party of India:

> In 1935, the Indian students in the college invited me to join them in welcoming Pandit Jawal Nehru...The most exciting event of the day was Pandit Nehru's address, which held every listener spellbound. He told the audience that he had come direct from jail, on his way to Switzerland to see his ailing wife. All good citizens in India were in jail, and no Indian worthy of his nationality was outside the jail. And he said, "Isn't India itself one large British jail? One thing is certain and incontrovertible. It is a question of time for India to become independent, and be left alone to direct its own affairs according to its will[10]

His steadfast commitment to 'One Nigeria' led him to become a useful ally of 'fellow travellers' especially in the articulation of policy. Many of the turnings in Nigeria's political journey were presaged by him with uncanny precision in several of his writings and speeches. For example, an article of his, *Lagos Won't Be 'No Man's Land'*, in the Daily Times of 5 June 1956, he wrote:

> Lagos is not an unoccupied arid desert. It is the land of the Lagosians, most of whom have no other homes and who live in Lagos. If the present tendency to autarchy in the Regions continues, then the Lagosians will soon demand that

another site be found elsewhere for the Federal Capital. Surely there must be some spot far away from Lagos where the East, the West, and the North have common boundaries. It is there that these "autonomous" regions with "residual powers", should meet and jointly chant the chorus "East for Easterners, West for Westerners, North for Northerners and the devil take the rest"[11]

Twenty years later, in 1976, a decision to move the federal capital from Lagos to Abuja was taken and justified on the basis of Abuja's unique quality as a place where the East, the West and the North have common boundaries. A significant number of other such prescient contributions suggests that H.O. Davies either had the ears of those in power or they had his ears. Either way, neither jail nor exile was ever his portion at any stage of his political career.

Under his stewardship the objective of the Nigerian Youth Movement was to be a truly national movement with a constructive nationalist agenda that would, ordinarily, have made all but the most hardened imperialist comfortable. The aim of the Movement was 'the development of a united nation out of the conglomeration of the people who inhabit Nigeria.... We will combat vigorously all such tendencies that would jeopardize the unifying process....' [12]

OBAFEMI JEREMIAH AWOLOWO

Born, on 6 March 1909, in rural Ikenne, in Ijebu Remo, Yoruba land, his family lineage had been wholly traditional until the arrival of the Christian faith in Ikenne in 196 when his father became one of the first converts. Notwithstanding, his grandmother who was the biggest influence on him, in his early years, remained an *Ifa* worshipper.

The death of his father, a successful farmer and timber merchant, in 1920, when he was just 11 years old, saw him transformed from a young boy with a comfortable upbringing and with an assured educational future into an Oliver Twist-like character in the service of various masters in Abeokuta in desperate quest for a means to pay his way through school to fulfil his late father's ambition for him to become a teacher or a clerk:

> *In the course of this chequered period of my young life, I attended four schools, namely: Ibara Anglican, Ogbe Wesleyan, Itesi Wesleyan and Itesi Roman Catholic. In the same period my clothes were reduced almost to tatters and rags, and there was a brief period when all I had for a decent apparel was a pair of shorts and a shirt...[13]*

This experience would have fed into his decision, as Premier of the Western Region, to introduce free education for all school children.

Fiercely competitive in all things, he had excelled in wrestling and as a centre-forward in football in his youth. The passion for competition extended to academics and made him instinctively hostile to anything that might suggest an acceptance of a status of inferiority to any man, white or black. His virulent hostility to colonial rule meant that he could not bring himself to work for the colonial administration. Work as a journalist with the *Nigerian Daily Times* was only a means to an end; that end being a career in law. On the journey he tried his hand at various commercial ventures ranging from money-lending, transportation and cocoa trading; experiencing boom and bust along the way before the award of a contract to supply the army barracks in the West, and in Kaduna, with yam and yam flour finally enabled him to embark on his law studies in the UK.

For Awolowo the political unity of his Yoruba people was his first priority. While in London studying law, he copied Nnamdi Azikiwe's initiative in forming the Igbo Federal Union to establish the Yoruba cultural organisation, Egbe Omo Oduduwa, which he then brought back to Nigeria on his return in 1948[14]. Later, in 1951, he took the initiative of launching the first modern political party in Nigeria with the Action Group, complete with party manifestoes and professional electoral campaigns.

His philosophy for Nigeria was shaped by his one-nation outlook for the Yoruba people: His commitment was to a united Nigeria rather than 'One Nigeria' and so he was implacably opposed to a unitary Nigeria. He was equally hostile to a federal arrangement which was unbalanced whether because some of the federating units were much larger than others or because the federating units were too small to effectively balance the power of the centre. He insisted upon true federalism with the federating units being organised on the basis of their ethnic identities or linguistic ties:

> *Nigeria is a country of various tribes, some of which have lived together in harmony for many years before the advent of the British, some were unknown to one another in the past and were only brought together for the first time by British administration. Some share similar customs, traditions and culture and are traceable to the same ethnic origin while others differed from each other as Aborigines of Australia from the Zulu of South Africa. In dividing Nigeria into regions it is therefore necessary to group together only people who, through affinity or general experience, are known to be capable of working together harmoniously. The guiding principles in the division of the country into regions must therefore be: ethnic classification, cultural affinity, common problems and, perhaps, administrative convenience[15]*

This position was the polar-opposite of the British outlook for post-colonial Nigeria. His thinking on the issue, coupled with his education and his dogged commitment to principle, made him the most feared, and, at the same time, the most respected, of the Nationalists in British circles. He would end up in jail on charges of high treason.

ANTHONY ERONSILE ENAHORO

Anthony Enahoro was the youngest, and physically the smallest, of the quartet. What he lacked in age and size he made up in his precociousness.

His grievance against British colonial rule was personal. He alone, amongst the quartet, was able to claim descent from a first tier ruling family, the Benin royal family. In the course of the British conquest of Benin, his great-grandfather had been killed. His grandfather, Okoje, was captured by the British as a young man and exiled by them on no less than three occasions during his lifetime:

> Upon the death of Overami, Okoje was returned from exile to resume the Stool of his fathers, although he was to be exiled twice again – to Benin and Ibadan – before he died, full of years, in his own home in 1944. Now, he was the current Onoje of Uromi, only recently returned from his last exile, an old man with the fire of rebellion still in his veins, never to be fully reconciled to British rule...[16]

The young Enahoro grew up on tales of his grandfather Okoje: 'this great man, my boyhood hero and god, whom the wicked British had orphaned, captured after battle and exiled three times'[17] from his grandmother. He had made an early resolution to find a way to get even. His father's conversion to Catholicism did little to quench the fire of rebellion and vengeance which he had inherited. That fire was being, unwittingly, stoked on a daily basis as he fulfilled his duty of reading the newspapers to his mother while she went about her chores[18].

Although born in Uromi, in Benin country, he had been raised in Owo, Yorubaland, from his infancy before attending Kings College in Lagos for his secondary education. His first language was, therefore, Yoruba. His father's plan was that he should study for the Bar and so he had had him tutored to the highest level in English. But the rebel child had his own plans. On finishing at King's College he decided to go into journalism as the shortest route to the career in politics on which his mind was set:

> ...perhaps in preparing me, as he thought, for college, Father had overprepared me and the additional six years at King's had made me a man before my time, so that I believed that I was fairly well equipped for adult life. Howbeit, while some of my colleagues dreamt of great careers at the Bar and others had visions of themselves as brilliant surgeons; while some aspired to the noble profession of the blackboard and chalk, and others had already applied to enter the Civil Service with its security and better wage prospects, I saw myself as a crusader setting wrongs right, denouncing injustice, changing the world, building a new life for our people[19]

He joined Azikiwe's *West African Pilot* in 1943 before becoming editorial chair of its sister paper the *Southern Nigerian Defender*. At the age of just twenty-two he was appointed editor of a leading publication, the Daily Comet, one of the ones he had been reading to his mother.

As a young political activist, he found himself coming under the influence of the three older nationalists in different ways. He cut his teeth in journalism in Azikiwe's stables, while he received his early political influence from H.O. Davies as a member of one of the 'Youth Circles' which Davies organised. Initially impressed by Davies's 'One Nigeria' philosophy, in the end it was Awolowo's ethnic federalism that won him over. The combination of Awolowo and Enahoro would make the Action Group a formidable political force.

Enahoro's battle with the British, and later with the political order that the British left behind, would see him repeatedly jailed for sedition before being forced into exile on two occasions after. His 1963 flight to Britain on a first round of exile following charges of high treason, saw him detained in Brixton prison. The debate in the British Parliament over the Nigerian Government's demand for his extradition not only filled the front pages of the British newspapers, it caused a permanent change in Britain's extradition laws. Such was the political storm that blew up over the extradition of this small, yet, extraordinary man that it led to the fall of the Conservative Government of the day notwithstanding that the extradition request was only granted on the strict condition that the death penalty would not be imposed.

BENJAMIN NNAMDI AZIKIWE

Of the individual life experiences of the quartet before they entered national politics, Nnamdi Azikiwe's was the hardest and the most moving. His story is an African tragedy of epic proportions: a man of great potential who set out to do the best for himself and for all Africans but whose judgment calls, at critical junctures, led to disastrous consequences for his Igbo people.

Azikiwe was an Igbo man who was born in Zungeru, Hausaland, on 16 November 1904. His father was a clerk in the West African Frontier Force, one of the educated Southerners on whose support the British administration of the North depended. As a result, Nnamdi Azikiwe was a Southerner who spent his childhood in the North. He was 'to all intents and purposes a Hausa Boy [speaking] that language very fluently'[20]. At the age of eight his father sent him to their native Onitsha to learn the Igbo tongue. At the age of ten he was moved again, to Lagos, following his father's transfer there. Now he was being raised as a Yoruba youth of the Lagosian kind:

In Bamgbose Street we also lived near the Akereles, John the eldest son of the popular contractor, was very kindly. Up to that time I had not met any boy who was such a humanitarian during my stay in Bamgbose Street. His three brothers, Alaba, Oni and Abiola, were real Aguda products. I do not say this in derision, but I mean that they were the life of our neighbourhood and they made things hot for boys who were not strong enough to resist the affronts and bullying pranks of other Aguda boys[21]

His close friendship with a Yoruba youth in the neighbourhood by the name of Francis Adedayo Alaba, an assistant head printer of the CMS Press in Lagos, implanted in him an early interest in the printing industry: "I went so far as to tell him that with his knowledge of printing we could start a newspaper".

In Lagos, Azikwe attended the Wesleyan Boys High School in Broad Street Lagos. After a year his father sent him back to Onitsha to be raised as a young Igbo man, continuing his education at CMS Central School there. By the time Azikiwe had finished the first stage of schooling he had to support his mother (she had divorced his father after the latter took a second wife) so he took up an appointment at the school. At the age of sixteen his father once again directed him to relocate to Calabar, to enrol at the Hope Waddell Institute there to resume his education.

At the Institute, he became exposed to the story of Liberia, then the only independent state in West Africa, from Liberians teaching there and also from the writings of Marcus Garvey. The next stage of his educational odyssey, as directed by his father, was to return to the Wesleyan Boys High School in Lagos as a boarder. This eclectic socio-cultural upbringing extended to his religious exposure as well:

As a Christian, I have been many-sided denominationally, due to chance and circumstance. At the tender age of nine I was a catholic. At ten I became an Anglican. At twelve I was a Methodist. At sixteen I became a Presbyterian. At eighteen I was a soldier of the Lord (Hallelujah!) in the Salvation Army. At nineteen I left the emotional for the intellectual side of Christianity and became a student Bible Expositor (now known as a Jehovah's Witness). At twenty-one, I entered the Baptist fold. At twenty-five I was reaffirmed in the Presbyterian faith[22]

Whilst attending service at Tinubu Methodist Church during his second stint at Wesleyan Boys High School, he became exposed to the teachings of Rev. Dr. James Emmanuel Kwegyir Aggrey. A book which Aggrey gave him *Negro Education: a study of the Private and Higher School for Coloured People in the United States* now directed his ambition towards America. Another book, *From Log Cabin to the White House, a biography of President James A Garfield*, which was conferred on him as a prize by the school, now became the road map for his life and convinced him that he had to go to America.

A speculative letter sent to the Principal of Howard University in America earned him an introduction to Storer College and a promise of support with admission to the College provided he could pay his way to America. Since his father had declared that he was unable to provide any financial assistance, he went to work as a clerk in the Treasury Department of the Colonial Service to raise some money for his adventure.

His first attempt to leave Nigeria for America via Liverpool as a stowaway found him ending up only in Accra where to keep body and soul together he joined the Ghana Police Force. He was not long there before his mother tracked him down to deliver his father's plea for him to leave the job and return to Nigeria with a promise that he would help fund his journey to America. His father had become converted to his cause after a racial insult from a young colonial officer colleague had made the older Azikiwe realise the limitations of his own position as a civil servant. The incident having affected the older Azikiwe's health and pushed him into taking early retirement from the service, he now handed over £300 from his life savings with his blessings to the young Azikiwe to go to America in pursuit of education and success.

Azikiwe left Nigeria in 1925 to enrol at Storer College. There, living the Black-American experience, he became immersed in the story of the Slave Trade, abolition, the American Civil War and the civil rights struggle. At college, he excelled in his studies and in sports as a pentathlete, and a boxer. However, soon after completing his studies at Storer, in June 1927, he found himself unemployed, on the edge of starvation and attempting suicide on a train line:

> *Four weeks had passed since I lost my job and no new job was in sight. By now I was worth one dime in all the world. I had rationed my funds so frugally that I went on a diet for a long time, and at times had one meal a day. When no job was coming, I reduced this to a cup of coffee and two thick slices of bread. But it was in vain*[23]

By this act he had given notice that he had no use for his life. He was rescued from the path of the train at the last minute by a passer-by who took him to the Pittsburgh YMCA. There he came under the influence of Rev. Dr. A.M. Lamb, a white Presbyterian minister:

> *Placing his aged hand on my head, he said to me, 'it is the unseen hand of Providence that saved you early this morning and brought me here my son*[24]

In America Azikiwe did every lowly job imaginable to pay his way including sweeping, dishwashing, coal-mining and working as a road labourer and lift operator in between repeated bouts of unemployment. Despite all his hard work, he had to leave Howard University with his studies unfinished because he owed tuition fees. It was only after more toil and struggle that he was able to gain admission into Lincoln University to finally finish his first degree before enrolling at Columbia University to study journalism. Once again, though, he ran out of money and had to drop out of Columbia. He returned to Lincoln, which gave him a teaching assistantship to pay for his studies. Finally, he returned to Columbia to enrol for a PhD in political science. It was the hard experience of life in America which led him to the following admission in the preface to his autobiography:

> *Since attaining manhood, I have had to fend for myself in a world where idealism and materialism are usually opposed to each other. In the course of my life's odyssey, I have been convinced that I must be idealistic to justify my existence as a human being; but I must also be materialistic to adapt myself to the concatenations of a materialistic world. To steer between these two, it became necessary for me to be eclectic and pragmatic; to draw the best from each philosophy and make it work to my advantage in the light of reason and experience[25]*

From Azikiwe's varied life experiences, his upbringing in the North, West and East of Nigeria, one might have expected that he would have become Pan Africanist in political outlook and a 'One Nigeria' man. The external influences which turned him into a jingoistic champion of his Igbo ethnic group lies at the heart of the Nigerian disaster story and the tragedy which was to befall his people.

GOVERNOR BERNARD BOURDILLON

The high-level thinking on future colonial policy in Africa, and on the future of the Nigerian colony in particular, was underway even as World War II and the negotiations for American entry into the war were going on. Those tasked with the responsibility were Margery Perham and Bernard Bourdillon. The former was Fredrick Lugard's biographer, the latter was his disciple whose influence on the internal political configuration of Nigeria was almost as great as the influence that Goldie and Lugard had had on the country's external boundaries.

To say that Bourdillon walked in the footsteps of Lugard is no exaggeration. Like him, he had started his colonial service in India where Lugard had first acquired his taste for 'indirect rule', before, like Lugard, moving to Uganda[i] to take up his first governorship appointment. As Lugard had done in his own time, it was from Uganda that he arrived

---

i   After short stints in Iraq and Ceylon (now Sri Lanka) as Governor of Nigeria in 1935 to take over from Cameron. Lugard began the process of extending indirect rule to the South but it was Bourdillon who completed it. Under the system, the educated natives' political participation would be tempered by the influence of the traditional rulers with the Native Authorities serving as a form of electoral-college in selecting candidates for the representative assemblies.

In both India and Sri Lanka, he had witnessed what the Lugardists considered to be the intoxicating effects on colonial subjects of missionary education. His comments on education policy, which he first articulated while Governor of Uganda, were straight out of the Lugard manual:

> *Education, he argued, had to be built slowly and upon a secure foundation of primary teaching, biased towards agriculture, while too much secondary education was a 'positive menace'. Purely academic teaching would not, in his opinion, help to produce 'national character', while a too rapid spread of higher education would overstock the employment market and yield 'a large crop of discontented unemployables, who produce all sorts of political troubles and do no good to themselves or the country'. Much better to concentrate on providing elementary education for all[26]*

He was, as his biographer depicted him, 'a twentieth-century colonialist'. His thinking was in terms of how to strengthen and sustain the British Empire rather than how to bring it to an end: *'He believed that Britain would be ruling Nigeria for several more generations'*[27] and at the outset his aim was to put in place a model of governance that would secure Nigeria's position within the Empire for the foreseeable future.

Essentially, the plan was for a slow and protracted introduction of democratic practices to the South to keep the educated natives at bay whilst devising special arrangements for the North that would protect and preserve the feudal order and the pact with the Fulani. It was a race against time. At its core, it was simply the revival of the plan that had been aborted earlier following Lugard's forced departure in 1919. The mission was to perfect the unconsummated amalgamation of 1914 by creating a *'united Nigeria'*. Bourdillon was determined to succeed where his mentor had failed in the endeavour to make the switch from direct to indirect rule in Southern Nigeria:

> *It was during 1937-38 that, true to his policy of gradually improving what existed, he took the decision to introduce indirect rule in the colony area of Nigeria (the colony comprising Lagos itself and the districts of Badagri, Epe and Ikeja)*[28]

This time the 'unity' was to be a unity of institutions, methods and policies and not simply a union in the person of the governor. As a minimum, it meant a shared model of governance for North and South and a common education policy. In both respects, it was the practices prevailing in the North that were to be applied in the South and not *vice versa.*

A battle of wits now ensued between the educated natives, determined to make it through to the Promised Land, and the defenders of the Empire, equally determined to keep them out:

> *In 1937 Margery Perham urged that officialdom persevere in the development and modernization of the native authority system, and that the educated elements be integrated into that system, but she cautioned against admitting them to the central superstructure or giving them any further powers in the Legislative Council[29]*

If there was any daylight to be found between Bourdillon and Lugard it was only in their method. While the latter, the soldier, had sought to achieve the policy objective by direct confrontation with the educated natives, Bourdillon went about the same objective using the more slippery art of diplomacy earning great acclaim for the relationship that he cultivated in the process. His tactic was to make some concessions to the native contribution to the war effort in some of the constitutional reforms. Thus whilst prior to the war the policy had been one of complete exclusion of the educated natives from central and local government:

> *Two educated Africans (Sir Adeyemo Alakija and Justice S.B. Rhodes) were appointed to the governor's Executive Council in 1943, but both were considered by the nationalists to be "safe" government men. Before 1943 no African had participated directly in policy formulation at the central executive level. Furthermore, with few exceptions, Africans were excluded from the various functional councils and boards appointed by the government to advise on specific problems[30]*

While Lugard had sought to keep the troublesome elements at arms' length and to browbeat them, Bourdillon drew them close. It was a masterful public relations exercise bordering on a confidence-trick. He promised dialogue, actively courted their society and provided material support at opportune moments to key players who were prepared to accept the offered hand. He is reported to have helped Nnamdi Azikiwe's publication 'West African Pilot' secure new offices in February 1939 after it had been evicted from its Broad Street premises.[31] So skilfully did Bourdillon play this hand that he won the radical groups over completely:

> *[In] a mere fifteen months – he had...helped to lay secure foundations of goodwill and co-operation between the colonial authorities and the NYM, an*

organisation which had become unquestionably the main focus of Nigerian nationalism when it achieved electoral success for the first time[32]

Members of the NYM now sat on his Legislative Council which they might have been expected to keep their distance from and, in 1937, he became a patron of the London-based West African Students Union.[33] On 29 October 1938 Bourdillon was meeting with the NYM to talk about Hitler's demand for territory in Africa.[34] His popularity amongst those who were supposed to be leading the battle against the colonial government, of which he was the first representative, was summed up in the following passage:

> *The NYM declared that Sir Bernard was a sportsman and a gentleman; and on the eve of his departure on leave on 19th May 1938 around 400 members held a torchlight procession to Government House to bid him farewell, an unprecedented event not simply in Nigeria but in the whole of British Africa.... and it was around this time that the - 'pork pie'- hat which the governor habitually wore started to become remarkably popular. It was known and sold as the 'Bourdillon'. 'Nobody should be without one' ran the advertisement, and very soon nobody was*[35]

The fundamentals of Bourdillon's covert scheme to keep the educated natives from power had been decided upon in 1937 although the implementation of the main planks only began in 1939 following Bourdillon's publication of his *'Memorandum on the Future Political Development of Nigeria'*. Even though he avoided consulting with the educated natives on the proposals in the Memorandum, he was not without opposition from those who he did consult. Ironically the most vociferous opponent of the proposals was a Briton, Theodore Samuel Adams, the Chief Commissioner for the Northern Provinces (1936-1943), who had a reputation for being a 'rabid anti-Southerner'[36]. Drawing upon his experiences in Malaya, and the failed efforts to fuse Chinese and Malay people into one community, Adams saw the two societies, north and south Nigeria, as being too different to make any attempt to unify them meaningful let alone sustainable:

> *Just as the differences between the Colony of the Straits Settlement and the Malay States has necessitated separate legislatures and local finance. The possibility of these different units coming more closely together is a possibility only and is one of the last stages in a remote development. For several generations in Nigeria too, one should look on the various parts as 'united' in the Governor and in no other authority*[37]

But Bourdillon had strategies to ensure that the Chinese domination of the Malays would not be replicated in Nigeria by Southern domination of Northerners.

PROMOTING DIVISION IN THE SOUTH

While Yoruba and Fulani antipathy can be traced to the 1804 jihad of Uthman Dan Fodio, the difficulties between the Yoruba and the Igbo are of more recent genesis; as the two nations share no borders or pre-British colonial interaction, the enimity is entirely the product of the politics of the period between the build-up to the Second World War and Independence in 1960.

Its beginning can be pin-pointed to the action taken by Governor Bourdillon, on 1 April 1939, when he reversed the amalgamation of the Eastern and Western provinces of Southern Nigeria that had created 'one South' and which had been in effect since 1906. The measure had not been precipitated by any agitation for the division from the people of the South-east or the South-west. It was also devoid of any intrinsic logic since the South was territorially smaller than the North, had fewer ethnic groups and was almost wholly Christian. Despite the warm and constructive relationship he had with the Nigerian Youth Movement, involving dialogue and consultation over many issues, there is no evidence that Bourdillon consulted them on this critical issue of the reversal of the southern amalgamation.

The claim that 'Nigeria falls naturally into three regions, the North, the West and the East' made by Bourdillon's successor, Sir Arthur Richards, was pure sophistry which contradicted every scholarly comment on record on the point. Eme O. Awa in his book *Federal Government in Nigeria* cites the writings of Lord Hailey, Margery Perham, Lord Lugard and Bernard Bourdillon himself in evidence against the notion.[38] The scheme of amalgamation which E.D. Morel had proposed in 1911 saw a Nigeria of four regions, two in the North (the Northern and the Central Province) and two in the South (the Western and the Eastern Province).

Bourdillon's biographer, Robert D. Pearce, conscious of the charge that his man deliberately fractured an existing consensus in Southern Nigeria, whilst leaving the North as one, makes an attempt to defend his man:

> .....to concentrate on Bourdillon's decision not to divide the north in 1937 is to sensationalise the issues. His actions ought to be judged in relation to the needs of the time rather than unpredictable future consequences[39]

The weakness in the argument is that the decision was no reflection upon the needs of the Southern Nigerians. More importantly, the future consequences of the omission to split the North in the same way, far from being 'unpredictable', were in fact known and the move was drawn directly from British experience in India, which had been a British colony for much longer than Nigeria (since 1858), and where the nationalist campaign for independence was much further advanced.

In India, as in Nigeria, there were two principal stakeholder groups divided on religious lines: In India, it was the Hindus and the Muslims while in Nigeria it was the Christians and the Muslims.

In keeping with the Empire's general policy of keeping interference with Islamic ways to a minimum, western education had been extended only to the Hindus who, consequently, were at the vanguard of the agitation for independence. As with the Yoruba in Nigeria, it was the Hindus of Bengal (seat of the then-capital of British India, Calcutta) who had been identified as the most vocal.

In 1905, the British Viceroy of India, Lord Curzon, had implemented a partition measure to divide and distract the chasing pack of Indian nationalists:

> *....as the largest, most populous and most troublesome administrative unit in British India, Bengal posed a worthy challenge. With a population, twice that of Great Britain, which was predominantly Hindu in the west and Muslim in the east, the administrative case for a division of the two brooked little argument. Curzon therefore pushed ahead...He was not unimpressed by the view that Bengal's highly vocal critics would also thereby be partitioned*[40]

Although the partition of Bengal was reversed in 1911 by then the damage had been done to the common front which had been emerging between Muslims and Hindu nationalists against British rule. From this point on Muslim nationalists who had worked side by side with Hindu nationalists within the Congress Party felt the need for a party of their own separate from what was now being depicted and perceived as a 'Hindu-dominated Congress Party'. Within two years of the partition in Bengal the All India Muslim conference was convened which led to the creation of a political party by the same name. The separation was compounded by elections in India in 1937 in which the British introduced the concept of 'separate electorates' and reserved seats to give maximum recognition to the now separate Islamic political voice in the Hindu dominated country.

Once such political identities are awakened in the struggle for power, they cannot be easily put to rest again. Through this process of imperial political engineering the Congress Party, which had historically been the party of all Indians of all communities and transcending all religious differences, became 'the party of the Hindus'. The Muslim League became 'the party of the Muslims'.

Bourdillon having started his colonial service in India, in 1908, at a time when the effects of the 1905 Bengal partition were still unfolding, and having left in 1918 some years after the attempted reversal of the partition, would have had first-hand knowledge of the effects of such sectarian measures. It was this Machiavellian precedent from

British-India that was applied to Nigeria in 1939 to sow the seeds of division between the nationalists of Southern Nigeria.

THE POISONING OF THE SOUTHERN NIGER

The new three region structure was consolidated in the new constitution which Governor Richards introduced in 1946. But the retreat to regionalism was only a measure to split the Southern consensus; the end game remained a unified Nigeria:

> *...in fact this measure represents not the division of one unit into three, but the beginning of the fusion of innumerable small units into three and from these into one....*[41]

The division of the South having been implemented without consultation, elections in 1946, and in 1951, now served to crystallize the new divide which had been introduced into the polity.

The Nigeria Youth Movement (NYM) was to the Nationalists what the Indian National Congress had been to their counterparts in India. It had been intended as a secular organisation for all Nigerians regardless of ethnicity and religious and linguistic differences. Just as the Congress Party in India had, originally, been the shared platform of the Muslim leader, Mohammed Ali Jinnah, and the Hindu leaders, Mahatma Ghandi and Pandit Nehru, so too the NYM had boasted the heavyweight-collective of Nnamdi Azikiwe, H.O. Davies, Obafemi Awolowo and Anthony Enahoro. Having begun with so much promise it suddenly died a complete death with accusations and counter-accusations of tribalism.

The allegation against Azikiwe, which led to him being summonsed before the Central Executive Committee of the organisation in October 1940 to explain why he should not be expelled, was that in his efforts to galvanize and prepare his Igbo people for the post-colonial age that was dawning, he had overstepped the line of what was acceptable to the Nationalist cause:

> *But Dr Azikiwe went about it in a manner which disgusted those of us who were used to describing citizens of Nigeria as Nigerians or Africans, and regarding their achievements as reflecting credit on Nigeria, indeed Africa, as a whole. The following are typical of the titles of front page news items and of editorial articles in the Pilot.*
> *1. 'Ibo Young Man to Sail to U.K.' is the heading of a front page story and picture on September 23, 1938. The young man is Mr Jaja Wachuku, now Speaker of Nigeria's House of Representatives.*
> *2. '14th West African Student, 10th Nigerian, 8th Ibo in U.S.A.' another front-page*

story on January 28 1939. The 8th Ibo is Mr Nwafor Orizu, now Senator in Nigeria's Upper House.

3. 'Ibo Medical Student Passes Exam in First Class Honours'. Yet another front page story, on June 26, 1940, of the brilliant success of Dr S. O. Egwuatu.

4. Editorials:

> *I. 'A Model Union (August 8, 1938) in praise of the Ibibio State Union.*
>
> *II. 'One Year Ago' (August 18, 1938) celebrating the first anniversary of the call to the Bar of the first Ibo lawyer, in the person of Mr Justice Louis Mbanefo, now Chief Justice of the Eastern Region High Court.*
>
> *III. 'The Ibo Are Coming' (December 31, 1938) – The very title is sufficiently indicative of the contents.*

These are but a few examples of the publicity given to Ibos as a group. But as against these, the achievements of the Yorubas and, in particular, the academic laurels of their scholars received, if at all, inconspicuous notice in the Pilot.[42]

However, to say that Azikiwe caused the break-up of the NYM, after he started to promote a distinct Igbo nationalist agenda, is to view the events from ground level only. The timing and suddenness of the emergence of 'tribalism' within the NYM has everything to do with the colonial government's agenda to divide and rule because parallel developments can be seen within the Congress Party of India around the same time:

> *But in 1938...Jinnah too foresaw the danger of a 'Congress Raj' at the federal centre. Accusations of Hindu discrimination against Muslims in the already Congress-run provinces were probably much exaggerated, but they received wide publicity. To the call of 'Islam in Danger', the League began a drive for the mass support which had hitherto eluded it...The Leagues claim to represent the majority of Muslims at least began to acquire some substance[43]*

Azikiwe, personally, had no reason, neither on account of experience or ideology, to be anti-Yoruba. He had grown up as a Lagos boy and it was to Yoruba colleagues and acquaintances that he had turned during his years of struggle. When making his preparations to enrol at Howard University, it was Babajimi Adewakun, an outgoing student at Howard to whom he reached out and who promised to '*hand over.....his job as a dishwasher*' on leaving to help him meet his board and lodging expenses;[44] it was Akintunde Dipeolu of the University of Chicago who inspired him to ditch his English name 'Ben'; it was Ladipo Solanke in London to whom he wrote in the autumn of 1929 when he '*needed a comforter*';[45] it was H.O. Davies with whom he lodged whilst passing through London and it was his '*boyhood hero, Herbert Macaulay*' with whom he sought employment in the *Lagos Daily News* when he was first trying to return to Nigeria from America. Again, it was H.O. Davies who worked with him as an 'unpaid organising manager' when he was starting his newspaper the *West African Pilot*.[46]

Besides, having had such a high level of exposure to African-American political issues during the years of struggle in America, his ideology was rabidly pan-Africanist. The first speech he delivered, on his homecoming, was full of pan-Africanist enlightenment for his people:

> *Social regeneration implied the treatment of all Africans as brothers and sisters irrespective of tribe, so as to crystallise a sense of oneness and identity of community interest. No longer should Africans draw a line of distinction, based on tribal or linguistic factors, but they should appreciate the universal affinity of all African peoples*[47]

Yet, it was Azikiwe who, soon after joining the Nigerian Youth Movement which had been birthed on ideals of oneness, began drawing very bold lines of distinction based on 'tribal or linguistic factors' culminating in the death of that organisation. That this started around the same time that Jinnah started to play the sectarian card in India leads to the conclusion that the change in Azikiwe was due to influences beyond himself. The explanation is to be found in the ground which the Bourdillon was laying in the South for 'tribalism' to germinate.

AZIKIWE'S NEW YEAR RESOLUTION

That Azikiwe on his way back home, after a nine-year sojourn in America, chose to spend the summer of 1934 in London is not particularly remarkable especially given the correspondence that he had been having with the West African Students union from America and with friends of his in London, like H.O. Davies. That in the course of that short stay in London he ran into the Empire's chief strategist for colonial policy (and later Lugard's biographer), Margery Perham, and spent a weekend at her country home in Abingdon, Berkshire, may have just been a happy coincidence. What followed cannot be so described.

Azikiwe, in his autobiography, notes that Perham gave him special mention in her work *Native Administration in Nigeria* which was published in 1937, the same year as his formal entry into the Nigerian political stage, and the same year in which Bourdillon decided upon the reversal of the amalgamation of Southern Nigeria:

> *On page 361 of her book, cited above, I detected a direct reference to me. She said:*

'The ambitions of the educated should also be met by doing everything possible to find or create opportunities for them within the native administrations. This is not always easy. It is fortunate that the majority of the educated have hitherto been from the Yoruba country, where the local governments are large enough to employ some, at least, of their more civilised members.

But what scope, to quote a recent example, can the rudimentary Ibo groups offer to one of the tribe who has spent ten years at American universities accumulating academic qualifications'[48]

By the time of his encounter in London with Miss Perham, Nnamdi Azikiwe had become disillusioned with life.

In 1930, renewed money problems had forced him to abandon his Ph.D. programme at Columbia and return home. He calculated that his prospects at home, as a pioneer of the new educated Igbo elite, would be better than whatever he could hope to achieve in America. Before he set off, he sent various applications for employment in Nigeria. What he met was a concrete wall of unemployment. He had applied for work to the Education Department and the Police Department of the colonial administration and to the newspapers and the various Christian missions. He had applied to the Nigerian banks and finance companies for a loan to start his own newspaper. All to no avail. He had scaled all obstacles to attain the highest level of education and an appointment as a lecturer in political science in America, only to find himself unemployable in his homeland. The stark reality was that under a colonial regime occupied with calculations on prolonging its hold on its colonies, educated natives, particularly those tutored in political science in America (the first rebel colony of the Empire) were the least desirable of all undesirables. What was now apparent to Azikiwe was that the colonial government controlled virtually all the gateways to employment in Nigeria which his education led to:

...the scar of 1776 [American Independence] was to be likened to the differences between two friends: like chinaware, it might be patched up, but it was always visible. The scar of 1776 was the price the African who was educated in America was bound to pay for having dared to proceed to America where one could imbibe the spirit of 1776.....[49]

Even an attempt to get employment with the Ethiopian and Liberian Governments – the latter being a country on which he had become something of an authority whilst teaching in America - soon brought home to him the realities of his Pan-Africanist ideals. The realisation that he 'was a 'foreigner' even in Africa' led him to make the following resolution, before leaving America, to reset his value system:

On the last day of the year 1933, the realities of unemployment inspired me to make a New Year resolution in the form of a solemn vow, made up of five points. Here is the text:

> *Having ardently sought for the opportunity to better my lot in life;*
>
> *Having bravely crossed the Atlantic Ocean in quest of knowledge and wisdom;*
>
> *Having passed through the crucible of unemployment and worked hard as an unskilled labourer and a menial worker;*
>
> *Having worked and whistled my way through university, partly because of my faith, perseverance and diligence, and partly on account of the charitable disposition of kind-hearted human beings;*
>
> *Having succeeded in realising my dreams for academic honours, because of my supreme determination, resoluteness and will power, in spite of man-made handicaps and other imponderables of human life;*
>
> > *I, Benjamin Nnamdi Azikiwe, hereby make this solemn vow, before God and man:*
> >
> > *First, that henceforth, I shall dedicate my life to the emancipation of the continent of Africa from the shackles of imperialism, and to the redemption of my country from the manacles of foreign rule.*
> >
> > *Secondly, that in order to earn an honest livelihood, henceforth, I shall, devote my energies either to work on my own or to work for others, with the sole aim of accumulating wealth to ensure that I shall never be in want.*
> >
> > *Thirdly, that I shall utilise my earned income to secure my enjoyment of a high standard of living and also to give a helping hand to the needy.*
> >
> > *Fourthly, that, henceforth, I shall be charitably disposed towards all human beings and do all I can to be philanthropic so as to make life less irksome for the underprivileged.*
> >
> > *Finally, that henceforth, I shall strive, to my utmost, to live as a true Christian; forgiving those who offend me, forgetting the evils perpetrated against me, and praying fervently to God to forgive my sins and to forget my shortcomings.*
> >
> > *Made at Houston Hall, Lincoln University, December 31 1933*[50]

After so many years of honest endeavour to improve himself, he had come full circle to what seemed a life with no future. He was effectively back to the point of hopelessness which had driven him to his earlier suicide attempt. The only escape that opened to him from his desperate state was an opportunity in the Gold Coast (Ghana) to help establish a new newspaper, *The African Morning Post*.

He was driven to bare his soul in an exchange of correspondence with one Dr.

Thomas Jesse Jones, Educational Director of the Phelps-Stokes Fund to whom he wrote to announce his plan to return to Africa:

> *I have come to the end of the road....My immediate aim is to aid in bringing about mutual understanding between the people of Nigeria and the British Government and missions in Nigeria...it might be of advantage to join hands with the efforts of the government and the missions. This seems to be practicable because such a connection should benefit the Africans. In the past, I must confess that I had doubted the possibility of such a programme. Probably the flame of youth was responsible. But with the passing of the years and as one grows older, it becomes evident that the only practical and workable way is the co-operation of the kind advocated by the later Booker T. Washington. I sincerely believe that I will co-operate fully and can be used as a means of better understanding between the indigenous Africans of my country and the various agencies of the British Government and missions in Nigeria*[51]

Azikiwe's admission of defeat in his personal struggle against the British colonial powers, and his declaration of his new readiness to work with them, formed the basis of his emergence as the political leader of the Eastern Region and goes to explain the special relationship that developed between Azikiwe, the British and the Fulani political leaders of the North.

Through Perham's agency, Azikiwe while still in London, in quick succession, had meetings with Sir William Edgar Hunt, the Lieutenant Governor of the Southern Provinces; Major Hanns Vischer, formerly Director of Education for the Northern Provinces of Nigeria, and with the Colonial Office team.[52] What seems to have happened is that Perham and her friends implanted a fear of Yoruba domination of post-colonial Nigeria into Azikiwe's mind in much the same way as they were to implant fears of Southern domination in the minds of the Northern political leadership to bestir them into competition.

The British side wasted no time in delivering on their part of the bargain to make Azikiwe leader of the Igbos with the mission of arousing and uniting them into a political force to compete with the Yoruba.

Heralded as the first indigenous Igbo graduate, ahead of his homecoming into Nigeria,[53] arrangements had been put in place for the 'Committee of Igbo Gentlemen' in Lagos and across the East to prepare welcoming parties at which 'the dawn of a new era in educational and cultural aspirations of the rising generation of the Ibo country and Nigeria' would be proclaimed before audiences ranging from 10,000 in Onitsha to 20,000 in Calabar[55]. In Port Harcourt the Chairman of the occasion was Rev. L.R. Potts Johnson, in Enugu it was Rev. A. W. Howells while in Aba it was Mr S.I. Simon. At each gathering what Azikiwe called 'a heavy purse' was given to him. The one that took place on 26 November 1934 at the Masonic Hall in Onitsha was a special one for 'non-native African residents of Onitsha' where he was enjoined to aim for the 'accomplishment of the prayer of the Christ: "That all may be one"'.[55]

With his degrees in political science, and with the speaking opportunities that had been arranged for him by his new friends in the Colonial Office, by the end of this tour of the Igbo country, in November 1934, Azikiwe was the undisputed political leader of the Igbos and the main political figure in the Eastern Region. The Pan-Africanist had been turned into an ethnic champion. To the extent that he spoke against tribalism it was aimed at the need for unity of:

> *I welcomed the two [Igbo] delegations and informed them that, first and foremost, I was a son of humanity and a citizen of the world. I submitted that my place of birth was an accident: neither Onitsha nor Nigeria nor even Africa could correctly claim me, because I was of the earth, and I belonged to the earth, irrespective of geographical and other man-made boundaries. But I did not want to be too idealistic in my view of the mission of man in the world. So I asked them what were the tribal affinities of their constituencies. They replied that they were all Ibo-speaking people. Then I questioned why a house should be divided against itself*[56]

Following this tour of the Igbo nation, Azikiwe left Nigeria to take up his job with *The Morning Post* in Accra where he would learn his trade in political journalism. Controversy soon followed him as he was castigated as 'a bird of passage' who had nothing at stake in [Ghana] but to pit brother against brother'.[57]

At the public gathering at the Native Court Hall, Onitsha, back in November 1934 before his departure for Accra, there was one speaker of special significance whom Azikiwe refers to as his 'friend, counsellor and guide'[58]. The man, John Moray Stuart-Young, was a homosexual, a paedophile, a master forger and an ex-convict[59]. For all these reasons, he had been an outcast from English society but now he was a pillar of society in Azikiwe's hometown, Onitsha, where he lived for over thirty years before his death. His body remains buried there.

Stuart-Young had relocated to Nigeria in 1905 to reinvent himself and he did so to great effect including awarding himself the academic title of 'Dr John Moray Stuart-Young' even though he had never been to university. Starting out in the palm oil trade in Onitsha as a common '*palm oil ruffian*', he soon became one of the richest European traders in Nigeria[60]. This spectacular rise from a 'poor white' to merchant prince gave him the means to indulge his passions from his home the quaintly-named the '*Little*

House of No Regrets', New Market Road, Onitsha. First amongst his passions was his passion for young boys:

> *Several local historians and senior men in Onitsha testify to Stuart-Young's passionate lifelong interest in young African men. He subsidized and sponsored many local youths during his thirty years in the town; he advised and trained several bright boys in clerical skills, and he offered employment and accommodation to other youths before and after their marriages. In this way, he built up an extensive network of proteges and manservants in Onitsha[61]*

It was a passion for the indulgence of which Stuart-Young might have been expected to have been stoned to death in Igbo country but, not only was he a white man in colonial Nigeria but he was one who had been adopted by Onitsha society as one of their own. His death, on 28 May 1938[62], was mourned throughout the papers of the Eastern Region with his funeral being attended by thousands. Azikiwe, himself, led the tributes:

> *In the West African Pilot.... [Azikiwe] takes charge of producing his friend's memory and reconstructs him as the exemplar of a hoped-for postcoloniality, a leader of "renascent Africa", and a model to Nigerian youths. "I wonder if the people of Onitsha will have the sense of duty and admiration for this white friend of the blacks," he writes, "to erect a monument dedicated to the sacrifice of this hero to the cause of inter-racial cooperation, and thus make the tomb of 'Odeziaku' a national shrine[63]*

'Odeziaku' – a misspelling of 'Odoziaku' meaning the keeper of the wealth - was the Igbo name which Stuart-Young had been given by his adopted community. It was testimony to his acts of philanthropy towards many Igbo youths in Onitsha.

Though Odeziaku Stuart-Young abhorred racial discrimination, yet he was an imperialist of the Lugard school, going so far as to refer to educated natives as 'criminals'[64]. A prolific writer, he used his regular columns in West African newspapers to propagate his imperialist views leading his biographer to wonder "how local editors could have tolerated these opinions". The explanation may have been in the financial support that Stuart-Young had been giving to these publications.

Azikiwe had left the United States with no money. The difficulties he had faced in finding any employment at all on his return had driven him to make his New Year resolution of 1933. He had approached the banks for loans to start his newspaper without success only to tell H.O. Davies that 'people from his home town had contributed sufficient money to found a press to be known as the West African Pilot'[65]. It is more likely than not that Stuart-Young was one of the key financiers of the trailblazing newspaper which Azikiwe launched after his apprenticeship in Accra. This would explain the editorial licence that Odeziaku Stuart-Young enjoyed in his contributions. It was in the knowledge of the financial support that Stuart-Young had given to so many Igbo youths, to the point that he had lost his fortune by the time of his death, that Azikiwe personally paid for his corpse *'to be transported home to Onitsha from the hospital in Port Harcourt where [he] had been receiving care'.*[66]

Azikiwe returned to Nigeria from Accra, in July 1937. His return coincided with the publication of Bourdillon's Memorandum on the Future of Nigeria. Newspapers being, then, the chief weapons of political warfare, Azikiwe effectively returned with an invading army:

> *When I left Accra, bound for Lagos, I arranged for all the printing plant and machinery of the printing press to be shipped to my new sphere of operation. Because of the friendly attachment existing between me and some members of the staff of The African Morning Post, quite a number of these personally loyal workers pledged to serve me wherever I decided to print and publish newspapers. Because of this remarkable demonstration of loyalty and faithfulness, I can correctly claim that at least one-fifth of my original staff that started the West African Pilot had followed me from Accra, either as former employees or as admirers who were willing to join the crusade for the mental emancipation of Africa*[67]

Interestingly, on his return, in his role as the Igbo champion, Azikiwe chose to join the Nigerian Youth Movement rather than to set up his own group. That by October 1940 he was being summoned by the group to a disciplinary hearing, on charges of violations of the group's fundamental ideals, suggests that he joined the group to break it up. By this time the restraining influence of Odeziaku who had preached 'the brotherhood of man" and "our oneness, our identity.... Our common humanity'[68] on Azikiwe was no more.

Even though members of the organisation persuaded Azikiwe to withdraw the resignation from the group which he had tendered in protest at the hearing, the damage had been done. On 20 February 1941, he used the medium of his West African Pilot to announce his resignation from the Nigerian Youth Movement[69] thereby signalling a formal parting of ways between East and West amongst the nationalists.

In the aftermath of the fallout amongst the nationalists within the NYM, in 1942, H.O. Davies accepted a job, as Marketing Officer, with the colonial government which the NYM had been at the vanguard of campaigning against. In 1943 Azikwe signalled the formal end of the nationalists consensus and the beginning of ethnic-based political associations when he launched the Igbo Federal Union with himself as its President[70].Obafemi Awolowo responded to the development by forming Egbe Omo

Oduduwa in London in 1945.

These developments effectively marked the death of the NYM. An attempt to revive the organisation as a 'Joint Council' under the leadership of the elder statesman Herbert Macaulay, so as to form a united front amongst the nationalists to negotiate a post-war deal with the colonial authorities was again frustrated by Azikiwe's intervention:

> ...the Joint Council was formed, and the parties agreed to share representation on the Legislative Council and on the Lagos Town Council...In September [1943] – one month after Azikiwe, dejected and embittered, returned from England – Macaulay resigned from the Joint Council. This ended the first effort to achieve a national front[71]

The Nigeria Youth Movement died a complete death when Davies and Awolowo both left Nigeria in 1944 to study law in England, returning in 1947 and 1948 respectively. The stage was left to Azikiwe who, in the same year 1944, moved to establish the National Council of Nigeria and the Cameroons (NCNC) as the main political voice of nationalism with Herbert Macaulay, then age eighty, as President of the party. The appointment was shrewd as two years later, on 7 May 1946, the old voice of Lagos politics died while on a tour of the country with the NCNC. His funeral in Lagos "was the largest in Nigerian history, with more than 100,000 in attendance"[72]. With Azikiwe delivering the eulogy personally, and then succeeding him as President of the NCNC, the legacy of Macaulay's Lagos political base was firmly in NCNC hands. The Macaulay legacy coupled with the special situation of Lagos being part of Yorubaland but also, as the national capital, being populated by many from other Regions now gave the NCNC a credible foothold in Lagos.

Nevertheless, Azikiwe did, with British help, deliver on his primary mission of arousing and inspiring the Igbos into competition with the Yoruba:

> Village improvement unions sponsored scholarships, and Ibo students flocked to secondary schools in what is now the Western Region. By the late 1930s the Ibos were more heavily represented than any other tribe or nationality in Yaba Higher College and in most Nigerian secondary schools. Thenceforward the number of Ibos appointed to the African civil service and as clerks in business firms increased at a faster rate than that of any other group. By 1945 the gap between Yorubas and Ibos was virtually closed. Increasing numbers of Ibo barristers and doctors began to arrive from England. By 1952 the number of Ibos (115) enrolled at University College, Ibadan, was nearly equal to the number of Yorubas (118)[73]

But, the effort came at a cost in East-West relations which worsened progressively. By the summer of 1948, when Awolowo returned from his law studies in London, the new rivalry was bordering on conflict:

> We were bunched together by the British who named us Nigeria. We never
> knew the Ibos, but since we came to know them we have tried to be friendly and
> neighbourly. Then came the Arch Devil to sow the seeds of distrust and hatred....
> We have tolerated enough from a class of Ibos and addle-brained Yorubas who
> have mortgaged their thinking caps to Azikiwe and his hirelings[74]

The rejoinder from the Igbos, through Azikiwe's West African Pilot, was no less gutural:

> Henceforth, the cry must be one of battle against Egbe Omo Oduduwa, its leaders
> at home and abroad, uphill and down dale in the streets of Nigeria and in the
> residences of its advocates...It is the enemy of Nigeria; it must be crushed to the
> earth...There is no going back, until the Fascist Organization of Sir Adeyemo
> has been dismembered[75]

The climax of Azikiwe's hubris was in his1949 address following his election as President
of the Igbo State Union:

> ...it would appear that the God of Africa has specially created the Ibo nation to
> lead the children of Africa from bondage of the ages...The martial prowess of the
> Ibo nation at all stages of human history has enabled them not only to conquer
> others but also to adapt themselves to the role of preserver....The Ibo nation
> cannot shirk its responsibility...[76]

The South would never again be united under a single political umbrella.

PROMOTING UNITY IN THE NORTH

If Bourdillon's handiwork in stirring up ethnic rivalry and political competition between
the Igbos and the Yoruba has to be inferred and deduced from events and circumstances,
what he did to build political unity in the North, and to play the thus-united northern
team against the now-divided South, is a matter of written confession by the man on the
ground who made it all happen, Sir Bryan Sharwood-Smith, the Lieutenant-Governor
of Northern Nigeria up to independence.

In his 1970 memoir. 'But Always as Friends: Northern Nigeria and the Cameroons
1921-1957', Sharwood-Smith gives a comprehensive account of the evolution of the
British relationship with the North, 'First as Masters', 'Then as Leaders', 'Finally as
Partners':

In the Britain of 1951, the Northern Region of Nigeria was little but a name. Nigeria, to the interested, was the Nigeria of the South with its eloquent political leaders, its clamant press, its academic links with the United Kingdom, its university graduates, and its student unions. The North, to the few who were aware of its existence, was still a stagnant backwater, quaintly feudal or incorrigibly archaic according to the viewpoint of the individual. Few in Britain seemed to realize that in the crucible of nationalist politics a new North had been born and that its leaders now faced a challenge so daunting that they needed all the sympathy and encouragement they could get. For public opinion in Britain to refuse that sympathy, either out of ignorance or from political bigotry, seemed to us to be morally wrong. It would also be politically stupid. There were Muslim states and communities in other parts of Africa, Egypt for instance, whose attitude toward all we in Britain stood for was the reverse of friendly. Why make them a present of the good will, now ours, to help them further policies that would not, at this stage, benefit the peoples for whom we are still responsible? Why also risk Nigerian unity by antagonizing the more stable and more administratively experienced half of the country?[77]

The lessons from India in the aftermath of the First World War had been well learnt, not least that excluding the educated natives from the administration of the country was a policy with a limited shelf-life. The only way to avoid the country coming under the control of the much-feared and despised nationalists was to abandon the policy of screening the North from political interaction with the South. However, that policy having been the orthodoxy for so long, special effort was going to be required, first to persuade the northern leaders to buy into the need for engagement with the South and, beyond that to avoid southern rule.

As had been done with Azikiwe and the Igbos, the plan was to fast-track the North's preparation to meet the challenge by using the fear of southern domination as their spur to action. It was this policy that, ultimately, led to the military coups of 1966 and the Biafran War.

THE ROUSING OF THE NORTH

As with the disunity of the South, the real groundwork for the Bourdillon plan for building unity in the North began in 1939 when the Barewa College Old Boys Association met in Kaduna and began to espouse the idea of "one north"[78]. Also, Bourdillon's biographer noted that his policy in the North took on a new urgency and directness as from 1942:

Bourdillon told his officers bluntly that the Emirs would have to be 'democratised' and a place found for educated Africans in northern native administration, for the next few years were likely to be of 'supreme importance in the political history of this country'.

Bourdillon had at last taken off the kid-gloves he had been using since 1937. Why had he changed his attitude, and why indeed had he taken so long to do so? There are several answers[79]

In suggesting answers to these questions, the biographer omitted the most important which was that the timelines that Bourdillon had been working to, had to be radically shortened following the publication of the Atlantic Charter in August 1941 and the loss of Singapore and Malaya to the Japanese in the Spring of 1942. These events, combined with the weakening grip on India, made the thinking on Nigeria more critical.

The new note of urgency manifested in Bourdillon's publication of 'A Further Memorandum on the Future Political Development of Nigeria[80] in October 1942 which followed a tour of the North that Bourdillon embarked upon to solicit the views of the British colonial officers in the region about how the North could be effectively unified with the South without the nationalists taking control:

> *It was about this time that Sir Bernard Bourdillon, when on tour in the North, invited senior Administrative Officers to set out, quite informally and with complete frankness, what their personal views were on the future political development of Nigeria. He especially wished to know what we thought could be done to break the isolationist attitude of the North and make it one with Nigeria as a whole. Among other points that he made was his conviction that it was high time that Nigerians were admitted to the Administrative Service. What would be the attitude of the chiefs to such a step?*
>
> *My own personal reaction to the general question, I remember was that there was no point in arguing that the North and South wee interdependent economically and politically. Still less was it any use telling the Northern chiefs and people that if they wanted to preserve their own traditional way of life they must accept the South and learn to meet it on reasonably equal terms, instead of pretending that it did not exist. Logic had no part in the problem. Nothing short of a biological shock, such as, maybe, the introduction of a few Southern D.O.'s would persuade them of the danger.*
>
> *Sir Bernard Bourdillon's conclusions, formed as the result of these inquiries, pursued throughout Nigeria, would pave the way to the major constitutional changes which would be introduced two years later by his successor Sir Arthur Richards....And it was to be these changes, or rather the invasion of the North*

by Southern politicians in reaction to them, that were to produce the biological shock that was so much needed[81]

BRYAN SHARWOOD-SMITH

What was intended to be the final solution to the problem of how to keep Nigeria out of the hands of the educated natives was a plan to groom and produce a new class of educated elite in the North who would provide the essential link between Lugard's Native Authority system and the future national parliament. This new class who were to bridge the past with the present were the sons of the Emirs and the Sultans.

Since Barewa College had been established precisely for the purpose of promoting northern unity by educating the sons of the elite from across the North in the one school, the exercise was a relatively easy one. The one likely obstacle to the implementation of Bourdillon's plan, Theodore Adams, had been taken care off with the award of a knighthood in 1942[82] before leaving Nigeria in March 1943 destined for retirement.[83] The way was now clear for Bryan Sharwood-Smith to rouse the North for political engagement with the South.

Although his father was a parson's son and his mother was the daughter of a vicar, the high point of Sharwood-Smith's career was to be the strengthening of the Islamic North against the Christian South. After military service in the First World War, in France and India, he chose to join the Colonial Service, in preference to going to Cambridge, where he quickly moved from District Officer to Governor of Northern Nigeria. Having arrived in Nigeria in January 1921, he only, finally, left the country in September 1957. Fluent in Hausa and with competent Fulani, he was the most trusted adviser of the Northern political leadership.

Sharwood-Smith knew the thinking of the northern leaders: that, left to themselves, they had no appetite for a unified Nigeria; that, within a united Nigeria, their only concern was to protect what they had and to avoid domination by the more educated South; but that if the South was seen to be moving to threaten their isolation they would be forced to react. The NCNC's fundraising rallies in the North, ahead of its mission to London, were just the opportunity that Sharwood-Smith was looking to exploit:

> *Southern politicians were to be heard for the first time in the market places of the North, or at least in the market places of those towns that had large settlements of Ibo and Yoruba and other Southern tribes. And the Northern leaders were not to relish the experience, which more than anything else cured them of any surviving illusions that they could continue to ignore the world around them.*
> *...All in all, the NCNC delegation had done the North, and Nigeria as a whole, a*

great service. The years of apathy were now ended, and though at the time the contrary seemed the case, the road to a united Nigeria lay at last open[84]

What remained was to put together the Northern team that was to be played against the Southern leaders. Sharwood-Smith was responsible for the recruitment exercise.

AHMADU BELLO

Ahmadu Bello's lineage traced directly back to the Fulani conquest of Hausaland little more than a century before his birth in 1910. His great-grandfather, Sultan Bello, was one of the two sons of Uthman dan Fodio, the leader of the jihad.

Just a few years before Bello's birth, the British had invaded and conquered the Sokoto Empire. His uncle, the Sarkin Musulmi (Commander of the Faithful) of Sokoto, Mohammed Attahiru I, had been killed in battle after refusing to come under British rule. His successor, Mohammed Attahiru II, was more amenable and Bello was of similar persuasion:

> *Whatever the rights and wrongs of the attack on Kano and Sokoto may be, the British were the instrument of destiny and were fulfilling the will of God. In their way they did it well. Even at the actual time there was no ill-will after the occupation[85]*

Ahmadu Bello, as the descendant of those who had established the Fulani Empire within the Nigeria space, was an obvious choice as leader of the Northern team. His father, who had worked as a District Head in the system of Native administration then prevailing in the North, died when he was six but his upbringing was nevertheless comfortable within the extended family network.

Schools on the western models prevailing in the South being unknown then in his village, pre-school education took the conventional form of instruction in Arabic and the study of the Koran.[86] At the age of ten he went to Secondary school before attending Barewa College to train as a teacher. A keen sportsman, he enjoyed the English pastimes of cricket and Eton Fives. In common with others from the North, who emerged from Barewa College, he started life as a teacher before, in 1934, being appointed District Head of his home district of Rabah.

Bello was a reluctant recruit to the Nigerian political scene. The death of the reigning Sultan, in 1938, had, momentarily, raised the prospect that he would fulfil his personal ambition of becoming the next Sultan. Alas, the development coincided with the roll-out of Bourdillon's plan for the North in which had been scripted to occupy a different office.

Ever since the British conquest of the Sokoto empire, although the responsibility for choosing the new Sultan, and Emirs, rested with the Traditional Selectors, their choice was subject to the veto of the chief representative of the British Government in the North, who at this time was Sharwood-Smith. It was the British who had, in fact, introduced the title "Sultan", as they had done with the "Alake" in Egbaland, to establish a clear hierarchy within the community of chiefs.[87]

The two main candidates for the Sultanate were Bello and the Sardauna Abubakar with Bello being the popular choice only for his selection to be trumped by British action:

> *At this point, many apocryphal stories arise as to what happened. One of the most recurrent is that the Selection Council recommended Ahmadu, but when the decision was taken to the Resident (John Carrow), he insisted that the succession, as of right, ought to go to the "son" of the Sultan. The council argued that Abubakar was not really the "son" of the Sultan, but his nephew. The Resident replied, with certainty, that he had often heard the Sultan refer to Abubakar as his son, and that as his son he was entitled to the succession*
> *Abubakar III was selected as Sultan, and within a short period of time, his title of "Sardauna" is given to the runner up, Ahmadu who, for all practical purposes, then becomes known as...Ahmadu, Sardauna of Sokoto[88]*

The British intervention changed the destiny of the two contenders: Abubakar would live a long life as Sultan while Ahmadu Bello, the new Sardauna, would live a short dramatic life as premier of the North.

As part of the preparation for his role, in 1948 the British Council arranged for him to visit England, for a short course in local government. In contrast with the experience of the nationalists in the South who had to fend for themselves while abroad, arrangements had been put in place for him to stay in the home of an English family while attending the course[89]. In several other respects his path to his destiny was cleared for him by decisive interventions by Sharwood-Smith.

The personal relationship between Ahmadu Bello and the new Sultan, Abubakar, was never good and was worsened by the fact that one of the first acts of the new Sultan was to sentence Bello to a term of imprisonment for one year following a conviction by the Sultan's court on charges of embezzlement which he was only spared from serving on appeal to the British[90]. The hostile relationship between the two leaders meant that in steering Bello through to his appointed political destiny Sharwood-Smith often had to force the issue:

> *The Sardauna was regarded as a "pushful prince, popular and generous, with lots of trouble with the Sultan". When Waziri Abbas died, Sardauna wanted his seat in the House of Assembly, and was nominated by Sir Eric Thompstone,*

*then Governor of Northern Nigeria. The Sultan refused to accept the Sardauna
as a nominee by show of hands at the electoral college. The Sardauna sent Abba
Jiddum Gana a note saying that the Sultan did not want him to have the seat.
Abba Jiddum Gana went to Captain Money, who took him to the Governor, and
put the case to him. The Governor then telephoned Sokoto and asked the Senior
Resident (Sharwood-Smith) to intervene. This was done and Sharwood-Smith told
the Sultan to stop blocking the Sardauna, because he was western educated....*[91]

When it came to party formation also, Bello's experience was very different from that of
Awolowo, in the West, with the Action Group and Azikiwe, in the East, with the NCNC.
The Northern Peoples Congress (NPC), when it was formed on 1 October 1951, was not
his brainchild but, by 1954, he had emerged as the leader of the party. Again, this was
largely due to behind-the-scenes work by Sharwood-Smith.

Like Azikiwe in the East, being one of the first of a new generation to be trained in
Western ways, the role that had been mapped out for Bello was to be the champion of
his people. At the headline level, at least, this was to be all the people of the North and
only indirectly his Fulani people. The ground for his Northern unification drive had
been prepared well ahead of him with the creation, in 1922, by Governor Hugh Clifford
of what was to become Barewa College as a school through which all the leading political
figures from the North would pass.[92] In keeping with Bourdillon's masterplan, the old
boys association of Barewa College is reported to have started espousing the 'One North'
ideology in 1939.[93]

Bello's outlook for Nigeria was wholly shaped by this 'One North' vision. His priority
was to screen the North from Southern influence and control, the fear of which had been
instilled in him and his colleagues by Sharwood-Smith and the Colonial Office. As a
result, he wanted as little as possible to do with the South and, at times, veered towards
complete separation of the North from the South.

The closeness of his working relationship with Sharwood-Smith, and the
understanding between the Fulani leadership and the British dictated that his position
on Independence differed greatly from the nationalists':

> *...we were never militant 'nationalists' as some were. We were sure that in God's
> good time we would get the power. The British had promised this frequently and
> we were content to rest on these promises....*[94]

TAFAWA BALEWA

If 'One North' was to have meaning it meant that all sections of the North had to be
brought within the NPC fold under the leadership of the Sardauna. It was a task only

British authority could bring about. The manner in which Sharwood-Smith went about it varied with the territory.

In Bauchi, the man who Sharwood-Smith and his team had identified to partner with Bello was Abubakar Tafawa Balewa, a product of Barewa College. In common with many of the leaders in the North, Balewa was a teacher. He had been selected to represent Bauchi in the Northern House of Assembly and had joined the NPC at the same time with the Sardauna. Indeed, the accounts suggest that he was the popular choice to be leader of the NPC if only to check the influence of Sharwood-Smith but, on receiving reports to this effect on the eve of the party's convention in Jos in 1954, he is reported to have renounced the leadership in favour of Bello[95]. That the decision was influenced by Sharwood-Smith and his team can be deduced from another account:

> *The Jos Convention was perplexing because Balewa was the choice of many. Yet Kano lorries came, which supported the Sardauna, and Borno supported the Sardauna wholeheartedly. In fact, Borno/Kano/Sokoto/Zaria supported the Sardauna, and the Sardauna even had some supporters from Bauchi. Balewa's support came from Adamawa and Bauchi. Balewa was younger than the Sardauna and was very charismatic. But many supporters came from the NAs and they supported the Sardauna[96]*

This was how, in the North, Ahmadu Bello, from the North-West and Tafawa Balewa from the North-East were able to work together under a single political umbrella covering the whole of the North, while in the South, Awolowo from the West and Azikiwe from the East ended up forming rival political parties. Awolowo and Azikiwe were both devout Christians just as the Sardauna and Balewa were devout Muslims. The distance from Awolowo's home town in Ijebu-Remo to Azikiwe's hometown in Onitsha was far shorter than the distance from the Sardauna's Sokoto to Balewa's Bauchi. The fault and credit lay not in the individual actors but with Bourdillon and his team who devised and implemented the policy of promoting "One North" while at the same time creating a divided South.

The political unity of the North was made all the stronger by the clear line of authority in the power relationship that existed between Ahmadu Bello as the Premier of the Northern Region and Tafawa Balewa as the Prime Minister of the Nigerian Federation which appears in the biography of H.O. Davies:

> *I remember when we were in front of the Sardauna's house when the Sardauna was not yet in the lounge, we all including the Prime Minister, had to wait in front of the door. When the Sardauna arrived in the lounge and had taken his seat, the door was opened for us to go in. I observed that the Prime Minister took off his shoes before he entered and naturally all of us had to do the same. When we got*

in, the Sardauna was sitting on the chair and the Prime Minister, on entering, sat on the floor in front of the Sardauna. We all had to do the same or kneel down[97]

THE ADAMAWA FULANI, THE KANURI AND THE MIDDLE BELT PEOPLES

Adamawa and Bornu presented a very different challenge to Sharwood-Smith's quest to bring the whole of the North under Bello's leadership. Forceful action was required:

> *The time had now come for drastic action in two specific administrations, both headed by powerful chiefs, where corruption and misrule had become a public scandal. Indeed, all chiefs must be made to realize that great changes lay ahead and they must adapt themselves to those changes. The two administrations in question were those of Adamawa and Bornu. Such matters were my personal responsibility, and it was to Adamawa that I went first* [98]

It was back to the Lugard pacification tactics of old as Sharwood-Smith gave the Lamido in Adamawa a straightforward choice between accepting retirement to another Emirate on a pension – effectively exile – or being forcibly deposed. The Lamido in Adamawa chose retirement. The Shehu of Bornu was not so easy.

It will be recalled that Bornu had been brought into the Empire by acquisition from France rather than through conquest by Lugard as with the rest of the North. This and the distinct Kanuri language had compelled the British to settle for a light grip on the territory. It was very different from the intimate relationship they had with the Fulani.

The Kanuri people, having driven the Fulani out of Bornu when Uthman dan Fodio had attempted to carry his jihad into their land, were never going to willingly accept coming under Fulani leadership through the person of Bello. Only with a show of British military readiness to force the situation, and with Sharwood-Smith sitting by his side, did the Shehu of Bornu give in to the changes insisted upon[99].

As for the non-Muslim peoples of the Middle Belt, in Jos, Benue and Niger, Sharwood-Smith adopted a more diplomatic approach by impressing upon the leadership of the NPC the imperative of giving key players from these regions a role on the Executive Council of the party. Ahmadu Bello's appointment as Premier of the Northern Region in 1954 gave him the platform and authority with which, with the guidance and assistance of Sharwood-Smith, he was able to make the necessary changes in leadership across the North:

> *The number of successions to traditional leadership which occurred between the time Sardauna becomes Premier in 1954 and Independence in 1960 is considerable...during the same period (1954-1960) a number of Chiefs are deposed, abdicate or voluntarily "resign"...the general pattern is for*

appointments to be made of younger, western-educated men, or of men who have allied themselves with the Sardauna in one way or another[100]

AMINU KANO

One Northerner who was not selected by Sharwood-Smith, and who was therefore less amenable to his plan, was Aminu Kano. Despite having been colleagues with Balewa at Barewa College and the University of London's Institute of Education, he pursued a political path which took him into collaboration with Nnamdi Azikiwe.

Aminu Kano had been a member of the Arewa organisation out of which the NPC was born, alongside Balewa and Bello, before breaking away to form the Northern Elements Progressive Union (NEPU) as the first political organisation in Northern Nigeria, on 8 August 1950. The break was ideological: He, and other young Northerners, wanted to dismantle the feudal order which NPC was bent upon preserving. This socialist, class-based ideology marked NEPU as a threat to the 'One North' agenda. It manifested in NEPU standing in opposition to NPC's 'North first' outlook and in Aminu Kano lining up with Azikiwe and his 'One Nigeria' position.

The intrinsic appeal of NEPU's reform agenda for the North was obvious. It was only inconvenient to the British plans. The moral dilemma for those responsible for implementing the policy was revealed by Sharwood-Smith himself:

> *I had always been a fervent believer in the Lugard doctrine and in the part that the chiefs of the North must play in the administration of the country, but I had always instinctively felt, also, that it was wrong that they should be forever sacrosanct in their persons and that the system that they represented should remain inviolate for all time. Surely neither common justice nor sane politics could permit the continuation in office of men in whose name, or at whose instance, the poor and helpless were oppressed. Yet, to take just one example, there was a chief in Niger Province who represented all that seemed to me objectionable in a ruler. As a judge he was venal, as an administrator he was extortionate, his word was valueless, and his fingers were forever sticky with other men's honey. His people disliked and despised him, yet he would not change. It seemed that no other course remained short of deposition. But when I made my case to my Chief Commissioner, he replied, "What, Sharwood Smith! Depose a Second-Class Chief? Heav'n forfend!" So other and less effective means had to be sought to contain his cupidity and spare his subjects distress*[101]

The key political actors in the North and in the South having emerged or been selected, the race for power at independence was set to begin with the British as the umpires of the contest.

7. The Independence Show

Mr Lennox- Boyd's success is due to his real affection for the colonies and to an infinite capacity for taking pains. It has also been due to a cheerful willingness to discard, where need be, the conventions of Whitehall.

British Prime Minister Anthony Eden

THE IGBO CHALLENGE

A number of factors combined to ensure that, despite the relationship with Azikiwe, his Igbo people were going to pose the biggest problem for the Colonial Office plan for the continuation of colonial rule in Nigeria.

To begin with, they were democrats by habit lacking the tradition of rule by chiefs or by Emirs. The system of indirect rule through traditional rulers, which the Colonial Office favoured, had been impossible to apply to them. The attempt to install a system of rule by Warrant Chiefs created by Colonial Office had failed after the women's uprising of 1929. To compound matters, Azikiwe's hold on the people was of recent manufacture and did not run deep. Added to this was the fact that British interaction with the Igbos, situated as they were in the eastern hinterland, was relatively recent compared with the longer trading experience with the coastal communities in the South.

The third, and most significant, factor was a bi-product of the action which the strategists in the Colonial Office had taken to fast-track the Igbos to compete with the Yoruba in the field of education. With no traditional rulers in Igboland to temper the demands of the young educated Igbos, the relationship between the Colonial government and the Eastern Region became increasingly difficult and heated. In their grand-planning to check and contain the power and influence of the first group of educated natives from the south-west, the British strategists had created a new group of educated natives in the south-east.

Azikiwe himself was far from dependable. He was often torn between his instincts as an anti-colonial campaigner born of his education and American experience and the bond that he had struck to work with the British. The colonial government's plans for self-government after the war was a theme that he had visited previously in his *Pilot* newspaper. He returned to the issue more directly in the edition of 14 November 1940:

> *Are Nigerians fighting to maintain the status quo or are they... to expect a new world order after this sacrifice is over? We want the Governor to tell us...*[1]

This was, of course, the same question that the American President Franklin Delano Roosevelt was asking of British Prime Minister Winston Churchill in the negotiations which were on-going between them over America's entry into the Second World War and over the terms of the Atlantic Charter. The answer that came back from the Governor in a speech in December 1940 was unyielding:

> *The correct but perhaps rather brutal answer would be that it is unusual for a man to expect a reward for failing to cut his own throat*[2]

With this answer, the Bourdillon mask had slipped. The rebuff, followed by the publication of the Atlantic Charter on 14 August 1941, was to signal a hardening of the relationship between the nationalists and the colonial government.

GOVERNOR ARTHUR RICHARDS

In character and style, Governor Richards' appointment was the colonial government's response to the changing relationship with the nationalists now that the empire had come through the attack by Hitler's Germany and outlived the champion of decolonisation, U.S. President Roosevelt. It was an attempt to reassert the authority of the Empire. The days of the warm and personal style of Bourdillon were over; it was now to be a matter of hard talking on both sides.

When Bourdillon had first set out for Nigeria, from Liverpool, back in October 1935, his companion on the ship was Sir Arthur Richards who was then the Governor of the Gambia.[3] While Bourdillon had prepared the ground for the injection of 'regionalism' into the nascent politics of Nigeria it was Richards, with the help of Bourdillon's parting gift, 'A Final Memorandum on the Constitutional Future of Nigeria', published in August 1943,[4] who concretized it by converting what were regional centres of administration into political units. Richards found further assistance from Lord Lugard, now age eighty-five but still keen to offer advice to the new Governor on 'Nigeria and its progress'.[5]

The new Constitution which Richards introduced in 1946 ran into difficulty much sooner than the British had expected. Whilst offering the trappings of democracy by establishing an embryo parliament in the form of a new all-Nigeria Legislative Council, the separate Houses of Assembly for each of the three regions - with a House of Chiefs in the North alone – it was built upon the defective foundations of the skewed regionalism that Bourdillon had introduced. Precisely because it had been designed to minimise the influence of the educated natives, it had been imposed without any consultation:

> *Yes Sir Bernard did have criticisms to make, and in particular that Nigerians had not been consulted enough or given sufficient opportunity to discuss the proposals. The new scheme was hastily rushed through the LegCo, local opinion was not sounded, and such an ex cathedra imposition of reforms was a maladroit example of the way a colonial government should not behave. It is scarcely surprising that Nigerian nationalists had similar criticisms to make about the way their constitution had been thrust upon them[6]*

Even though they had no law-making powers - their role being confined to deliberation and advice on legislative proposals from the Legislative Council - still the composition of the Regional Houses of Assembly left little room for the truly unofficial voices to be heard. In the Western House of Assembly for example, where the educated natives were most vocal, the closest the Assembly came to having representatives of the people were the seven to eleven members who were selected by the Native Authority from amongst their number. But since the Native Authority was effectively made up of traditional rulers, this was no representation at all.[7] With the balance of official and unofficial members being replicated in the Legislative Council (21:28), and with the unofficial members being drawn from membership of the Regional Houses of Assembly, this arrangement where there would be representative government but not by way of direct elections was never going to satisfy the nationalists:

> *Nationalists...strongly resented the system of election provided for in the Richards proposals. No change was made in the number of Legislative Council members elected directly by Nigerians. Only the people of Lagos and Calabar were given the opportunity to elect representatives directly to the Legislative Council, a privilege they had exercised since 1923. All other representatives were to be elected indirectly through the native authorities[8]*

As if the Richard's Constitution was not provocation enough for the Nationalists, the colonial government went further, in 1945, to pass a number of insensitive new laws. In one, it reserved to itself the power to remove traditional rulers.[9] In the circumstances where these traditional rulers had been brought into the political stream to control and contain the embers of radicalism in the first place, to go further to vest in the colonial government power to depose and appoint them as it pleased, such that they held their status and office at the sufferance of the Governor, was a step back rather than a step forward towards self-government. Another law proclaimed all land as belonging to the Imperial government exclusively[10] while yet another vested all mineral resources in the country in the same body:

> The entire property in and control of all minerals, and mineral oils, in, under, or upon any lands in Nigeria, and of all rivers, streams and water courses throughout Nigeria, is and shall be vested in the Crown[11]

For the nationalists who had been expecting rapid political changes towards self-government in recognition of the country's sacrifices in men and materials for the British war effort, these new laws suggested that the Imperial hold was being tightened rather than loosened. This was all the provocation they needed to rally the people to their cause. A general strike was called in June 1945 led by the trade union leader Michael Imodu with Azikiwe's papers providing strong support.[12]

The Richards government reacted by banning two of Azikiwe's Lagos Newspapers, *West African Pilot* and Daily Comet on 8 July 1945. The ban only served to further enhance Azikiwe's reputation amongst the young Igbos, and in the country at large, as the champion of the fight against colonialism. A master of the media arts in his own right, Azikiwe now mobilized an international campaign based on allegations of plans to assassinate him.[13] Borrowing from an initiative that he had seen used to good effect during his time in Accra, he decided to take the battle to the streets of London and to the editorial pages of Fleet Street. To fund the mission the NCNC had first organised a fund-raising tour of Nigeria:

> In June 1947, the long-awaited NCNC delegation to London left Lagos to lodge a formal protest with the Secretary of State for the Colonies, having, as they claimed, a mandate from the people. The delegation was reputedly "national", for it was composed of the following persons: Nnamdi Azikiwe (Ibo), Adeleke Adedoyin (Ijebu Yoruba), Dr Abu Bakr Olorun –Nimber (Ilorin Yoruba), Mallam Bukar Dipcharima (Hausa), Chief Nyong Essien (Ibibio), P.M. Kale (Bakweri Cameroonian) and Mrs. Funmilayo Ransome-Kuti (Yoruba)[14]

The political situation had reached a new crossroads. The disaffection felt by the nationalists with the Richards constitution could no longer be ignored. In 1947, with its hold on its Indian empire slipping, Britain could not afford for Nigeria, its biggest colony in Africa, to go the same way.

GOVERNOR JOHN MCPHERSON

On 5 February 1948, Sir John McPherson replaced Arthur Richards as Governor of Nigeria. McPherson was no stranger to the issues. From 1937-1939 he had served as Principal Assistant Secretary for Nigeria and, in that capacity, would have been a key aide to Bourdillon at the time he prepared his First and Second Memoranda.

Under McPherson, there was an acceptance that the policy of shutting the educated natives out of the administration of the country's affairs had failed. The strategy now was to contain their influence. In May1948 a Nigerianization Commission was established to make recommendations for the active recruitment and training of Nigerians for the responsibilities which lay ahead with self-government. Three months later, in August 1948, McPherson announced proposals to conduct a detailed review of the hated Richard's Constitution. Ahead of the new constitutional changes there was to be full consultation by way of a national conference:

> ..... a series of conferences [were to] be held, first at village and divisional level, and then at provincial level, when the various Provincial Conferences would make recommendations to be considered by Regional Conferences....The views of the four Regional Conferences were then to be considered by a Drafting Committee, ... and then a General Conference, and the resolutions of this Conference would then be debated in the Regional Houses and by the Legislative Council before being submitted to the Governor and the Secretary of State for the Colonies[15]

But retreat by the colonial government was not surrender. Every concession to the nationalists was offset by a forward measure towards McMillan's vision of a 'Third British Empire' which was to be realised by granting Independence on Britain's terms; to retain influence after power may have gone.

In the meantime, Azikiwe's speeches became increasingly strident in tone borrowing from his experience from America to stoke the passions of his young followers:

> The people of Nigeria cannot continue to accept as their destiny the denial of human rights. We, too, have a right to live, to enjoy freedom, and to pursue happiness like other human beings. Let us reinforce our rank and file in the fight for freedom, no longer suffering in silence and whining like a helpless dog, but striking back with all the force at our command when we are struck, preferring

to suffer the consequences of pressing forward our claim to a legacy of freedom, than to surrender our heritage to despoilers and usurpers. Be of good cheer, my compatriots...Freedom is within our grasp. Shall we let it slip away? Shall we relapse into the dungeon of fear and the servitude of hesitation? Let us no longer quake or doubt about our capacity to enter into our rightful heritage. Why not deal one blow in a gamble for national liberty? Let there be no mistake about our future. We are determined to discard the yoke of oppression. We shall be free. History is on our side. In this hour of national peril, Nigeria expects every patriot to stand firm in the cause of justice and righteousness. God knows we hate none but we love our country. Long live Nigeria and the Cameroons[16]

THE IVA VALLEY MASSACRE

The Zikist Movement was a movement of Igbo youths in the main who were dedicated to Azikiwe's narrative of struggle against the imperial government but impatient with his methods. Formed shortly after the end of the war, in 1946, they found more inspiration in the tactics of Ghandi's India.

Before the, belated, announcement of the discovery of oil in 1956, coal was the chief energy export from Nigeria. Iva Valley coal mine, in the suburbs of the city of Enugu had been in operation since 1917. Its contribution to the British war effort in both the First and Second World Wars had been significant. In late 1949 the miners at the mine decided to take industrial action to protest over pay. The management of the colliery called in the police to deal with the striking miners. When the British officer commanding the force directed the police to open fire, twenty-one miners were killed and fifty-one were wounded. The Zikist Movement was provoked into violent reaction.

In April 1950, the Movement was outlawed after a police raid on the homes of the members following an assassination attempt on the Chief Secretary to the government. The rising tone of the defiance is illustrated by the speech made at the trial of one of the accused:

> *Later during his trial, the secretary of the movement, a twenty-four-year-old ex-serviceman, defied the judge in these terms*
> *"...with the immense resources and the coercive state machinery behind you and the Government you represent, I do not as a Zikist recognize the right of this court to try this case...You are a symbol of that imperialist machine which I and my colleagues abhor; therefore I am not pleading before this court..."[17]*

Azikiwe's stirring rhetoric had been the inspiration for the young radicals. However, when crisis came he quickly retreated:

In 1950, more Zikists were gaoled, and the Movement proscribed. Most painful of all, Azikiwe repudiated the Movement which bore his name, and even went to the lengths of ridiculing its imprisoned members. Raji Abdallah, lampooned in the Pilot, resigned from the NCNC. Okoye remembered with undiminished bitterness, in later years:

Dr Azikiwe's denial of the Zikists before the Cock crowed [thrice] is painful but understandable. After preaching a revolution for a decade he....was terrified when he saw one...Prudence without courage is mean, without loyalty weak[18]

With Azikiwe's repudiation, the Zikist Movement, which had been inspired by him, died a death, never to recover, just as the Nigerian Youth Movement had done before it.

THE NATIONAL CONFERENCE OF 1950

But the twenty-one miners killed at the Enugu coal-mine did not die in vain. The incident served to animate the nationalist campaign and to unify the groups as never before. They combined to form a National Emergency Committee which used the incident to give a more aggressive push for Independence: "not self-government in seven years' time as originally conceived, but self-government now"[19]. The colonial government needed to do something to take the steam out of the growing radicalism of the Eastern Region. To draw Azikiwe and his NCNC organisation closer they made him a member of the new Nigerianization Commission.[20]

This Iva Valley massacre coming, as it did, on the back of the international profile that the NCNC London mission to the Colonial Secretary had generated for the nationalist cause, was to be the last attempt by the colonial government to control the rising tide of nationalism by force of arms. The forceful action taken against the Zikist movement was counter-balanced by arrangements for the national conference which McPherson had set into motion in 1949 by way of regional conferences and which climaxed in a final general conference held in Ibadan in January 1950.[21] The constitutional consultation exercise in the Eastern Region was especially sensitive:

The significant feature of the 1948 reforms in the east, however, was the scrupulous manner in which the government avoided giving the impression that the new system was being imposed upon the people. An all-African select committee of the Eastern House of Assembly toured the entire Eastern Region and conferred with native authority councils and tribal unions, as well as with prominent nationalists....By the end of 1949, the people of the Eastern Region (and to a lesser extent elsewhere) were so thoroughly involved in discussions about their political and economic future -local government reform, constitutional revision, and development planning- that even the most militant nationalist had difficulty in finding an issue or an audience[22]

With the goal of Independence now firmly in view the discourse became focused upon the form that self-government in Nigeria should take. It was one thing for Nigerians to unite against colonial rule, but how far should that unity go in the context of self-rule? The position taken by each region on the issue was dictated by the party leaders.

THE SOUTH WEST POSITION

In the Western Region and nationally, the Yoruba leader Obafemi Awolowo, was beginning to make his presence felt. For him there was a structural failing in the idea of a united Nigeria and he saw the amalgamation of 1914 as a fundamental obstacle to the country's viability:

> *Since the amalgamation (of Northern and Southern Protectorates of Nigeria) all the efforts of the British Government have been devoted to developing the country into a unitary state. This is patently impossible*[23]

His vision was for a united Yorubaland 'within the Federal State of Nigeria'. He saw the three-region structure introduced by the Richard's Constitution, not as the first step towards a unitary state as the British saw it but, as the first step towards a true federal system in which 'each group, however small, is entitled to the same treatment as any other group, however large...opportunity must be afforded to each to evolve its own peculiar political institution'.

THE NORTH'S POSITION

The starting point in Ahmadu Bello's position was that, left to themselves, the North wanted nothing to do with the South at all and it was only the pressure from the British that had brought them to the table. From this standpoint, the structure he favoured was the one that would best preserve the North's way of life. On the issue of the governance structure for Nigeria, his vision was not far removed from Awolowo's regionalism:

> *Nigeria is so large and the people are so varied that no person of any real intellectual integrity would be so foolish as to pretend that he speaks for the country as a whole*[24]

To begin with, the NCNC's position was little different from that of the Northern and Western Regions. Such difference as existed was only in the detail of the application of the principle of federalism to the Nigerian situation. But then Azikiwe suddenly changed his stance:

> ....*Azikiwe had advocated a federal system for Nigeria, with eight protectorates, some of which would roughly coincide with tribal boundaries. At the Kaduna National Assembly of the NCNC, held in 1948 after the inauguration of the Egbe Omo Oduduwa, the NCNC further defined its stand in its Freedom Charter, advocating a federal system based strictly upon tribal units. Thus its federalistic aims were quite similar to those which the Egbe supported. Indeed it would seem that the NCNC was nudged into such a position by the action of the Egbe. In any event...the Ibo organized the Ibo State Union and other groups followed suit; for example, the Edo National Union, the Ibibio State Union... and the Warri national Union were organized. Finally, at the NCNC convention held in Kano, in September 1951, the NCNC leaders suddenly decided to abandon federalism and switch to a unitarian position...*[25]

Azikiwe had taught political science at graduate level in America before entering Nigerian politics. He could hardly have been confused about the relative merits of a federal versus a unitary government for Nigeria. Indeed, his preference for federalism was long-standing and well known. He had argued the case for it unequivocally in his publication *Renascent Africa* as far back as 1937 and he had been consistent in this view ever since. This sudden conversion, in late 1951, of Azikiwe and the Igbo leadership to the Colonial Office view that federalism risked a break-up of the country and that the goal of a united Nigeria would be more quickly achieved through a unitary structure was dramatic and fatal.

The effect of Azikiwe's shift was to put his Igbo people firmly in the camp of the British and at odds with the North and the West. Only in 1967 as the Biafran war loomed did the Igbo leadership insist on a return to regionalism as a condition of calling off its plan to secede from Nigeria by which time it was too late and the consequences were dire.

AZIKIWE'S CRISIS

The Nigerian Constitution that was laid before the British Parliament, on 29 June 1951, fully reflected Bourdillon's grand design. By the stipulation that 'Nigeria shall be divided into three Regions which shall be known... as the Northern Region, the Western Region and the Eastern Region' it entrenched the division of Southern Nigeria into two.[26] Each of the three Regions was to be headed by a lieutenant governor and they were to meet in the centre in a House of Representatives which was to be made up of one hundred and thirty-six elected representatives from the three regions.

A balanced federation would have dictated a principle of equality between the regions with each region having the same number of representatives in the House of Representatives. But federation was not the agenda. The outcome of what was supposed to be a dialogue between Nigerians to decide for themselves and in their own interests on the political arrangements they were going to be responsible for running was distorted and corrupted by the interests and behind-the-scenes tampering of the imperial umpires. With Bourdillon's measures for the northern awakening having started in earnest only just before his departure in 1943, it was clear by the time this national conference was taking place in 1949 that the North had not had sufficient time to prepare for the encounter. This led to the situation where the British were batting for the North while at the same time playing the role of umpires of the match. Bourdillon's biographer argues strenuously against the suggestion that it was this interference that distorted the contest:

> *Bourdillon's success in February 1943 owed much to the progressive feeling which, though latent, did exist in the north. It was also the culmination of the excellent relations with the Emirs which he and his wife had been fostering since 1935.....Nor can the governor's achievement be gainsaid by the assertion that he won over the Emirs by promising them as many seats in the central council as the eastern and western provinces put together, a rather shady deal that redounded to the constitutional detriment of Nigeria and ultimately to the civil war of the 1960s. There is no evidence for this view...[27]*

That the author had not opened his mind to the available evidence is clear from the fact that he made no reference to Sharwood-Smith's memoir nor to Sharwood-Smith himself even though the memoir had been published in1969, almost twenty years before his biography of Bourdillon. This is curious given Sharwood-Smith's self-proclaimed leading role in implementing Bourdillon's plans in the North. The denial is certainly not consistent with the advice which Sharwood-Smith was to give in similar circumstances to Tafawa Balewa in preparation for the 1957 Constitutional Conference on what to insist upon to secure the North's position in an independent Nigeria.[28]

The upshot of the conference was that instead of equilibrium between North and South, the Northern Region was allocated the same number of Representatives as the two southern Regions combined with the consequence that the North could never be out-voted even if the two Souths joined forces but in the event of any division between the them the North could ally with one or the other.

This 50:50 divide had been sold to the southerners as a compromise from the 56:44 split that it was said the North would have been entitled to insist upon had seats been allocated on the basis of the population count between the Regions.[29] This, of course, depended upon the validity of the population claim.

The claim was dubious. Not only because the British, who had taken sides in the contest, were the ones making the claim but also because there had been no proper population count, in the sense of census, prior to the McPherson Constitution being laid before the UK Parliament in June 1951: such an exercise made little sense under the colonial regime since, outside of Lagos and Calabar, the people had no vote. The regime had always relied upon population estimates only. The only census conducted by the colonial regime started in 1952 by which time the constitutional arrangements which the figures were supposed to legitimise had already been promulgated. Coming, as it did, after the assertion that the North was more populous than the South, the exercise was tainted from the outset.

Bias aside, the questionable reliability of the count is evident from the following account given by Mr John Hilary Smith CBE, Deputy Secretary to Prime Minister Balewa until just before the first coup of January 1966:

> *I worked on the census full time as an ADO in Kano province, the only expat involved full time...Enumeration began on 7 July and in the far north coincided with the first rains. As everyone hastened to plant the fear was that there might be no counting at all. Lazy enumerators, often schoolboys in a generally illiterate society and not all keen bush trekkers, might opt to ignore isolated homesteads and, in deference to Islamic practice, there was no actual headcount. The head of each household had to list all those within it. It was easy to forget a child or two*[i]

Despite over it, the 1951 Constitution still represented a significant milestone for the nationalists. Even though it would still be the colonial power, in the person of the lieutenant governors, that was making the laws, now the laws were going to be made "with the advice and consent" of the Regional House of Assembly of which the Educated Natives would, at last, now be members. The promised land of an independent democratic Nigeria was now firmly in sight. They resolved that the new five-year parliamentary term which this constitution ushered in in 1951 would be the last under British rule.

This was the state of play in Nigeria when Churchill returned to power as Prime Minister of Britain in October 1951. The key members of his cabinet ensured that there would be consistency in the British position in the countdown to independence for Nigeria. His Foreign Secretary was Anthony Eden who would take over as Prime Minister in April 1955. His Defence Minister was Harold MacMillan who would become Prime Minister

i   Letter to the Author dated 24 August 2007

in succession to Eden in January 1957. These three leaders were supported during their tenures by three forceful characters who held the office of Colonial Secretary in succession: Oliver Lyttleton (October 1951 - July 1954); Alan Lennox-Boyd (July 1954 - October 1959) and Ian Macleod (October 1959 - October 1961). In these men, the nationalists faced formidable opposition to their agenda for Nigeria.

The challenge was compounded by the fact that while the British team were united in their objective of securing the best arrangements to secure British national interests post-Independence, on the Nigerian side there was no common ground, not even on the headline issue of ending British rule. The seeds of disunity which Bourdillon and his team had sown amongst them very quickly manifested in the first trial run of the new Constitution with the elections to the new Regional Assemblies in November 1951.

With only one Northern House of Assembly to which all Northerners could aspire for election, regardless of whether they were North-East, North-West or North-Central, elections in the North passed with little rancour. The Northern Peoples' Congress (NPC) held the Northern House of Assembly unopposed. The idea of leaders in the North campaigning before the masses for their votes was of course alien to the Caliphate tradition and so special provision had been made in the Constitution for indirect elections with the Emirs effectively acting as an electoral college. No Independent candidates made it to the Northern House of Assembly. Even Aminu Kano, the NEPU leader, failed to make it through.[30]

In contrast, the arrangements for the South, where there were now two Regional Houses of Assembly, saw unbridled competition. Not only were there many more political parties, many more candidates campaigned and were elected as Independents. By the end of the exercise, the Pandora's Box of ethnic politics had been well and truly opened between the Yoruba and the Igbos in the Western House of Assembly and between the Igbos and the smaller ethnic groups of the Eastern Region in the Eastern House of Assembly.

To shield the North from an invasion from southern political influences, the British framers of the constitution had taken care to ensure that elections to the national House of Representatives would be indirect with members of the House of Representatives being elected from amongst the members of the House of Assembly of each region.

Since, the only way to national politics was through the regions there was little point in political parties extending their campaigns outside of their region. What was envisaged was that the political parties would confine their activities to within their own regions. This was the line taken by both Bello's NPC in the North and Awolowo's Action Group in the West. Azikiwe's NCNC, however, decided to contest both the Western House of Assembly and the Eastern House of Assembly.

In the East, although many stood as Independents, NCNC was the only political party. Having won the largest number of seats in the Eastern House, it simply invited successful Independents to come under its political banner. The elections to the Western

Region House of Assembly ended in controversy with NCNC claiming that it had won the largest number of seats in that House also and that Azikiwe was only cheated of the premiership of the Western Region[31] by Yoruba members of the NCNC 'cross-carpeting' to the Action Group.

THE 'CROSS-CARPETING' CONTROVERSY

The door had been left open for Azikiwe's attempt on the Western Region by the timetabling which ensured that the elections in the Western Region took place ahead of the others.[31] The plan was to exploit the two weakest links in Awolowo's Action Group's hold on the Western Region: the two major cities, Lagos and Ibadan. In Lagos Azikiwe and the NCNC had already inherited the political legacy of the dominant Lagos politician Herbert Macaulay. In Ibadan the key political figure was Adegoke Adelabu supported by the then Alaafin of Oyo.

The claim that NCNC won the largest number of seats in the Western House of Assembly in these elections has been controversial. In Azikiwe's own account, written in 1970 when he had time for reflection, he stops well short of conviction and of the claims made on his behalf by some commentators:

> *Towards the end of 1951 I stood for another election, this time to the Western House of Assembly, as a representative of Lagos, under the Macpherson Constitution, and I topped the poll...The NCNC was under the impression that it had won the [Western House of Assembly] election with 43 members out of 80. As it turned out, 20 of the legislators who were known or regarded as NCNC members or supporters or sympathisers decided to align themselves with another party[32]*

Not only did NCNC not have a party manifesto in these elections it also did not publish a list of members as the parties were required to do.[33] The party was including in its count candidates who had successfully stood on other platforms or as Independents whom it calculated upon bringing into its fold. Azikiwe as much as confirms this in his narrative when he proceeds to identify sixteen out of the twenty 'legislators who disappointed the hopes of the NCNC'. However, none of the 'sixteen' is referred to by Azikiwe as an 'NCNC member': one is identified as the 'Legal Adviser of the NCNC at Sapele'; he refers to another as having 'been a supporter and sympathiser of the NCNC from time immemorial'; the remaining fourteen are listed as 'supported by the NCNC'. Of the sixteen, only seven were Yoruba and so the claim that Azikiwe and his NCNC were robbed of victory in the Western Region elections in 1951 due to cross-carpeting was false; the claim was simply part of the grand plan to stir up Igbo-Yoruba antipathy.

In the context of a multi-ethnic state, whose citizens only enjoyed freedom of movement between each other's historic lands courtesy of the over-arching British rule, and at that only within living memory, the very idea that the Igbo-dominated NCNC, under Azikiwe's leadership who had positioned himself as the champion of his Igbo people, could while ruling the Eastern Region unchallenged, also rule the largely Yoruba Western Region was a case of an ideal running way ahead of its time.

Azikwe's failed attempt to dominate Western Region politics was to backfire on him dramatically as the first sitting of the new House of Representatives, on Tuesday 29 January 1952, found him in the embarrassing position where he had no seat in the House. Not being a member of the Eastern House of Assembly, he was ineligible despite that House being under the full control of his NCNC party. At the same time he had no support for his candidacy in the Western House of Assembly whose leadership he had gambled upon winning. The Igbo leader found himself stuck in opposition in the Western Region House of Assembly:

> *In the Western Region, where the AG was in power, Azikiwe was the leader of the opposition; in the Eastern Region, where Azikiwe's party was in power, the leadership of the government was entrusted to Eyo Ita, his lieutenant. Thus on the eve of a new era in Nigerian constitutionalism, Azikiwe, who had contributed so much to the national awakening in the country, and who had made the strongest bid for national leadership, found himself without formal power in any regional government or in the federal government. Furthermore, some of his ablest lieutenants either were private members of the eastern legislature or were not members at all. Most of the members of that chamber had been elected as independent candidates, but had been invited by Azikiwe to join the NCNC; some of them held ministerial appointments. While Azikiwe and his immediate lieutenants lacked formal power, some of those who possessed it did not owe loyalty to the NCNC. Azikiwe's residence in another region further endangered party discipline, then in an embryonic stage[34]*

Azikiwe was in a political wilderness from which only British intervention could rescue him, thus exposing his dependency.

The only way he was going to get to the House of Representatives was through the Eastern Region House of Assembly. His manoeuvrings to find a way in led to the first major constitutional crisis in the country which exposed the ethnic fault lines within the Eastern Region. In his autobiography, Azikiwe glosses over this crisis:

> *Before the end of 1952 a crisis loomed in the ranks of the NCNC as a result of the unwillingness of certain NCNC-appointed Federal and Regional Ministers to toe the party line. (This is a long story which I hope to expand in a later volume.)*

Consequently, I was drafted to contest an election into the Eastern House of Assembly and regularise this irregularity[35]

The promise of more to come in a later volume was never delivered upon.

To get back into the Eastern Region House of Assembly, Azikiwe needed that house to be dissolved. However, a drafting error in the 1951 Constitution meant that it was not possible to dissolve any Regional House of Assembly without a dissolution of the Federal House of Representatives.[36] Without an amendment of the Constitution by the British Parliament, Azikiwe was locked out of active involvement in central politics.

"THE MISTAKE OF 1914 HAS COME TO LIGHT"

In the wake of the controversies thrown up by the 1951 regional elections, the competition between Awolowo's Action Group and Azikiwe's NCNC now reached a new intensity. In the new vote-chasing climate, the end of colonial rule was the guaranteed vote-winner on which neither of the lead protagonists was prepared to be outbid:[37]

> *In the subsequent electoral contest between the NCNC and the Action Group in the Western Region (including Lagos), politicians and their followers became irrevocably committed to, if not prisoners of, the mutual target date their electoral competition had established. Thereafter it would have been political suicide for either party to slacken its drive toward that "year of destiny"...As Chief Anthony Enahoro stated, "1956 is a position from which it is impossible to retreat".*

On 31 March 1953, the Action Group's Chief Anthony Enahoro rose to move a motion "that this House accept as a primary political objective the attainment of self-government for Nigeria in 1956".

Anthony Enahoro 1953 SELF-GOVERNMENT MOTION

'Mr President, Sir, I rise to move the motion standing in my name, "that this House accepts as a primary political objective the attainment of self-government for Nigeria in 1956. "

'Sir, this motion is an invitation to the Honourable Members of this House to associate the highest legislature of our land with the expressed desire of the peoples of this country, whose views we all represent, for political autonomy in 1956. It seeks to provide representatives from all parts of the country with an opportunity to exchange views on the most burning question of our time. It is an invitation to this House to make a declaration of objective with regard to Nigerian freedom.

'I do not propose, Sir, to go into the arguments for self-government because I am satisfied that it is generally accepted on all sides of the House that self-government for this country at some future date is a desirability. Therefore I propose to deal with this motion in two main parts and very briefly – namely, of what significance is such a declaration of objective and secondly, why should the objective be 1956?

'Sir, I believe that a declaration of objective by this House has become a matter of supreme importance in our march towards self-government. For the time being, this Legislature is the supreme voice of the people of this country, although not all the majority decision which have been taken in this House in the past could hope to survive the test of a referendum. It is essential in my view, to assess by a formal motion of this nature the honest feelings of various sections of this House and to discover to what extent these feelings may truly reflect the aspirations of the politically conscious citizens of this country.

Self-government is after all, sir, a subject on which it is of the first importance that people should believe rightly, and I cannot overstress the great inspiration and succour which various political parties in this country would derive therefrom if the demand for self-government in 1956 were to enjoy the full force of the backing of the highest legislature of the country.

'Some Honourable Members may feel that the issue of self-government is not one for this House to decide. It may be argued that it has very little to do with the present administration of this country, but speaking for this side of the House, sir, we have always felt that the House of Representatives should serve a dual purpose in our political progress. Firstly, that it is our duty to utilise the powers which we now enjoy in this House to further the expansion of our economy and of our social services and to remove obstacles on the road to freedom; but secondly and perhaps even more important, we must use this House of Representatives itself to continue the fundamental struggle for national freedom. One of the basic moves in the furtherance of that struggle - and even though we carry it on with less violent methods than the people of Kenya have found it necessary to employ, it is nevertheless a struggle – is a statement of our goal and that is why, in my view, it is necessary for this House to express an opinion on this subject.

'A declaration of objective, sir, is important in other respects. We and our people can be likened to builders. We have set out to build a new state. From the multitude of tribes in the country we are striving to build a new and modern structure. Self-government is merely the foundation of that structure. This work of construction is a romantic idea to me, and I am sure that Honourable Members will agree with me that we are all proud and honoured to be the architects and that we should be grateful to Providence that this task has fallen upon our generation. But among the responsibilities which accompany this great honour and privilege is the important decision which none but ourselves can make, as to when we shall strike the first sod in this new edifice.

'Many Honourable Members, sir, have had houses built for them. Others like myself may only have seen them built. In the North I have seen peasants construct their own hamlets. For many years these poor peasants must have planned and dreamed of their own little homes. They did not just sit by and hope that Providence would create a new home for them. They did not say to themselves, "I shall lay the foundations of my new home as soon as practicable." That is not planning. On the contrary, I am sure that they must have examined their own earnings and their business prospects over a period, then considered their commitments and found out where savings might be made here and there, and they could say to themselves "by the grace of Allah, I shall lay my foundation in three or five years' time."

'Now, the builders of a nation, as we are, are no different from these poor peasants. That is why in places like Russia, England, India and other countries, the Government sets out a declaration of objectives embodied in five-year plans, and all that this motion asks of this Legislature is to follow in the footsteps of these great and wiser nations and to establish a political objective towards the attainment of which we can bend the energies of our own people.

'Many years ago, sir, when I was a young man and I entered public life, the popular slogan was "Self-government in our lifetime". But as the country advanced, this slogan went out of vogue and the new catch-phrase was "Self-government as soon as practicable". That is many years back. As I have said, I do not wish to deal with the arguments for self-government and how the desire for freedom grew, but anybody who has kept pace with political advancement or with the trends of political thought in this country in the last seven years will agree that the bare idea of self-government is no longer attractive, is no longer enough.

'Whether it is expressed as "Self-government in our life-time" or "Self-government in the shortest possible time" or "Self-government in as soon as practicable", it has ceased to be a progressive view, because Nigerian nationalism has moved forward from that position. The question in the public mind since the end of the war has been, "Self-government, when?" What time, what date? That is the question which this motion now invites Honourable Members, who should be true representatives, representatives of that same public which is demanding an answer, to answer.

'There is a third reason, sir, why a declaration of objective is important. We do not want to part with the British people with rancour. For many years they have ruled us. We are not an unreasonable people, and like a good house servant, it is only fair that we should give our masters notice of our intention to quit, so that they can effect arrangements either to employ new servants or to serve themselves. We do not wish to take them by surprise. On the contrary, we wish to invite them to co-operate with us in the attainment of our objectives.

'Honourable Members may remember that the Indian cause alienated a lot of sympathy in the United Kingdom because of what was regarded as the indecent haste with which the British evacuated or withdrew from India. The British mind, essentially a conservative mind, does not like things thrust upon it all of a sudden. We all know that. This motion is designed therefore to acquaint the British public with what we are thinking, with what we are feeling so that our agitation in 1956 for self-government will not to come to them as a surprise. This motion will also afford the British Government sufficient time within which to arrange gradual withdrawal and progressive transfer of power to Nigerians.

'Sir, a declaration of objective, such as this, is essential for a fourth reason. It is now accepted by the highest international bodies that there should be a time limit for self-government for Colonial territories. I may mention here, without giving anything away, that one of the questions which the recent British Labour Party Delegation to West Africa asked my party was what the House of Representatives thought about self-government for Nigeria in 1956. The Trusteeship Council of the United Nations Organisations has requested governments administering Trust Territories to fix target dates when territories will attain self-government. The International Confederation of Free Trade Unions has also declared its acceptance of the principle that a time limit should be set by occupying powers and Imperialist Governments for self-government for dependencies.

'Even in Britain itself, a large body of opinion is growing in support of this principle. I well recall, sir, that when I was in England last year, Mr Fenner Brockway, the well-known Socialist M.P., said in the course of Colonial affairs debate in the

202

House of Commons: "I should like to urge upon this House and particularly upon the Secretary of State for the Colonies that if we are to secure the confidence trust and co-operation of peoples in the Colonial Territories, the best way to do it would be in discussion, consultation and agreement with them to fix a target date when in each respective Colony the goal of self-government should be secured. And I believe that if it were possible to pursue such a policy, we would change the psychology of the Colonial peoples."

'I myself think that was a very correct assessment of our psychology. It is clear that such international organisations as I have mentioned and men like Mr Brockway are thinking along the lines of this motion and I think it is up to this Legislature, representing the peoples of this country, to strengthen their hands.

'That, sir, is very briefly the first part of my argument explaining the significance of a declaration of political objective.

'Now, sir, if it is agreed that an objective should be declared, what should it be? It may be asked, "Why pick on 1956? Is not 1956 an arbitrary date?" What considerations have led to the decision on this date?

'Mr President, two of the many factors which have influenced our selection of this date are the factor of convenience and the factor of previous commitment. 1956 is convenient, sir, because it is the year which will see the end of the present constitution. The Constitution Order-in-Council is dated 1951 and is supposed to expire in five years. It is public knowledge that all true nationalists have made up their minds that this is the last constitution prescribing a dependent status which the people of this country can tolerate.

'To recommend a date earlier than 1956 would be to put a premature end to the life of this constitution, and although I myself can contemplate such a course with pleasure, we know too well how strenuously some sections of the country would resist it. In addition, most of the programmes and policies of the Regional Governments to educate and prepare our people for freedom are based on five year plans, and I think it would be unwise, to say the least, to interrupt the process of maturity of these programmes with the upheaval that constitutional changes might occasion.

'To settle on a later date would mean a further period in national slavery, a prospect which I do not think any Honourable Member would welcome. We might, if we settled on a later date, have to draw up yet another interim constitution and waste time and public funds to arrange new elections, still as a subject people, at a time when our sister colony on the gold Coast and our kinsmen in the West Indies and places like Malaya will most assuredly be free independent nations. It seems to me, therefore, that we cannot afford to put the date forward and it would be inadvisable to set it back. Convenience therefore dictates 1956.

'The arguments on the grounds of previous commitment are even stronger. There may be some doubt as to whether any particular political party is fully representative of the people, but there can be no doubt whatsoever that any unanimous view approved by the majority of political parties must represent the true feelings of the politically conscious citizens of any country, and 1956 from this point of view enjoys the advantage of unanimity. The Action Group, the NCNC, the Northern Elements Progressive Union, the Askianist Movement, the Convention People's Party have all publicly declared for self-government in 1956, and I am confident that today – on this historic day in the political annals of this country – I am confident that the Northern People's Congress will take the opportunity of this debate to associate themselves with the declared objective of all other true nationalists in this country.

'Sir, the Action Group, the NCNC, the Northern Elements Progressive Union, and indeed all true nationalists who interviewed the Labour Party delegation left them in no doubt that 1956 is their irrevocable choice. I myself, in the course of my tour of the United Kingdom last year, gave many interested organisations and our own students over there to understand that we are deeply committed to 1956. I am sure that Chief Bode Thomas, Chief Arthur Prest, Mr Arikpo and Mr Nwapa who represented us abroad last year in their ministerial capacities, could not have failed to make this claim. Chief Bode Thomas has even gone further to publicise our ambitions in Canada and New York to world personalities. All these great people and organisations are looking forward to the emergence in 1956 of the largest and greatest Negro nation in the world as a free independent country.

'We have all at one time or another held out high hopes for 1956 to our own people at mass meetings, at public lectures, in the press and through other media our people are expectant. We have, all of us, whether it is the Action Group or the NCNC or other parties, promised at one time or another to lead them to the Promised Land in 1956. We cannot go back on our plighted word. You will understand, therefore, Mr President, that on these three grounds of previous commitments, 1956 is a position from which it is impossible to retreat, and that is why this motion recommends it to this House for adoption.

'Mr President, there are one or two minor points to answer on this subject, such as "shall we in fact be able to rule ourselves in 1956? Shall we have enough knowledgeable men and women? Are there any grounds for the fear on the part of some Members from the North that they will be dominated by the South? I shall leave those questions, sir, to be dealt with by my Honourable Friends who will speak after me. For the moment, I hope I have said enough to show why it is of paramount importance that this House should set a target date for self-government and why that date should be 1956.

'One final observation I would like to make is upon the attitude of the Special Members of this House and of the Ex-Officio Members to this motion. I believe, sir, that the subject of self-government is an issue between Nigerians and the British Government. It is nothing to do with my good and honourable friends, the Special Members or with my equally good and honourable friends, the Ex-Officio Members. I hold the view that no non-Nigerian has the right to express an opinion in this House on this subject or seek to influence the course of this debate on the time that we may choose to strike for freedom. We are the elected representatives of our people and that applies to all Nigerians here. We are all elected by some process. We as the elected representatives of our people, do not require the assistance of aliens to help us to decide when we should be free. I would therefore appeal to the Special members to refrain from speaking and from voting on this motion, whatever their private feelings may be.

'The Ex-officio Members, Sir, are in a similar position. Their functions in this House relate to the work of certain specified departments of government. Perhaps they have the interests of Nigeria at heart. Perhaps they have not. Their private feelings are entirely their own concern and are of no consequence in this debate. The subject of this motion is not covered by the portfolio of any Ex-Officio Member. I would like, therefore to appeal to them in all sincerity to stay out of this debate sir, and to let us Nigerians argue our own demands and desires and differences among themselves. We will go into the lobbies, sir, to decide the future of our own people and of our own children. None of the officials has a stake in this country, and I mean no offence at all when I describe them as mere birds of passage. They are here today, sir, but being out of the Colonial service, they may well be elsewhere tomorrow, by transfer or by retirement. I beseech them, therefore, not to take any course which might lead to an estrangement between us and them.

'Mr President, the whole country – I might even say the whole world - is awaiting the verdict of this House on this motion. News of what we say here today will travel far and wide. I do not know how many Honourable Members read the English press. They may have noticed in the Daily Telegraph an account of the debate which took place here last week on nudity. I am sure that any Honourable Member looking back now and reading an account of that debate will feel thoroughly ashamed of the decision of this House. I appeal, sir, to all sections of this House not to let us repeat the mistake of underestimating the extent of overseas interest in the proceedings of this House. Our minds are irrevocably made up on the issue of self-government in 1956. Sir, I beg to move'.

With Enahoro's motion the Action Group had lobbed a political grenade into the new House of Representatives and all political parties had to take a position.

Up until this point the relationship between the Awolowo led Action Group and the Ahmadu Bello led Northern Peoples' Congress in the House of Representatives had been constructive: they were united by opposition to Azikiwe's drive for a unitary Nigeria. This dramatic move for independence on Nigerian terms brought about a dramatic realignment of the political forces within the House of Representatives. While the issue reunited East and West it served to drive a firm wedge between North and South.

The NPC, which had never had any appetite for mixing its political fortunes with the Southerners in the first place, and which had only agreed to do so under British pressure and in the expectation that British rule would continue for some time to come while it prepared itself for the new political game, was now being invited to commit political suicide. The move was to drive the NPC leadership closer to the British:

> , the relationship between Ministers and British civil servants on Executive Council was such that we could, in many ways, have described ourselves as a genuinely bi-racial government. There were, of course, occasional misunderstandings and clashes of temperament, but a consciousness of common purpose persisted throughout...the British, were not the "enemy". The "enemy" lay beyond the Niger in the persons of the political leaders and their followers who desired independence for Nigeria before the North was ready, in order, the North was convinced, to dominate the whole[38]

Britain, under Churchill, had no intention of giving in to the nationalist demands for independence in 1956. It was not just that they were not going to be dictated to by the word-of-mouth-only demands of the nationalists, there were other considerations. The British Empire in India had been lost only very recently in 1947 and Britain had no intention of losing its largest colony in Africa so soon after. Also, 1956 was the year in which Sudan was due to be decoupled from Egypt and December 1956 was the deadline that the Americans had given for British withdrawal of all their troops from the Suez Canal in Egypt.

At a more strategic level the North and the Army, both of which the British were counting upon to keep power out of the hands of the nationalists, had not been fully-readied for their role. The defence strategy was a simple one of playing for time although achieving it required sophisticated parliamentary manoeuvres for which the Nationalists were no match. The first move was to use parliamentary procedures, with the help of the NPC leadership, to prevent the nationalists' Independence motion being debated:

> On the day of debate in March 1953, the Council of Ministers, unable to avoid the motion, had placed it last of the eight on the Order Paper, confident that it could

not be reached by the end of the day's sitting and would therefore lapse. We had an answer. Notice of five or six of the motions stood in the names of N.C.N.C. members. One after another, they begged to withdraw and not to move[39]

The next move of the 'bi-racial' team in the North was for Ahmadu Bello to move a motion to amend the Enahoro motion by substituting 'as soon as practicable' for 1956. Although this amending motion was seconded neither the original nor the amending motion made it through to debate because another member of the NPC team had been lined up to move a motion adjourning the whole debate.[40] The move took the Action Group and the nationalists by surprise.

Confronted by the starkness of the North's decision to delay Independence from colonial rule, pandemonium followed as tempers flared and abuses were exchanged on the floor of the House. The country was thrown into its first national political crisis as the Action Group members and NCNC members staged a walkout and the Action Group Ministers tendered their resignations. The following day, the Sardauna is said to have closed the adjournment debate for the House with the words, 'The mistake of 1914 [when the Protectorates of Northern and Southern Nigeria were united] has now come to light'[41].

Lagos was the venue for this House of Representatives meeting and the Lagos political crowds rained abuses upon the Northern delegates. When the southern press and political parties joined together to deride the NPC members as imperialist stooges the northern leaders began to reconsider their options for separate existence from the South.

When ethnic clashes broke out in Kano in May 1953 after the Action Group decided to take its campaign for self-government in 1956 direct to the people of the North, a new urgency was injected into the matter, as thirty-six people were killed with many more injured. That the victims were mainly Igbos is ironic given that this was essentially a stand-off between the West and the North.

The North was now threatening to secede with shouts of 'Araba' meaning separation. The secession of the North threatened catastrophe for British plans for influence post independence as they would have felt compelled to take action to stop the secession attempt by the very group they were depending upon for post-independence influence.

Behind the scenes, the Colonial Office wasted no time in launching a charm offensive to the North to dissuade them, underlining the fact that the imperative of keeping the North in political union with the South was a British one. On 7 April 1953, Sharwood-Smith wrote to the Colonial Office:

Substantially, what has occurred is that the Northern Members of the Central Legislature, resentful of, and disgusted at, the manoeuvres, manners and methods of the Southern political leaders and their followers, have found themselves mentally back where their representatives were at the opening of the Ibadan Conference, with their worst fears realised. They are now in effect demanding a complete reassessment of the position with a view, in their present frame of mind, to asking for separation with some form of association at the Centre to protect their interests. This can be taken as the worst possible alternative of all and we hope to improve on it appreciably as time passes[42]

Azikiwe had been reduced to watching the constitutional crisis surrounding Enahoro's Independence Motion from the visitors' gallery of the Federal House of Representatives having manoeuvred himself out of central politics. Fortunately for him, his need for the help of the British to get back in was more than matched by their need for him to be there as a counterweight to Awolowo in order to avoid the danger of the South being reunited under the personality of a single leader.

The British duly made the constitutional changes and the way was clear for Azikiwe to return from political wilderness in the Western House of Assembly to contest new elections in the East as a pathway to the House of Representatives. After the Eastern Region House of Assembly was dissolved, new Regional elections were held in May 1953 in which Azikiwe was successful allowing him to formally assume the leadership of the Regional Government in the East.

But, by removing the Eyo Ita government in this way, Azikiwe had damaged what unity there had been between the Igbos and the minority groups of the Eastern Region. This was to have consequences for Eastern Region unity later on.

THE APPEASEMENT OF THE NORTH

On 21 May 1953, a telegram arrived in the Colonial Office. It contained warning of a hardening of the North's determination to put as much distance as possible between itself and the South:

> *In the aftermath of the 31 March self-government debate in the House of Representatives...separatist sentiment grew stronger among Northern political leaders. The day after order had been restored following the Kano riots, the Northern Region House of Assembly debated the motion (the so-called 'Eight-points Motion') outlined in this document; the motion was carried without any dissenting vote and was passed by the Northern Region House of Chiefs on the same day. In effect the motion called for regional autonomy in all but the most limited spheres; there would in effect be no central government for Nigeria and only a restricted central agency*[43]

Sensing that the situation was spiralling out of control, on the same day, the colonial government announced that it was convening a conference in London to revise the McPherson Constitution.[44] This was the conference, above all others, which cast the mould for the political order of the soon-to-be-independent country. Its importance was reflected in the fact that it was conducted under the chairmanship of the Colonial Secretary Oliver Lyttleton. A sense of the way in which the exercise was managed can be gleaned from the following comments by Anthony Eden:

> On our party's return to office in 1951 the post of Colonial Secretary had special significance. Whoever held that office would have to guide and influence hopes and ambitions in every continent. Mr Oliver Lyttleton, now Lord Chandos, did this work brilliantly and selflessly. He charted the course for the Conservative administration in colonial affairs…His successor may be said to have chosen himself. Mr. Lennox-Boyd has given his whole life to the study of colonial problems and colonial territories and today commands unrivalled knowledge and experience. He has held the Colonial Office with distinction and acclaim in a period of endless harassment. Colony after colony, inspired or infected by the universal bacillus of nationalism, has tried to run before it could walk. With patient care and parental indulgence, the Colonial Secretary has led their first footsteps. His guiding hand has always been there, unobtrusively. If all his charges have not grown up with the code of conduct in which he had instructed them, that is not the fault of their patient guardian. Mr Lennox- Boyd's success is due to his real affection for the colonies and to an infinite capacity for taking pains. It has also been due to a cheerful willingness to discard, where need be, the conventions of Whitehall[45]

The British desire for a 'united Nigeria' was completely at odds with what the Northern political leadership were insisting upon at this time which was a loose federation with effectively no central government as security against Southern domination. The way the Colonial Office sought to reconcile the British agenda with the North's concerns was to produce a Nigeria united under the control of the North. In the wake of the crisis following the Enahoro motion for Independence, they recognized that a temporary retreat from the goal of a unitary Nigeria was necessary. This appears from the Colonial Office's reply, on 18 April 1953, to Sharwood-Smith's letter of 7 April 1953:

> We firmly believe that unity is in the best interests of all regions of Nigeria, but we recognise that the only solution for present difficulties, and probably the only hope eventually of achieving and preserving that unity, lies in some modified and looser form of association at the Centre[46]

The 1953 conference marked the beginning of the journey towards this end game.

The key objectives of the British for the Conference were to make changes to the structure of the federation that would reassure the North that there was no likelihood of it ever coming under the rule of the South whilst, at the same time, managing the demands of the nationalists in the South for self-rule. The key elements of the strategy were (1) A new constitution with a looser federation; (2) The excision of Lagos from the Western Region; (3) The division of the British-Cameroonians to achieve a population shift in favour of the North; (4) A compromise position between North and South on self-governance and (5) Federal Elections in 1954.

THE NEW CONSTITUTION

The constitution that emerged from the conference (known as the Lyttleton Constitution, after the conference chairman) federated the Northern Region, now further enlarged by the integration of what was British Northern Cameroon, with, now, four units in the South: The Western Region; the Eastern Region; the Southern Cameroons and the Federal Territory of Lagos. It provided for a House of Representatives, made up of 184 members with ninety-two seats for the Northern Region and ninety-two seats shared between the four units in the South (with forty-two seats each for the Western and Eastern Regions; six seats for the Southern Cameroons and two seats for Lagos). The other major feature to protect the North was the establishment of a civil service for each Region in place of the unitary civil service. It was the dismantling of these constitutional safeguards in 1966, in an attempt to create 'united Nigeria', by the first military government, that was to take the country back to the crisis of 1953.

THE EXCISION OF LAGOS FROM THE WESTERN REGION.

Nigeria was a British creation and so long as the country remained under British rule it was an easy thing for the state to treat all the subjects of the colony as one people and for the people to relate to each other as such. With the open borders under the protection of the colonial government, a level of migration was achieved by the more mobile ethnic groups than would otherwise have been possible. The chief beneficiaries of this state of political and economic union were the entrepreneurial and industrious Igbos whose possibilities were only constrained by their limited and land-locked territory.

Lagos, having been a British colony since 1861, and having served as the seat of the colonial government since 1914, had become a magnet for seekers of opportunity and fortune from all over the country. Being historically part of Yorubaland, non-Yorubas were to be found residing there in much greater quantities than Yorubas would be found living outside of Yorubaland.

The Egbe Omo Yoruba, with its mission statement of working to "unite the various clans and tribes in Yorubaland and generally to create and actively foster the idea of a single nationalism throughout Yorubaland" had an obvious interest in having the colony of Lagos treated as part of the Western Region. Azikwe, the Igbo champion, with an eye on the interests of the large Igbo community in Lagos, and the many more overseas who might be expected to settle in Lagos on their return, argued for Lagos to be kept separate from the Western Region. Given his personal experience in the aftermath of the 1951 regional elections Azikiwe had a special interest in ensuring that the link between Lagos and the Central Legislature was free-standing and not dependent upon the Western House of Assembly acting as a form of electoral-college.

It was not, however, a purely Yoruba-Igbo divide as many Yorubas in Lagos, like H.O. Davies, viewed themselves as a separate breed from their fellow nationals on the mainland. With the NPC and NCNC taking a common stand with the British on the issue, the decision of the conference was that, from 1954, Lagos should be excised from the Western Region and stand independently as the Federal Capital Territory.[ii]

From the British perspective, the move represented an important bargaining chip for use in more crucial constitutional discussions which were to follow.

THE DIVISION OF THE BRITISH-CAMEROONIANS

Of the many unfortunate experiences of colonialism in Africa, that of the people of the land that the Germans called "Kameroon" has been amongst the most unfortunate having, almost literally, been hung, drawn and quartered at different points in time between the Germans, the French and the British.

It will be recalled from Chapter Three that the original British plan was for Cameroon to be part of Nigeria until this plan was frustrated when Germany stole a march on them and claimed the territory. Then, in the aftermath of Germany's defeat in the First World War, Cameroon was divided on a West-East basis by the League of Nations and given to Britain and France, respectively, to govern as League of Nations mandates. Through this process a generation of Cameroonians found themselves speaking the three main languages of Western Europe, English, French, and German, and, in the process, being exposed to their contrasting cultures. Now the people of British-Cameroon were to find themselves being used as pawns in the Nigerian political gerrymandering exercise.[iii] The strategic objective of the colonial government was to achieve a population shift in favour of the North. The census of 1952, for what it was worth, had suggested that the North was more populous than the South and, with independence now in contemplation,

ii   This decision was reversed in 1957
iii   Even so, the results of the first census count taken in [1963] showed the South to be more populous which led the Sarduanna to order Balewa to do a recount

the division of Cameroon was one of the measures that had been fixed upon in an attempt to legitimise the claim. The plan was to make British Northern Cameroon an integral part of the North and to prepare the ground for excising the southern part of the territory from the South.[iv]

With the territory running alongside the eastern boundary of Nigeria and mimicking Nigeria's geographical north-south and Muslim-Christian divide, it fitted very conveniently into Nigeria's political matrix. The fit was made all the neater, in the North, because the vertical line that the European powers had drawn to demarcate the old boundary between Nigeria and German Cameroon ran through several ethnic groups in its path. Thus, in the North, the Kanuris are to be found on both sides of the old border.

Without disclosing the true end game, the Colonial Secretary had promised the delegates from British Southern Cameroon a separate Southern Cameroon Region[47] and in October 1954 Southern Cameroon became a Region with its own House of Assembly and Legislature. No such pledge had been given to the people of British Northern Cameroon. Instead, active measures had been taken by the Colonial government to fully integrate the territory into Northern Nigeria. To this end the area had been designated 'the Sardauna Province' in honour of Ahmadu Bello the Sardauna of Sokoto[48].

THE COMPROMISE ON SELF-GOVERNANCE

The nationalists having staked their credibility publicly on Independence in 1956, and the North, on the other hand, having passed a resolution expressly rejecting self-government in 1956, the colonial government needed to bridge these opposing positions. It seized upon the northern objection to Independence in 1956 to justify its refusal of the nationalists' requests. To neutralize any popular resentment over the decision, it was announced that the new Queen, Elizabeth II, would visit Nigeria that year. The concession made to the nationalists was that any region that wanted self-government for itself in 1956 could demand it. But as for Nigerian independence, the colonial government's strategy was to avoid committing to a date.[49]

THE 1954 FEDERAL ELECTIONS

Keeping the main southern parties divided having been a key pillar of the British strategy to ensure Northern rule, an election in which the two parties fought head-to-head for

---

iv   In contrast, the whole of Eastern Togo (the other former German colony on the West Coast of Africa which was similarly divided on an East/West basis between Britain and France) was integrated into British Ghana without distinction between north and south

power and influence in each other's home base was needed. The Lyttleton Constitution, which came into force on 1 October 1954, took care to prescribe indirect elections only in the North and in Southern Cameroons. In contrast, it provided for direct elections in the South thus ensuring that the real contest would be between the NCNC and the Action Group. With seats in new House of Representatives at stake, the competition between these two main parties of the South assumed another level of intensity.

The Action Group having restricted its own campaign for the 1951 elections to its own Western Region[50] only to see Azikiwe's NCNC, not only campaigning in both the Eastern and Western Regions but, claiming victory in the West, now moved to take its own message into NCNC territory.[v] The plan was to exploit the new fissure within the East that had been exposed in the wake of Azikiwe's dissolution of the Eyo Ita-led Eastern Region government. Awolowo's brand of federalism, with the federating units being the ethnic groups, had a ready appeal to the eastern minority groups especially in the light of Azikiwe's switch from federalism to unitarism. The NCNC in turn was campaigning to break up the Western Region by supporting the campaign to carve out a new Mid-West State.

These federal elections in November 1954 were to be the first elections for national offices in Nigeria. Already the outlook for the democratic experiment was unpromising given that the elections were to be based on the questionable census count of 1952. In the end the NPC won eighty-four out of the ninety-two northern seats while NCNC won sixty-three out of the ninety-two southern seats with Action Group winning only twenty seats. The upshot was that the House of Representatives was effectively controlled by an alliance of the NPC and NCNC.

The next crucial election was the 1956 regional elections. The last time these elections were held, in 1951, they had produced the controversy over the results in the Western Region. Depending on the outcome of this new round of elections, the Western Region was expected to formally request self-government. That expectation fed into much more controversial action by the colonial authorities with enduring consequences for democracy in Nigeria.

THE MISSED ROAD

It was at this point, in 1955, that two equally strong-willed characters, with opposing values and opinions of the British national interests, entered the Nigerian political stage. One was the new Governor General of Nigeria, Sir James Robertson who took the Colonial Office viewpoint. The other was a colonial officer, Harold Smith, who took the line of the British people. The clash between these two characters was to expose the underhand machinations of the Colonial Office in a major way.

v   The NPC also did not field candidates outside its Region (see *Oil, Politics and Violence - Nigeria's Military Coup Culture*, Siollun, p. 12)

Robertson was a veteran of the Sudan Political Service. He had joined the service in 1922 and, since 1945, had been functioning effectively as Governor of Sudan, a country which is almost the mirror image of Nigeria with broadly the same North-South Islamic-Christian divide and which was plagued by the same anxieties about domination, by one side of the other, following the end of British colonial rule. In Sudan, with the seat of colonial government having been in Khartoum in the North, with Arabic as the lingua franca of governance and with the South not having had the benefit of the same level of exposure to education as its counterparts in Nigeria, it was the Christian South that stood in fear of Northern Islamic domination.

As in Nigeria, whereas British policy before the Second World War had been one of separate development for North and South, following the war and the prospect of having to grant independence to the territory, the policy suddenly changed, in 1946, to integration of North and South. The other parallel was that integration was to be achieved on the basis of the template of governance prevailing in the Islamic North being extended to the Christian South. Having overseen the arrangements which saw Sudan to independence in 1956 on this basis, Robertson's brief was to achieve the same outcome in Nigeria.

Harold Sean Smith was a colonial officer different from the norm. For one thing, when he arrived in Nigeria, in 1955, he came with his wife and his daughter who had been born just the year before, the same year in which he had finished at Magdalen College, Oxford where he had read Politics, Philosophy and Economics. His dedication was to country and principle but not necessarily to the policies of the government of the day. His father had served in the First World War, and he himself had seen more than three years of service with the RAF in the Second World War in Egypt. Through his mother's pressure he had been brought up with inner strength, never to submit to defeat whatever the physical cost:

> *Despite his weight of seventeen stones and being sixty years of age, Sir James Robertson, KCMG, the Governor General of Nigeria, seemed very alert and fit. He was a bluff, hearty man with a greying moustache, and I supposed he could be a genial and warm person to his friends. He saw before him a man half his age, six foot tall, lean in face and build, with a pale complexion and black hair*[51]

In the Colonial Office plan for the defence of the empire there was a distinction to be drawn between decolonisation and independence. There would be elections but no electoral contests. How this was done in the 1956 elections to the Regional Assemblies was revealed by Harold Smith in his unpublished memoirs:

Harold Smith at the Ministry of Labour, 1955

Harold Smith at work at the Ministry

At this juncture the order arrived which was to change my life. It had come through the chain of command apparently from the Governor General [Robertson] himself. It was addressed to me personally. Perhaps my work had come to the Governor General's attention? I was much too modest to make that assumption. The order directed me to arrange for all Nigerian staff of the Department and all departmental vehicles to proceed to the Minister [Festus Okotie-Eboh]'s constituency for the duration of the election campaign to work under the Minister's orders and to get his [NCNC] candidate elected. This was a covert operation and a cover story was needed. I was to devise a survey of migrant labour covering the Minister's constituency.

My reply was brief. 'No,' I wrote on the minute sheet. 'This would be a criminal act'[52]

It is no exaggeration to say that the tactics to which the combination of Robertson and McPherson resorted in the implementation of the Colonial Office's plan were responsible for the failure of democracy in Nigeria. This was where the practice of rigging elections and the corruption of the political system began:

The British authorities played a decisive part in the selection of politicians for ministerial posts. Once the politician became a Minister he was made, and he became a much more powerful politician. The essence of colonial rule is that politics is banned for the people of the country while the colonial regime engages in full time politics. The notion that colonial administration functions without politics would be laughable to those administrators or political officers engaged in the trade.

The politics of the colonial regime are employed in the selection, destruction and manipulation of the leaders of the native people....The major aim of all this is to encourage friends of the colonial regime, people who are 'sound,' that is prepared to betray their own people's interests for personal advancement, and to put down irresponsible elements, that is to say nationalist politicians who act in their people's interests and cannot be bribed.

A major proportion of the politicians who made Nigeria notorious for corruption after Independence were selected by the British before Independence. The politicians and leaders and men of eminence not chosen were often honest, trustworthy and responsible people. Why were these people not brought in by the British? The answer is that the British needed people they could control. They sometimes selected crooks whom they knew they could control after Independence. Balewa, the leader from the North, was of course the exception, as was Awolowo. Balewa was so pro-British that he hardly needed manipulating. He was sound because he took advice from his band of British advisors[53]

THE FINAL GRIP ON AZIKIWE

This was the backdrop to the Constitutional Conference which was to take place in 1957 following the decision of the Western and Eastern Regions to formally request self-government for their regions in 1956. This was the conference that was supposed to prepare the Nigerian political class for the Promised Land of self-rule. The preparatory Conference had taken place in January 1956 and the main event had been scheduled to start on 19 September 1956. However, in July 1956, the colonial government suddenly announced an investigation into Azikiwe and his African Continental Bank on allegations of corruption. The start of the Conference was now postponed to await the outcome of the investigations.

Party funding is always an issue within any electoral system. The Foster-Sutton Report published on 16 January, 1957 confirmed what the colonial government already knew which was that Azikiwe had been using customer deposits of his African Continental Bank to prop up the failing enterprises through which he had been funding the NCNC's activities:

> *The funding of the political parties was the key not only to Nigerian elections but also to their results. The British knew where every penny came from. If the British chose not to investigate claims that the West were diverting six million pounds of official funds from the Marketing Boards into the Action Group treasury, it was because the NPC in the North was obviously also being financed by the Native Treasuries. In the East the Foster-Sutton Tribunal into Zik's African Continental Bank (ACB) found that it was insolvent. The principal use made of the public deposits in the ACB was to finance Zik's various business ventures. In 1955 the Eastern Region Finance Corporation invested large sums in the ACB, money which had come from the Eastern Region Marketing Board. In turn Zik financed his party, the NCNC. In 1955 the ACB and Zik's businesses were virtually bankrupt. In 1959 the Development Board took over the ACB [54]*

Adegoke Adelabu, the leader of the Ibadan Party and NCNC ally, had been jailed for the same malpractice following a similar investigation by the British but Azikiwe in jail was of no use to them. The whole reason Azikiwe had been rescued by them, in 1953, from the political wilderness of leader of the opposition in the Western Region, was to serve as a counterweight to Awolowo. More importantly, he and his NCNC party were needed as alliance partners for the North against the Action Group. With his enterprises in financial distress, his only source of campaign funds having been effectively sealed off with this investigation, and with the possibility of jail term for fraud hanging over him, from this point on Azikiwe, and through him the NCNC, were firmly back under the control of the strategists in the Colonial Office. Funding for the NCNC now came from other sources:

> *Not all the party leaders were aware, as were Zik and [Festus] Okotie-Eboh, of the fact that British firms were financing the NCNC and that the British Government was actively participating in election rigging and chicanery to ensure that the North with the assistance of the NCNC ruled Nigeria in the British interest after Independence....Okotie-Eboh's ever growing wealth allowed him to play an independent role in politics, even defying his own party when necessary. He financed the NCNC and was probably more powerful than Zik. When criticised in the House of Representatives in 1960 for his dubious property deals, like selling the Department of Labour's trade testing headquarters, a deal put through by British civil servants, he threatened to expose similar deals in the Western Region. Okotie-Eboh and some of his colleagues were more at home with the British-backed NPC Northern leaders than they were with the Igbo leaders of the NCNC. It has been suggested that, as an Itsekiri, Okotie-Eboh could not plunder the Eastern Region, so had to be given licence to pillage the Federal Government - a licence from Sir James Robertson he exploited to the full. To put such a crook in charge of the Ministry of Finance was so unprincipled as to be beyond belief. It convinced me that on a personal level Sir John MacPherson, the Head of the Colonial Office and former Governor General, and Sir James Robertson, the Governor General, thought little of the Nigerian people and cared nothing for democratic values*[55]

In the wake of the corruption scandal surrounding Azikiwe, who was the leader of the House, the Eastern House of Assembly had to be dissolved, once again, to allow new elections to be held, which took place on 15 March 1957. At these elections Azikiwe obtained a fresh mandate to represent the people of the Eastern Region at the Constitutional Conference which was now to be held between May 23 and June 26 1957.

THE LANCASTER HOUSE CONFERENCE OF 1957

The venue for the 1957 Conference was Lancaster House, a stately building in London's St James's district. The choice of venue was ironic because the building had been donated to the Foreign and Commonwealth Office, in 1913, by Viscount William Lever, the founder of Lever Brothers, an imperialist who had made his fortune from the manufacture of soap whose principal raw material was Nigeria's palm oil.

A key objective of the British at the 1957 Conference was to secure agreement *'to the creation of an office of Federal Prime Minister and to an all-Nigerian Federal Council of Ministers presided over by the Governor-General, whose members would be appointed by the Governor-General on the Prime Minister's recommendation'.*[56] The principle was innocent enough to sell but the devil lay in the choice of prime minister. There was no plan for the post to be filled by electoral contest. This was politics by selection and it was Governor Robertson who would be selecting the person who would be the first prime minister. Long before the idea of the new office was presented to the delegates at the Conference, he had made his choice in Tafawa Balewa of the NPC. This is clear from an exchange of correspondence, in February 1957, between Tafawa Balewa and Sharwood-Smith:

> House of Representatives, Lagos
> 10th Feb. '57
>
> DEAR SIR BRYAN,
>
> I am forced to write to you on my personal problems. It is not common with me to worry people with my difficulties but I trust you as a father and hence I am writing.
>
> I am now thinking very much about my future. The climate of Lagos is not suitable to my health and I am never happy here though I find the work most interesting and the people respect me generally. I have been doing my best to assist in making the federation work though I myself do not believe that the present type of federation can exist without the British Administration. There is much talk now about a Prime Minister for Nigeria after the Constitutional Conference and my name is being freely suggested as one. Now I do not like to be a Prime Minister under the present arrangements and I also do not like to continue with my stay in Lagos. I am very tired of politics and I am seriously thinking of retiring quietly at the end of this year. I cannot see in what other capacity I can serve the N. Region and so I hope to take up my N.A. Education work again. You will appreciate the delicate situation in which I am now placed and so I think of quitting politics without any fuss. I have been discussing this matter with my colleagues for some time but they do not seem to appreciate my difficulties. Some of them even say to my face that only death can free me from Lagos! If I act it will be without their knowledge…No British Administrator knows more about us in the North than you do and so I come to you for…guidance in helping me to solve my personal difficulties. I appeal to you as a son to a father.
>
> Yours….
> Abubakar T. Balewa[57]

The grooming of Balewa for his role as Prime Minister had in fact begun long before. He had been one of two Nigerian ministers who represented Nigeria at the 1953 West African Forces Conference which held in Lagos in April 1953[vi]. He also attended the meetings of the West African Military Council which followed. Tragically, Balewa's colleague's comment that only death would free him from Lagos was to prove a prophesy as Sharwood-Smith's response, on 19 February 1957, made it clear that he had no choice but to fulfil the role for which he had been chosen. His only comfort was to be the assurance that neither he nor the North would be left to walk alone in the cause:

> *Abubakar accepted my advice. In the meantime, preparations were going forward for the 1957 Constitutional Conference, and before leaving Lagos for London he wrote to me again. He wished me to prepare for him, personally two papers. In one he asked me to set out what, in my view, were the essential requirements for a new nation aspiring to independence. In the other paper he asked me to lay down what I thought should be the minimum safeguards that the North should demand before finally committing itself to independence.*
> *....The first paper presented no great difficulty. But when it came to the second, I had to stress that constitutional safeguards would not be worth the paper on which they were written, once a legislature made up its mind to scrap them.*
> *It had also to be remembered that, in the ultimate resort, it would be the armed forces of the state, the army and the Nigerian Police, on whose discipline and loyalty the government of the day might have to depend, maybe for survival. It was therefore of great importance that the composition of both forces, both as regards officers and men, should represent a reasonably balanced cross-section of the major ethnic groups in the federation[58]*

With this vital tip-off on the trump-card which control of the army and police represented within any democratic arrangement, the North was ready to take on the educated natives who had only been schooled in the art of constitutional government:

> *On May 23 the delegates assembled in Lancaster House. The Secretary of State, Mr Lennox Boyd, presided, and, this time, the Regional Governors were present in addition to the Governor General. But our part was largely played in personal discussions in less formal surroundings. In the Conference chamber it was for the politicians to hold the stage[59]*

The conference went into adjournment in June 1957 to await some reports and resumed on 29 September 1957. By this time, Azikiwe was in firm alliance with the

vi   The other being Dr Eni Njoku, see N.J. Miners, The Nigerian Army 1956-1966, p. 18

NPC and the British against the common foe, Obafemi Awolowo and his Action Group members.

Awolowo was uncompromising in his insistence upon self-rule. The fact that Ghana had gained independence on 7 March 1957 only added new urgency to the demand. The consensus that had previously held between the NCNC and the Action Group over ending colonial rule by 1956 suddenly fell apart. When the Action Group proposed a motion to demand independence for Nigeria in 1957 the NCNC and the NPC combined to amend it to substitute 1959 for 1957.

The decisions made at the conference included the grant of regional self-government to the Eastern and Western Regions. The position taken by the northern delegates was that they did not want regional self-government until 1959. This was a clever ruse by the British and NPC team which the British were then able to use to partially justify their award of the post of Prime Minister of the Federation to the North. In their vulnerable state over the party funding controversy, Azikiwe and the NCNC were in no position to object. For Awolowo and the Action Group, the proposal to return Lagos to the now-to-be-self-governing Western Region was tendered as a sweetener.

At this point he Action Group realised the game that the British were playing, leading Anthony Enahoro, who had moved the abortive independence motion in 1953, to observe: 'it began to look, ironically, as if those who were least disposed to urge the withdrawal of the imperial power might be its heirs'.[60]

THE MINORITY QUESTION

One of the big issues at the 1957 Conference was the provision to be made for the minority ethnic groups within each of the regions. The Action Group's position was that the independence constitution should make express provision for the creation of new states but in terms which provided that no new states should be created 'without the consent, signified by a two-thirds majority of the legislatures of the states concerned as well as of the Federal Parliament'. The exception was to be the long-standing demands for the creation of Calabar-Ogoja-Rivers (COR) State in the South East, Mid-West State in the South-West and Middle-Belt State in the North. The NCNC argued for an arrangement that would see the country divided into seventeen states while the NPC maintained that the structure should remain as it was.

The different positions taken by the three main ethnic groups on the issue was understandable given that Nigeria was not the creation of any of them: Only the British Colonial Office had the moral authority to deal with the issue. The problem was that the preservation of the 'One North' identity which they had created was critical to British planning at the time. The only way they could effectively avoid the break-up of the North was to maintain a consistent line against the creation of any new states in any region ahead of Independence. What they did was to park the issue by the appointment, in 1958, of a Commission of Enquiry known as the Willinks Commission. Ahead of publication of its Report, in July 1958, the Colonial Secretary had announced that the Commission 'will recommend no new states'[61]. This was a defining moment in the history of Nigeria.

The Willink Commission Report had been the last opportunity for the Colonial Office to bequeath a more balanced and stable Nigeria to posterity in line with the earlier recommendation of four regions which E.D. Morel had made. While the report openly acknowledged the problem, in keeping with the official line, it turned its face against the obvious solution:

> *In each of the three Regions of Nigeria we found either a minority or a group of minorities who described fears and grievances which they felt would become more intense when the present restraints were removed and who suggested as a remedy a separate state or states....In each Region, we came to the conclusion that – on its own merits – a separate state would not provide a remedy for the fears expressed[62]*

Pushing the new country out to independence whilst pregnant with these agitations for self-determination, and new states, could only lead to one outcome.

In a move calculated to drive a wedge between the Action Group and the minorities over the issue, the Colonial Office presented the Action Group with a choice between postponing Independence to allow the issue of new states to be resolved or postponing the creation of new states to allow independence to happen. There could only be one answer since the ending of colonial rule at the earliest possible date was a matter of honour for the Action Group,

The only concession that the Report appeared to make to the problem was that certain areas in the Eastern and Western Region should be designated 'Special Areas' which were to receive special attention. In the Eastern Region these areas were the Niger Delta and the Calabar and in the Western Region, the Mid-West Area. As to the, arguably, greater needs of minority groups in the Northern Region, such as the Christian-Tiv in the Middle Belt areas and the Muslim-Kanuri in the North East, the Report was silent.

What the Report had, in fact, done was to flag the areas in the two Southern Regions that were going to receive 'special attention'. The nature of that attention would only become clear on the eve of two major political crises; first in the Western Region, with the declaration of a state of emergency, and later in the Eastern Region, with the declaration of the State of Biafra.

Writing in July, 1958, four months ahead of the Independence elections that were to take place in November 1959, Lennox-Boyd was already anticipating the outcome:

> *The vast Northern Region is still well behind the others in "progress". Two-thirds of its 18 million people are strict Muslims, accepting the authority of their Emirs. Educational progress is still slow and there is no prospect for a generation of the Region being able to replace from its own resources the overseas officers who have served them so well. The North fears and dislikes the more educated Southerners and if they were not economically bound to the Federation would be glad to be quit of it....I understand that at the Federal elections late next year the Northern Peoples' Congress and the NCNC (who are normally kept apart by mutual suspicion and by Northern dislike of Dr Azikiwe) alarmed by the determination and organising ability of the Action Group are likely to combine to keep the Action Group out of power. Such a combination would offer no great reassurance for competent or courageous Federal Government. The tribal divisions that remain in Nigeria are so deep that the unity and stability of the country cannot yet be taken for granted[63]*

Lennox-Boyd's suggestion that the idea of a coalition between North and East to stop the Action-Group came from the Nigerian parties rather than from his office fails scrutiny. The timing of his July 1958 memorandum, referred to above, ties in with a meeting which had taken place earlier in May 1958 between Nnamdi Azikiwe and the Sardauna of Sokoto which Anthony Enahoro suggests was the occasion on which the NPC and NCNC alliance was brokered:

> *The Action Group and the N.C.N.C. had drifted apart since the brief accord of 1953. My people in Ishan have a proverb: 'Those with similar aesthetic tastes are more likely to quarrel over a maiden.' So it was with the Action Group and the NCNC. The two parties were rivals for the leadership of the nationalist and progressive movement. They both claimed to be socialist. They were both most active in the same area – Southern Nigeria. They both appealed to the same audiences and the same interests. They could either be the closest of allies or the most violent of opponents. The latter was the case by May 1958 when Dr Azikiwe had sprung a surprise on the country and, it was said, on N.E.P.U., his party allies, by paying a visit to the Sardauna of Sokoto at Kaduna. It may have been at this meeting that an understanding was reached in broad terms for the N.C.N.C. and NPC to work together, if neither party was in a position to control the Federal Government...[64]*

In the hard game of politics, the Colonial Office team were entitled to put British interests first and they did. The "tribal divisions" (which were in fact ancient national divisions) made it unlikely that any single party was going to be able to command an absolute majority such that the only issue was which party was going to lead the inevitable coalition government. But all pretence of the Colonial Office being a disinterested umpire of an electoral contest for power finally evaporated with the last act to usurp the democratic choice of the Nigerian people when the Independence elections did eventually take place in December 1959.

With the results showing NPC with one hundred and thirty-four seats; NCNC with eighty-nine seats and Action Group with seventy-three seats, and before all the votes had been counted, the Colonial Office rushed to swear-in the NPC's Tafawa Balewa as Prime Minister[65], thus delivering a fait accompli. It was a desperate final measure to close off the possibility of an alliance between the Action Group and the NCNC which was then under active discussion between the two parties.

INDEPENDENCE DAY

The choice of the date on which Independence would be granted to Nigeria had, throughout, been a matter which the British had reserved for their discretion.
When the time came, they chose 1 October 1960. That 1 October was the day, in 1954, on which the NPC had been formed cannot be put down to mere coincidence. 1 October was also the date, in 1954, on which the Lyttleton Constitution gave birth to the new House of Representatives under NPC control.

The rigging of the first national elections in Nigeria was only one of 'the conventions of Whitehall' that the Colonial Office discarded. The elections could, of course, have been rigged to give the North an outright victory. That this did not happen was because a coalition government of the North and part of the South had the advantage of making northern rule more acceptable to the South whilst the presence of southerners in the government served to restrain some of the excesses of northern rule which might otherwise have manifested.

These lessons in democracy in action which the British gave as their parting gift were not lost on the winners nor on future generations of Nigerian parliamentarians. The rigging in favour of the 'Kano rulers' was explained and confirmed fairly recently by the late Sir Peter Smithers:

> *I was Parliamentary Private Secretary at the Colonial Office through almost the whole of the period of decolonisation, I was one of the three man mission which visited Africa in 1952 to consider the federal structures which it was proposed to establish in Africa, I was present at most of the negotiations*

for independence including that of Nigeria, and....I had, therefore, a rather comprehensive view of the process of decolonisation and of the establishment of Nigeria in its present boundaries.

....The concept of Nigeria in the mind of Alan Lennox-Boyd, the Secretary of State at that time (I was his Parliamentary Private Secretary and thus his eyes and ears in the House of Commons) was that Nigeria should be established as a large and powerful state, rich in resources of many kinds, which would be an element of stability amidst the numerous small African states resulting from the dissolution of the French Empire. On the face of it this was a reasonable view and I agreed with it at the time. We did not then have the benefit of experience generated by the problems of multi-racial states which we have since seen manifested in the former USSR, in Yugoslavia and elsewhere. It is now clear that the policy was mistaken, and that it would have been better to set up a number of smaller states corresponding with the pre-colonial ethnic boundaries. At the same time it must be pointed out that to have done this would have involved the demolition of existing administrative structures, involving a good deal of confusion and hardship at the very outset of independence. There existed an excellent administrative machine ready for the new Nigerian Government to take over....The attraction of the Kano rulers was that they had long and successful experience of government. They therefore offered an obvious choice to head the new experiment. It was in fact difficult at that time to see an alternative for the early stages of independence[66]

On 1 October 1960 the coalition government of the NPC and the NCNC took office with Tafawa Balewa as Prime Minister precisely as the Colonial Office had ordained. But the event that symbolized the new relationship between the British and the Fulani was the formal return of the flag of the Caliphate, with its motto in Arabic 'Victory comes from God alone', which took place the following month:

The final token of the changed status of the Queen's Own Nigeria Regiment was a ceremony that took place on the durbar ground at Sokoto in November 1960. The flag of Sultan Attahiru Ahmadu, kept since 1903 by the first battalion as a trophy of their victory, was paraded and solemnly handed over to the reigning Sultan of Sokoto in the presence of the premier of the Northern Region[67]

Writing in 1969, Sharwood-Smith attributed the inspiration for the title of his memoirs to the speech given on Independence Day, 1 October 1960, by Balewa:

We are grateful to the British officers whom we have known, first as masters and then as leaders and, finally as partners but always as friends....[68]

BOOK 3.
THE END GAME

8. The Short Road from Independence to Biafra

"What if a man should take upon him to be king?"
Oliver Cromwell

THE BRITISH ARMY IN NIGERIA

In front of the main entrance to the British Houses of Parliament at Westminster stands a statue of a soldier with his sword in his right hand and the Bible in his left. It is a permanent reminder to the parliamentarians that democracy, in England, was fathered by the army.

Oliver Cromwell, monarchist, defender of the faith, parliamentarian and soldier, was the man who instituted rule by a parliament of the people. This was after he had beheaded the king on 30 January 1649 and, by so doing, put an end to the tradition of despotic rule of monarchs. The first parliament having fallen short of his expectations, he chased them out in a military coup on 20 April 1653. Only afterwards did he bring back both king and parliament to share power on the terms of a new constitution drawn up by his army.

Ever since the reign of Cromwell, British statesmen have known that the control of the army is the lynchpin of all government. As they were making their preparations for the grant of independence to Nigeria, the officials of the British Colonial Office had this important lesson of history firmly in mind. Sharwood-Smith had made clear the imperative of Northern control of the army and the police force in his confidential advice note to Balewa.[1] The point was reiterated by Sir Peter Smithers in his letter in which he explained that control of the police and the army had been the chief difficulty. That the North controlled the security forces at independence was, therefore, no accident.

The shape of the armed forces in Nigeria had evolved according to the needs, and sensitivities, of the colonial government. In the beginning when the military objective had been the conquest of the Fulani Empire, the West African Frontier Force had been recruited from amongst 'the Hausa, the Yoruba and Nupe'.[2] After the First World War, the Colonial Office conducted a review of its policy of recruitment to the West African Frontier Force. The report, which was produced by the Inspector General of the forces in 1923, identified the tribes that should henceforth be recruited from:

> *Southerners were perceived as 'timorous and secretive in character.... Almost entirely pagan, and much addicted to fetish worship and are inclined to be suspicious of Europeans'. They were not recruited into the military in large numbers because it was felt that they lacked fighting spirit and did 'not possess the qualifications necessary to make good soldiers'. As for the Northern ethnic groups, it drew a distinction between the Muslim Far North and the pagan Lower North, but found that they were 'of a franker and bolder disposition'. It found that the Hausa of the Far North were 'brave, intelligent, easy to discipline and show a remarkable spirit of devotion to their officers'. Similarly, the Fulani, also of the Far North, were found to demonstrate 'a decided power of command' necessary for a good non-commissioned officer. Although the pagan tribes of the Lower North had many of the military attributes of the tribes of the Upper North, however, they were not considered as intelligent[3]*

The comment that the southerners lacked fighting spirit was a convenient untruth which was to be much repeated to explain northern domination of the armed forces. There was more to the matter than the report was admitting to.

The real reason was that the lessons of the 1918 armed-challenge to British rule, by the combined forces of the Egba and Owu Yoruba tribes, while the First World War was going on, had not been forgotten. That uprising was the only all-out war between the British and the natives since the Amalgamation and though it had ended in defeat for the Egba and Owu rebels, it had also led to the recall of Lugard as governor-general. The claim that the southerners did 'not possess the qualifications necessary to make good soldiers', on the other hand, is less open to question since the armed forces of a state depends upon the unquestioning commitment of its members to the state's defence.

Thus the report's recommendations were a reflection of the colonial administration's assessment of where the long-term threats to its longevity would come from. Having already determined that the level of education that had been allowed in Southern Nigeria had been a grave policy error for the empire's longevity, there was little appetite for compounding that error, and increasing the threat, by recruiting, and training, military personnel from the South in great numbers.

These political considerations meant that at the time of the report, the Nigerian army was seventy percent northern[4]. It was only the exigencies of the Second World War, which required educated Nigerians to be trained to do the work that had previously been done by British officers, and to fight in the densely-forested regions of India and Burma, that the recruitment policy was modified.[5] At the end of the war, after the empire's needs had been met, most of these Nigerians who had seen combat were quickly de-mobilized.

NIGERIANIZATION OF THE ARMY

At the onset of the nationalist struggle for independence following the end of the war, the Nigerian army was really the British Army in Nigeria. Although Nigerians had formed the bulk of its fighting force since its creation, as the West African Frontier Force, the officers were almost exclusively British. It was not until 1948 that Lt. Laud Victor Ugboma became the first Nigerian to be commissioned. That the security services would be last aspect of governance that a colonial power would expose its subjects to, stood to reason. Thus, whilst the drive to promote Nigerians to senior posts in the public service had started in 1948, with the creation of a Nigerianization Commission, that initiative did not extend to the army.

It was the sudden hardening of the American stance on de-colonization, in the wake of Suez, coupled with the near break-up of the Federation following the 1953 Independence motion crisis, which now injected urgency into the task of assembling a Nigerian army that would preserve the Nigeria legacy.

Although they were now resigned to the need to bring in educated natives into the Nigerian army, there was still an important judgment to be made about which part of the South the new recruits were to come from and which sections of the army they were to be recruited into.

Having decided upon a political alliance of the North and the East to rule the country at independence, it followed that the composition of the army should reflect the political order that it was to protect:

> *In view of the backwardness of the Northern Region in education it is very surprising that the first five regular officers to graduate from Sandhurst were all Northerners. In 1954 only 85 boys from the North passed the School Certificate Examination, compared with 1,334 boys in the South. All five Northerners had been at the same school, Government*[6]

At the same time, there was a conscious drive to recruit Igbos into the army at senior levels:

Easterners had predominated among the cadets taken for officer training in the period from 1955-1958, when selection was entirely in the hands of British officers[7]

The ethnic stratification of the officer class of the new Nigerian Army was to be the last act of the British Empire in Nigeria. In the situation where, at independence, two-thirds of the officers in the Nigerian Army were from the East, a clash for supremacy between the two alliance partners, North and East, would only be a matter of time.

The army being the ultimate guarantor of political control, the North had little to fear so long as it was essentially a northern army. But a sudden surge in the recruitment of Igbo officers would mean that the North would no longer be sure of the loyalty of the armed forces and this was bound to feed anxieties. This manifested in the Balewa government introducing a quota system into army recruitment to stem the Igbo tide. In the meantime, the challenge for the British, remained what to do with the graduates who had now joined the army:

No attempt was made to advertise for graduates to enter the Army before 1960, either for the fighting arms or the technical corps. There were quite a number of Nigerian doctors who had qualified abroad who might have been attracted into the Army earlier, but none was commissioned before 1961. There was one unexpected graduate recruit in 1957: Odumegwu Ojukwu, who had taken his B.A. in History at Oxford in 1955 and then served as assistant district officer in the administrative service for two years, was commissioned in March 1958[8]

The suspicion of educated natives was of course long-standing. The concerns over the new graduate class coming into the army was grounded in the fear that they would have been exposed to radical, possibly communist, thoughts in the course of their undergraduate studies. At the outset the policy was to contain the risk by keeping this suspect group away from the fighting corps:

Two graduates were commissioned before Independence, Ojukwu in 1958, and Olutoye in 1960. The latter had a B.Sc. degree and was mostly employed in the Army Education Service, rising to the head of it in 1964. Three more graduates were given combatant commissions after 1960: Rotimi and Ifeajuna in 1961 and Ademoyega in 1962. Rotimi had been a cadet at school at King's College when the first unit was formed there; Ifeajuna was an outstanding athlete who had won the gold medal for the high jump at the Commonwealth Games; Ademoyega had been an administrative officer in the Federal public service for a short time between graduating and joining the Army. After these three no other graduates were given combatant commissions...all other graduates who entered the Army after 1960 were given 'direct commissions' and were recruited specifically to practise their professional skills as doctors, engineers or teachers....These officers had no more than the most perfunctory military training and generally served in the headquarters or technical units. As they would not normally be in command of any considerable body of troops, these graduates posed no threat to the government[9]

THE ATTEMPT TO BRIDGE THE NIGER

Against the background of the extreme measures that had been taken to ensure an NPC victory in the independence elections, the British were in no doubt that the rickety alliance, which they had forged between the North and the East, would not hold.

It was a marriage of the strangest bedfellows and not just because of the Muslim-Christian divide. The one alliance partner was driven by individual aspiration and industry; the other was communal and authority-led. The East, and principally the Igbos, were natural democrats and egalitarians amongst whom the institution of hierarchy through chieftaincy was a recent import that had failed to take root. In contrast the lead partners in the North were aristocratic and traditional. This was an alliance of convenience with the sole objective of sharing power and of keeping the political opponents, in the West, out of power.

The alliance was under constant threat with entreaties by Awolowo to Azikiwe for a substitute alliance between East and West:

> *...I hold it as a fact that if the Action Group and the NCNC, both of which parties have a monopoly of political following in the South, and at least one-third of the political followership in the North, could come together then, they would serve a catalyst to the political system in the North to ensure the creation of more states in the Northern Region, entrench liberal democracy in the country and infinitely increase the tempo of progress in the Federation as a whole.*
>
> *I also hold it as a fact that such combination is sure to win a landslide victory at a subsequent federal election. In all these connections I hold it as a fact that in view of the standing and stature of Dr Nnamdi Azikiwe in the politics of the country the most important step towards the solution of the problem of the North, the problem of Nigeria and the problem of taking over power in the Federation would be to contrive to bring him back into politics and to combine and bring together under his leadership all the truly nationalist, progressive and radical elements in the Federation[10]*

232

Nnamdi Azikiwe's Compound in Onitsha

With Balewa installed as Prime Minister, to keep power the Northern Region only had to remain 'One' and to secure an alliance with either the Eastern or, alternatively, the Western region. To put Awolowo's desired alliance between the East and the West further out of reach the British crowned the alliance between the North and the East which they had engineered by appointing Azikiwe to the ceremonial office of governor-general of the Federation. The events that followed in the immediate post-Independence years were dominated by the West's efforts to replace the North as the East's alliance partner:

> "I was to make direct contact with Dr Azikiwe myself. But the two of us having been opposed politically for upwards of two decades, I had to prepare the ground. I wrote him a nice letter when he became Governor-General. I took time to attend all the functions which were held to make his inauguration as Governor-General....Eventually, on 15th of August 1961, I met Dr Azikiwe himself at 5 p.m. in London. I used that meeting as a sort of attempt to break the ice. On the 20th of December 1961, in Nigeria, at the State House, at 12.30p.m., I met Dr Azikiwe again. That was after I had been conferred the Doctor of Laws Degree of the university of Nigeria, Nsukka. "On that occasion I made it absolutely plain to Dr Azikiwe that I was prepared to serve under him and that in the event of his wanting to stand for the presidential election, I assured him of all Action Group votes as I was not going to stand as a candidate myself"[11]

Awolowo's efforts to build an alliance with the East were doomed to failure because the North, with the support of the British Colonial Office, had its own strategies to ensure that that alliance would never happen. At its core was what looked like an innocent appeal for unity, an all-party alliance, under Balewa:

> To further this overriding need for unity, my colleagues in the Council of Ministers and I have decided to give the country a lead by inviting the leaders of the Action Group to form with us a truly National Government composed of members of the main parties in the Country, and here I must pay tribute to Dr Azikiwe, to Chief Awolowo, Dr Endeley and to the leader of my own party, the Sardauna of Sokoto, for supporting me in this decision. I and my Colleagues of the N.C.N.C. and N.P.C. hold out our hands in welcome to the Action Group members of the Council and I promise you that we shall do our utmost to ensure that the deliberations of the Council are held in an atmosphere devoid of strife and narrow party prejudice[12]

It was a strategy that would split the Action Group and throw the Western Region into crisis before using the breakaway party from the Action Group as new alliance partners to replace the NCNC.

234

What followed, over the ten years following Independence, was determined action to neutralize the threat to Northern rule by the use of the army spawning the Western Region political crisis of 1962 and the military occupation of the Region; the Treason Trials of 1963 leading to the imprisonment of the main political actors in the South West; the uprising in the Tiv Division leading to the military occupation of that area from 1964; the political crisis in the Western Region in 1965 leading to a virtual civil war in that region; the first military coup in January, 1966; the military countercoup of July 1966; and the Biafran war of 1967 leading to the military conquest of Biafra in January 1970.

THE 1962 WESTERN REGION CRISIS

Balewa's appeal for national unity was an easy one for him to make; it was in reality the offer of a poisoned chalice. For Awolowo it posed a dilemma.

If the Action Group rejected the hand that the NPC was offering, it would be labelled un- patriotic. If it accepted it, its message for future electoral contests against the NPC would be compromised. The problem, as Awolowo saw it, was not going into an alliance for the sake of national unity per se, but going into an alliance with the NPC:

> *When I delivered my lecture in London one of the students asked me whether I could work under Balewa and I said I could not because both of us do not operate on the same wavelength. I opposed the participation of my party in a National Government because I felt that such participation would mean the disappearance of the Opposition which in the view of democrats is the soul of democracy. I would not take office under Balewa at any time. If the Prime Minister had been Dr Azikiwe I would gladly work under him. I would not work under the Sardauna. He is the fountain of authoritarian rule in the North and of oppression in Nigeria[13]*

The problem for Awolowo was that there were some within his party who were keen not to miss out on this first opportunity to taste power. There was also the thinking was that if Action Group members joined the national government they would have the opportunity to build closer relationships with the NCNC and woo them from within.

The compromise, between opportunity and principle, which Awolowo thought he had found was to put forward Samuel Akintola, the then deputy leader of the Action Group, and Ayo Rosiji, the then Federal Secretary to the party, to join the Balewa-led coalition government whereupon they became Federal Ministers.[14] It proved a fatal move as the NPC was now presented with an opportunity to groom these Action Group members of the national coalition government to open up the divide between Awolowo's camp and Akintola and his followers. Enahoro explained the divide as follows:

Ever since Independence Day, debate had raged within the party over the future of the Western Region and of the party. Some members wanted the Action Group to join an all-party coalition government at the Centre. Others suggested that the Western Region should secede from the Federation. Some that the party should seek accord with the N.C.N.C., others with the NPC. In the end, two schools of thought predominated; the one, led by Chiefs Akintola and Rosiji, leaned towards the N.P.C. and desired to join a national coalition at any cost, and the other, led by Chief Awolowo and myself, preferred the N.C.N.C. and suggested what became known as a Progressive Front comprising the N.C.N.C., Action Group, N.E.P.U. and U.M.B.C.[15]

As the crisis within the party grew, attempts were made to reconcile the irreconcilables but deeper currents were at work. As Awolowo, himself, put it:

Chief Akintola's chief complaint at the meeting for settlement in February 1962 was that I made unfavourable reference to the advisability of the Action Group participating in a National Government. I never wanted National Government because I felt it would spell the doom of the Opposition and consequently of Parliamentary democracy. In order, however, to please the Obas and Chief Akintola, and those who shared his views, I interviewed the Prime Minister, Sir Abubakar, on the 6th of April 1962 to discuss with him the possibility of the Action Group participating in a National Government. Up till that day, though Sir Abubakar had always expressed his preference for a National Government in the Press and the public and to Chief Akintola and Chief Rosiji, he had never thought it fit to mention it to me[16]

In May 1962 the party moved to charge Akintola with disloyalty and anti-party activities. Although he had pleaded guilty to the charges and apologised for his conduct,[17] he refused to step down from his position as Premier and Deputy Leader. When a petition to remove him from the posts was acceded to by the stand-in Governor of the Western Region, Akintola commenced High Court proceedings claiming that he had the support of a majority of the members of the Western Region House of Assembly. A meeting of that Assembly, called by the party to test his claim, turned into a fracas which Enahoro narrated as follows:

When the House met on 25th May 1962, Chief Awolowo and I were sitting in the distinguished guests' box behind Mr, Speaker. Supporters of Chief Akintola and the N.C.N.C., who were at that time indisputably the minority, commenced a fight in the Chamber. N.C.N.C. Members marched across the floor and waded into A.G. Members. One N.C.N.C. supporter lifted the mace from its place of rest and tried to hit Mr. Speaker but, missing him, smashed it on the table and broke it. A Minister, Kessington Momoh, was struck on the head with a sharp instrument and bled freely[18]

The NPC-NCNC government quickly rushed to suspend democracy in the Western Region by declaring a state of emergency on 29th May 1962. Enahoro continued:

So within four days of the riotous assembly at Ibadan, the Federal Government had suspended the Western Government and Legislature, adopted a mass of stringent regulations, appointed an Administrator and restricted leading politicians. Had it all been arranged long beforehand? The Federal Government was not accustomed to such speed[19]

From this point forward the Western Region was effectively under military occupation by a Nigerian army composed principally of Northern troops under the overall command of a British officer. The region would remain under military occupation until the Biafran War.

BREAKING UP THE ACTION GROUP'S POLITICAL BASE

The British stand against the creation of new states ahead of independence had forced the issue to return later with greater force and under an administration with far less moral authority to deal with it. It is no exaggeration to say that all the post-independence crises in Nigeria can be traced back to this decision because, left in the hands of the three dominant ethnic groups the issue of the creation of new states simply became a political weapon for use in emasculating rival regions.

The creation of new states had been one of the key, potentially-vote-winning, policies being pushed by the Action Group in the territory of both the North and the East. With the Western Region being the least heterogeneous of the three Regions (the Edo people being the only significant minority group), it had been an easy policy for the party to push. In contrast, the East had many minority groups and the North had even more, especially in the Middle Belt area. The Action Group saw in the policy the prospect of cutting the North down to size by undermining the One North policy. To this end it built close relations with the Christian Tiv in the Middle Belt and with the Muslim Kanuri in the North East both groups who were known to defend their independence from the Hausa-Fulani. Once more, the NPC with the support of the British Colonial Office and its NCNC allies, were to beat the Action Group to the punch.

Had the colonial government responded to the demand for the creation of new states it would have been hard-pressed not to do something in each of the three regions equally: It would not have carved a new Mid-West State out of the Western Region without taking similar measures in the Eastern and Northern Regions especially since the Western Region was the smallest and least heterogeneous of the three. But a new Nigerian coalition government, made up of an alliance of the Eastern and Northern Regions could do precisely that. It was telling that the act to create the Mid-West Region, and effectively break up the Western Region, was published by the Federal Government on 24 May 1962, the eve of the crucial meeting in the Western Region House of Assembly on the back of which a state of emergency in the Region was declared.[20]

THE STATE OF EMERGENCY IN TIV COUNTRY

The treatment given by the NPC-NCNC government to the Tiv minority in the Northern Region, who were allies of the Western Region, could not have been more different from the new region that had just been created for the mid-westerners.

Due to their mountainous terrain and their fighting spirit, the Tiv had never been easy to conquer. The British found the task difficult and the Fulani found it impossible. Now that the British were leaving the Tiv were deeply hostile to the idea of being handed over to Fulani rule as part of the One North policy. Being Christians within the predominantly Muslim North, they felt their minority status twice over.

The Action Group's policies towards minorities, and specifically the party's proposal of a Middle Belt state to be carved out of the North, had an obvious appeal to the Tiv. For this reason the United Middle Belt Congress ("UMBC") under the leadership of Joseph Tarka became a close ally of the Action Group.

In the NPC's calculation, this was a dangerous liaison which, if not attacked, had the potential to give the Action Group a bridgehead into the North. With nothing to offer the Tiv to rival the Action Group's proposed Middle Belt State, the solution adopted was to frustrate the democratic aspirations of the UMBC with the aid of Tiv traditional rulers on the Native Authority. The trouble had started in the run up to the November, 1959 independence elections:

> By the time the first explosion came in August 1960, the UMBC supporters in Tiv
> Division had exhausted their patience and tolerance for the local functionaries
> of the NPC regime. The Government having made it impossible for legitimate
> opposition voices to be heard made itself vulnerable to violent aggression....
> Those targeted were the clan and kindred heads, court presidents and members,
> tax collectors and, generally, known supporters of the NPC. The 1960 uprising
> which first began in Yandev near Gboko soon spread like wild fire to other parts
> of Tiv Division[21]

The response of the NPC-NCNC government to the uprising was ruthless. It dissolved the Native Authority and imposed collective punishment on all Tivs by requiring every adult male to pay reparations for the riot damage. The failure of the same NPC-NCNC government that had carved the Mid-West State out of the Western Region to redress the Tiv grievance in the same way led to a heightened sense of grievance. This, coupled with the arrest and imprisonment on charges of treason of the UMBC leader Joseph Tarka, led to a bloodier uprising in 1964. The Balewa government's response was to send the army in:

> *Of course, this was not the first time the Army would be deployed to Tiv Division since Independence...But the November 18, 1964 order was the first time when a massive military force involving a whole battalion (3 NA) including the Recce Squadron was being mobilised for an Internal Security Operation...Troops were never withdrawn again thereafter until the outbreak of the civil war*[22]

Thus, in the run up to the Biafran war, the Western Region and its allies, the Tiv, in the Middle Belt, were both under effective military occupation. The 'special attention' that was to be given to the Niger Delta and Calabar was still to come.

AND THEN DANCE WITH THE REMNANTS OF THE WEST

The final act in the NPC-N.C.N.C. government's systematic dismantling of the threat from the Western Region was the announcement, on 17 September 1962, that the police had uncovered a plot to overthrow the Government. Awolowo, Enahoro, and the Tiv political leader Joseph Tarka were now charged with treason.

Tarka's position was remarkable; just months before, in June 1961, he had been acquitted of a separate charge of treason against what had been the Government of Northern Nigeria.[23] Fate smiled on him again as he was acquitted of all charges. His co-accused, Awolowo and Enahoro, were sentenced to prison for ten and twelve years respectively.

After the Supreme Court dismissed their appeals on 1 July 1964, what was expected to be a long period of forced removal from the political stage began for Awolowo and Enahoro. This, what seemed at first their misfortune, turned out to be good fortune as their incarceration at the time of the first military coup in January 1966 perhaps saved their lives when other political leaders were murdered. At the same time their survival contributed to giving the coup the colouration of an anti-North plot. In the meanwhile, the Action Group stood decapitated.

When the state of emergency in the Western Region was lifted in January, 1963, instead of the NPC-NCNC alliance government directing new elections, it simply appointed Akintola as Premier, in succession to Awolowo, in a new administration made up of Akintola's followers and members of the Western branch of the NCNC. Awolowo's Action Group, which had been the official opposition to the NPC-NCNC alliance, had effectively ceased to exist.

But in aiding the emergence of the Akintola faction from the Action Group, the NCNC had unwittingly joined with the NPC to prepare the ground for its own replacement as an alliance partner.

THE BATTLE OF THE COUNT

The next round of federal elections, scheduled for December 1964, were to be the first that Nigerians would be conducting for themselves. With the Action Group decapitated and effectively neutralised, it was looking like a two-way contest between the NPC and the NCNC with the NPC controlling the Northern Region and the NCNC now controlling almost the whole of the Southern Region (after winning the February 1964 elections in the new Mid-West State). The omens for free elections were never good.

Both former alliance partners, NPC and NCNC, had benefited from the rigged Independence elections. Each understood the importance of the census since seats in the federal parliament were to be apportioned according to the population of each region. With the political parties reflecting regional, and ethnic, divides it was clear to the contestants that the crucial first step to winning the next, and indeed, possibly all future elections in the country, was to win the census due in 1962.

Since neither of the former alliance partners trusted the other, a Briton, Mr J.J. Warren, was appointed to head the count.[24] Even so the exercise ended in controversy when the results suggested that the South was more populous than the North, notwithstanding the British manipulation through the division of the Cameroons.[25] Harold Smith put the census controversy into context:

> *The massive power of the North rested on the census figures produced by British officials in the early 1950's. All attempts to confirm those census figures since have proved a failure and this has become the most bitterly contested issue in Nigerian politics. After the census in 1962 it was found that the Northern Region no longer had a numerical majority over the rest of the country combined. The NPC leaders found these results unacceptable and cancelled the results. The 1962 census returns were never officially published. In a fresh census in 1963 the North improved on its 1962 figures. If Southerners had thought that the new figures would end the North's absolute majority they were to be bitterly disappointed. It was little wonder that Awolowo commented bitterly that for himself and his party 'the twilight of democracy and the rule of law in Nigeria is changing into darkness'[26]*

While the census dispute was still raging, the western-branch of the NCNC led by Chief Fani-Kayode, who was then the Deputy-Premier of the Western Region, decamped from the party to join with Akintola's followers to form a new party, under an old name, the Nigerian National Democratic Party (NNDP)[i]. By this move Akintola had contrived to take back from the NCNC the political legacy of Herbert Macauley in the Western Region.

After the Eastern Region's challenge to the census figures was rejected by the Supreme Court on 29 August 1964, the Federal Government proceeded to release the final census figures suggesting a total population of 55, 620,268 of which 29, 758, 875 was said to be in the Northern Region, giving the North a comfortable majority over the South with 53.5% of the total. With the census battle thus having been won and lost, the stage was now set for the showdown Federal elections.

BEFORE BREAKING OFF THE ALLIANCE WITH THE EAST

Ahmadu Bello, the leader of the NPC, was never one to mince his words for long. With Awolowo in prison, and Akintola having been installed as Premier of the Western Region, Bello effectively brought the alliance with the Eastern Region and the NCNC to an end with the following declaration:

> *Even if my party fails to get the required majority in the next federal elections, it will definitely not enter into a coalition with the NCNC...the Ibos have never been true friends of the North and never will be[27]*

On 26 September 1964, the NPC-NCNC alliance government was formally dissolved. Fifteen months later, on 15 January 1966, Ahmadu Bello and Prime Minister Tafawa Balewa would be murdered in a military coup and by July 1967, the former partners, the North and the East, would be at war in the Biafran War. The build up to crisis and conflict began with the Federal elections of December 1964.

THE END OF THE FIRST REPUBLIC

Having failed with its challenge to the 1964 census figures, the NCNC knew that there was little hope for a fair electoral contest against its former partner.

When the head of the Western-branch of the party, Samuel Akintola, demerged the NNDP from the NCNC and went into alliance with the NPC under the banner-name of the Nigerian National Alliance (NNA), the NCNC was left with no alternative but to go into alliance with those members of the Action Group who were still loyal to Awolowo

---

i   The Nigerian National Democratic Party was the name of Nigeria's first politicalparty formed in 1923 by Herbert Macauley

under the name the . However, with Awolowo in prison and Azikiwe trapped in the presidency, this coming together of the decapitated parties was a poor shadow of the southern alliance that Awolowo had been pushing for all along.

With the NNA effectively controlling the North and, through Akintola, also the Western Region, the UPGA knew that to stand any chance of victory in the elections it had to win seats in the Northern Region. A hard task was made impossible by the no-holds-barred tactics adopted by the NPC-controlled Federal Government:

> *The campaign was marked by a fair amount of thuggery by 'party stalwarts'. Conditions were so bad in Tiv Division that the Army had to be sent in...certain NPC officials in the North showed an excess of zeal when they forcibly prevented certain UPGA candidates in the far North from filing their nomination papers, and so secured the unopposed return of sixty-seven NPC candidates*[28]

Faced with the prospect of being out-muscled in the electoral contest, the UPGA decided to boycott the elections in the mistaken assumption that its rival had any interest in a fair contest. When the NNA claimed victory by default in the East, and in the Federation overall, the UPGA refused to accept the result.

Azikiwe, the former leader of the Eastern Region, but who had been kicked upstairs to the largely-ceremonial office of President of the Federation in October 1963, was now drawn into the fray to decide who would form the new government: his former party in the East or his former partners in the North.

He initially resisted Balewa's demand to be re-appointed Prime Minister to the point that President and Prime Minister were not on speaking terms. But suspending the constitution in the face of the stalemate depended upon his authority being accepted by the army. With a British general, Maj. Gen. Welby-Everard, still the general officer commanding the Nigerian army, there was little prospect of him getting British support for anything but the return of Balewa to power. In the end, it was Balewa's NNA that he was forced to call upon to form the new government. After this, very public, standoff between Prime Minister and President, the administration had little prospect of making it through to the next scheduled elections.

The importance of the post of the commander of the army having been highlighted by this episode, and having been previously stressed by Sharwood-Smith, it is a curious thing that when in February 1965 Major-General Welby-Everard had to be replaced by one of four Nigerian brigadiers, Maimalari, Ogundipe, Ademulegun or Aguyi-Ironsi, it was the Igbo man, Aguyi-Ironsi, who was appointed rather than the Northerner, Maimalari, especially since, as it will emerge later in this account, Aguyi-Ironsi appears not to have had the best credentials.

'OPERATION WETIE'

The already-heated political situation in the country was made worse when regional elections in the Western Region followed in October 1965. At these elections Akintola was looking to be legitimised as the political voice of the people of the Western Region. For the NPC, victory in these elections for its alliance partner would put the party in a position where it would, effectively, be in control of the whole of Nigeria excepting only the Eastern Region.

With the memory of the imprisonment of their leader Awolowo still fresh, an insurgency broke out in the Western Region when the NPC-NNDP alliance partners resorted to the same bullying tactics they had used in the federal elections in the East to produce an improbable victory for Akintola's NNDP:

> *The plan to foreclose any chance of an electoral victory for the NNDP's opponents was multi-faceted. Opposition candidates and voters were often intimidated or prevented from filing nomination papers or voting. Even where opposition candidates managed to stand for election and win in results declared at polling stations, radio announcements would announce a different set of results with NNDP candidates being declared "unopposed" winners. The NNDP was shockingly declared the winner of the elections against all expectations. Many westerners could not understand how a party they loathed and voted against could have possibly gained a legitimate victory. Akintola's retention of power led to even greater violence in the Western Region. Protests, arson and murders placed many parts of the Western Region into a state of near anarchy, which earned the Region the nickname of the "wild west"[29]*

While the federal government had been quick to declare a state of emergency on the back of the fisticuffs within the Western Region House of Assembly in 1962, it was content to stand back and watch the West burn even though estimates suggested that more than two thousand people had been killed in the violence which trailed the announcement of Akintola's electoral victory. The Federal government's indifference to the bloodshed in the Western Region was all the more remarkable given that the Briton, Major-General Welby-Everard[30] was still the head of the army at this time and, another Briton, John Hilary-Smith, was serving as Deputy Secretary to Prime Minister Tafawa Balewa. Everything pointed to the blind eye being a policy decision.

THE 1966 COUPS

It was while the West was burning that the first military coup in the country occurred on Saturday 15 January 1966. Of the many mysteries surrounding this coup the most intriguing is how a soldier with the nickname 'Ironside' emerged as Nigeria's first military ruler.

Maj. Gen. Johnson Thomas Umunnakwe Aguiyi-Ironsi is said to have acquired the nickname while he was serving with a United Nations peacekeeping force in the Congo. It is suggested that the nickname 'Ironside' had been given to him by British officers as a 'corruption of his surname 'Ironsi' with reference to various military historical parallels on account of his feats of valour'. Only that it appears that his surname was not actually 'Ironsi' - a word with no obvious meaning or common usage in the Igbo language - but simply 'Aguiyi' - which means crocodile. Thus, it seems that what happened was that his nickname was corrupted to form part of his surname.[ii]

Further, the suggestion that he was an exceptional soldier is not borne out by the available evidence. The following is an extract from a magazine interview that Maj. Chukuma Nzeogwu, the lead actor in the coup that brought him to power, is reported to have given in May 1967:

> [Ejindu]:   *Tell me, what do you think of him [Ironsi] as a soldier*
>
> [Nzeogwu]:   *I am afraid I cannot tell you that. But I will say that as a person he was very well liked and as the Supreme Commander, his orders were promptly carried out.*
>
> [Ejindu]:   *If he joined the Army as a gunner, he must have progressed as a military strategist?*
>
> [Nzeogwu]:   *Yes, if he had, he could have done so. But he actually joined the Army as a tally clerk and was a clerk most of the time[31]*

Nzeogwu's assessment does not stand in isolation. Its thrust is supported by another account of Ironsi's performance in Congo:

> *Lt.-Col. Ironsi's inexperience must also have added to the difficulties at Bukavu. When he was second-in-command of 1 QONR[32] he had not gone to the Cameroons but had been left behind in Enugu to supervise the rear details. At Bukavu he found himself faced by unusual difficulties which would have taxed an experienced battalion commander. But he was evidently held partly to blame. When 1 QONR returned to Nigeria in May 1961 Ironsi was posted away to London to the obscure position of military adviser to the Nigerian High Commission, and he did not hold another command in the Nigerian Army until October 1964[33]*

---

ii   The use of double-barrelled names amongst Igbos at this time was also a rarity

The timing of the coup was also curious given that it occurred just three days after the close of a Commonwealth Conference that had been held in Lagos from 10 to 12 January, to discuss the unilateral declaration of independence by the white-minority government of Rhodesia. This being the first time that such a meeting of Commonwealth heads of government was being held outside London, it would be reasonable to expect that intelligence gathering on security issues would have been of the highest order, not least because of the virtual civil war that was then raging in the Western Region at this time as graphically recounted by the British Prime Minister at the time, Harold Wilson, in his memoirs:

> *We arrived about 10.00pm on 10th January....Sir Abubakar and I drove to the city, along a road that I came to know so well three years later. There was great enthusiasm at the roadside, but behind the cheers sounded the ominous if distant crackle of insurgent gunfire, which from time to time we were able to hear from the heavily guarded conference hotel...*
>
> *The conference ended in an atmosphere of unity, even euphoria...Abubakar full of justified pride, insisted on riding with me to the airport. Again we heard the rifle-fire. As we turned into the airport entrance he said to me, 'You have a great future as Prime Minister of our mother country. You are fortunate. One thing only I wish for you, that you never have to become Prime Minister of a federal and divided country.'*
>
> *That was on Wednesday, 11th January. On the Saturday, 15th January, he was dead, and his body was later found in a ditch, the victim of a communal uprising[34]*

What is more, Chukwuma Nzeogwu, the driving force behind the coup, was already on the watch of British intelligence:

> *Chukwuma was not only very vocal in his views about East-West relations, he even went as far as visiting Hungary in the summer of 1959, to see things for himself. Unknown to him, the British intelligence had been on his trail[35]*

Adewale Ademoyega, who together with Nzeogwu and Ifeajuna, was one of the three lead coup plotters said that 'throughout 1965, Nzeogwu spoke freely and openly to some young officers about his plan to stage a coup'.[36] In fact during the planning stages of the coup, according to Gen. Olusegun Obasanjo's account, a formal report had been made, by one Capt. Udowoid to Brigadier Ademulegun, of Nzeogwu's activities in 'brainwashing officers against the government':

> *Captain Udowoid quoted Chukwuma as saying to junior officers, "wait until the day you will look at the senior officers through the sights of your rifle".*

> *Brigadier Ademulegun who was a victim of the coup, received the letter and referred it to Colonel Shodeinde, another victim of the coup, and Chukwuma's commandant, for his comments.....Brigadier Ademulegun reported the case to Army Headquarters in Lagos, and described Chukwuma as "a young man in a hurry" who should "be closely watched"[37]*

Obasanjo does not say what the response from Army Headquarters was and neither the brigadier nor the colonel lived to tell the tale after the coup.

THE 'IGBO COUP' CLAIM

Above all else, the most intriguing aspect of the tale of Ironsi's emergence as Nigeria's first military ruler is the coincidence of the nickname 'Ironside' with the 'Old Ironsides' nickname of Oliver Cromwell, Britain's first military ruler following a coup. Still the coup was said to be an Igbo coup to seize power from the North.

Those propagating this view point to the fact that not only did an Igbo Maj. Gen. Aguiyi-Ironsi emerge as the new military ruler, the lead actors in the coup plot, with one Yoruba exception - Adewale Ademoyega - were Igbos. That the coup succeeded in eliminating its main targets in the North, the Premier of the Northern Region Ahmadu Bello and the Federal Prime Minister Tafawa Balewa, and their allies in the West, Premier Samuel Akintola and Chief Festus Okotie-Eboh (Awolowo and Enahoro languishing safely in prison), while those who might have been targets in the Eastern Region, President Nnamdi Azikiwe and Premier Michael Okpara, were left untouched, lent support to this view. However, the claim that this was an Igbo coup targeted at Northerners is not credible considering other factors that have emerged.

In the first place, the victim count does not take account of the fact that Brig. Ademulegun and Col. Shodeinde, the two most senior Yoruba officers in the army were killed.[iii] Also, Maj. Onwuatuegwu, after killing Shodeinde, simply arrested the governor of the Northern Region, Sir Kashim Ibrahim when he might have been eliminated if the Igbo power-grab story is to be believed.[38]

More importantly, the lead actor, Chukwuma Kaduna Nzeogwu, certainly did not see himself as pursuing any Igbo agenda. He was one of the Igbos who had been born and raised in the North, in Kaduna. His best friend was Olusegun Obasanjo, a Yoruba man. His politics was pan-Africanist in the mould of Azikiwe. When asked about whether the coup was driven by a tribal agenda, his response was categorical:

> *In the North, no. In the South, yes. We were five in number, and initially we knew quite clearly what we wanted to do. We had a short list of people who were either*

---

iii   These two, along with Aguiyi-Ironsi, were amongst the first five commissioned officers in the Nigerian army

*undesirable for the future progress of the country or who by their positions at
the time had to be sacrificed for peace and stability. Tribal considerations were
completely out of our minds at this stage. But we had a set-back in the execution.
Both of us in the North...did our best. But the other three who were stationed in
the South failed because of incompetence and misguided considerations in the
eleventh hour. The most senior among them was in charge of a whole brigade
and had all the excuse and opportunity in the world to mobilize his troops
anywhere, anyhow and anytime. He did it badly. In Lagos, even allowing for
one or two genuine mistakes, the job was badly done. The Mid-West was ever
a big problem. But in the East, our major target, nothing practically was done.
He and the others let us down*[39]

Ademoyega is equally emphatic in dismissing the suggestion that the coup was driven
by an ethnic agenda:

*Contrary to the load of wicked propaganda that had [sic] since been heaped
on us, there was no decision at our meeting to single out any particular ethnic
group for elimination or destruction. Our intentions were honourable, our views
were national and our goals were idealistic. We intended that the coup should
be national in execution so that it would receive nationwide acclamation.*[40]

What seems clear is that a coup of the kind that Fl. Lt. Rawlings was to later carry
out in Ghana, a non-partisan and across the board elimination of those who had
been identified as the enemies of a united Nigeria, is what the lead coup plotters had
planned. As well as ending the bloodshed in the Western Region that the Balewa
government was neglecting, a key objective had been to re-orient the army. In the
words of Ademoyega:

*If the Army was made to see itself as part of the people, to embrace the same
ideology as the people under a revolutionary and not a political party system
and if the Army was turned into a productive arm of government , then it would
neither have been used as an instrument to sponsor political riots, as was the
case in the days that Lieutenant-Colonel Hassan U. Katsina governed Northern
Nigeria, nor could it have been used as an instrument of pogrom , as it was used
in the days that Gowon took over the reins of power in the Federation. It would
also not have been used as an instrument of arson, looting and brigandage as it
was used during the civil war.*[41]

The economic order was to have been changed so that Nigerians could 'produce most
of the things that they needed for the betterment of their lives'. There was to have been

a program of mass education and the system of traditional rulers had been marked for abolition according to Ademoyega:

> *The posts of obas, obis, emirs and amanyanabos constituted the greatest anachronisms in the Nigerian Society of 1965. These natural rulers were useful instruments of corruption and compromise, first under the British and later under the Nigerian politicians. Of what use to the society were those glorified idols that had eyes but would not see and had ears but would not hear, but merely served as conduits to pass a bribe to the people in order to miscarry social-justice? Many of them were diabolical and their continued existence is inimical to social take-off and progress.[42]*

In the area of foreign policy, the plan was for Nigeria to live up to its independence by putting an end to 'her total dependence on NATO weaponry'. That the plans were never carried through was because the coup was hijacked by the conservative forces within the army without the people actually realising what had happened:

> *Hardly...could the people tell much difference between the Nzeogwu group of revolutionaries and the Ironsi group of reactionaries. More so because Ironsi did not publicise this difference and deliberately refused to tell the world that Nzeogwu and his group had been clamped in jail.[43]*

The coup was only given an 'Igbo' colouration as an excuse to deal with the Igbo challenge to Northern rule. Far from being driven by ethnicity, the most remarkable feature of the January coup is that a significant number of the principal actors in the coup were the first graduates to enter the Nigerian army:

> *By January 1966, the Nigerian army had seven graduates with combatant commissions. Lt Colonels "Emeka" Ojukwu and Victor Banjo, and Majors Olufemi Olutoye, Adewale Ademoyega, Emmanuel Ifeajuna, Emmanuel Udeaja and Oluwole Rotimi. All seven were southerners and either Igbo (Ojukwu, Ifeajuna, Udeaja) or Yoruba (Banjo, Olutoye, Ademoyega, Rotimi). Three or four of these graduates were involved conceptually or physically, in Nigeria's first military coup. Banjo and Ifeajuna were students together at the University of Ibadan. Banjo and Udaja had degrees in Mechanical Engineering from the Royal Military College of Science, Shrivenham, UK. Ojukwu had a degree in history from Lincoln College, Oxford University[44]*

The combined intellectual capacity of the principal military actors in the January, 1966 coup and the Biafra sequel is certainly interesting; in this they were a completely different class from their army colleagues who went on to rule Nigeria. Emmanuel Ifeajuna had, literally, leapt to fame, by winning a gold medal in the high jump at the British Empire and Commonwealth Games in 1954. He had followed this achievement with a science degree at the University of Ibadan before joining the army in 1960. Adewale Ademoyega, the Yoruba man in the coup plot, received a degree in history from the University of London before joining the army in 1962. Odumegwu Ojukwu was arguably the most educated soldier of them all having attended CMS Grammar School, Kings College, Lagos, Epsom College, and obtained a master's degree in history from Oxford University.

That these graduate-soldiers all ended up on the Biafra side of the divide at the start of the conflict, and all, with the exception of Ojukwu and Ademoyega, were killed in one way or another by the end of the War, suggests that the long-standing War Against Educated Natives was being played out within the Nigerian Army.

What is clear is that the lead actors in the January 1966 coup were radicals and intellectuals, rather than Igbo 'tribalists'. It was the educated natives, whose presence in the army had been of such concern to the British, who were rising against the 'gangsterism and disorder, corruption and despotism' of the new order that the Colonial Office manipulations had brought about:

> *Among the senior officers arrested, officers with degrees and officers who had spent at least two years in England at Sandhurst were prominent. Of the fourteen captains and officers of higher rank, eight had been to Sandhurst. Although there were only six graduates in the Army who held combatant commissions, three of these were accused of taking part in the plot (Lt.-Col. Banjo, Major Ifeajuna and Major Ademoyega)*[45]

The impression that it was an Igbo coup for the Igbo's to grab power from the North came from events and circumstances beyond the control of the coup plotters. First was the fact that most of the leading minds of the coup were from the rank of majors in the Nigerian Army, and due to the recruitment policies that were in place while the army was under British control, most soldiers of that rank were Igbos:

> *The Nigerianization program unwittingly stratified the army on ethnic lines. By the mid-1960s the army's most senior officers were career soldiers who had originally enlisted as NCO's and then risen through the ranks. Most of these were Yoruba (Samuel Ademulegun, Babafemi Ogundipe, Ralph Shodeinde, Robert Adebayo). Immediately behind them in seniority were the first Sandhurst-trained generation of army officers. These men were largely Kanuri Muslims from the north (Zakariya Maimalari, Umar Lawan, Kur Mohammed) Johnson Aguiyi-Ironsi was the only member of the*

army's top stratum that was not Yoruba or Kanuri. The Lt-Colonels were ethnically diverse (e.g. Ejoor, Ojukwu, Kurubo), but many of the majors were Sandhurst-trained Igbos and most junior officers like lieutenants and NCOs were Northerners who had been encouraged to join the army's infantry by an army recruitment campaign by Northern politicians. This meant that when the senior strata of the army officer hierarchy ended their careers, their successor commanders would inevitably emerge from the middle-grade officer ranks dominated by Igbos. These Igbos would be directly commanding mostly Northern subordinates. The psychology of this relationship was later to prove fatal[46]

Thus far from the army being the one detribalised institution in the country it was itself ethnically stratified.

Had the coup been an Igbo plot driven by tribal sentiments, it is odd that all the lead Igbo actors were young Igbos who had spent all or most of their lives living in the North, who were more comfortable speaking Hausa than Igbo, and whose connection with the Igbo heartland was tenuous to the point that they barely could find the way to their family compounds in the East unassisted. Again, it would seem that the Igbos were doing their utmost to headline their tribal agenda. Thus, although the Council of Ministers meeting, of 16 January 1966, which handed over power to the army included members from other ethnic groups, it was an Igbo man, Dr Nwafor Orizu, the Senate President, who made the public announcement that a fellow Igbo, Aguyi-Ironsi, was taking over.[47] The picture of a brazen Igbo takeover was then completed when the new Igbo leader appointed his fellow Igbo, Francis Nwokedi, to recommend the dismantling of the federal arrangements that had been the North's insurance against the threat of Southern domination.

The narrative that the coup was an Igbo attack on Northerners is further undermined by the fact that, not only did Aguyi-Ironsi leave his personal security in the hands of Northern soldiers, his administration gave preferential treatment to Northern politicians. Whilst the administration had no qualms over arresting and detaining members of other political parties, it left NPC politicians untouched even though, as the party in power, it was the excesses of this party of the North that had precipitated the coup.[48]

THE NIGER DELTA REPUBLIC

The special relationship that existed between the Fulani North and the Ijaws of the Niger Delta requires explanation.

The patchwork of ethnicities within each of the major regions meant that each had fault lines that would force a ruption on any increase, real or perceived, in the power of the dominant ethnic group. In the Eastern Region, the Ijaw people of the Niger Delta were to the dominant Igbos as the Tiv ethnic group were to the dominant Hausa-Fulani in the Northern Region. Just as the Action Group had been hard at work courting the Tiv's so the NPC had been cultivating a relationship with the Ijaws.

It was the Ijaws who first reacted to the January coup that produced the new Igbo leadership when, on 23 February 1966, little more than a month after the coup, Maj. Isaac Adaka Boro declared the independence of his Ijaw people from Nigeria and the creation of the 'Niger Delta Republic'. The Ijaw revolt lasted just twelve days before it was crushed by Nigerian forces making it 'the Twelve Day Revolution'.

For the insurrection Isaac Boro received a long jail sentence but, in May 1967, in the run-up to the outbreak of the Biafran war, he was granted an amnesty by the Federal Government. It should come as no surprise that after his amnesty he joined the Federal side against Biafra, with all the propaganda value that brought to the Federal cause. He was then killed, though 'in mysterious circumstances', on 16 May 1968 before the war's end.

In the use of force to crush the Ijaw secession, the Igbo-led Federal Government had set a precedent for the Federal reaction to the Igbo people's own secession attempt when it came. In the meantime, they had created a vengeful neighbour at their rear within the geographical space that they would soon call 'the Republic of Biafra'.

THE 29 JULY 1966 COUNTER-COUP

For one into whose lap power had so suddenly dropped, and who had no track-record in political science, it is curious that Aguyi-Ironsi seemingly had a clear view about the constitutional order that Nigeria needed. Within days he was declaring that 'All Nigerians want an end to regionalism' and in February he had set up his one-man commission of enquiry to report on the means by which a 'united Nigeria' could be delivered.

On 24 May 1966, Aguyi-Ironsi proclaimed a new Decree, Number 34, by which he abolished the Regions and declared "Nigeria ceases to be what has been described as a Federation. It now becomes simply the Republic of Nigeria". This was a strange move in the climate of the times. The North's opposition to a unitary Nigeria was common knowledge: They had threatened to pull out of the federation altogether in the wake of the constitutional crisis following the Action Group's 1953 Independence motion and had only been persuaded to remain in the union by British assurances that the federation with the South would be a loose one.

Beyond the curiosity surrounding his name, Ironsi was no stranger to the Colonial

Office having been aide-de-camp to Governor McPherson. Added to this was the presence of his British predecessor, as head of the Nigerian Army, Major-General Welby-Everard, 'on a return visit to Nigeria when the coup happened'.[49] And then there is the coincidence of the January 1966 coup with a spate of coups occurring around this time in various African States that had recently attained independence from European powers: Gabon (February 1964), Algeria (June 1965), Congo-Leopoldville (November 1965), Central African Republic (January 1965) and Ghana (February 1966). Writing around the time of the July 1966 counter-coup in the New Left Review, one Roger Murray made the following observation:

> *During the past three years, action initiated or prosecuted by the military has determined the overthrow of no less than eleven African Heads of State, and has seriously endangered four further regimes. Eight of the successor regimes are headed by military men. Over the last six months, coups have proceeded at a feverish rhythm[50]*

In the aftermath of the January 1966 coup in Nigeria and the unification decree, it was said of the 'Ironsi' administration that:

> *...As far as can be discerned, they aimed to restore the political institutions of the old colonial era, re-creating in a new guise the hierarchy of governor, residents and district officers, united in a single public service and advised by subservient natural rulers[51]*

This was a sudden and fundamental shift of political direction. It was a direct assault on everything that the North, under Ahmadu Bello's leadership, had been holding out for. Bello's murder, followed by the removal of the buffers against southern domination that he had erected -especially the regional civil service - was bound to produce a violent reaction. Maj. Gen. Philip Efiong, the second in command to the Biafran leader Gen. Ojukwu, is blunt in his assessment of the events leading up to the countercoup:

> *...there was good reason to believe that there was a British-backed plan for a Northern reprisal action. The Ahmadu Bello University had, for instance, become a centre for counter insurgency planning under the instigation of a former British officer who had once served in the Nigerian army[52]*

The reaction came, on 29 May 1966, just five days after the promulgation of the Decree, with the first round of a series of murderous pogroms against Igbos in the North. Then came the counter-coup, on 29 July 1966, led by Lt. Col. Murtala Mohammed beginning with a wholesale slaughter of Igbo officers within the barracks, starting in Abeokuta and repeated across the various barracks in Lagos, Kaduna and Kano. Care was taken to ensure that "weapons were issued to Northerners only". This elimination of Igbo officers was a first step in a war to come:

> *After dawn on 29 July the massacre of officers and men of Eastern origin took place all over Nigeria with a speed, precision and uniformity of pattern that took away any subsequent excuse of spontaneity*[53]

'Ironsi' had spent just 194 days in office before he was murdered in this counter-coup. By the end of his short tenure, Nigeria had been returned to something very close to the colonial model: a unitary government with a unified public service, free of political parties and elections.

The next most senior military figure after 'Ironsi' was Brig. Ogundipe, a Yoruba. But this was about power not seniority. Northern officers having made it clear that they would not accept Ogundipe, he did not press his claim. Only a Northerner would be acceptable. '[W]ith Maimalari, Kur, Largema and Pam all dead, [Yakubu Gowon] was now the most senior surviving Northern officer in the Nigerian army'.[54] As a Christian from the Middle Belt, his appointment had the attraction of playing down the Muslim-Christian divide whilst restoring power to the North. Like 'Ironsi', who he was succeeding, he too was close to the British administration having served as chief administrative officer (Adjutant-General) under Welby-Everard until the Briton completed his tour of duty in February, 1965.

In the aftermath of the counter-coup, Nigeria was back to a unitary government under Northern control. The restoration of direct Fulani control would have to wait until the Biafra secession was crushed.

THE ROAD TO BIAFRA

One man on whom Gowon's credentials as the most senior Northern officer made scant impression was Col. Ojukwu, the Governor of the Eastern Region.

EMEKA OJUKWU

Odumegwu-Ojukwu Chukwuemeka was born in November 1933, like Nnamdi Azikiwe, in Zungeru, Northern Nigeria, to Igbo parents. By the time the family moved to Lagos at the end of the Second World War, his father, Sir Louis Odumegwu-Ojukwu was probably the richest man in Nigeria, the Aliko Dangote of his time.

Like Azikiwe, Ojukwu spoke the three main languages Igbo, Yoruba and Hausa to different levels of fluency.[55] He had received the best education that money could buy:

Kings College Lagos, Epsom College in Surrey; one year of a law degree at Oxford before obtaining an honours degree in Military History there. On returning home he joined the Civil Service as an Administrative Officer in the Eastern Region before joining the Nigerian Army in 1957. With these credentials, if any Nigerian could be said to have been 'born to rule' Nigeria, it was Chukwuemeka Odumegwu-Ojukwu.

However, at this point in time, the very existence of 'Nigeria' was in question. There was no enthusiasm for it within the three major regions: The Western Region was still in ashes from the insurgency. In the wake of the slaughter of their people that had occurred on 29May and 29 July 1966, the Igbo were abandoning Nigeria for their homeland:

> *Even after Lt.-Col. Gowon was installed as supreme commander, he was unable to prevent further murders, as that of Major Ekanem when he had been summoned to Military Headquarters. Within a few days all Easterners in the Army were either dead, in prison or had escaped to the East. Those still alive were later returned to Enugu, in exchange for the Northern soldiers who had formed part of the battalion there. In all, according to a list issued by the Eastern Region Government, at least 43 officers and 170 other ranks were murdered d during the counter-coup[56]*

Even the Hausa-Fulani had been heard shouting 'Araba' –'separate'- during the May pogroms against Igbos. The evidence suggests that they were bent on this course right up to the moment that Gowon was appointed Supreme Commander and Head of the Supreme Military Council on 1 August 1966. A close examination of the speech that Gowon delivered on that occasion suggests an eleventh-hour change of plan because, having explained the sectional killings in the January coup, and the May and July pogroms, he presaged a dramatic announcement with the following words:

> *I have now come to the most difficult part, or the most important part, of this statement. I am doing it, conscious of the great disappointment and heartbreak it will cause all true and sincere lovers of Nigeria and of Nigerian unity both at home and abroad, especially our brothers in the Commonwealth.*
> *As a result of the recent events and the other previous similar ones, I have come to strongly believe that we cannot honestly and sincerely continue in this wise, as the basis of trust and confidence in our unitary system of government has not been able to stand the test of time. I have already remarked on the issue in question. Suffice to say that, putting all considerations to test – political, economic, as well as social – the basis for unity is not there, or is badly rocked, not only once but several times*

After this build up, what came next was an anti-climax:

> *I therefore feel that we should review the issue of our national standing and see if we can help stop the country from drifting away into utter destruction*

Rather than a declaration of 'Araba', it was simply a call for a conference. All the signs were that Britain had, once again, stepped in to stop the North from seceding:

> *[The Northerners] had shouted for it in May and had it in their minds ever since. Now was their time to make it a reality. Was there anybody in their way? Certainly, none. Was there anything to stop them? Yes – self-interest. Who could use this to stop them? Their friends, especially the international ones – the British and the Americans and of course, some faithful Nigerians who still believed in the continuity of the nation.*[57]

When Gowon was formally appointed as Supreme Commander and head of the Supreme Military Council on 1 August 1966, Ojukwu could not bring himself to accept his authority and he had just cause. Gowon was his junior within the rank-conscious army heirarchy and, besides, decisions of the Supreme Military Council were supposed to be made by consensus and not by majority. The country had effectively divided into two and the countdown to Biafra had begun.

THE ABURI ACCORD

The prize for both former partners, North and East, was the support of the West. However, the race for the West's sympathies had been skewed against the East even before it began by those advising Ironsi when they had advised him against granting the plea for amnesty that Awolowo had made in March, 1966 on behalf of himself and his colleagues. On 3 August 1966, Gowon released Awolowo and Enahoro from prison to the adulation of their Yoruba and Edo people. Together with the release of the Ijaw leader, Isaac Boro, these moves ensured the isolation of the Igbos amongst the big four ethnic groups in the South.

The North's U-turn from 'Araba' set in motion the arrangements for an ad-hoc constitutional conference which was to take place in Lagos in September 1966. The conference saw a reversal of positions by the former partners, the East and the North. The Igbos, who had all along been the chief advocates of 'One Nigeria' with a powerful centre, were now holding out for a confederacy, while the Hausa-Fulani, who had all along been insisting upon the loosest federal arrangement, now insisted upon the type of unitary government the 'Ironsi' administration had pushed through.

That the northern position was completely contrary to the proclamation that Gowon had made, just days before, viz. 'that the basis of trust and confidence in our unitary system has not been able to stand the test of time' was evidence of external influences being brought to bear on the situation. The northern agenda had also taken a more sinister turn. It was no longer simply a matter of northern rule. They were bent upon a crushing the Igbos permanently.

Even as the conference was going on, the third in the series of pogroms against Igbos in the North started in mid-September. It reached a crescendo:

> *On 29 September 1966 Colonel Gowon made a radio broadcast apparently intended to bring the violence to an end. In it he said: "It appears that it is going beyond reason, and is now at the point of recklessness and irresponsibility"...far from abating, the pogrom on that day exploded from a blaze into a holocaust[58]*

According to one account, the number of Igbos killed "ranged from 10,000 to as high as 30,000".[59] The Army who might have been expected to be the last restraint on civilian excesses were in fact leading the slaughter:

> *On the afternoon of Saturday October 1, 1966, the 5th battalion's troops mutinied and opened fire as their commander Major Kyari addressed them on the battalion parade ground. The rampaging soldiers were so out of control that even Northerners who tried to restrain them were murdered....The troops raided the battalion armory, broke out of the barracks and headed into town to pick up local civilian [thugs] whom they asked to take them to locations where they could find Igbos...Igbos trying to escape were not spared. At Kano Airport, the soldiers set upon a crowd of Igbo refugees boarding a southbound flight and killed them. Some were dragged out of the plane cabin and shot. Igbo workers at the airport were also hunted down and killed, sometimes inside the terminal. The soldiers also made their presence felt at the railway station where Igbo civilians were waiting to board trains to escape. Many of the Igbo would-be passengers and railway staff were shot dead[60]*

To take the heat out of the situation it was agreed, on 9 August 1966, that all troops should return to their regions of origin. While eastern troops returned to the East, northern troops remained in the West and Lagos on the excuse that the West had no troops of its own to fill the security vacuum that would arise were northern troops withdrawn. When the delegates from the South made compliance with the agreement a condition of their continued participation in the ad hoc conference, the northern response was uncompromising. On 30 November 1966, Gowon simply announced the dissolution of the Ad Hoc Constitutional Conference and the appointment of a committee to draw up a new constitution.

By reneging on the agreement on troop withdrawal after the East had complied, the North had put itself in a position where it had unchallenged control of all Regions apart from the East thus ensuring that the war would be fought exclusively on Eastern territory. As a result Ojukwu now insisted on all future talks being held in neutral territory, outside of Nigeria. Aburi, in Accra, Ghana, was the chosen location for the meeting of the Supreme Military Council which took place on 4 and 5 January 1967.

A number of agreements were reached in Aburi which, had they been honoured, would have averted the war. The use of force to resolve the crisis was renounced; the ad hoc conference on the future shape of Nigeria was to be resumed; the decrees which had been passed to change the government from federal to unitary were to be identified and repealed and the agreement of 9 August 1966 for Northern troops to withdraw from Lagos and the Western Region was to be implemented and complemented by a 'massive recruitment of Yorubas into the army'.[61]

There was no room for controversy about what had been discussed and agreed at Aburi Accord because the discussions had been recorded:

> *...Aburi is probably unique in the annals of historic confrontations. The entire two day's proceedings, apart from two short breaks, were recorded by the Ghanaians who, afterwards, gave each military governor and Gowon a copy of the tapes.....For once the outsider can be the fly on the wall of history and hear what the leading characters said, the way they said it at the time they said it, cutting through the web of conflicting interpretation and propaganda that later throttled the truth...*[62]

The war happened because the northern leadership was bent upon a military solution and so reneged upon all that had been agreed at Aburi.

THE AWOLOWO AND OJUKWU PARLEY

The North having beaten the East to the punch with the release of Awolowo, on 6 May 1967, the Gowon government sent him to Enugu at the head of a four-man delegation to meet with Ojukwu to make a final appeal. Just a few days before, on 1 May 1967, Awolowo said in a speech in Ibadan:

> *If the Eastern Region is allowed by acts of omission or commission to secede from or opt out of Nigeria, then the Western Region and Lagos must also stay out of the federation.*

This has been interpreted to mean that Awolowo had pledged Yoruba support for Igbo secession. However, as in Aburi, the meeting of the two leaders was recorded and the transcript belies the post-war propaganda.[63]

The North having brought the Western Region, the Mid-West and the Niger Delta on side with the release from prison of Awolowo, Enahoro, and Isaac Boro, the Igbo leadership realised they were isolated. Ojukwu's attempt to use this meeting with Awolowo to form an alliance with the Western region was coming at the eleventh hour in the May month in which the independent state of Biafra was to be declared. To Ojukwu's suggestion that they could now use the meeting at hand to discuss a common front for the South, Awolowo's response was unequivocal:

> *It will be something near fraud for us to sit down here and discuss in terms of the South especially as this delegation was sent here by a body consisting of the Northern delegation[64]*

Awolowo's concern to ensure that any discussion with Ojukwu with a view to a common front for the South was in the open was hardly surprising given that barely nine months had elapsed since he was released, on a pardon from the government that he was representing at this meeting, from a long term of imprisonment following a conviction for treason. What the transcript of the parley shows is Awolowo making it clear that with the Western Region and Lagos still under Northern military occupation, the Yoruba were not ready to follow the Igbos if they decided to go ahead with secession:

> *And I may say in this connection of Southern solidarity – I am sorry to go into what happened in the past -in 1953 there was an understanding between the banned NCNC and the banned Action Group; we entered into an agreement, which I hope we will use sometime, to the effect that if the North remained intransigent we would declare a Southern Dominion. This was signed by myself and Zik and I still stand by it; but we prefer that you should send your delegates to this meeting, so that we should, known to everyone, enter into negotiations among ourselves and present a common front to the North. Then nobody can accuse us of conspiracy or trying to divide the country into two parts. I want you to look at it from our point of view. If there were no Northern soldiers in the West the position would be different. And even if by the time I return home the Northern soldiers have gone I still do not want to be accused of perfidy. The issue at hand is not enough for us to say we do not like the North[65]*

Rather than encouraging the Igbos to make the unilateral move for Biafra, the path which Awolowo recommended to Ojukwu was for the Eastern delegation to attend the conciliation meeting and to join in a united southern political front with a view to securing at least moral support internationally if a split later became unavoidable:

The main concern of these delegates is to ensure that Nigeria does not disintegrate, and I would like to see Nigeria bound together by any bond because it is better than breaking the whole place up because each unit will be the loser for it. The economy of the country is so integrated that it is too late in the day to try and sever them without risking the death of one or both of them. So we have come, therefore to appeal to you to let Eastern representatives attend the meeting of the [Nigerian National Conciliation] Committee.

I do not want to put myself in a position where I will be treated as an advocate of the Eastern cause. Let the Eastern delegates go there, make their case and then as a member of the Committee I will get up and say I support this entirely. If at the meeting the East and West present what they want for a new Nigeria whether temporarily or permanently, and the North says "no, we are not going to have it", I will go out and address a World Press Conference and send our case to that body and say that this is what we have done and the North has turned it down. I will then take any step that is necessary to bring into effect what we want. The North needed to be in a position of being presented with the United front of the South[66]

The Eastern position was all the more tragic because it appears that the NCNC had also failed to stand with the Action Group when, at the 1954 Conference, the latter had proposed that the Constitution should contain a right for any region to secede:

Perhaps most significantly the issue of secession was addressed. The AG had urged that such a right should be included in the constitution. The NCNC, in light of its sentiments for Nigerian unity, took a stand against this and was strongly supported by Lyttleton, a decision that confirmed the collapse of the AG-NCNC pact[67]

THE DECLARATION OF BIAFRA

On 27 May 1967 the Eastern Region Consultative Assembly meeting in Enugu gave Ojukwu a *mandate* 'to declare, at the earliest practical date, Eastern Nigeria a free sovereign and independent state by the name and title of the Republic of Biafra'.

On the same day Gowon responded by announcing the division of Nigeria into twelve states. In the Western Region, the creation of three states (Lagos, Mid-West and Western states) was cosmetic since the Mid-West and Lagos were already in existence. The reconfiguration of the Northern Region into six new states (North West, North

259

East, North Central, Kano, Benue-Plateau and Kwara) was more administrative than political. The real change was in Ojukwu's Eastern Region where three states were created:

> *East-Central State comprising the present Eastern Region excluding Calabar, Ogoja and Rivers Provinces. South-Eastern State comprising Calabar and Ogoja Provinces. Rivers State comprising Ahoada, Brass, Degema, Ogoni and Port Harcourt Divisions*

What, on its face, looked like an even-handed exercise to balance the numbers of states in the North and the South was in fact a manoeuvre to further isolate the Igbos within the Eastern Region by bringing the minority groups in the Region on to the side of the government and leaving the Igbos potentially landlocked in the event of secession. At the same time, the areas which contained the Eastern Region's oil were being separated from the core Igbo areas in the new East Central state. This move had been foreseen in the Willinks Commission Report in which the areas within the new Rivers and South Eastern States had been earmarked for 'special attention'. In his speech announcing the creation of the new states Gowon in fact made express reference to the Report:

> *The country has a long history of well-articulated demands for states. The fears of minorities were explained in great detail and set out in the report of the Willinks Commission appointed by the British in 1958*

The Willinks Report was, in other respects, uncannily prophetic in flagging up the threats to the country that lay ahead: Paragraph 42 was especially insightful in speaking of 'the absence of institutional roots and dependence upon characters who could disappear from the stage'.

Ojukwu, and the Igbo leaders now found themselves between the devil and the deep blue sea. They could choose to remain within Nigeria in a land-locked oil-stripped Igbo enclave or they could gamble on seceding with the entire old Eastern Region with all Nigeria's known oil reserves. At 2.00am on 30 May 1967, Ojukwu declared the Eastern Region the 'sovereign state of Biafra'.

Gowon's response was to draft into his administration the key political figures in the Western Region and the Mid-West, whom he had earlier released from jail, by appointing them to the Federal Executive Council. Awolowo was given the post of Vice-Chairman and Federal Minister of Finance while Enahoro was made Information Minister: one was responsible for financing the war effort against; the other was responsible for defending it publicly. With Gowon at the head of affairs, to the outside world, it looked very much like a war between fellow Christians. Meanwhile the appointments of these southerners to these key posts dealt a final blow to forming a common southern front against the North and in due course they and other southerners would be given the credit and the blame for the manner in which the war was prosecuted.

What Ojukwu had to lose from delaying secession is not clear because there had been no more pogroms since September/October 1966. In the intervening six months most Igbo survivors had returned to Igbo territory. That the events within Biafra were under the influence of fifth-columnists (supporters of the federal government clandestinely working against the Biafran regime from the inside) is strongly suggested by the timing of the declaration.

Although, strictly speaking, Biafra was declared at 2.00am on 30 May, 1967, it might as well be regarded as having occurred at the close of 29 May, 1967 as had many of the significant events in the North's march to political dominance in the country. The first of the North's pogroms against the Igbos had occurred on 29 May, 1966 and the two which followed had been carried out on the 29th of the month. In 1962, it was on 29 May that the state of emergency was declared in the Western Region when that region came under Northern military occupation and it was on 29 September, 1967 that Enugu, the political capital of Biafra, fell to the federal army. Even, pre-Independence, in 1957, the final constitutional conference had taken place on 29 September. A careful study of other key events in Nigeria's political history will highlight the recurrence of the 29th day of the month if not 29 May itself.

The significance of 29 of May is to be found in the imperial struggles between the two faiths, Islam and Christianity and specifically in the fall, on Tuesday 29 May, 1453, of the then capital of the Christian Roman Empire, Constantinople, to the forces of Islam led by Sultan Mehmet II.[68] The 29th of May therefore appears to a deeply symbolic day for the Islamic north.

INTERNATIONAL OIL POLITICS

That colonial empires had ceased to be politically acceptable in the new world order did not mean that the economic benefits from the former colonial territories were to be forsaken. On the contrary, post-war reconstruction imperatives in Europe meant that the economics of colonisation was more crucial than even before. Access to crude oil, in particular, was vital.

Although, as we have seen, the search for oil had started in Southern Nigeria as far back as 1906 and production had begun in 1908, it was only on 15 January 1956, in the last years of colonial rule, that it was announced that oil had been discovered 'in merchantable quantity' in the Niger Delta area. This announcement would change Nigerian economics and politics forever. On 30 April 1956, Shell Darcy Petroleum Development Company changed its name to Shell-British Petroleum Development Company.

The importance of Nigeria's oil to Britain came into clear focus with the outbreak of a new round of war between the Arabs and the Israelis in the Six Day War, in early June, 1967, just weeks before the first shots were fired in the Biafran War:

> *Virtually all the Mid-West's oil, a third but a growing proportion of the total production, was shipped out through the Bonny terminal in the East via the Trans- Niger pipeline. The Federation's only oil-refinery, near Port Harcourt, was also under Biafran control. Therefore any sanction imposed by the Nigerian government against Ojukwu was bound to boomerang on Lagos. This helps to explain why oil shipments were exempted from the general blockade of Biafra during the month of June while Shell/BP was trying to nose its way out of its nasty dilemma*
> *The oil companies' principal interest was to keep the oil flowing, protect their multi- million-pound installations, pay their dues and offend neither side[69]*

Britain had been accused of aiding the Israelis and the Wilson Government, already struggling with economic crisis, was thrown into further crisis as Arab states combined to close the Suez Canal and cut off its oil supplies:

> *The economic consequences of this June week were extremely serious for Britain. The closure of the Canal alone, it was authoritatively estimated was costing Britain*
> *£20 million a month on our balance of payments. No less serious was the loss of Middle East oil. We had to seek to replace this from other areas at higher price and, in the main, at much higher freights. Supplies from Libya, the one source west of*
> *the Canal, were cut for a time. Nor could we make up any substantial part of the loss from Nigeria, our other short-haul source. Within weeks, the civil war there cut off all our Nigerian supplies too. We had to shop for supplies in the US and Latin America, at high cost, high freights and in competition with other hard-hit countries. We had many anxieties for the following winter[70]*

Against this background, the British position on Biafra's attempt to secede with all the oil which they had found was never going to be neutral.

Any hope for a peaceful resolution of the standoff between the federal government and the Biafrans evaporated with this Arab-Israeli war. Any embarrassment on the part of the Wilson Government over the fact that even as the drums of war against Biafra were being beaten, the same government was resisting calls for a military response to white Rhodesia's own secession in November 1965, or at least an economic blockade, made no difference. Energy security apart, there was the other imperative of preserving the legacy of the Berlin Conference in defiance of the "winds of change" because the logic of Biafra was otherwise inarguable. With a population of fifteen million, a dominant ethnic group with a distinct language and with oil in abundance, it was a viable independent state.

The Igbo people's political case, having been slaughtered in great numbers in the North, was as legitimate as those of the Jews in Nazi Germany, indeed more so because theirs was not an appeal for the creation of a homeland but for a release from an involuntary political union. Further, Southern Cameroons had been released from the same political union by a referendum while Eastern Nigeria was to be locked into the union by a full- blown war.

The Organisation for African Unity (OAU) had been established in 1963, to preserve the integrity of the African states which had been forged through the Berlin Conference principles. Before this, in 1949, the British Commonwealth had been established effectively as a holding station for former British colonies as they left the Empire. In reality, it was 'Empire-lite', operating under a more inclusive brand.

THE BRITISH PARLIAMENTARY DEBATE ON BIAFRA

As head of the Commonwealth, Britain had a special interest in preserving the borders of the group's member states. Nigeria was, after all, Britain's creation.

Britain had expertly piloted its creation through the various political storms that had threatened its existence including the North's threat to pull out of the union in the aftermath of the 1953 independence motion crisis. The British Colonial Office had gone further to carefully manage the independence struggle to ensure the succession to power by local leaders of its choosing. With the co-operation of these friendly successors, Britain had been able to exercise continuing influence on key policies and appointments right up to the run up to the war: A Briton had been head of the Nigerian army until February 1965 and another served as the Deputy Secretary to Prime Minister Balewa until the time of the January 1966 coup.

The fighting started in July 1967. A year later, what it had been predicted would be a quick police operation was now a full-blown bloody war which was dominating British newspaper headlines. In the House of Commons, the debate on the Biafran War, which took place on 27 August 1968, was reminiscent of the great debates of the nineteenth century in the same House over the equally emotive issue of abolition.

The war was at a critical stage. Azikiwe sat and watched the debate from a seat that had been reserved for him in the cubicle of the Sergeant-at-Arms.[71] The choice before the House was whether to compel the federal government to call a ceasefire or to allow it to press ahead with, what was expected to be, the final push to overwhelm the Biafrans. George Thomson, the Secretary of State for Commonwealth Affairs put the government's case thus:

> The Nigerian forces, like the forces of many Commonwealth countries, were trained and equipped on British lines long before independence. Under successive British Governments, they have naturally looked largely to us for re-supply. When the time came that they most needed supplies, they counted on our willingness to allow them to purchase from the United Kingdom.
> Neutrality was not a possible option for Her Majesty's Government at that time. We might have been able to declare ourselves neutral if one independent country was fighting another, but this was not a possible attitude when a Commonwealth country, with which we had long and close ties, was faced with internal revolt. What would other Commonwealth countries have thought? After all, some other Commonwealth countries face dissident minorities who may be tempted to break up their countries to achieve secession....
> I come to the question of whether, if we were to cut off our supply of defence equipment unilaterally, a peace agreement would be made more likely. We would I believe lose our capacity to influence the Federal Government if we were to take such a step ... [72]

An especially articulate statement of the opposing case came from Stanley Henig, an academic political-scientist and Labour MP:

> I want to put three essential questions. They are essential to what is being done in our name, which is something I bitterly regret. The first is the legal question. By what right do we claim to judge what should happen in Nigeria and what is or is not good for the Nigerian people?....My right hon. Friend the Foreign Secretary has told us that the aim of all of us is One Nigeria. Why? If the Nigerian want one, two, three or ten Nigerias it may be a matter of regret, but it is their business not ours.
> Secondly, there is the political question. Why have we made the choice that

264

we have made? Why have one Nigeria as against two Nigerias or the right of secession? Would it not have been better for us to have declared neutrality to show that we were not involved?

Finally, there is the moral question....We have supplied arms in order to get influence. That policy has failed. We have no influence, for the war is spreading. It may be that we could stop the war now by ceasing to supply arms but is it a moral position for a British Socialist Government, whom I support, to be supplying arms for use in a civil war by men to kill each other and for that Government to say, "when this is over, we have bandages and food for you and we shall give you aid and patch you up again."[73]

Harold Wilson was in no doubt as to the strength of feeling in the country against his government's decision to supply arms to the federal side. The thought of their government being responsible for Biafran deaths was anathema to the British people who were already the most vocal critics of America in the Vietnam War then in progress. Wilson knew that if Biafra went to the vote his government would be defeated which would bring an end to his administration. To avoid this outcome he made sure that there would be no vote on the matter:

But the pro-Biafrans decided to organise a vote and since many Government supporters had gone home expecting that there would be no vote it became clear that we could be defeated. In these circumstances the under-secretary, Bill Whitlock, was instructed by the whips to 'talk out' the debate, i.e. not to sit down just in time for a division to be called (there were not enough dissidents to carry a closure motion). His action further intensified the anger of those of our people and of the Conservatives who supported the Biafran line.

In the evening, as I was dealing with papers before going off to resume my holiday, there were sounds of a great commotion in Downing Street. A large group of Biafran students, after a protest meeting in North London, had surprised the police by converging on Downing Street, where they lit an enormous bonfire which was kept going by petrol. It could easily have caused damage, but they then suddenly rushed the door of No.10, surprising the custodians and almost succeeding in entering in strength. In the mood they were in, who knows what damage they would have done, but enough custodians just managed to get their shoulders to the door to hold it and lock it. From that day on the front door defences were strengthened[74]

While the federal government side could count on British government support, the Biafrans were largely on their own.

Conflicted between sympathies flowing from its own war of independence from the British Empire and its special relationship with Britain and also its own war in Vietnam, the United States, under President Lyndon Johnson, adopted a position of strict neutrality and imposed an embargo on the supply of arms to both sides.

The Soviet Union, which might have been expected to support the Biafrans, took the side of the federal government alongside the British. The decision is to be understood in the context of the USSR's own vulnerability to dissident minorities who might wish to secede. The attempt by a new government in Czechoslovakia to introduce liberal reforms in early 1968 was a secession from the communist order, in all but name, which was crushed when Soviet troops invaded Czechoslovakia on 20 August 1968, just days before the House of Commons debate on Biafra. Recognising that Nigeria was a major sphere of British influence which they stood little chance of prising away, the USSR was content to take a purely commercial position on the war. They would supply the federal government with the war-planes and bombs which the British Government had drawn the line against supplying. Any moral credit the British government might have earned for this stand was, however, lost by the interest free loan which it made available to the federal government to acquire these weapons from the Soviets and also by the decision to maintain all other war supplies.

The only support the Biafrans found was from the French. With Biafra sharing a border with French Cameroon, which itself adjoined French Equatorial Guinea and oil-rich Gabon, the prospect of de-coupling the oil-rich region from Nigeria, through a low-risk proxy war, was attractive to Gen. de Gaulle's France. At the very least French support for Biafra could be a useful bargaining tool.[iv] For this reason French support for the Biafrans was tactical rather than wholehearted; it stopped short of formally recognising Biafra as an independent state.

INSIDE BIAFRA

Even after the mass murder of the Igbos in the pogroms, support for secession from Nigeria was far from unanimous amongst Igbos. The leave camp were not helped by how the people had been forced to consider the secession option in extremis and a leadership had had no time to develop a considered exit plan. There was, therefore, a strong remain camp who advocated reconciliation with Nigeria, especially in the early days before the

---

iv   The fact that an accord with Cameroon over the oil-rich Bakassi Peninsula was signed by the Gowon government within months of the Biafra War's end in January 1970 has led to strong suspicion that a deal, even if only in principle, had been done at some stage during the conflict

fighting began. The remainers were bolstered by the several non-Igbo ethnic minorities who found themselves on the Biafra side by reason only of the accident of geography that placed their homelands in the old Eastern Region. These were the peoples of the areas marked out for 'special attention' back in the Willinks Report and their position would be heavily emphasised by the Commonwealth Under- Secretary, William Whitlock, in the House of Commons debate:

> *It must be remembered that the pipelines, the oil installations and the ports of the Eastern Region are mainly in the non-Ibo tribal areas. Thus Colonel Ojukwu's concept of a separate State for Biafra could be achieved only by subordinating the wishes and interests of 5 million non-Ibos to those of the 7 million Ibos in the region.*
>
> *If Colonel Ojukwu were to succeed in his aim, he and the Ibos would acquire for themselves a territory rich in agriculture, and containing the great oil installations and reserves, all this at the expense of Nigeria as a whole*[75].

FINANCING THE WAR EFFORT

With no foreign help to rely upon the Biafrans were forced to rely upon themselves. The war effort was to throw up the best and the worst of their people.

The responsibility for getting the people's army to at least look like a fighting force fell on Timothy Chukwuemeka Modu, the Nigeria country representative for Blackwell Young & Company Ltd. a City of London-based company and the official buying agent for the Biafran Government. Blackwell's role produced the paradox that the British were supplying both sides in the war. Shell Petroleum Corporation, too, was not to be left out in the double act:

> *Shell, though hit on its production side, made a killing in sales. To the chagrin of its competitors in Nigeria, it won the lucrative contract of supplying the Federal armed forces. Then, through a complicated operation run from The Hague, it supplied the bulk of the aviation fuel for the relief and gun-running airlifts into Biafra via Sao- Tome and Libreville. The relief organisations and the Biafrans settled their accounts in dollars through a Paris bank*[76]

Precisely when preparations for war began on the Biafran side is not clear but there is evidence that it started soon after the third, and bloodiest, round of pogroms on 29 September 1966: An undated 'Secret' letter from Mr T.C. Modu to 'Major General P. Effiong, Chief of Staff, Biafra Army', discussing military I.D. Cards to be 'produced by BEEYWYSE in both silver and gold letters' talked in terms of 'our possible intake of these identity cards to a total number of 30,000' and 30,000 yards of 'Olive Green Khaki materials'; an invoice from Blackwells, dated 12 January 1967, for £13,500.00 in respect of '60000 pairs' of 'Black Ankle Boots, grained chrome leather uppers, direct moulded sole and heel, vulcanised rubber, No. P.45, as sample 'Beewyse' brand', was addressed to 'Store Officer, Nigerian Air Force, Enugu, Nigeria', as opposed to the Biafran Army.

Another instruction to Modu, dated 21 February 1967, from the Secretary to the Government of Eastern Nigeria approves the procurement of '3000 blankets and 6000 pairs of socks (with reinforced heels and toes) at prices 30/- and 5/8d per pair respectively' and gives an indication of the sense of imminence of war with the note 'I would urge that your overseas principals be pressed to take prompt action on the order as the blankets and socks are urgently required by Government'. An order for 10,000 steel helmets, matchetes jerrycans, ponchos, binoculars, compasses, officers' uniforms and swords, military watches, belts caps and buttons followed in April 1967.

To secure the supply lines to Biafra, in the face of a trade embargo now placed against the territory by the federal government, on 5 June 1967 Blackwells issued a new certificate in respect of Modu now designating him as 'a Sales Agent for this Company in West Africa', rather than Nigeria, stating that 'it is necessary for him to visit our offices from time to time to discuss and negotiate business'.

The start of the fighting was precipitated by a tug-of-war between the federal side and the Biafrans over £7million of oil receipts that were due to be paid by Shell-British Petroleum for the first-half of 1967. In a classic legal conundrum, both sides claimed ownership. What was at stake was not only vital resources for the war effort but also, because of the British Government's stake in British Petroleum, tacit political recognition of whichever side the money was paid to. An Aburi-type meeting to broker a compromise between the competing claims was held in New York at the end of June 1967:

> *The Biafrans put forward a suggestion that 57.5 per cent of the revenues deriving from operations in the East should be paid to the Biafran government by Ojukwu's deadline of 1st July. The rest should go into a suspense account pending a political settlement. The companies agreed but the Nigerians flatly rejected it. They went further. Any attempt by the companies to deny the Federal government its normal revenues would be countered with an extension of the blockade to tankers and the terminal at Bonny. The industry, the Nigerians warned, would grind to a halt[77]*

With the Biafrans threatening to stop all oil production on their territory, the British oil companies agreed to make a token payment of £250,000 to them. The federal side reacted by imposing a full blockade on 2 July 1967 and the fighting started four days later. In the meantime, the £250,000 pledged to the Biafrans went missing within the international payment system:

> *But one mystery remained. What had happened to the 'token' payment of £250,000? Stanley Gray had written a letter to Ojukwu, which was delivered on 1st July, promising him the money but stressing that he was acting under duress. The Biafrans originally asked that it should be paid into the African Continental Bank in London where they had their main UK account. However, they suddenly changed their minds, probably fearing an attempt by the Nigerians to recover it through legal action, and gave instructions for it to be paid into a numbered account in Geneva. The money never arrived. The Bank of England, presumably instructed by the Treasury (i.e. the British government), refused exchange control permission and the money was frozen[78]*

Isolated, landlocked and now shackled by a crippling trade embargo, all that the Biafrans had to fight for was survival. A letter, dated 26 August, 1967 from Modu to the General Manager of the African Continental Bank in London reported that, 'There are thousands and thousands of people enlisting themselves in the Army, Militia and Civil Defence....The news which B.B.C. have been carrying about the capture of places in Biafra is completely false'.

The reality of Biafra's existence as a country was confirmed by the contents of a letter from the Enugu branch of Azikiwe's the African Continental Bank, to its London branch dated 14 September 1967. The word 'Nigeria' in the address had been overtyped and replaced by the world 'Biafra' and, somewhat ironically, the telegraphic address for the bank was 'ZIKBANK'. The letter reported an adverse turn of events that London's 'Midland Bank has refused to add their confirmation to the [letter of] credit established in favour of Messrs, Blackwell Young and Company Limited...on account of the present malaise besetting our Republic'.

What the Biafrans lacked in financial resources and weaponry they made up for in gallantry and a highly effective international media campaign. The daily television images of the suffering of Biafran women and children, from the combined effects of the policy of starvation and bombing, caught the imagination of the British people. Their biggest handicap, however, was the presence in their midst of so many who were not committed to the cause but who found themselves on the Biafran side of the front by accident or by the design of the federals. Harold Smith offers the following insight into the role of Francis Nwokedi:

> *The Eastern Treasury was taken over and Francis Nwokedi was despatched by Colonel Ojukwu, the Biafran leader, to travel abroad buying arms. Francis*

was an extremely efficient and highly experienced former head of the Foreign Service so that what purportedly happened seems extraordinary. It appears that very few arms were obtained for the very large sums of money taken out of Biafra. It was claimed that Francis and his mission were duped by unscrupulous arms dealers. Twenty million dollars of foreign exchange were rapidly depleted in dubious deals. Yet those involved were the cream of Nigeria's civil service. Twenty million dollars was an awful lot of duping!

The Nigerian Government responded by cancelling Nwokedi's passport and belatedly trying to stop the flow of currency from the East. Francis had once been the dutiful advisor to the British, and then after Independence to the British-backed northern rulers of Nigeria. When Ironsi took over, Francis was by his side and, now Ironsi was dead, he was General Ojukwu's lieutenant and right hand man[79]

THE BETRAYAL OF BIAFRA

Apart from those amongst the minority ethnic groups within the Eastern Region who, as a matter of conscience, did not buy into the Biafran cause, there was the added complication of the former Nigerian army officers who had been implicated in the coup and who appear to have been transferred to prisons in the region as part of advance war planning strategy.

Ojukwu had been persuaded to release them from prison in January, 1967 at the time of the Aburi accord. If the theory that the January, 1966 coup was an Igbo plot had any merit, these coup-plotters might have been expected to have been loyal to the Biafran cause but the opposite appears to have been the case. Principal amongst these was Nzeogwu the leader of the coup plot.

Having first been held in Kirikiri maximum security prison in Lagos following his arrest, by a series of transfers he ended up in the Eastern Region. In May, 1967, days before the declaration of Biafra, he had made his opposition to secession clear:

> *Secession will be ill-advised, indeed impossible. Even if the East fights a war of secession and wins, it still cannot secede. Personally I don't like secession and if this country disintegrates, I shall pack up my things and go. In the present circumstances, confederation is the best answer as a temporary measure. In time, we shall have complete unity*[80]

That he had no loyalty to the Biafran cause and may, in fact, have been working with the federal side, is suggested by a letter that he wrote to Olusegun Obasanjo, on 17 June 1967, just a couple of weeks before the outbreak of the war:

270

You have no doubt heard a lot of rumours about my relations with Ojukwu. We obviously see things quite differently after what he did to my supporters in January 1966. He is also worried about my popularity among his own people. I was to be put back into prison, but he was afraid of the repercussions. Right now I am not allowed contact with troops nor am I permitted to operate on the staff. One gentleman's agreement which we have is that I can carry on with whatever pleases me; you can't be in any doubt about the fact that if I have financial and logistic support, I will create a new Nigerian Army inside Biafra!! With Ibo, Hausa, Yoruba & all other ethnic groups. Let me know whether anyone in authority there in Lagos is ready to support me. If he is, I like contact to be established soonest[81]

It was perhaps not surprising that Nzeogwu was killed soon after hostilities commenced on 6 July 1967. The intriguing element is that he was killed on 29 July 1967 – the very anniversary of the countercoup.

Even more beguiling is the care that the federal forces took to retrieve his corpse, two days later, and to fly it to Kaduna to be buried in the military cemetery even while the war was going on.[82] On one level this honour that was paid to him in death, and the fact that his family escaped the war crimes inflicted on men, women and children from his home town Asaba, can be put down to special favour from his friend Obasanjo. That it was an act of appreciation from the very highest level can, however, be discerned from the fact that even while he was in Kirikiri prison in Lagos, he had been receiving VIP treatment:

Ifeajuna and my colleagues in the South made such a nonsense of this affair with result that people are accusing us of being one-sided. The so called loyalist troops under the influence of the Supreme Comd, egged on by certain tribalists, encouraged private soldiers & NCO's to cane & maltreat some of these offrs & the men now in Kiri-Kiri whilst they were under detention in the FEDERAL Guard and in 2 Bn. They were beaten with Kobokos daily, starved and forced to drink urine at gunpoint. Nwobosi nearly had his eyes poked out with a rifle muzzle and Oyewole who is still admitted in the military hospital had his forehead and nose smashed to bits with a rifle in the presence of Ekanem, Capt Iwe, Maj Ally and a few other loyalist offrs. If you see the men here in prison you will be sorry for them. Koboko & Bayonet wounds all over the face & body! It is terrible.
In fairness to them, (loyalists) they were probably acting so, in order to please some faction of the army that felt the human loss, but that is not how to soldier. We get VIP treatment in the prison & all the warders & prisoners respect me as head of the revolutionary group[83]

The special treatment afforded to Nzeogwu is curious because it was he who had murdered the revered northern leader, Ahmadu Bello. It is all the more curious that it is said that he received a full military burial in Kaduna, the political capital of the North, with a twenty-one gun salute.

Victor Adebukunola Banjo was another former officer in the Nigerian army who was also a firm believer in 'One Nigeria' who found himself in prison on the Biafra side of the front until he was released by Ojukwu in January, 1967. He had been named and jailed by the 'Ironsi' regime as having been one of the coup plotters although there is reason to doubt the truth of this:

> No one has been able to say exactly how Victor Banjo became involved with the January revolution for him to be detained by Ironsi. But Victor Banjo became the only colonel in the Nigerian Army, detained for a major coup - a thing he had absolutely no knowledge of. In fact Banjo was so opposed to the January revolution and revolutionaries alike, that he even called and threatened the Nzeogwu group at Kaduna, soon after Ironsi took over Lagos[84]

He too was killed not long after hostilities commenced. His real offence appears to have been that, as a graduate in mechanical engineering, he was one of the new generation of educated officers who the army regarded with suspicion.

Why those who had been implicated in the coup, but who were not committed to Biafra, remained in the Eastern Region up until the outbreak of war, in July 1967, requires explanation. That Ojukwu appointed Nzeogwu to take charge of the Nsukka front when he was known to be loyal to the ideal of 'One Nigeria' also requires explanation. In the case of Victor Banjo, he is said to have ended up joining the Biafran Liberation Army which Ojukwu set up to liberate the Western Region from northern occupation only after General Gowon had rebuffed his appeal for release:

> After Gowon was installed in power from August 1966, Lieutenant-Colonel Banjo made several overtures to him for his (Banjo's) release. Gowon refused to release him, even though he (Gowon) knew perfectly well that Banjo had not played any part in the coup. The only condition he gave Banjo was the latter could be transferred back to a prison in Lagos. Banjo did not accept the offer.[85]

The Biafran Liberation Army's mission of taking the battle into the Western Region would have been ambitious in normal circumstances given the distances and the logistical challenges. With the Biafrans already facing extreme challenges in defending their own enclave, the move is difficult to comprehend.

Azikiwe's Mausoleum in Onitsha

Ojukwu's appointment of Banjo as head of the Biafran Liberation Army, to lead the Biafran counter-attack against the Nigerians also does not sit well with the claim that the Igbos had already been betrayed by the Yoruba leader, Awolowo, into declaring secession. In this climate in which truth was hard to separate from fiction, it should come as no surprise that Victor Banjo's fate was to be accused and tried with Emmanuel Ifeajuna (and two others, Maj. Philip Alale and Sam Agbam) for treason against Biafra.

As the story goes, on 9 August 1967, it was reported that the Liberation Army had captured the Mid-West and had reached Ore in its drive to capture Lagos when the operation was sabotaged by Banjo and Ifeajuna by halting the advance on Lagos. It was said that the decision was made as part of a plot to overthrow Ojukwu and end the war through reconciliatiion with Nigeria. Their plea of innocence having been dismissed after a trial, they were executed on Ojukwu's order on 25 September.

The Biafrans fought on bravely against impossible odds, until such will to fight as they still had was finally destroyed by a propaganda coup that was handed to the federal side when Nnamdi Azikiwe, who since the outbreak of the war had been holded up in London, writing his autobiography (ultimately published in 1970), landed in Lagos, on 17 August 1969, to be received by Gowon:

> *Zik had become a prize-catch for the federal government, and General Gowon... immediately saw in his return to the fold, if for nothing else, the propaganda value which he exploited to good advantage: With one stone therefore, General Gown was able to kill the proverbial two birds. By taking Zik along with him to the OAU summit at Addis Ababa in September 1969, he was able to finish Biafra off diplomatically once and for all. And secondly, the grand reception and the courtesies accorded Zik on his return to Nigeria, helped in no small way in destroying the myth of Biafra, by removing the morbid fear that had gripped all Biafrans concerning the alleged intentions of the Nigerians to annihilate all Biafran males of ten years and above, which was no doubt the mainstay of the Biafran resistance[86]*

Just as he had abandoned the radical Zik Movement, who had drawn their inspiration from his speeches, when the group was outlawed in April 1950, so again, Azikiwe, who had been responsible for igniting Igbo nationalism, abandoned those whom he had inspired in their hour of need. On 28 August he made the following pronouncement:

> *Knowing that the accusation of genocide is palpably false, but bearing in mind the widespread killing of 1966, which must always haunt our memories, why should some people continue to fool our people to believe that they are slated for slaughter, when we know that they suffer mental anguish and physical agony as*

a result of their being homeless and their places of abode having been desolated by war and their lives rendered helpless[87]

Ironically, just three months before, on 30 May 1969 (the second anniversary of the declaration of Biafra), Bruce Mayrock, a twenty-year old American of Jewish descent who was a medical student at Columbia University in New York, burnt himself to death in front of the the United Nations building, in protest over the genocide in Biafra.

THE WAR'S END

The General Elections which were looming in Britain in the summer of 1970 was a significant influence on the war coming to an end in that January. Biafra was Britain's own Vietnam, a war that was competing for the headlines at the same time.

The Nigerian army was viewed as conducting a proxy war for Britain's oil interests with just cause. The army had been put together and trained by Britain: General Gowon, the leader of the federal forces, had been trained at Sandhurst; the Biafran forces were led by Colonel Ojukwu who had been trained at Eaton Hall, Chester. It was Britain that was providing the arms and the credits for the prosecution of the war.

Harold Wilson had hoped for a short war. As the conflict became drawn-out the moral ground on which he was standing became more difficult. He needed a quick end to the war but the end had to be on terms of Biafran acceptance of the principle of a united Nigeria i.e. Biafran surrender. A quick victory meant a resort to more desperate measures including aerial bombardment of the Biafrans by hired Egyptian pilots. In the words of Ademoyega:

> *Now, talking about air raids, it is extremely necessary to speak the truth here and now, that the Federal forces performed horror. These raids, even as perceived from behind bars, were indiscriminate in their choice of victims: detention camps, refugee camps, prisons, hospitals, markets, schools, private and public homes, churches and every conceivable target – even trees and grasses [sic]. Those raids were of severe intensity and extent and were ceaseless, producing a most horrifying and most disgusting spectacle that could be perpetrated in any community of human beings*[88]

The ceasefire sought by the Biafrans could not be granted as it was seen as a delaying tactic; only unconditional surrender would be acceptable.

The hard line taken by the Wilson government meant more hostile headlines and more desperate efforts for the final victory. Wilson's Labour Party simply could not go to the country to renew its electoral mandate whilst this war was still filling the front pages of British newspapers and the nightly TV news with images of horrific civilian suffering. Reports of atrocities committed by Nigerian forces against Biafrans had already forced the Wilson Government to compel the Nigerian government to recall the offending commanders, Benjamin Adekunle and Murtala Mohammed, from their commands. In March, 1969, increasingly concerned about the stalemate that was developing, Wilson decided to fly to Nigeria for a personal assessment of the progress of the war effort. That he had ownership of the conflict was clear in the commitments he wanted from General Gowon:

> *I wanted to be satisfied about the willingness of the Federal Government to negotiate on anything not involving dismemberment of Nigeria....In the event of a military victory, he should let the Colonel slip through his hands to safety abroad*[89]

It should come as no surprise that the war ended precisely in accordance with Wilson's script when, at 2.00am, on 11 January, 1970 Col. Ojukwu boarded the last flight from Biafra to safety.[90]

POST-WAR PROPAGANDA

The Biafran war was essentially a falling-out between two former political allies, the Northern Region and the Eastern Region: the Hausa-Fulani and the Igbo. Their party alliance, the NPC-NCNC alliance, had controlled the Nigerian political space and the army had been dominated by Northerners and Easterners with only a token representation from the Western Region and the war had its genesis in the slaughter of Igbos living in the North. However, come the end of the war, in January 1970, an observer might have thought that the war had been between the Yoruba and the Igbo.

A Yoruba man, Obafemi Awolowo, was the Minister of Finance who was said to be responsible for the policy of starvation as an instrument of war that accounted for most of the deaths on the Igbo side. In an army in which the Yoruba representation had been fairly insignificant, the Yoruba officers suddenly took centre stage. The one division led by Col. Benjamin Adekunle, a Yoruba man born to a Fulani mother, the Third Marine Commando Division, was the spearhead of the federal assault on Igbo land. In the final act of this tragedy, it was the same Marine Commando Division, by now under the command of another Yoruba officer, Col. Olusegun Obasanjo, that carried out "Operation Finishing Touch", the January, 1970 final assault on the Biafrans. There was much more than a sense of irony in the image of the Yoruba man, Obasanjo, accepting the surrender of the Biafran forces from their commander Maj. Gen. Philip Efiong.

276

In the prologue to his memoirs on the Biafra War, Efiong narrates the story of a meeting long before the war, in November 1965, with a mysterious old man, who had come in to see him on the pretext of a show of appreciation for admitting his nephew into the army:

> *After a while, he looked at my palms and started telling me about the crisis the country was going to go through and the enormous bloodshed that was going to follow. Of course, I was very sceptical and told him that he was probabaly seeing the bloodshed in the West. Operation Wet-ie was already on, I pointed out to him. He shook his head and went on to say that he had seen me in the midst of a crisis that was more like a war. To cut a long story short, the old man left me in no doubt about the ugly prospects, and said that he would do all that was necessary to protect me because I was a good man. He also asked me to remember him when everything he had told me came to pass. I gave him an indulgent simile before he left.*
>
> *At the end of the War in 1970, I sought out Nicholas Anyanru, then a lieutenant colonel in the supreme headquarters of Major General Yakubu Gowon, head of state and commander-in-chief of the Nigerian Armed Forces. He recalled the meeting with the old man but told me that the man had not been his uncle. Anyanru had met him for the first time by mere coincidence at the ordnance depot gates, and he had insisted on seeing me. When he told me that he had never seen the man again and did not know his name or where he had come from, it became even more significant that what the man had told me had come to pass[91]*

Much more was to come in terms of the damage to future southern relations from the post- war rehabilitation policy, again credited to Awolowo, whereby Igbos were to receive £20 each to restart their lives following a change of currency that had reduced the value of their pre-war savings to zero. In a country that had never been able to count the living properly, figures for the dead from the Biafran war are unreliable. They range from one million to close to three million.

The old partnership between North and East had died with the Biafra war, at least for the time being. The new partners were the North and the West symbolized by that image of Obasanjo accepting Efiong's surrender on 15 January 1970, ending the dramatic events which had begun precisely four years earlier, on 15 January 1966. This symbolic act confirmed Obasanjo as the principal military figure amongst the Yoruba and, with the Eastern Region's defeat, in the whole of the South. It would become the platform for the major role that he would now play in the country as it prepared to enter a long phase of military rule.[95]

9. From General Obasanjo to President Obasanjo

"In the retrospect of 40 years it is clear that this was a grave mistake which has cost many lives and will probably continue to do so. It would have been better to establish several smaller states in a free-trade area".

Sir Peter Smithers

MILITARY RULE

With the slogan "No Victor, No Vanquished", the soldiers, under the leadership of General Gowon, set to putting the broken union back together again.

The experience with democratic self-rule had been short-lived, spanning barely six years from independence. But, if the politicians had been inexperienced the soldiers were even more so because Nigeria's military independence came much later than political independence. For the first five years of civilian self-rule, up until 9 February 1965, the Nigerian army was still being run by a Briton. Not only were the soldiers militarily inexperienced, they were young compared to their political counterparts. General Gowon, the most senior figure in the army, and the head of state, was a mere thirty-five years of age. The army having been so hurriedly put together, and with so little exposure to the sobering discipline of combat (their experience, typically, being limited to UN peacekeeping in the Congo) and with low educational attainment, were the least-equipped institution for the challenge of rebuilding the broken mega-state.

The charade of Nigeria as a nation having been so brutally exposed by the blood-letting of the pogroms, and by the Biafra war, the only bonding agent that remained with which to build some sense of common purpose was the opportunity of financial patronage i.e. corruption. The oil boom of the 1970s came just in time to restore hope in the waning Nigeria project. The trigger for the boom was a new round in the Arab-Israeli wars in 1973.

With Syria and Egypt receiving weapon supplies from the Soviet Union, the USA moved to supply weapons to Israel. The war quickly turned into a global economic war when, on 17 October 1973, the Organisation of Arab Oil Exporting Countries (OAPEC) imposed an oil embargo against the U.S. and several other industrialised countries. By the time the embargo was finally lifted in March 1974, world oil prices had quadrupled from $3/barrel to $12/barrel. This suddenly transformed Nigeria into an oil-rich state. With the Biafran war over, and infrastructure needing to be rebuilt, the country's new-found oil wealth first masked, before then exposing the limited competence of the young soldier-rulers.

With the country now awash with oil revenues, Gowon, the northern-Christian, had served his purpose as the acceptable face of Northern rule. His removal from power on 29 July 1975 by Murtala Muhammed was achieved by exploiting popular disenchantment over the announcement of a delay to the return to civilian rule scheduled for 1976.

Unlike Ojukwu who, after the coup of January 1966, had refused to be subordinated to Gowon, his junior in rank, just because he was a northerner, Obasanjo, although senior to Muhammed by age and rank, accepted to serve as his second-in-command. This act of deference cleared the way for Muhammed to be sworn in as head of state. Nigeria was back where it had been when the British left, under Fulani-northern rule but now with a unitary structure under a military regime.

MURTALA MUHAMMED

A Fulani native of Kano, Muhammed had attended Barewa College before joining the Nigerian Army in 1958 and attending Sandhurst for his officer training.

He had been at the centre of all the key political ructions in Nigeria from his leading role in the bloody counter-coup of July 1966, his service as aide de camp to the military administrator in the Western Region during the 1962 crisis, down to his ignominious role in the massacre of civilians, including women and children, in Asaba during the Biafran War.

While, the earlier coups of January and July 1966 had represented fundamental changes in the political matrix, the driving force for the coup which brought Murtala to power was more about the man at the top. Gowon had enjoyed nearly ten years in power and Murtala wanted his turn on the grand stage. Perhaps because his tenure was so short, it was possible to put an enduring gloss on his blood-soaked past.

As it happened, the delay timetable for the return to civilian rule which he had used to justify Gowon's removal was, in fact, extended further by his new regime when, on

1 October 1975, it announced a new date of 1 October 1979. The announcement of an anti-corruption programme, and a plan to create seven new states coupled with the promise of a new constitution for the country, was sufficient to buy the customary early popularity for the new regime. The real boost to its popularity came from a new radicalism in external affairs which was clearly demonstrated in Nigeria's role in the struggle for Angolan independence.

When, in November 1975, South African forces, with American CIA backing, intervened in the war against the Peoples Movement for the Liberation of Angola (MPLA), the Murtala Muhammed regime, in a departure from the position taken by the OAU, and in defiance of U.S. wishes, decided to assert its independence by giving formal recognition to the MPLA regime. The move ensured the withdrawal of the South African forces, in December 1975, but at great cost to Murtala Muhammed himself: He was assassinated, in Lagos, on 13 February 1976 in what was reported to be an attempted coup. With a count of 199 days in office, Murtala had ruled for only five days longer than 'Ironsi'.

The leader of the attempted coup, Col. Buka Suka Dimka, was a Christian from Gowon's ethnic group and it was suggested that Gowon was behind the plot to take back power having been in nearby Togo at the time. With Ojukwu already in exile in Ivory Coast, Gowon's subsequent exile to Britain meant the military leaders from both sides of the Biafran War were now exiled from Nigeria.

Once more a popular northern leader had been killed in a coup at the hands of a Christian. The prospect of power passing down to his deputy, a southern Christian, was viewed with concern in many quarters not least by the man himself, Obasanjo. For this reason he went to great lengths to deny interest in the succession[1]. For their part, the northerners were sensitive to a situation where another northerner would succeed a northern-Muslim who had himself succeeded a northern-Christian. Thus, despite his protests, everything pointed to Obasanjo, the southern-Christian, as the man for the job.

OLUSEGUN OBASANJO

Obasanjo's Owu people were one of the Yoruba tribes that were once militarily powerful before they were conquered in the Yoruba civil war of the mid-nineteenth century. Power had subsequently shifted to their neighbours, the Egba.

Born to a man who, having failed as a farmer, then failed as a father by abandoning his young family while Obasanjo was in his teens[2], the young Obasanjo found refuge from poverty in the colonial army in Nigeria. There, like other young soldiers he became firmly wedded to the ideal of 'One Nigeria'. Plain good fortune does not adequately explain Obasanjo's career; a better explanation can be found in the meaning of his rather uncommon Yoruba surname '*Obasanjo*' viz. The ruler rewards the faithful servant.

He had joined the army in 1958, as an officer-cadet, at the age of twenty-one[3] alongside Benjamin Adekunle, just as the army was embarking upon its Nigerianization drive and attended Mons, in Aldershot. Unlike Adekunle he failed to win selection for further training at Sandhurst. However it was to be a recurring theme of Obasanjo's life to ultimately trump his betters in the power game, in the process often reaping from ground which they had ploughed. Thus, while it was Adekunle who had had the command of the Third Marine Commando Division that had spearheaded the federal assault on Igbo land in the Biafran war, it was Obasanjo who, in May, 1969 was appointed to replace him to carry out 'Operation Finishing Touch' to end the war and receive the laurels of the Biafran surrender. Similarly, while the academically-brilliant Awolowo made three unsuccessful bids to become President of Nigeria, Obasanjo, who never went to university, would rule the country three times in all. Also, while it was Moshood Abiola who would later make the breakthrough to win a presidential election, it was Obasanjo who would harvest the mandate. Although there had been officers from the South who were more senior in rank than Obasanjo, Murtala Muhammed had retired all of them supposedly in a purge of possible threats to his regime. In this way, Obasanjo became the most senior officer from the South when he was appointed Chief of Staff, Army Headquarters. It was the least that Muhammed could do as payback for Obasanjo stepping aside for him.

In all, Obasanjo played his part, of the reluctant heir to power, skilfully. He spared no effort in eulogising the memory of Murtala Muhammed. The Lagos International Airport, in Ikeja, was named after him and he adhered faithfully to Muhammed's policies and programmes. So much so that, under Obasanjo's rule the North achieved several key strategic objectives. The land ownership rules prevailing in the North were extended to the South by the Land Use Decree, which was passed into law in 1978: the Decree had the effect of vesting the ownership of all land and mineral resources contained within the land in the state. Contracts for the construction of a steel mill in Ajaokuta (Kogi State) were signed. In addition, the decree to establish a new Federal Capital in Abuja which had been passed in the last days of the Murtala Muhammed regime, on 4 February 1976, was promulgated.

The big challenge remained the constitutional arrangements to restart the democracy game.

BANISHING TRIBALISM

In the thinking of the soldiers and their advisors, the collapse of the First Republic had been due to the "tribalism" of the political class. The solution was for the men of the armed forces, as de-tribalised Nigerians to draw up a constitution and a political order that would banish tribalism forever. In this thinking the soldiers conveniently overlooked the fact that it was the slaughter of Igbo soldiers by fellow soldiers from the North within shared barracks which had led to full-blown inter-ethnic warfare resulting in the deaths of millions.

One of the other perceived mistakes was said to be the system of parliamentary government in which a government team was directly shadowed by an official opposition team, with weekly parliamentary confrontations between the Prime Minister and the Leader of the Opposition, and in which the executive was made up of elected representatives of the people. In its place a system broadly modelled upon the U.S. presidential system of government was introduced.

The result was a poor imitation which lost sight of the important feature of American federalism. The draftsmen failed to appreciate, or more likely closed their minds to, the balance of power between the arms of government which serves as a guard against Federal excesses. They also ignored the fact that the daily encounters under the parliamentary system, between the Cabinet and the Official Opposition, served as a similar check on the excesses of the executive. These blind spots meant that the presidential system, which the Obasanjo regime introduced, bore a close resemblance to military and colonial rule with the only difference being the requirement for the president to renew his mandate every four years. A system of governance providing for such limited accountability paved the way for the reign of corruption.

The Constitution Drafting Committee came up with several prescriptions towards the abolition of "tribalism". There was the National Youth Service Corps under which young graduates were required to spend the year following their graduation working in a part of the country other than their state of origin. The thinking was that by emulating the practice within the armed forces wherein soldiers were posted to serve in different parts of the country this would make civilians de-tribalised like the soldiers. Also, there was the principle of Federal Character under which public bodies were required to observe a policy of equal representation between the ethnic groups in appointments.

Biafra had been possible because there was a strong Igbo identity. It failed because not all in the Eastern Region were Igbos. In the aftermath of the Biafran defeat and surrender, the Obasanjo regime could be confident that the threat to the 'One Nigeria' project from the East had been dealt with. The concern now was to neutralise any threat from the Western Region which had always been the most homogenous of the three regions and following the carve-out of the Mid-West State, it was now, more than ever before, made up of a single-ethnic group.

The Obasanjo regime resolved to break up the Western Region by creating new states to facilitate the emergence of new loyalties. As a result, what had been 'Western State' was split into Ondo, Ogun, and Oyo States with Lagos State having already been carved out as a separate State from the old Western Region. Equivalent, although less significant, measures were taken in the East and in the North. East Central State, which had been the core Igbo area, was split into Anambra and Imo States. In the North, North Eastern State became Borno, Gongola and Bauchi States; North Western State became Sokoto, Niger and Federal Capital Territory; and Benue-Plateau State became the separate States of Benue and Plateau. In the new arrangement, there were a total of nineteen States, thus reversingthe parity of states between North and South that had apparently been conceded with Gowan's twelve-state measure just before the war.

Seven states remained unchanged (except for minor boundary adjustments); Kano, Kwara, Lagos, Mid-West, North-Central, Rivers and South-Eastern. All nineteen states were given new names without geographical links in order to erase memories of past political ties and emotional or regional attachments[4]

The most significant prescription was a requirement for political parties to be 'national'. This, it was thought, could be achieved by making it a condition of registration as a political party that the party should have offices in at least two-thirds of the states in the federation.

The stipulation only succeeded in making the process of registering parties prohibitively expensive. It failed in the central objective of avoiding 'tribal' based parties as the five political parties which emerged through the process were, almost without exception, a reincarnation of the parties of the failed First Republic. Awolowo and his Action Group resurfaced with the Unity Party of Nigeria (UPN) as the predominantly Yoruba party. Although the Sardauna and Balewa were now deceased, their party, the NPC, returned, in name, as the National Party of Nigeria (NPN) but, in substance, as the party of the Hausa-Fulani under the leadership of Alhaji Shehu Shagari. Aminu Kano who had been the leader of the Northern Elements Progressive Union, as the voice of the radical North, initially returned as a member of NPN before breaking away to set up his own party, the Peoples Redemption Party (PRP).

The only real departure from the old mould was Alhaji Waziri Ibrahim a Kanuri businessman from Bornu in North East Nigeria. His Nigerian Peoples Party (NPP), when it was formed, was a coalition of the North East and South East of Nigeria. It was effectively the old NCNC (which had been prominent in the North-east) but now led by a non-Fulani northerner in place of Azikiwe.

Not only did the party undermine the Hausa-Fulani NPN's appeal in the North-east (confirmed when the party won both Borno and Gongola States) but it posed the larger danger of a broad alliance against the NPN since it contained prominent members of the old Western arm of the NCNC. With Azikiwe having retired from party politics, there would be nothing to stop this North-east with South-east alliance further allying with Awolowo's UPN of the South-west.

There can be but few precedents in history for one who has served as a head of state, above sectional politics, to return to the mire of the partisan struggle for votes as Azikiwe did but, by one means or another, Azikiwe was persuaded to return to the fray. He did so not by forming his own party but by joining the NPP before then using his power and influence over Igbo members to get the party to adopt him as its Presidential candidate in preference to Waziri Ibrahim. The move forced Ibrahim to leave, with his Kanuri followers, to form a new party, the Great Nigerian People's Party ('GNPP').

Azikiwe's late intervention had the effect of taking the country back to square one in its political journey as he then took the now predominantly-Igbo NPP into alliance with the NPN, thus reproducing the old alliance of North-west and East. The reward for Azikiwe and his followers was eight positions within the new NPN/NPP alliance government.[5]

THE TWO-THIRDS OF NINETEEN DEBACLE

A new dimension introduced to the political arena is what can be described as a judicial electorate. As part of the measures to outlaw 'tribally-based' parties, the constitution had stipulated that:

> *A candidate for an election to the office of President shall be deemed to have been duly elected to such office where... (i) he has the highest number of votes cast;[6] and (ii) he had not less than one-quarter of the votes cast at the election in each of at least two-thirds of all the states in the Federation*

When the votes were tallied, Alhaji Shehu Shagari of the NPN was credited with 5,688,857 million votes with Awolowo of the UPN coming in second with 4,916,561 million votes and Azikiwe coming third. Shagari had the highest number of votes cast but the issue was whether he had met the 'not less than' stipulation. He had, unquestionably, in twelve of the nineteen states, but in Kano he had attained only 19.9% of the total votes cast.

Awolowo and the UPN argued that not less than two-thirds of nineteen states meant thirteen states so that Shagari was not entitled to be sworn in as President without a run-off election between him and Awolowo. The prospect of a head-to-head contest between Awolowo and Shagari, without the splintering influence of Azikiwe and others, offered no attraction to the NPN.

Before the Supreme Court, the NPN's lead counsel, Richard Akinjide, argued that two-thirds of nineteen was twelve and two-thirds and that since Shagari had won 25 percent of two-thirds of the vote in the thirteenth state, he had met the constitutional requirement. With only one dissent, the court accepted this argument or the alternative argument that the constitutional provisions had been 'substantially complied with' without affecting the result. With this, the Second Republic was born with a heavy cloud over its legitimacy. Nothing had changed and nothing had been learnt. It was not long before the resurrected alliance of North and East fell apart once more.

With no ideology binding the alliance partners corruption became the only cause. A sudden collapse in the oil price saw the economy run completely out of control and the country mired in astronomical debt. Given the desperate state of the economy, exceptional measures were going to be required to return the failed alliance to power. The Shagari government sought to curry electoral support by granting pardons to the two central characters in the Biafran war who had been in exile for different reasons, Gowon and Ojukwu.

The subsequent, 1983, presidential election, which was again plagued with allegations of vote-rigging, saw Shagari returned as president with a disputed 47% of the vote with Awolowo far behind with 31% of the vote and Azikiwe still making his influence felt with 14%. This time the arithmetic was such that there would be no judicial contest but history was, nevertheless, to repeat itself when, on 31 December 1983, the army took over and dismissed the political class.

The Second Republic had run aground even more quickly than the First despite all the political reforms introduced by the soldiers.

MUHAMMADU BUHARI

Daura, the town where Muhammadu Buhari was born, is to the Hausa people as Ife is to the Yoruba people in that it was the spiritual home of the Hausa people before the Fulani takeover.

Buhari was the last of his father's twenty-three children. His father having died when he was a mere four years of age, it was almost inevitable that he would join the army in the footsteps of his ancestors who played a front-line role in expanding the Fulani Empire:

> Muhammadu's maternal grandfather, Sarkin Dogarai, was the head of the Daura Infantry and the Police chief. His maternal great-grandfather, Kauri Daura Lawal, was the head of the Armed Forces during the period of the ferocious battles between the Hausas and the Fulanis for dominance in Daura in the early 1800s. Buhari's paternal great-grandfather, Adamu, was the son of a Kuran Kukawa, who was the head of the Army during the fierce battles with the Rabe of the old Borno Empire[7]

Buhari joined the army in 1962. Like his contemporaries, his own active military service before Biafra was limited to participation in the UN Peacekeeping Force in Congo. In August, 1975 he was appointed Military Governor of Borno by the new Murtala Mohammed regime before serving as Federal Commissioner of Petroleum and

Energy in 1976, the beginning of a long, and close intimacy, with Nigeria's oil and gas sector. He first came to public prominence as the commander of the armoured brigade which, in April 1983, reportedly drove out Chadian forces who had invaded Nigerian territory. In December of the same year he took power in a military coup that toppled the Shagari administration.

THE WAR AGAINST INDISCIPLINE

Where the Obasanjo regime had put Nigeria's problem down to 'tribalism', the cure for which was supposed to have been lessons in de-tribalisation from the soldiers, Buhari now put the problem down to the indiscipline of the people and the press and the corruption of the politicians. Buhari had justified the coup with a military equivalent of a jihad speech:

> "While corruption and indiscipline have been associated with our state of under-development, these two evils in our body politic have attained unprecedented height in the past few years. The corrupt, inept and insensitive leadership in the last four years has been the source of immorality and impropriety in our society"

The cure was to be further instruction from the soldiers and so he decided upon a programme of enforced discipline for the people through a crash training course. At the same time he sought to banish corruption by arresting and imprisoning the corrupt politicians for exemplarily long terms.

His Deputy, Major General Tunde Abdulbaki Idiagbon, a native of Ilorin, Kwara State, was the public face of the administration who led the 'War Against Indiscipline' that the administration launched against the people. The key objectives of the 'War' were to instil into Nigerians the culture of queuing, work ethics, punctuality, nationalism and patriotism, abolition of corruption and environmental sanitation. Buhari missed out on the opportunity to leave the country a constitutional legacy of his own because on 27 August 1985 he was overthrown in a bloodless coup by General Ibrahim Babanginda.

However, it would soon become clear that the fundamental problem was the indiscipline and corruption of the soldiers themselves.

IBRAHIM BABANGIDA

The Nigerian who has had the most enduring influence on the political landscape of Nigeria was General. Of the Gbagi ethnic group in central Nigeria, he had been orphaned in 1955 at the age of fourteen.[8] In common with many other orphaned youths he found a ready career in the army and so he enrolled at the Nigerian Military Training

College in December 1962 before going on to the Indian Military Academy[9]. His first war experience was Biafra.

Having, along with his colleague Sani Abacha, been at the heart of previous coups that had brought two Fulanis, Murtala Muhammed and Buhari, to power, this time Babangida was resolved to enjoy the experience himself.

Perhaps the only thing Babangida understood well about governance was the art of courting popularity and of keeping enemies on edge. Thus, the coup to change the northern guard was timed to play upon the unpopularity of the Buhari regime in the midst of the economic gloom that had taken hold of the country. It was quickly followed up with a demonstration of the utmost ruthlessness.

Major General Mamman Vatsa, a native of Nupe, was a cultured soldier, an author of several books and a poet. More significantly, he was a close friend of Babangida having been the best man at his wedding. On 23 December 1985, the Babangida regime had Vatsa arrested on suspicion of plotting a coup. He, along with several of his co-accused, was then executed after a military trial. The execution of such a friend on mere suspicion of coup plotting, without evidence of an actual attempt, was intended as an early warning from the master coup plotter to all other would-be imitators. Indeed, it has been said that:

> of the 117 people executed for coup plotting in Nigeria's history, 78 were executed by the Babangida regime[10]

A new phenomenon emerged in the politics in Nigeria when, in October 1986, Dele Giwa, the editor-in-chief of the popular political magazine *Newswatch* was killed in his home by a parcel bomb. The incident, coming after Giwa had undergone a series of interviews at the behest of the State Security Services, caused suspicion to fall on the Babangida government.

Newswatch was one of the publications which had uncovered the story that the regime had, in January, 1986, without any prior discussion or consultation, upgraded Nigeria's observer status with the Organization of Islamic Communities to full membership. In what was supposed to be a secular state because of the broadly equal numbers of Muslims and Christians, this was a provocative move. It was all the more incendiary because of its timing, coming on the back of three successive baton changes between Muslim leaders since Obasanjo's handover in 1979: Shagari, Buhari and Babangida. The pace of drift between the tectonic plates of Northern and Southern Nigeria became measurable from this point on as other measures taken began to give a distinctly religious appearance to the agenda of the administration:

> The reshuffles led to a massive regional and religious polarization of senior positions in favour of northern Muslims. The Head of State, Defence Secretary,

Chairman of the Joint Chiefs of Staff, Chief of Army Staff, Chief of Air Staff, Chief of Navy Staff, Inspector-General of Police, Minister of the Federal Capital Territory, National Security Adviser, Director of Military Intelligence and Director-General of the State Security Service (i.e. all the positions that really mattered) were all northern Muslims[11]

THE ORKAR COUP ATTEMPT

These actions and repeated postponements by Babangida of the timetable for the return to civilian rule led to a coup attempt against the regime on 22 April 1990 led by Major Gideon Orkar and other colleagues from the Niger Delta Region. It was the first sign that the rest of the country was beginning to see through the charade and to call time on Northern-led military rule. The coup attempt failed but not before Orkar had made his speech headlining the structural imbalance within the body politic:

> *"We wish to emphasise that this is not just another coup but a well conceived, planned and executed revolution for the marginalized, oppressed and enslaved peoples of the Middle Belt and the south with a view to freeing ourselves and children yet unborn from eternal slavery and colonization by a clique of this country. Our history is replete with numerous and uncontrollable instances of callous and insensitive dominatory repressive intrigues by those who think it is their birthright to dominate till eternity the political and economic privileges of this great country to the exclusion of the Middle Belt and the south...*
> *In the light of all the above and in recognition of the negativeness of the aforementioned aristocratic factor,[sic] the overall progress of the Nigerian state a temporary decision to excise the following states namely, Sokoto, Borno, Katsina, Kano and Bauchi states from the Federal Republic of Nigeria comes into effect immediately until the following conditions are met.*
> **The conditions to be met to necessitate the re-absorption of the aforementioned states are as following:*
>> *(a) To install the rightful heir to the Sultanate, Alhaji Maccido, who is the people's choice.*
>> *(b) To send a delegation led by the real and recognized Sultan Alhaji Maccido to the federal government to vouch that the feudalistic and aristocratic quest for domination and oppression will be a thing of the past and will never be practiced in any part of the Nigeria state.*
> *By the same token, all citizens of the five states already mentioned are temporarily suspended from all public and private offices in Middle Belt and southern parts*

of this country until the mentioned conditions are met. They are also required to move back to their various states within one week from today. They will, however, be allowed to return and join the Federal Republic of Nigeria when the stipulated conditions are met. In the same vein, all citizens of the Middle Belt and the south are required to come back to their various states pending when the so-called all-in-all Nigerians meet the conditions that will ensure a united Nigeria. A word is enough for the wise"

Biafra had been an attempt at a defensive secession of the East but Orkar's proclamation was an attempt to expel the North.

Proof that the coup was not "a well-conceived, planned and executed revolution" was that it was quickly crushed by the Babanginda regime. Yet the declaration was a significant marker: while it had brought dancing on some streets of the Middle Belt and the South, it led to somber reflection and calculation in the North. The declared objectives of the abortive coup had raised the stakes of the political game at the centre. What had hitherto been thought, but not spoken, was now out in the open.

The northern administration made a small retreat on one front, by announcing the suspension of Nigeria's membership of the Organization of the Islamic Conference in August 1991, whilst making a big advance on another front as Babangida embarked upon a radical programme to reshape the Nigerian state. The creation of several new states on 27 August 1991 effectively atomized the federation and by so doing reduced the scope for concerted action in the future. This was followed quickly by the move of his seat of governance from Dodan Barracks in Lagos (which had been captured by the Orkar coupists) to Abuja in December 1991. Up until this point Abuja as the seat of government was still a plan.

JUNE 12TH

In the aftermath of the coup-attempt, Babangida now quickly announced a programme for return to civilian rule that saw a census count undertaken in November 1991 ahead of planned elections in 1992 with a promise to hand power back to civilians on 27 August 1993. In the meantime he embarked upon a radical experiment towards creating a diarchy: the joint rule of soldiers and civilians. Military officers were retired from the army but then retained in office as part of the Federal Military Government whilst, at the same time, civilians were brought into the administration:

> *Although civilian involvement in military regimes was not new, the level of civilian participation in the Babangida regime was unprecedented, and far exceeded that of prior military regimes*[12]

In another departure from previous military regimes, and to underline the fusion of military and civilian rule, he resorted to calling himself 'President' as opposed to 'Head of State'.[13] All the signs were that the regime was testing the waters to assess the viability of a conversion of a military ruler into a civilian leader, as Flt. Lt. Rawlings had recently done in Ghana. However, doubts over the prospects of pulling it off set the stage for what was intended to be a transition to civilian rule that was to end all transitions.

On the two previous occasions when the democracy game had started, a northerner had taken power. The pattern was to be broken in the course of Babangida's elaborate arrangements.

A carefully orchestrated plan saw a gradual withdrawal of military officers from governance, and their replacement by elected civilians. The process of disengagement had worked up progressively from local government, to state, then to the National Assembly, until the final stage of federal presidential elections, only for the Babangida regime to then ban the freely-formed parties.

In a naïve attempt to fast-forward a country made up of hundreds of ancient nations into a western-type two party system, the regime now decreed the creation of two parties the Social Democratic Party ("SDP") and the National Republican Convention ("NRC"). The attempt to escape 'tribal parties' which the multi-party system was believed to bring about only served to push the country into the deeper abyss of the North-South divide. The party whose name began with "S" quickly became identified with the South while the one with the name beginning with "N" equally quickly became associated with the North.

The divide was compounded when a Yoruba southerner, Moshood Kashimawo Abiola was chosen by the SDP as its standard-bearer for the presidential election while the NRC chose a northerner Bashir Tofa. With Babagana Kingibe, a Kanuri Muslim from the North East, as a running mate, and with Abiola himself being a southern-Muslim, the SDP constituted a formidable alliance between the South and the North-east. With only two parties in play, this time around there was no room for Azikiwe to play the role of the makeweight. In this head-to-head contest between Abiola and Tofa, the odds favoured an Abiola victory.

The realization came to the Babangida regime too late. The votes were already being counted when, at a point in the vote tally where Abiola was believed to have won nineteen out of the thirty states, the prospect of the power loop between the Army and the North being broken for the first time since independence suddenly loomed. The Babangida regime was faced with a choice between allowing the democratic contest to take its course or calling a stop to the exercise and allowing the mask of army-neutrality to slip. It chose the latter course and so, on 23 June 1993, Babanginda announced the annulment of the elections and withheld the results.

With this, the country had come full circle from the crisis over the census count of 1962, the results of which were similarly annulled and withheld. The annulment of the presidential elections by the very same northern military ruler who had been the target of the Orkar coup now brought the issues of northern domination that had been aired in the coup speech back into full focus. If a southern-Muslim, who had garnered so much electoral support across the Muslim-North, could ultimately be denied his mandate, there was little reason for other southerners to have any confidence in the system.

In an address, on 23 June 1993, to explain the annulment of the elections, Babangida admitted his regime's manipulation of the process:

> *"In particular, during the course of handling the interlocking relationships between the old and new political forces and institutions, some problems had arisen leading us into a number of difficulties and thereby necessitating our having to tamper with the rules and regulations laid down in the political programme. As a result, the administration unwittingly attracted enormous public suspicions of its intentions and objectives. Accordingly, we have experienced certain shortfalls and conflicting responses to the pulls and pushes of governance in the course of policy implementation"*

SANNI ABACHA

With Abiola, and his supporters, insisting upon his mandate it was clear that Babangida had to go. The transition having been so thoroughly mishandled, a direct handover to civilian rule was not viable; but neither was yet another military ruler from the North tenable.

The solution was a technical in-house coup which saw Babangida 'step aside' for Gen. Sanni Abacha as head of the armed forces. At the same time a civilian was appointed to head a new Interim National Government. Careful calculation had gone into the choice. He was to be a southerner like Abiola, a Yoruba like Abiola and from the same Egba tribe as Abiola. The man was Ernest Shonekan.

Shonekan was a former chairman of Cadbury's Nigeria. He was a career corporate man who had never shown any interest in politics before his sudden emergence as head of state on 26 August 1993. His appointment had been intended simply to take the heat out of the political situation. The illusion of power lasted only eighty-four days before Abacha pushed him aside, on 18 November, 1993:

> *"Fellow Nigerians, the events of the past months, starting from the annulment of the June 12 presidential election, culminating in the appointment of the former Head of State, Chief Ernest Shonekan, who unfortunately resigned yesterday,*

*are well known to you...we require well thought-out and permanent solutions
to these problems if we are to emerge stronger from them. Consequently, a
constitutional conference with full constituent powers will be established soon
to determine the future constitutional structure of Nigeria. The constitutional
conference will also recommend the method of forming parties, which will lead
to the ultimate recognition of political parties formed by the people"*

The mask of the Nigerian Army had slipped at least for the nationalists. Hitherto they
had looked upon the army as the embodiment of the unity of the country which the
civilians aspired to and as the salvation of Nigeria whenever civilian rule was breaking
down. Now it was clear that the army was in fact sectional. With Orkar's ghost still
roaming the land, those who had been dis-enfranchised by the annulment, and the
south-western press in particular, were in no mood to allow the peoples' mandate to
be overridden with such impunity despite Abacha's warning of dire consequences for
defiance:

> *"This regime will be firm, humane and decisive. We will not condone nor tolerate
> any act of indiscipline. Any attempt to test our resolve will be decisively dealt
> with".*

The country was about to discover what the regime meant by its promise to be "firm,
humane and decisive".

The National Democratic Coalition (NADECO), a loose coalition of activists and
political figures, had formed, in May 1994, under the leadership of Chief Anthony
Enahoro, to champion the cause of the 'June 12 mandate'. With a heavy south-west
composition but with sympathisers all over, it was the organization that had encouraged,
cajoled, and imposed upon Abiola to stand his ground on the stolen mandate. On the
eve of the first anniversary of the 12 June 1993 elections, Abiola was again imposed
upon to declare himself president. Following his declaration, first Abiola decided to flee
the country, but then he turned back, deciding to meet his destiny. Returning on 23
June, he was arrested, charged with treason and imprisoned.

Apart from removing the last semblance of fair-play in Nigeria's political system, the
other destructive dynamic that Babangida's rule had unleashed in the country was the
liberal access to oil revenues and oil wells for close associates and friends of the regime.
The practice continued under the Abacha regime with Abacha himself reported to have
purloined billions of dollars and stashed them away in Swiss bank accounts.

This was an era in which America was turning its face against military rulers in
the third world. But with George Washington, Andrew Jackson, Dwight Eisenhower,
amongst others, as examples from its own history, there could be no objection to

military rulers who were prepared to swap their uniforms for suits and contest elections. The new template had been tested with Flt. Lt. Jerry Rawlings in Ghana in 1992 and Yoweri Museveni of Uganda was readying himself for the same conversion. Abacha started to prepare for the same costume change. To this end he first organized a National Constitutional Conference which sat from 26 June 1994 to 26 June 1995 to deliberate on a new constitutional arrangement for the country. In an attempt to bury Abiola's mandate by decree, the administration proscribed and banished the SDP and NRC parties that Babangida had created and, approved, instead, the registration of five new political parties. What at first appeared as a liberalising move to enhance freedom of association by the political class, and more choice for the electorate, turned into farce when each of the five parties, one by one, adopted Abacha as their presidential candidate in the planned elections. The outcome was famously labelled, by Chief Bola Ige, as the 'five fingers of the same leprous hand'.

NADECO led a very effective boycott of Abacha's constitutional conference and mobilized popular and international opinion against the regime. As the standoff between NADECO's position and Abacha's ambition hardened, the political language of the battle between the two camps took a dire turn. On 17 November 1994, the first anniversary of Abacha's coup, a bomb went off in Lagos marking the beginning of a low-level bombing campaign. The Abacha regime responded with a campaign of assassinations directed at the key figures in NADECO. The first victims were the financiers of the organization. In February, 1995 the publisher, Chief Alex Ibru, narrowly survived an assassin's bullet. The businessman Pa Alfred Rewane was less fortunate as he was shot and killed, in his home, on 6 October 1995.

The strugglers in the south-west were to find common cause with the activists in the Niger Delta when, the Ogoni activist and playwright, Ken Saro-Wiwa was tried by a military tribunal and sentenced to death by hanging. Abacha captured world headlines when, on 10 November 1995, shunning all pleas for clemency, he ordered the public hanging of Saro-Wiwa. This was done even as the conference of the Commonwealth Heads of State, that was leading the international call for mercy, was in session. The barbaric act led immediately to the suspension of Nigeria from the Commonwealth and to a downward spiral in the Abacha regime's foreign relations.

The regime confirmed its pariah status when Abacha's assassins shot and killed Abiola's wife, Kudirat Abiola on 4 June 1996, on the streets of Lagos. The evident ruthlessness of the Abacha regime now drove the chairman of NADECO, Chief Anthony Enahoro, and other prominent leaders into exile to continue the campaign from abroad. It now seemed that there was nothing that could stop Abacha from realizing his ambition to convert himself into a civilian president in 1998 and, with oil revenues at his command, there were those who were ready to support his ambition.

On 12 June 1997, the fourth anniversary of the June 12 elections, an organization by the name 'Youths Earnestly Ask for Abacha' was launched in Lagos under the leadership of one Daniel Kanu, as a campaign group to support Abacha's plan. Another organization, the National Council of Youth Associations organized a 'Two Million Youth March' in Abuja in March 1998 in support of Abacha. It was all in vain. Abacha and the army had gone too far now to turn back with any honour. With the murder of his wife, Abiola's resolve became steely and turned him into the accidental hero of the struggle for democracy in Nigeria.

The standoff quickly came to be seen as Abacha of the North versus Abiola of the South. With Abacha refusing to release Abiola from prison unless he agreed to give up his claim to the presidency and Abiola holding firm, as the fifth anniversary of the aborted June 12 election approached, it was Bill Clinton's US administration that took the decisive action to break the deadlock. Abacha died on 8 June 1998 and Abiola's death, in prison, quickly followed on 7 July 1998.[i]

Plans had been laid to ensure that there would be no political vacuum. The succession plan was simple. The programme of transition to civilian rule under a new constitution would be re-started with new elections. When the elections came the North would play the ball back to the South and to the Yoruba in particular. This would be done by ensuring that the North did not put forward one of their own to contest. However the winner of the planned election would be no ordinary Yoruba. He would be one of the North's choosing; a former soldier who would give the army a face-saving formula through which to salvage some degree of continued political relevance. That man would be the now-retired Gen. Olusegun Obasanjo.

Nelson Mandela's autobiography, *Long Walk to Freedom*, which detailed his journey from prisoner to president was published in December 1994. It seems more than just a few leaves were borrowed from this book when, Obasanjo, who had never shown the slightest revolutionary tendency was arrested and imprisoned by Abacha on 13 March 1995 on allegations of coup-plotting. This was all part of the setting for Obasanjo's costume change from former military ruler to born-again Christian, chairman of the Advisory Council of Transparency International and presidential candidate. The man who brokered the arrangement was General Abdulsalami Alhaji Abubakar who took over as military president on 9 June 1998 following Abacha's assassination.

Although Abdulsalami was another northern military ruler, he was one who made it clear that he had no lust for power by quickly announcing arrangements to hold elections within a year and to handover to an elected president. At the end of the week of mourning that he had declared for Abacha, his first act had been to release Obasanjo from prison on 15 June 1998: Obasanjo had spent precisely 3 years, 3 months and 3 days in prison, a curious coincidence with his cell number '333'. Just eight months later, he would be declared the winner of presidential elections on the platform of the newly formed Peoples Democratic Party. Even Mandela had not achieved the transition from prisoner to president so miraculously.

The election was notable for the North not fielding a candidate, so the candidates

---

i   See by the same author, *The Law, the Lawyers and the Lawless, Chapter 9*

of the two main parties, the Peoples Democratic Party and the Alliance for Democracy, retired Gen. Obasanjo and Olu Falae, were both southerners and both Yoruba. Equally significant was the fact that the new constitution, which the army had drafted, was not released until 5 May 1999, after the winner of the election was confirmed, and just days before Obasanjo was sworn in as the new president of the Third Republic on 29 May 1999.

The Olusegun Obasanjo edifice in Abeokuta

SHARIA AND MEND

Hot on the heels of the celebration of Nigeria's Independence Day by the new Obasanjo administration on 1 October, came a dramatic announcement, on 26 October 1999, by the governor of the north-eastern state of Zamfara, Ahmad Sani Yerima: Sharia criminal law was to be enforced Saudi-style, with amputations and beheadings, in the new millennium as soon as Saudi-trained judges were in place.

Although not in so many words, this was the North's riposte to the Orkar declaration. Just as the Orkar announcement of the expulsion of certain northern states from the federation had been welcomed with singing and dancing on some of the streets of the Christian south and Middle Belt, so too Governor Ahmed Sani's Sharia announcement saw jubilation on the streets of Zamfara and in other parts of the North. A clear challenge had been thrown down to the Constitution and to President Obasanjo. In substance, it was a call to Jihad by legislation, coming at the turn of the century with the usual justifications of the need to re-Islamize the society to fight immorality, crime and corruption.

Sharia law was not new to Nigeria. Its proper place within the setting of a secular state had also challenged the British colonial administration and the outcome had been a similar fudge:

> *Islamic, Maliki law coexisted with enacted criminal aw, a situation which continued until 1960 with the introduction of the Penal Code Law for Northern Nigeria 1959. However, the application of Sharia's criminal law was increasingly controlled and curbed by the British colonial administration and judiciary...Although it seems that in the early years of colonial rule amputation was still applied as a punishment for theft, the British soon abolished this and other Islamic penalties such as stoning and crucifixion...The Emirs' courts could pronounce capital sentences. Caning and flogging continued to be lawful punishments, but sentences imposing these penalties had to be confirmed by the Emir or the District Officer[14]*

The enactment pre-independence of the Penal Code Law for the Northern Region, 1959 was intended to take Islamic criminal law out of the hands of state governments and for the federal government to serve as a moderating influence on possible local extremism. It was this code and this objective that Zamafara's initiative challenged directly.

With the Nigerian Police Force a federal institution, the inevitable consequence was the emergence of Islamic vigilante forces 'hisba' groups to enforce the Sharia criminal code, creating the need for the state government to legalize and finance these forces in the interests of controlling them. In this way the Sharia states muddied the waters surrounding another pillar of the Nigeria federal structure, the prohibition on states having their own police forces.

There was every reason to expect a tough and decisive reaction by the Obasanjo Government to this early and fundamental challenge to its authority especially in view of the action the same government had taken, on 20 November 1999, against the Ijaw town of Odi after militants from the Niger Delta had killed twelve policemen. On that occasion, as a warning to others, Obasanjo had sent in troops who burnt down every building in the town saving only the bank, the Anglican Church and the health centre and killing scores in the process. However, to Zamfara's challenge there was no response.

These acts of omission and commission by the Obasanjo administration set off two similar reactions. In the Niger Delta the Ijaw people now found common cause with the late Ken Saro-Wiwa's Ogoni people. His Movement for the Survival of the Ogoni People (MOSOP) now bonded with the Ijaw militants to form the Movement for the Emancipation of the Niger Delta (MEND). Meanwhile in the North, Zamfara's lead was very quickly followed by other states, as one after another passed laws to re-Islamize its legal system.

It was widely suspected that Obasanjo's failure to take any steps to deal with the challenge to the Constitution was part of the price of his acceptance as President by the North. This would be consistent with a report which appeared in Next newspaper on 14 May 2009 that Nigeria had rejoined the Organisation of Islamic Conference on 11 April 1999 in the same quiet manner as Babangida had originally taken the country into the organization. The problem which Obasanjo's compromise over Sharia law brought for the continued viability of One Nigeria is that:

> *The introduction of Islamic criminal law is a state act with a highly symbolic value, as becomes clear from other countries where Islamic criminal law has been adopted. It is also an irreversible process. For a political leader to advocate its abolition would be political suicide*[15]

BOKO HARAM

It was against this background that Boko Haram emerged on the scene in 2002 coinciding with the call from Osama Bin Laden for a global jihad following the 9/11 attack on the United States and the American invasion of Afghanistan ("Operation Enduring Freedom"), the following month.

Earlier we saw that it was at the turn of an earlier century, in 1804, that the Mujaddid, Uthman d'an Fodio launched his jihad in north-west Nigeria that saw his Fulani people conquer the Hausa empire and that it was similarly at the turn of the century, in 1903, that Lugard launched the British equivalent of jihad to over-throw the Fulani hegemony while their French counterparts simultaneously over-threw the Bornu empire. It was, therefore, almost to be expected that some form of jihad would take place shortly after the turn of the millennium in the year 2000.

'Jihad' is nothing more than a political revolution with a claim of Allah's sanction. Those leading it make the same promises of tackling injustice, abolishing corruption and banishing poverty as every radical politician makes to advance his political ambition. It was in the name of establishing a truly Islamic state that d'an Fodio had launched his jihad in the nineteenth century. It was in quest of the same truly Islamic state that two hundred years later, in 2002, that Jama'atu Ahlisunnah Lidda Awati Wal Jihad (Congregation of Followers of the Prophet involved in the Call to Islam and Religious Struggle), which came to be tagged 'Boko Haram', came onto the Nigerian scene. The group's emergence appears to be the result of the convergence of three different but inter-connected influences: internal, regional and international.

With these developments on the global scene, what might have been intended by the Zamfara governor and his fellow governors in the north as a political gesture, and tolerated by President Obasanjo as such, was overtaken by events with the more violent jihadist agenda of Boko Haram under the leadership of Muhammad Yusuf.

World attention had already been called to the radically-altered state of Nigeria when on 22 March 2002 a Sharia court in Katsina State sentenced a 31-year-old woman to be stoned to death for bearing a child out of wedlock despite her defence that she had been raped. The international campaign for her release was still ongoing when Nigeria was scheduled to host the Miss World Beauty Contest in Abuja.

Islamists in Kaduna vented their protest against the country's decision to host the contest on their fellow citizens in riots on 23 November 2002 which, according to reports, saw more than two-hundred people killed and more than five-hundred injured. The excuse for the riot was a comment attributed to a young journalist, Isioma Daniel, in an article in the This Day newspaper, suggesting that the Prophet Mohammed would have approved of the contest and might have married one of the contestants. The contest was hurriedly relocated to London. When in March, 2003 the U.S. president George Bush and the U.K. prime minister Tony Blair together launched an invasion of Iraq ('Operation Shock and Awe'), it was to be expected that there would be repercussions in Nigeria.

The global 'War against Terror' now forced the Obasanjo government to take action against Boko Haram and the army succeeded in driving them into the Cameroon hills following a major clash in 2004. The group were scattered but not beaten[16] and a pattern of attacks and counter attacks emerged as the group attacked police stations and banks to secure ammunition and funds.

THIRD TERM AGENDA

In the meantime following on from the Odi massacre of 1999, trouble had been brewing in the Niger Delta. Odi town was part of Bayelsa State, and the elected governor of that state was a former Nigeria Air Force squadron leader Diepreye Alamieyeseigha. He had been re-elected in 2003 by which time he had amassed considerable wealth which brought influence not only with the Niger Delta militants but also potentially the opportunity to influence the outcome of the next presidential elections in 2007. In this latter regard it was significant that Vice President Atiku Abubakar, who was expecting to succeed Olusegun Obasanjo, had been a key backer of Alamieyeseigha's 2003 re-election campaign.

Obasanjo, for his part, had designs on amending the constitution to enable him to run for a third consecutive term. This 'Third Term Agenda' was to become the source of a major feud between the president and his vice-president with the latter alleging a breach of faith by the former with respect to an understanding that he would only serve two terms before standing down.

With party funding being the key to the outcome of contests in a political system devoid of any ideological divide, it appears that the removal of Atiku's ally, Diepreye Alamieyeseigha, from his position as governor of the largest oil-producing state in Nigeria was a key early measure towards the realization of Obasanjo's Third Term Agenda. It could not have been done without the assistance of the British Government when the Metropolitan Police arrested and detained the governor on charges of money laundering on 15 September 2005. The arrest and imprisonment of a serving governor of a sovereign state, who was entitled to immunity from prosecution in his own country, was an unprecedented act.

Amidst incredible claims that Alamieyeseigha had jumped bail and fled from Britain dressed as a woman, he was re-arrested in Nigeria and safely locked away until after the 2007 elections had been concluded. In the meantime, he had been stripped of all his resources. His impeachment paved the way for his deputy Goodluck Jonathan to step up to become Governor of Bayelsa State in 2005 without undergoing any election to complete his predecessor's term of office.

In the meantime, Alamieyeseigha's incarceration only served to spur on MEND's guerilla warfare in the Niger Delta as they attacked pipelines and other oil installations and sold directly accessed oil to fund their operations. With every barrel of thus 'bunkered' oil their operations grew more and more sophisticated to the point of attacking offshore oil platforms. Thus, as Boko Haram bombed and terrorized people in northern Nigeria, MEND was fighting its own war against the oil operators in the Niger Delta.

THE YAR'ADUA SAGA

Obasanjo ultimately failed in his bid to amend the constitution to allow him a third term but even so he took steps to make sure that Abubakar would not succeed him. He arranged for the party to select Umaru Musa Yar'Adua, the governor of Katsina State, as the party's presidential candidate for the 2007 elections with Goodluck Jonathan as his running mate. The ticket was a reflection of the two main challenges that the country faced: Boko Haram in the North-east and MEND in the Niger Delta.

Given what was known of the challenging state of Yar'Adua's health he was never going to last the term. It soon became clear that his presidency was simply a transition to Goodluck Jonathan's, albeit with more substance than the earlier transitional presidency of Ernest Shonekan. In the process both would depend on a high level of hand-holding from Obasanjo.

President Yar'Adua was sworn in on 29 May 2007 after what was regarded as the most rigged elections in the long history of election-rigging in Nigeria. With Goodluck Jonathan as his Vice President, the clear agenda was to take the heat out of MEND's activities in the Niger Delta and so one of the early measures of the new administration was the release of Dokubo-Asari and Alamieyeseigha.

The other challenge was Boko Haram. The Yar'Adua government met this to an extent when a security raid on the group's base in Bauchi on 26 July 2009 led to the capture of the group's leader Mohammad Yusuf who was then killed in police custody.

However, Yar'Adua's health now reached crisis point. The country's governance became a farce when he flew out of Nigeria, on 23 November 2009, for treatment in Saudi Arabia without authorising vice-president, Goodluck Jonathan, to act in his stead during his 'temporary incapacity'. Elements in the North, who considered that they had been short-changed by Obasanjo's selection of a northerner who was never going to complete his term of office, maintained that it was still their 'turn' and were strongly opposed to Goodluck Jonathan, a southerner, taking over.

Such was the level of secrecy maintained around the state of Yar'Adua's health that it led to all manner of speculation that he might be in a vegetative state or even dead, with the country being ruled by a corpse. The speculation was not helped by the elaborate exercise by which he was brought back into the country in enforced darkness, on 24 February 2010, when all lights at the airport were extinguished. Officially he died on 5 May 2010 and was buried on 6 May 2010. Once again, Goodluck Jonathan lived up to his name, achieving high office without an election, this time as president of the country.

THE 2011 ELECTIONS

The North-South controversy over the presidency was to re-surface in a major way less than a year later in the April 2011 presidential elections. The ruling party the Peoples

Democratic Party, reputedly had an unwritten rule that power was to rotate between North and South every two terms, so, since the South had occupied the office for two terms under Obasanjo, it was still the turn of the North to produce the party's candidate for the 2011 Presidential elections. This expectation of the northern elements in the party conflicted directly with the assumed ambition of Goodluck Jonathan and, more significantly, the expectations of his Niger Delta people who had never before had a 'turn' at the presidency despite producing virtually all the oil on which the Nigerian economy floated. When Goodluck Jonathan eventually confirmed that he was going to run for the presidency the North-South tension heightened.

The elections which were to have taken place in January 2011 were first postponed to 9 April 2011 before being postponed again to 16 April 2011 on the excuse of the late delivery of ballot sheets. In the meantime, another major political figure from the Niger Delta areas, the former governor of Delta State, James Ibori, who had the potential to upset Goodluck Jonathan's presidential ambitions, was arrested in Dubai at the behest of the Metropolitan Police and jailed in Britain. While he was safely locked up, the democracy game in Nigeria went on without him.[ii]

[ii]In the meantime, on 14 June 2010, Boko Haram reputedly joined forces with Al Qaeda in the Islamic Maghreb (AQIM) which promised to provide it with "weapons, training, and other support in order to expand its own reach into Sub-Saharan Africa not only to gain "strategic depth", but also to "defend Muslims in Nigeria and to stop the advance of a minority of Crusaders"[17]. A string of Christmas Eve bomb explosions in Jos, the capital of Plateau State, created scenes of carnage which were a sign of things to come in the country.

The announcement of Jonathan as the winner of the April 2011 elections produced an iconic map of the vote count that brought back into stark focus the two Nigerias that a century of amalgamation had failed to make into one with General Buhari, the northerner and Muslim candidate sweeping all of the Northern states and Goodluck Jonathan, the southerner and Christian candidate, taking all of the Middle Belt and South with the exception of Osun State.

The disappointed extremists in the North were to direct their anger at one of the important symbols of Nigerian unity, the National Youth Service Corp ("NYSC") as scores of Youth Corpers in Bauchi, and other northern states were slaughtered and raped. The very essence of the NYSC programme had been to foster unity by requiring young graduates to perform a year of national service in a state other than their state of origin. After this slaughter of the innocents many parents in the South became loathe to allow their young ones to serve in some states in the North.

---

ii On 1 October 2015, another political figure from the Niger Delta, Goodluck Jonathan's former Minister of Petroleum, Mrs Diezani Alison-Madueke, was arrested in London by British police

CHIBOK GIRLS

Operation Restore Order was a major military offensive against Boko Haram that was launched in May, 2013 following a declaration of a state of emergency in the north-eastern states of Yobe, Borno and Adamawa involving 8,000 Nigerian troops on a mission to reclaim territory that had effectively been lost to Boko Haram. If the plan was to deal with the Boko Haram menace to Nigeria's unity once and for all ahead of the planned celebrations to mark the centenary of the 1 January 1914 amalgamation of North and South Nigeria, it failed. It was in the centenary year that Boko Haram read the last rites on One Nigeria when it hit the international headlines with reports of the kidnap and abduction of more than 250 Christian girls from a school in Chibok in Borno State close to the border with Cameroon. The new leader of Boko Haram issued a video broadcast admitting responsibility for the act and declaring his intent to sell the girls into slavery.

With more than a touch of tragic irony, on 13 June 2014, in the centenary year of the amalgamation that was supposed to have created One Nigeria, the British Foreign Secretary, William Hague, announced that British military aircraft had been dispatched to Nigeria to help combat the extremist group Boko Haram. According to the report in the Times newspaper, he condemned the group's "twisted mission to deny education to girls" and "announced that Britain and the US would provide funding to educate a million more Nigerian schoolchildren, with a particular emphasis on support for girls".

Thus this history of Nigeria which started in the seventeenth century with British efforts to end slavery ends, in the twenty-first century, where it began.

10.
Coming to Terms with the Past

Germany has come to terms with the past, in a way that other nations should not only admire, but emulate. Wherever toxic history bubbles up, we should ban the politicians, nationalist protesters, propagandists and soldiers, and send in the historians, armed with plenty of footnotes.

Ben Macintyre, Times Columnist

This book opened with a discussion of the link between the Industrial Revolution that occurred in the West in the mid-19th century and the travails of the people of West Africa in the Slave Trade and it touched upon the arguments in a book written by Nicholas Wade, a former science editor for the New York Times titled *A Troublesome Inheritance: Genes, Race and Human History.*

In the book, Wade says that the Industrial Revolution marked the point at which the people of the West evolved into a new race different from the people of Africa and others races who have been left behind in terms of economic development. Having noted that the wealth gaps across the world in the agrarian period was relatively modest, he argues that the Industrial Revolution happened because 'productivity increased because the nature of the people had changed'. According to him, '"the rise of the West", over and above all other races, is an event not just in history but also in human evolution'. Even though recorded human history dates back over 200,000 years, Wade boldly pinpoints the period of 600 years leading up to the Industrial Revolution (i.e. from 1200 – 1800) as the period when westerners evolved into a new species of human beings.

Wade does not shy away from the implications of his claims of the emergence of a new super-race in the West to the state and condition of Africa:

Continuity in social behaviour is evident in Africa, which has consisted largely of tribally organized societies both before and after the episode of colonial rule. European powers prepared their colonies for independence by imposing their own political institutions. But these had been developed over many centuries for the European environment. Considering the long historical process by which Europeans had rid themselves of tribalism, it is hardly surprising that African states did not become detribalized overnight. They reverted to the kind of social system to which Africans had become adapted during the previous centuries

At the heart of the confusion in Wade's analysis the belief that 'Europeans rid themselves of tribalism' and the suggestion that Africans have yet to 'become detribalized'. The assumed detribalization of the West is nothing more than the product of sophistry arising from the abuse of language. In most commentary in relation to Africa and Africans, the word 'tribe' is used in a manner which, intentionally or otherwise, confuses the real issues: while commentators are precise in not referring, for example, to the English, Scots or Welsh as 'tribes', they carelessly and, in many cases, deliberately use the term when referring to the Hausa, the Igbo and the Yoruba and the many other ethnic groups in Nigeria, and Africa, even when, in terms of population, distinctiveness of language and culture, the difference of labelling cannot be justified on any proper and consistent use of the word. The use of different labels for the same phenomenon may be explained away as carelessness for the uneducated but it can only be regarded as calculated deception when done by those who should know better.

Through this play with words, the same issues which, in Britain, may be considered issues of Welsh, Scottish, or English 'national interest', are portrayed and perceived in the African context as lower-level 'tribalism' and, therefore, devoid of any basis in rational conduct and attributable only to baser instincts. It is such sophistry that underpins the nonsensical conclusion of the emergence of a new human race different from the rest.

Another common misconception which confuses the issues is the claim that these events that have shaped the Nigerian experience happened a long time ago and that after more than 100 years of political union and 50 years of independence, Nigerians should have become 'detribalized'. But the 2014 Scottish Independence Referendum is all the reminder needed that the past is forever here with us in the present. That the winding up of the successful and voluntary union 300 years on from its formation should even be contemplated to the point of a referendum is an obvious challenge to those who maintain that the British-made political union that is Nigeria that has resulted in the loss of so many lives is somehow sacrosanct.

The reality is that Nigeria was made by Britain in its own image. All the relationship issues that have plagued Nigeria and arrested its development can be found, on a smaller scale, within the British political union of English, Scots, Welsh and Northern Irish. Consider, for example the fact that after 300 years of voluntary and successful union with the Scots the English are seeking to solve the 'West Lothian question' by demanding a law to ban Scottish MPs at Westminster from voting on English-only matters so as to ensure 'English votes for English laws'. The Nigerian equivalent of the West Lothian Question became to what extent should Igbos living in the Western Region be allowed to shape the politics of the Western Region given that the Yoruba could never exercise the same influence over the affairs of the Eastern Region. It remains a central question in British politics:

> *You can put it to voters however you like, but people will never be persuaded that it is fair to allow Scottish voters to determine English-only questions when English MPs can't determine Scottish-only questions*

This book is being published in the year that marks the 50th anniversary of the Biafran War in which many millions lost their lives in a struggle to re-shape the political union that is Nigeria. As we go to print the clamour for Biafra is getting louder. In reaction to this development, on 6 June 2017, some Northern socio-political groups joined together to issue what has become known as the Kaduna Declaration in which they gave a 1 October deadline for all Igbos to 'quit' the North. Coincidentally, the people of British Southern Cameroon, who might have been part of Biafra, are agitating for separation from French Cameroon.

There is an irony in the fact that in this same year, Britain which created the political union before then dissuading the North and preventing the East from leaving it, is negotiating its own Exit from the European Union, a political union which it joined voluntarily after nearly forty-five years of membership. The popular concern over the control of immigration which has been the main driver for Britain's planned withdrawal from the European Union is a long way removed from the murderous pogroms that were conducted against the Igbos ahead of the declaration of Biafra and their subsequent marginalization.

The abuse of the control of resources has been at the heart of the Nigeria story from the very beginning and the Niger Delta has borne the brunt of it. It is more than coincidence that at the onset of the British colonization drive towards the end of the nineteenth century four major chieftains of the Niger Delta were "arrested" and exiled by the British: Pepple of Bonny, Jaja of Opobo, Nana of the Itsekiri and Koko of Nembe-Brass. In recent times, three major political figures have been arrested by the Metropolitan Police on allegations of "money- laundering", each of them from the Niger Delta: Diepreye Alamieyeseigha, the then Governor of Bayelsa State; James Ibori ex-Governor of Delta State and Mrs. Diezani Alison-Madueke, former Petroleum Minister in the administration of the only President from the Niger Delta, Goodluck Jonathan.

In an attempt to chart a way through the ethnic morass, President Jonathan convened a National Conference, in 2014, under the Chairmanship of Justice Idris Kutigi. The summation of this former Chief Justice of Nigeria was as follows:

> *Most of the southern delegates had said they looked forward to the conference recommending a restructuring of the country and establishing a true federalism that would be characterized by regional autonomy, resource control, state police, among other changes. But their northern counterparts wanted the status quo to remain in terms of the country's governance structure. They also sought for an increase in revenue allocations from the Federal Government to the states in the North. Going by these positions and those specially presented by the different blocs like the North, the South-West and the South-South, the recommendations of the committees seem to favour the North more than the South. Resource control is not going to happen as long as we (northerners) are part of Nigeria.*

This is what was denied to Nigerians in the 1960s and led to the Biafran war and it is the repeated refusals by those who were enjoying the status quo that had led to the ongoing attempt at a forcible restructuring of the country by Boko Haram.

From the static viewpoint of the record of unbridled corruption, military coups and chronic underdevelopment that has plagued Nigeria since its creation, it is possible to see how Mr Wade has been led to his implied conclusion that Nigeria, and by extension Africa's problem is a people problem. But this is to fundamentally misunderstand the country's dynamics, both in its origins and functioning:

> *The role of the Colonial Office was to see that the Colonial Empire was ruled on sound lines and opened to commercial development – not to found new nations*

It is the surface-level view that is so often taken as proof that concepts of democracy and the rule of law are completely unworkable for Africans. The proponents of this view, black and white alike, will point to the record of governance in places like Nigeria in support of their argument. Many educated Nigerians have also been led to the conclusion that the problem with Nigeria, and by extension Africa, is the people.

It has been the author's mission to show that the people of Nigeria are no different from the people of all other countries with their mix of the good, the bad and the ugly. This book is intended to be a reaffirmation of our common humanity and the universality of the solutions to these human social problems. There is no new human race; there is only one human race.

Nigeria's troubled history has spawned a sizeable and growing Diaspora community in Britain for whom the history and prosperity of Britain and Nigeria can never be viewed separate and apart. This book is intended to be part of the process by which Britain comes to terms with its past and resets the relationship with the people of Nigeria on whom it imposed political union.

Nigeria 2011 Electoral Map

BIBLIOGRAPHY

Achebe, Chinua, *Things Fall Apart*. London: Penguin Modern Classics, 2001

Ade-Ajayi, Professor Jacob, Festus, *A Patriot to the Core: Bishop Ajayi Crowther*. Ibadan: Spectrum Books Limited, 2001

Ademoyega, Adewale, *Why We Struck*. Ibadan: Evans Brothers Ltd, 1981

Ajayi, Sir Olaniwun, *Nigeria: Political Power Imbalance*. Ibadan: Safari Books Ltd, 2015

Awa, Eme O. *Federal Government in Nigeria*. Berkeley and Los Angeles: University of California Press, 1964

Awolowo, Obafemi, *Awo: The Autobiography of Chief Obafemi Awolowo*. Cambridge: University Press, 1960

Awolowo, Obafemi, *The People's Republic*. Oxford: University Press, 1968

Azikiwe Ifeoha, *Nigeria: Echoes of a Century*, Authorhouse UK, 2013

Azikiwe, Nnamdi, *My Odyssey: An Autobiography*. London: C Hurst & Company, 1971

Bello, The Sardauna of Sokoto, Alhaji Sir Ahmadu, *My Life*. Cambridge: University Press, 1962

Buchan, John, *Oliver Cromwell*. Cornwall: House of Stratus, 2008

Burns, Sir Alan, *History of Nigeria*. London: George, Allen and Unwin Ltd, 1955

Buxton, Thomas Fowell, *The African Slave Trade and Its Remedy*. London: Frank Cass & Co Ltd, 1967

Carland, John M.,*The Colonial Office and Nigeria 1898-1914*. California:Stanford University, Hoover Institution Press, 1985

Catterall, Peter, *The Macmillan Diaries: The Cabinet Years 1950-1957*. Basingstoke and Oxford: Macmillan, 2003

Catterall, Peter, *The Macmillan Diaries Vol II: Prime Minister and After: 1957-1966.* Basingstoke and Oxford: Macmillan, 2011

Coleman, James S., Nigeria: Background to Nationalism. Berkeley and Los Angeles: University of California Press, 1965

Davies Q.C., Hezekiah,Oladipo, Memoirs. Ibadan: Evans Brothers (Nigeria Publishers) Limited, 1989

Davies, Norman, The Isles: A History. Basingstoke and Oxford: Macmillan, 1999

Jorre, John, de St., The Brothers' War: Biafra and Nigeria. London: Faber and Faber, 2009

Douglass, Frederick, Narrative of the Life of An American Slave. New York: The New American Library, 1968

Eden, Sir Anthony, Full Circle: The Memoirs of Sir Anthony Eden. London: Cassell & Company Ltd, 1960

Efiong, Philip, The Caged Bird Sang No More: My Biafran Odyssey 1966-70. South Africa, 30 Degree South Publishers, 2016

Enahoro, Chief Anthony, Fugitive Offender: The Story of a Political Prisoner. London: Cassell 1965

Esposito, John L., The Oxford History of Islam. Oxford: University Press, 1999

Falola, Toyin and Matthew M. Heaton, A History of Nigeria. Cambridge: University Press, 2008

Falola, Toyin, and Abdullahi Mahadi, Martin Uhomoibhi, Ukachukwu Anyanwu, History of Nigeria: Nigeria Before 1800 AD. Longman Nigeria, 1989

Falola, Toyin, and Abdullahi Mahadi, Martin Uhomoibhi, Ukachukwu Anyanwu, History of Nigeria 2: Nigeria in the Nineteenth Century. Longman Nigeria, 1991

Ferguson, Niall, Empire: How Britain Made The Modern World. London: Penguin Books, 2004

Forsyth, Frederick, Emeka. Ibadan: Spectrum Books Ltd, 1982

Forsyth, Frederick, The Biafra Story: The Making of an African Legend. Barnsley: Pen & Sword Military, 2007

Froude, James Anthony, Disraeli: A Biography. London: New European Publication, 2004

Gailey, Harry A., *Lugard and the Abeokuta Uprising: The Demise of Egba Independence*. London: Frank Cass, 1982

Gibbon, Edward, *The Christians and the Fall of Rome*. London: Penguin Books, 2004

Gould, Michael, *The Biafran War: The Struggle for Modern Nigeria*. London: I.B. Tauris. 2013

Guedalla, Philip, *Palmerston*. Great Britain: Hodder and Stoughton, 1937

Hitler, Adolf, *Mein Kampf*. London: Pimlico, 1992

Isichei, Elizabeth, *A History Of Nigeria*. London: Longman Group Limited, 1983

Jakande, Lateef, K., *The Trial of Obafemi Awolowo*. London: Secker & Warburg, 1966

Johnson, Rev. Samuel, *The History of the Yorubas: from the Earliest Times to the Beginning of the British Protectorate*. Lagos: CSS Bookshops Ltd, 1997

Keay, John, *India: A History*. London: Harper Collins, 2000

Kwarteng, Kwasi, *Ghosts of Empire: Britain's Legacies in the Modern World*. London: Bloomsbury Publishing Plc, 2011

Louis, Wm. Roger, *Imperialism at Bay: The United States and the Decolonization of the British Empire 1941-45*. Oxford: University Press, 1977

Ludden, David, *India and South Asia: A Short History*. Oxford: Oneworld Publications, 2002

Lugard, Sir Frederick. D., *The Dual Mandate In British Tropical Africa*. Edinburgh and London: William Blackwood & Sons Ltd, 1929

Mason, Philip, *The Men Who Ruled India*. London: Jonathan Cape, 1985

Meredith, Martin, *The State of Africa: A History of the Continent Since Independence*. London: The Free Press, 2006

Miners, N.J. *The Nigerian Army 1956-1966*. London: Methuen & Co Ltd, 1971

Morel, E. D. *Nigeria: Its Peoples and Its Problems*. Memphis: General Books, 2010 reprint

Morgan, Giles, *Byzantium: Capital of an Ancient Empire*. Hertfordshire: Pocket Essentials, 2007

Nicolson, I. F., *The Administration of Nigeria 1900-1960: Men, Methods and Myths*. Oxford: University Press, 1969

Obasanjo, Olusegun, *Nzeogwu*. Ibadan: Spectrum Books Ltd, 1987

Ogun, Dele, *The Law, the Lawyers and the Lawless*. London: New European Publications, 2009

Oguntimoju, Dele, *Identity And Development: Lessons From Nigeria For Africa & Europe*. London: Economic Research Council, 2002

Paden, John N., *Ahmadu Bello, Sardauna of Sokoto: Values and Leadership in Nigeria*. London: Hodder and Stoughton, 1986

Pakenham, Thomas, *The Scramble For Africa*. Great Britain: Abacus, 1992

Pearce, Robert D, *Sir Bernard Bourdillon: The Biography of a twentieth-century colonialist*. Oxford: The Kensal Press, 1987

Pearce, Robert D, *Then the Wind Changed in Africa: Nigerian Letters of Robert Hepburn Wright*. London & New York: Radcliffe Press, 1993

Peters, Jimi, *The Nigerian Military and the State*. London: Tauris Academic Studies, 1997

Quigley, Carroll, *The Anglo-American Establishment*. California: G S G & Associates, 1966

Roosevelt, Elliott, *As He Saw It*. New York: Duell, Sloan and Pearce, 1945

Schama, Simon, *Rough Crossings: Britain, the Slaves and the American Revolution*. London: BBC Books, 2005

Sharwood-Smith, Sir Bryan, *But Always As Friends: Northern Nigeria and the Cameroons 1921-1957*. London: George Allen & Unwin 1969

Shasore Olasupo, A Platter of Gold: Making Nigeria 1906-1960. Lagos: Quramo Publishing, 2016

Shaxson, Nicholas, *Poisoned Wells: The Dirty Politics of African Oil*. New York: Palgrave Macmillan, 2007

Siollun, Max, *Oil Politics and Violence: Nigeria's Military Coup Culture*. New York: Algora Publishing, 2009

Siollun, Max, *Soldiers of Fortune*. Abuja: Cassava Republic Press

Smith, Harold, *A Squalid End to Empire: British Retreat from Africa*. Unpublished, www.genesisnigeria.com/articles.html

Staudenraus, P.J., *The African Colonization Movement: 1816-1865*. New York: Columbia University Press, 1961

Thomas, Hugh, *The Slave Trade: History of the Atlantic Slave Trade, 1440-1870*. Oxford: Papermac, 1998

Tharoor, Shashi, *Inglorious Empire: What the British Did to India*. London: Hurst & Company, 2017

Wade, Nicholas, *A Troublesome Inheritance: Genes, Race and Human History*. New York: The Penguin Press, 2014)

Wilson, Harold, *The Labour Government 1964-1970: A Personal Record*. London: Weidenfeld and Nicolson and Michael Joseph Ltd, 1971

ENDNOTES

INTRODUCTION
1 U.K. Times Newspaper 15 July 1998.
2 Bryan Sharwood-Smith, *'But Always As Friends'*, p.16
3 Sir Frederick D. Lugard, *The Dual Mandate In British Tropical Africa* p. 61
4 Chief Anthony Enahoro, *Fugitive Offender*, cover
5 Robert D. Pearce, *Sir Bernard Bourdillon*, p. 320
6 *Identity and Development: Lessons From Nigeria*
7 Letter to the Author

CHAPTER 1
1 Sir Thomas Fowell Buxton, *the Slave Trade and its Remedy*, p. 453
2 Hugh Thomas, *The Slave Trade*, p. 265
3 Thomas, p. 267
4 Thomas, p. 274
5 Niall Ferguson, *Empire: How Britain Made The Modern World*, p. 119
6 Ferguson, p. 122
7 Buxton, p. 442
8 Thomas, p. 597 quoting Johann Wolfgang Goethe
9 Simon Schama, *Rough Crossings*, p. 80
10 P. J. Straudenraus, *The American Colonisation Movement*, p. 15
11 Straudenraus, p. 1
12 Straudenraus, p. 4
13 Straudenraus, p. 5
14 New African Magazine, October 2011
15 New African Magazine, October 2011
16 Buxton, p. 442
17 Buxton, p. 298
18 Buxton, p. 354
19 Buxton, p. 302
20 Buxton, p. 398
21 Buxton, p. 441
22 Buxton, p. 453
23 Buxton, p. 288
24 Buxton, p. 290
25 Buxton, p. 290
26 Straudenraus, p. 8
27 Thomas, p. 575
28 Buxton, p. 375
29 Buxton, p. 491
30 Frederick Douglas, *Diary of an American Slave*, p. 67
31 Obiaku Christopher, History of the Exploration of Africa/Nigeria since 1788
32 Buxton, p. 420
33 Buxton, p. 510
34 Buxton, p. 502
35 Buxton, p. 242
36 Ade Ajayi, *A Patriot to the Core*, p. 29
37 Ade Ajayi, p. 41

CHAPTER 2
1 Edward Gibbon, *The Christians and the Fall of Rome*
2 Ade Ajayi, p. 72
3 Ade Ajayi, p. 91

4 Chinua Achebe, *Things Fall Apart*, p. 129
5 Nehemia Levtzion, *Oxford History of Islam*, p. 535
6 Jean Boyd and Shehu Shagari, *The Life and Legacy of Shehu Uthman d'an Fodiyo*, p. 52
7 Levtzion, p. 477
8 Levtzion, p. 519
9 Toyin Falola and others, *History of Nigeria*, vol. 2, p. 32

CHAPTER 3
1 Lugard, p. 17
2 *Dictionary of African Christian Biography*
3 Gailey, p. 17
4 Gailey, p. 18
5 *Dictionary of African Christian Biography*
6 Sir Alan Burns, *History of Nigeria*, p. 112
7 Burns, p. 39
8 Burns, p. 114
9 Burns, p. 123
10 Burns, p. 124
11 Ibid, Page 305
12 Johnson, p. 193
13 Johnson, p. 210
14 Johnson, p. 353
15 Johnson, p. 353
16 Johnson, p. 371
17 http:dacb.org/stories/Nigeria/townsend_henry.html
18 http:dacb.org/stories/Nigeria/townsend_henry.html
19 Johnson, p. 439
20 Johnson, p. 463
21 Johnson, p. 470
22 Johnson, p. 494
23 Thomas Pakenham, *The Scramble for Africa*, p. 200
24 Lugard, p. 3
25 Ferguson, p. 268
26 Lugard, p. 4
27 Johnson, p. 572
28 Johnson, p. 575
29 Johnson, p. 626
30 Burns, p. 135
31 Burns, p. 136
32 Falola, p. 115
33 Burns, p. 148
34 Burns, p. 149
35 Burns, p. 146
36 Adogbeji Salubi, *The Establishment of British Administration in the Urhobo country (1891-1913)*
37 Elizabeth Isichie, *A History of Nigeria*, p. 324
38 Burns, p. 157
39 Isichie, p. 324
40 UK Times news report, 26 February 1895
41 http:dacb.org/stories/Nigeria/townsend_henry.html
42 Burns, p. 172
43 Lugard, p. 29
44 Johnson, p. 573
45 Lugard, p. 35
46 I.F. Nicholson, The Administration of Nigeria 1900 to 1960, p. 152
47 Flint John E., *Frederick Lugard: The Making of an Autocrat*, p. 12, www.webafriqa.net/library/African_proconsuls/lugard_autocrat.html
48 Crowder Michael, *History Today, February 1986, Vol. 36, pg 23-29, Lugard and Colonial Nigeria – Towards an Identity.*
49 Gailey, p. 22

50 Gailey, p. 25
51 Gailey, p. 30
52 Gailey, p. 32
53 Johnson, p. 644
54 Burns, p. 161
55 Nicholson, p. 128
56 Ogunjobi Deji, *Historical Flashback, Vol 3 No.11, The British expedition of Kano in 1903*
57 Nicholson, p. 153
58 Carland, John M. *The Colonial Office and Nigeria 1898-1914*, p.128
59 Burns, p. 178
60 Burns, p. 183
61 Burns, p. 182
62 Burns, p. 184
63 Burns, p. 186
64 Nicholson, p. 131
65 Burns, p. 187
66 Flint John E., *Frederick Lugard: The Making of an Autocrat*, p. 6, www.webafriqa.net/library/African_ proconsuls/lugard_autocrat.html
67 Wikipaedia
68 Nicholson, p. 159
69 Carland, p.70
70 Nicholson, p. 131
71 Carland, p.91
72 Carland, p. 95
73 Journal of the Historical Society of Nigeria, Vol. IV No.3, Dec. 1968

CHAPTER 4
1. Nicholson, p. 48
2 Nicholson, p. 55
3 Nicholson
4 Nicholson, p. 84
5 Shasore Olasupo, *A Platter of Gold: Making Nigeria 1906-1960*, p.22
6 Carland, p. 106
7 Carland, p. 113
8 Nicholson, p. 45
9 Nicholson, p. 88
10 Nicholson, p. 144
11 Nicholson, p. 139
12 Nicholson, p. 132
13 Carland, p. 119
14 Carland, p. 132-133
15 Carland, p. 87
16 Carland, p. 195
17 Nicholson, p. 133
18 Lugard, p. 61
19 Coleman, p. 181
20 E.D. Morel, *Nigeria: Its People and its Problems*
21 Morel, p. 83
22 Morel, p. 83
23 http:dacb.org/stories/Nigeria/townsend_henry.html
24 http:dacb.org/stories/Nigeria/townsend_henry.html
25 Morel, p. 81
26 Morel, p. 83
27 Morel, p. 84
28 Lugard, p. 426
29 Lugard, p. 460
30 Lugard, p. 453
31 Morel, p. 84

32 Lugard, p. 454
33 Morel, p. 79
34 Morel, p. 85
35 Morel, p. 82
36Coleman, p. 97
37 Morel, p. 80
38 Lugard, p. 596
39 Nicholson, p. 42
40 Flint John E., *Frederick Lugard: The Making of an Autocrat (1858-1943)*, p. 42
41 Morel, p. 44
42 Gailey, p. 36
43 Gailey, p. 36
44 Gailey, p. 52
45 Gailey, p. 58
46 Lugard, p. 122
47 Crowder Michael, *Lugard and Colonial Nigeria – Towards an Identity?*, History Today, Vol. 36, pp 23-29 February 1986
48 Gailey, p. 75
49 Gailey, p. 91
50 Burns, p. 59
51 Obafemi Awolowo, *Awo*, p. 69
52 Shasore, p. 158
53 Isichie, p. 400
54 Shashore, p. 190
55 Enahoro, p. 74
56 Coleman, p. 225

CHAPTER 5

1 Adolf Hitler, *Mein Kampf*, p. 588
2 Hitler, p. 127
3 Elliot Roosevelt, *As He Saw* It, p. 24
4 Rooselvelt, p. 37
5 Roosevelt, p. 43
6 Anthony Eden, *Full Circle: The Memoirs of Sir Anthony Eden*, p. 332
7 Peter Catterall, *The Macmillan Diaries Vol 1*, p. 187
8 Eden, p. 133
9 Eden, p. 483
10 Eden, p. 523
11 Eden, p.541
12 Eden, p.556
13 Catterall, p. 603
14 Norman Davies, *The Isles – A History*, p. 909

CHAPTER 6

1 Davies
2 Sharwood-Smith, p. 4
3 Harold Smith, *Blue Collar Lawman*, Chapter 10
4 Awolowo, p. 129
5 Morel, p. 43
6 Coleman, p. 254
7 Coleman, p. 247
8 H.O. Davies, *Memoirs*, p. 2
9 Davies H.O., p. 47
10 Davies H.O., p. 314
11 Davies H.O., p. 68
12 Davies H.O., p. 315
13 Davies H.O., p. 95
14 Awo, p. 42
15 Awo, p. 169

16 Awo, p. 177
17 Enahoro, p. 8
18 Enahoro, p. 28
19 Enahoro, p. 45
20 Enahoro, p. 62
21 Nnamdi Azikiwe, *My Odyssey*, p. 9
22 Azikiwe, p. 19
23 Azikiwe, p. 66
24 Azikiwe, p. 100
25 Azikiwe, p. 103
26 Azikiwe, Preface
27 Pearce, p. 172
28 Pearce, p. 219
29 Pearce, p. 217
30 Coleman, p. 271
31 Coleman, p. 153
32 Pearce, p. 233
33 Pearce, p. 228
34 Pearce, p. 225
35 Pearce, p. 231
36 Pearce, p. 227
37 Pearce, p. 214
38 Pearce, p. 223
39 Eme O. Awa, *Federal Government in Nigeria*, p. 18
40 Pearce, p. 221
41 John Keay, *India: a History*, p. 464
42 Coleman, p. 276
43 Awo, p. 140
44 Keay, p. 494
45 Azikiwe, p. 114
46 Azikiwe, p. 141
47 Davies H.O., p. 87
48 Azikiwe, p. 229
49 Azikiwe, p. 208
50 Azikiwe, p. 181
51 Azikiwe, p. 174
52 Azikiwe, p. 178
53 Azikiwe, p. 210
54 Azikiwe, p. 239
55 Azikiwe, p. 245
56 Azikiwe, p. 243
57 Azikiwe, p. 225
58 Azikiwe, p. 258
59 Azikiwe, p. 235
60 Stephanie Newell, *The Forger's Tale*,
61 Newell, p. 99
62 Newell, p. 80
63 Newell, p. 159
64 Newell, p. 162
65 Newell, p. 115
66 Davies H.O., p. 87
67 Newell, p. 160
68 Azikiwe, p. 286
69 Newell, p. 113
70 Awo, p. 147
71 Awo, p. 165
72 Coleman, p. 260
73 Coleman, p. 291
74 Coleman, p. 333

75 Coleman, p. 346
76 Coleman, p. 346
77 Coleman, p. 347
78 Sharwood-Smith, p. 213
79 Paden, p.139
80 Pearce, p. 339
81 Pearce, p. 331
82 Sharwood-Smith, p. 148
83 Sharwood-Smith, p. 338
84 Sharwood-Smith, p. 340
85 Sharwood-Smith, pp. 160-161
86 Sir Ahmadu Bello, *My Life*, p. 19
87 Bello, pp 6-7
88 Sharwood-Smith, p. 51
89 John N. Paden, *Ahmadu Bello*, p. 112
90 Bello, p. 64
91 Bello, p. 58
92 Paden p. 131
93 Bello, p. 28
94 Paden p. 139
95 Bello, p. 86
96 Paden p. 153
97 Paden, p. 154
98 Davies H.O., p. 345
99 Sharwood-Smith, p. 243
100 Sharwood-Smith, p. 256
101 Sharwood-Smith, p. 195-198
102 Sharwood-Smith, p. 150

CHAPTER 7
1 Pearce, p. 275
2 Pearce, p. 275
3 Pearce, p. 195
4 Pearce, p. 352
5 Olaniwun Ajayi, Nigeria: Political Power Imbalance, p. 56
6 Pearce, p. 354
7 Awa, pp.11 and 20
8 Coleman, p. 280
9 The Appointment and Deposition of Chiefs (Amendment) Ordinance)
10 The Crown (the Public Lands Acquisition Ordinance)
11 (the Minerals Ordinance)
12 Coleman, p. 284
13 Coleman, p. 290
14 Coleman, p. 293
15 Coleman, p. 311
16 From Blackpast.org: Nnamdi Azikiwe, Zik: A Selection from the Speeches of Nnamdi Azikiwe, Governor-General of the Federation of Nigeria formerly President of the Nigerian Senate formerly Premier of the Eastern Region of Nigeria (Cambridge: Cambridge University Press, 1961).
17 Coleman, p. 301
18 Isichie, p. 408
19 Sharwood-Smith, p. 216
20 Coleman, p. 312
21 Sharwood-Smith, p. 215
22 Sharwood-Smith, p. 314
23 Awolowo, p. 173
24 Bello p. 67
25 Coleman, p. 347
26 Article 5(1)
27 Pearce, p. 341

28 Sharwood-Smith, p. 365

29 Awa, p. 32

30 Sharwood-Smith, p. 225

31 Awolowo, p. 228

32Azikiwe, p. 303

33Awolowo, p. 252

34 Awa, p. 41

35 Azikiwe, p. 305

36 Article 118(2)

37Coleman, p. 398

38 Sharwood-Smith, p. 258

39 Enahoro, p. 123

40 Enahoro, p. 263

41Enahoro, p. 264

42 CO 554/260, no 73

43 CO 554/261 no 127 inward telegram no.741

44 Coleman, p. 400

45 Eden, p. 383

46 CO 554/236, no 46A

47 Coleman, p. 58

48 Burns, p. 237

49 Awa, p. 51

50 Awo, p. 225

51Harold Smith, Blue Collar: A Squalid End to Empire, Chapter 8

52 Smith, Chapter 8

53 Smith, Chapter 8

54 Smith, Chaper 12

55 Smith, Chapter 12

56 A Memorandum on Nigeria's Constitutional Conference (1957-1958) and Background to the Willink Commission.

57 A Memorandum on Nigeria's Constitutional Conference (1957-1958) and Background to the Willink Commission.

58 Sharwood-Smith p.364

59 Sharwood-Smith, p. 366

60 Enahoro, p. 153

61 31 July 1958: "A Memorandum on Nigeria's Constitutional Conference (1957-1958) and Background to the Willink Commission" By Alan Lennox-Boyd, Secretary of State for the Colonies (1954-1959)
 July 1958: Report of the Commission Appointed to Enquire into The Fears of Minorities and the Means of Allaying Them: Conclusions and Recommendations

62 A Memorandum on Nigeria's Constitutional Conference (1957-1958) and Background to the Willink Commission.

63Enahoro, p. 163

64 Smith

65 Awolowo, *The People's Republic*, p.71

66 Letter to the Author

67 Miners, p. 69

68 Sharwood-Smith, colophone text

CHAPTER 8

1 Michael Gould, *The Biafran War*, p.23

2 Jimi Peters, The Nigerian *Military* and the State, p.55

3 Peters

4 Peters, page 58

5 Peters, page 60

6 Miners, p. 37

7 Miners, p.210

8 Miners, p. 49

9 Miners, p. 113

10 Lateef, K. Jakande, The Trial of Obafemi Awolowo, pp. 172-173

11 Jakande, p. 175

12 Jakande

13 Jakande, p. 189

14 Enahoro, p. 156

15 Enahoro, p. 177

16 Jakande, p. 179

17 Enahoro, p. 185

18 Enahoro, p. 186

19 Enahoro, p. 191

20 Enahoro, p. 186

21 Audu Bem, Tiv (Nigeria) Riots of 1960, 1964: The Principle of Minimum Force and Counter Insurgency, Dept. of History and International Studies, Nigerian Defence Academy, Kaduna

22 Audu

23 Jakande, p. 10

24 Ifeoha Azikiwe, Nigeria: Echoes of a Century, Vol.1, p.154

25 Frederick Forsyth, *The Biafra Story: The Making of an African Legend*, p. 19

26 Smith, Chapter 13

27 Forsyth, *The Biafra Story*, p. 21

28 Forsyth, *The Biafra Story*, p. 140

29 Max Siollun, *Oil, Politics and Violence: Nigeria's Military Coup Culture*, p. 19

30 Siollun, *Oil, Politics*, p. 26

31 Olusegun Obasanjo, *Nzeogwu*, p. 136

32 Queen's Own Nigeria Regiment

33 Miners, p. 81

34 Harold Wilson, *The Labour Government 1964-1970*, pp. 194-196

35 Obasanjo, p. 30

36 Adewale Ademoyega, *Why We Struck*, p. 69

37 Obasanjo, p. 30

38 Siollun, *Oil, Politics*, p. 45

39 Obasanjo, p. 135

40 Ademoyega, p. 83

41 Ademoyega, p. 47

42 Ademoyega, p.63

43 Ademoyega, p.161

44 Siollun, *Oil, Politics*, p. 30

45 Miners, p. 170

46 Siollun, *Oil, Politics*, p. 22

47 Siollun, *Oil, Politics*, p. 62

48 Siollun, *Oil, Politics*, p. 84

49 Siollun, *Oil, Politics*, p. 57

50 Murray Roger, *Militarism in Africa*, p. 35, New Left Review, July-August, 1966

51 Miners, p. 224

52 Philip Efiong, *The Caged Bird Sang No More: My Biafra Odyssey*, p. 78

53 Siollun, *Oil, Politics*, p. 102

54 Forsyth, *The Biafra Story*, p. 48

55 Siollun, *Oil, Politics*, p. 51

56 Forsyth, *The Biafra Story*, p. 216

57 Ademoyega, p. 168

58 Forsyth, *Emeka*, p. 72

59 Mark Curtis, *Nigeria's war over Biafra 1967-70 (An edited extract from Unpeople: Britain's Secret Human Right Abuses)*

60 Siollun, *Oil, Politics*, p. 134

61 John de St. Jorre, *The Brothers War: Biafra and Nigeria*, p. 95

62 Jorre, p. 92

63 Mobolaji Aluko, *The May Month that shook Nigeria*

64 Aluko

65 Aluko

66 Aluko

67 Page lxxi, Colonial Office Records

68 Giles Morgan, *Byzantium: Capital of an Ancient Empire*, p. 137

69 Jorre, p. 139
70 Wilson, p. 400
71 Efiong, p. 187
72 Hansard Vol 769 CC1433-5341
73 Hansard Vol 769 CC1433-5341
74 Page 561 Ibid
75 Hansard Vol 769 CC1433-5341
76 Jorre, pp. 388-389
77 Jorre, p. 139
78 Jorre, p. 141
79 Smith, Chapter 13
80 Obasanjo, p. 136
81 Obasanjo, p. 164
82 Obasanjo, p. 141
83 Obasanjo, p.150
84 Bernard Odogwu, *No Place to Hide*, p. 53
85 Ademoyega, p. 199
86 Odogwu, p. 157
87 Efiong, p.192
88 Ademoyega, p. 249
89 Wilson, pp. 629 and 632
90 Jorre, p. 398
91 Efiong, p. 21

CHAPTER 9

1 John Lliffe, *Obasanjo Nigeria & The World*, p. 48
2 Lliffe, p. 9
3 Lliffe, p. 12
4 Siollun, *Oil, Politics*, p. 189
5 Eghosa E. Osaghe, *Crippled Giant: Nigeria since Independence*, p. 129
6 Osaghe, p. 129
7 Professor Tam David-West, *Who Really is General Muhammadu Buhari*, p. 32
8 Siollun, *Soldiers of Fortune*, p. 62
9 Siollun, *Soldiers of Fortune*, p. 63
10 Siollun, *Soldiers of Fortune*, p. 450
11 Siollun, *Soldiers of Fortune*, p. 113
12 Ibid pg Siollun, *Soldiers of Fortune*, p. 223
13 Siollun, *Soldiers of Fortune*, p. 120
14 Prof. Dr. Ruud Peters, The Reintroduction of Islamic Criminal Law in Northern Nigeria, p. 12
15 Prof. Dr. Ruud Peters, The Reintroduction of Islamic Criminal Law in Northern Nigeria, p. 3
16 Africa Security Brief April 2012 J. Peter Pham

CHAPTER 10

1 Times Newspaper 7 September 2012
2 Awolowo, p. 209
3 Carland, p. 90

Index

326